SONG OF SOLOMON

by

Paige Patterson

MOODY PRESS

CHICAGO

Library of Congress Cataloging-in-Publication Data

Patterson, Paige.
  Song of Solomon.

  (Everyman's Bible commentary)
  Bibliography: p.
  1. Bible. O.T. Song of Solomon—Commentaries.
I. Title. II. Series.
BS1485.3.P37 1986   223′.907   86-5433
ISBN: 0-8024-2057-5 (pbk.)

1 2 3 4 5 Printing/EP/Year 90 89 88 87 86

Printed in the United States of America

SONG OF SOLOMON

The joy that Shulamith brought to the life of Solomon was first brought to her own parents. The cheerfulness and spontaneity of our daughter has daily brightened our household and invigorated even the most trying days. To my lovely daughter, Carmen Leigh, I gratefully dedicate this exposition, praying that her fondest dreams and expectations will be met as she follows the sound teaching of the Song of Solomon.

Contents

PREFACE

In a world awash with the debris of broken homes, crushed spirits, and fractured dreams, God's people need the message of the Song of Solomon as never before. The Song is a righteous antidote to a licentious society that has prostituted the sacred nature of human love. Hope exudes from its pages. If ever a book was written with a message more salient for a later generation, Solomon's ode is that book.

Though the symbols, metaphors, allusions, and vocabulary of the Song are frequently so obscure that dogmatism is unthinkable, its insights into the nature of successful love and delightful marriage are clear. I know that much light can yet emerge regarding this love song, and I have keenly felt the limitations of my own understanding. Nevertheless, the priceless message of this book needs to be expounded in the churches today. My prayer is that this brief commentary will encourage expository preachers everywhere to do the unimaginable—preach through the Song of Solomon. At the same time I have sought to help the lay reader curious about the message of the Song of Songs to gain an essential understanding of it.

Special gratitude must be expressed to the Old Testament division at the Criswell Center—Dr. Ken Mathews, Dr. Lamar

Cooper, Professor Ray Clendenen, and Dr. George Davis—for their suggestions and reading of the manuscript. Rabbi Yechiel Eckstein assisted with the location of modern Jewish materials and provided much encouragement. Martha Seaton, my executive assistant, contributed long hours beyond her assignment with the school to type and retype the manuscript. My student interns, Keith Ninomiya, Paul Carter, Mike Komatsu, and Ronnie Lowery, cared for a thousand items of minutia, freeing me to concentrate on this project. Special thanks to my precious family, Dorothy and the children, Armour and Carmen, for patience, support, and encouragement even when the research and writing tasks impinged on their time with husband and father.

INTRODUCTION

O, she doth teach the torches to burn bright!
It seems she hangs upon the cheek of night
Like a rich jewel in an Ethiope's ear;
Beauty too rich for use, for earth too dear!
So shows a snowy dove trooping with crows,
As yonder lady o'er her fellows shows.
The measure done, I'll watch her place of stand,
And, touching hers, make blessed my rude hand.
Did my heart love till now? forswear it, sight!
For I ne'er saw true beauty till this night.

(Shakespeare)

To love one maiden only, cleave to her,
And worship her by years of noble deeds,
Until they won her; for indeed I knew
Of no more subtle master under heaven
Than is the maiden passion for a maid,
Not only to keep down the base in man,
But teach high thought, and amiable words
And courtliness, and the desire of fame,
And love of truth, and all that makes a man.

(Tennyson)

I love thee with the breath,
Smiles, tears, of all my life!—and,
if God choose, I shall but love thee
better after death.

(Browning)

As unto the bow the cord is,
So unto the man is woman;
Though she bends him, she obeys him,
Though she draws him, yet she follows;
Useless each without the other.

(Longfellow)

Many waters cannot quench love,
neither can the floods drown it.

(Solomon)

The enchantment of a love song captivates the imagination of the pragmatist as well as the mystic. The poignancy of grief in tales that depict loss of lover or separation from the object of one's delight can knot the throat and moisten the eye of the most calloused. The Song of Solomon is such a poem, a sonnet rendered strange only by its literary setting. If discovered in the anthologies of sensitive poets, the Song would be notable but not particularly astonishing. Cradled as it is, however, in the wisdom literature of the world's most renowned Book of theology and ethics, Canticles (*Songs*, latinized; cf. Vulgate) has become the object of virulent assault, the focus of profuse praise, and a matter of ongoing debate and interpretation.

Song of Solomon is one of the five Megilloth, or scrolls (including also Ruth, Lamentations, Ecclesiastes, and Esther), that were read publicly and privately at the various Hebrew feasts. As such it belongs to the third section of the Hebrew canon, the *keṯubîm*, or "Writings." Peculiarities of the Song include the omission of God's name and indeed of any identifiable theological theme. The absence of discernible structure, together with the occurrence of almost fifty *hapax legomena* (words attested only once) and a large number of other rare words, does little to simplify the interpreter's task. The appearance of multifarious symbols, some of which are blatantly sensuous, complicates that task even further. Not unexpectedly, Franz Delitzsch begins his commentary by observing, "The Song is the most obscure book in the Old Testament."[1]

The extent of this obscurity may be illustrated by the divergent evaluations provided by both Jewish and Christian exegetes. The rabbinical school of Shammai vigorously opposed inclusion of the Song in the canon of Scripture, whereas the Babylonian school of Hillel viewed it as the zenith of biblical thought, eminently worthy of belonging to the canon. Among Christian commentators, Jerome recognized the value of Solomon's Song but suggested that no one read it before age thirty. C. H. Spurgeon did not advocate such strictures but believed the Song's mysteries yield themselves only to the spiritually mature, insisting that "its music belongs to the higher spiritual life, and has no charm in it for unspiritual ears. The Song occupies a sacred enclosure into which none may enter unprepared . . . the holy of holies, before which the veil still hangs to many an untaught believer."[2]

Crucial questions the reader must answer include the following. Does the sublime Song convey some profound spiritual insight, or is it merely a surviving Hebrew love song? Is the poem a unit or just a collection of lyrics possessing no essential connection? How many characters or groups appear in the Song? Should the book remain as a part of the canon of sacred Scripture, or should it be deleted? If significant meanings lie beneath the surface, what interpretive devices can be employed to unearth them and bring them to light?

Adding to the dilemma of the evangelical interpreter is the unwelcomed discovery that scholars whose insights are generally trusted haggle as much over the nature of the book as over its

1. Franz Delitzsch, *Commentary on the Song of Songs and Ecclesiastes* (Grand Rapids: Eerdmans, 1950), p. 1.
2. C. H. Spurgeon, *The Most Holy Place* (Pasadena: Pilgrim Pub., 1974), p. 89.

interpretation. One might safely venture that establishing the purpose of the Song of Solomon is more important to its verse by verse exegesis than for any other book in the Bible. Recent commentators Joseph C. Dillow and S. Craig Glickman argue that the Song is essentially a love song picturing the happiness and sanctity of human love with a focus on sexuality.[3] Delitzsch concurs: "This sunny glimpse of paradisaical love which Solomon experienced, again became darkened by the insatiableness of passion; but the Song of Songs has perpetuated it, and whilst all other songs of Solomon have disappeared, the providence of God has preserved this one, the crown of them all."[4] Otto Zockler adds that the "fundamental thought" of the Song is found in its "praise of the joyful happiness of wedded love."[5] But Spurgeon, following the Puritan lead, found the Canticles to be an exalted allegory with spiritual significance transcending its physical trappings. Nor is Spurgeon isolated in this conviction. The majority of Jewish and Christian commentators also have viewed the book thus. The modern Christian who wants to grasp all that God says to him must somehow extract the truth from this labyrinth of speculation.

AUTHOR

The Solomonic authorship of the Song has been questioned. However, even among more liberal thinkers, some allow that significant portions of the text originated in the Solomonic era. For example, Marvin Pope notes several reasons for assigning much of the book to that period. First, there is the mention of Tirzah (6:4), the capital of the Northern Kingdom under Jeroboam I. Pope notes it is unlikely that that city would have been mentioned in concert with Jerusalem by a poet of either kingdom

3. Joseph C. Dillow, *Solomon on Sex* (Nashville: Thomas Nelson, 1977) and S. Craig Glickman, *A Song for Lovers* (Downers Grove: InterVarsity, 1976).

4. Delitzsch, p. 3.

5. Otto Zockler, "The Song of Solomon," *Commentary on the Holy Scripture* (Grand Rapids: Zondervan, 1969), p. 17.

during the period of the divided monarchy. Second, extensive references to flora and fauna and a profusion of natural imagery are also in keeping with the approach generally accorded to Solomon. Finally, appealing to parallels to the Song in Ugaritic literature, Pope concludes, "No matter how late one places the final editorial operations, the antiquity of at least parts of the Song cannot be doubted in light of the Ugaritic parallels."[6]

Verse 1 of the text specifies that the Song was the work of Solomon, but many view this as a late editorial addition reflecting the popular rabbinical notion that Solomon wrote the Song in his youth, Proverbs in mid-life, and Ecclesiastes in seasoned maturity. But if this were allowed, Solomonic authorship cannot be tossed aside just because it is an ancient tradition. Actually, the reason provided for distrusting the early date of verse 1 is that the verse employs the word "which" (Hebrew, *'ăsher*), a term the critics allege Solomon would not have used. This assumption is nowhere adequately supported.

Theophile Meek is representative of scholars who beg the issue by charging that "No serious scholar today believes that Solomon was the author, and there are few who believe that the book was the work of a single hand. It is too repetitious for that and too disorderly in its content."[7] The principal reason for Meek's conclusion is the supposed disorderliness of the contents. Accordingly, Meek suggests that the book is simply a group of poems that developed along with the people across the centuries.[8]

So the critics fail to achieve unanimity regarding the degree of Solomonic participation. Because there is no substantive reason to depart from the opinion of the rabbis or conservative scholars who across the years have argued for the unity of the book and the authorship of Solomon, it is best to attribute the book to

6. Marvin Pope, *Song of Songs,* The Anchor Bible (New York: Doubleday, 1982), p. 27.
7. Theophile Meek, *The Interpreter's Bible*, vol. 5 (New York: Abingdon, 1956), p. 96.
8. Ibid., p. 97.

Solomon as the first verse suggests and the remainder of the Song purports. To the author himself no problem existed in the supposed disorderliness of the book, which is reflected in the decisions interpreters must make concerning the speaker in the book's various segments. An author often writes something perfectly lucid to him and his immediate readers that those removed from the text by several millennia may find obscure, disorderly, and even stylistically incomprehensible.

Still, the content of the book is in perfect accord with what the Bible reveals elsewhere about this tenth-century B.C. poet-king, who was blessed with remarkable wisdom. Since earliest evidences ascribe the book to Solomon and since the critics of the last two centuries have failed to show convincingly why Solomon could not have been the author, there is every reason to take the book at face value. First Kings 4:32–34 provides the matrix out of which such a conclusion can be reasonably drawn.

> And he spake three thousand proverbs: and his songs were a thousand and five. And he spake of trees, from the cedar tree that is in Lebanon even unto the hyssop that springeth out of the wall: he spake also of beasts, and of fowl, and of creeping things, and of fishes. And there came of all people to hear the wisdom of Solomon, from all kings of the earth, which had heard of his wisdom.

DATE

The question of date is inseparably linked to the question of authorship. If a Solomonic origin of the whole is rejected, then Pope's thesis is the most probable alternative. Pope attaches considerable credibility to the arguments of Chaim Rabin, of the Hebrew University in Jerusalem, who insists that at least portions of the Song must reflect Solomon's era. Pope also seems to follow the suggestion of Robert Gordis that the final redactions of the book were complete by the fifth century B.C., bringing the book to its present form.[9]

9. Pope, p. 26.

On the other hand, if the Song is viewed as the work of Solomon, then the date can be established with greater precision. Solomon ascended the throne in 971/70 B.C. and reigned until his death in 931 B.C. Since the Song identifies Solomon as king at the time of writing, the parameters for dating are set.

There is no way to determine with any greater certainty what the date of composition may have been. Certain presuppositions, however, are reasonable and lend probability to a time near the beginning of Solomon's reign, possibly before 965 B.C. For example, the text mentions the presence of 60 queens and 80 concubines (6:8)—both numbers falling considerably short of the 700 wives and 300 concubines reported in 1 Kings 11:3. Critics assert that the Kings numbers are exaggerated. A more logical assumption is that a summation of the harem's size as accumulated over Solomon's forty-year reign is found in the Kings account, whereas the numbers provided in the Song show the early composition of the poem.

Furthermore, it is not entirely certain that Song 6:8 should be interpreted as referring to the existence of a harem for Solomon's use. These queens and concubines could have been the residue of David's harem, inherited but not indulged by Solomon— Scripture indicates that severe problems surfaced with reference to the disposition of some members of David's harem (1 Kings 2:13–25)—or they could have been members of a royal wedding party. In any case the wholesomeness of the love portrayed in the Song of Solomon and the apparent exclusive devotion of Solomon to the Shulamite shepherdess suggest a time prior to the promiscuity of the king and the "turning away" of his heart (1 Kings 11:4). Add to this the ancient Jewish avowal that the Song was the product of the romance of the king's youth and the case for an early dating of the book seems probable.

INTERPRETATIONS

Interpretations of the Song of Solomon are almost as numerous as the volumes written on the subject. Generally these fall into seven rather distinct categories. The first, allegorical interpretation, encompasses the largest single segment of literature on the Song.

ALLEGORICAL INTERPRETATION

Allegorical interpretations of the Song have prevailed among both Jewish and Christian commentators. Jewish interpretations are drawn principally from the Talmud (ca. A.D. 150–500) and from the even more extensive and imaginative allegories of the sixth-century Targum to the Song. Several distinct approaches are discernible in this literature. Some viewed the Song as an expression of the union between Yahweh and His wife, Israel. The Targum expanded this to discover in the poem a historical allegory depicting Israel's experiences from the time of the Exodus to the advent of Messiah. This tradition has continued from the Middle Ages into modernity. In 1977 Jewish commentators produced a translation of the Song based on the comments of the medieval interpreter Rashi (Rabbi Solomon ben Isaac d. 1105) and an anthologized commentary gathered from talmudic, midrashic, and rabbinic sources. Rabbis Meir Zlotowitz and Nosson Scherman, who prepared the volume, support the allegorical approach. Incredibly, they suggest that "the only 'literal' translation of *Shir HaShirim* [i.e., the Song of Solomon] is allegorical." The difficulty of accounting for the maze of interpretations, many of them apparently mutually exclusive, was not missed, however. The compilers explain,

> The readers will note that the various commentaries often appear to be mutually exclusive. They are not; they complement each other just as each of the many facets of a diamond plays a part in enhancing the brilliance of a precious stone. As the Talmud says:
> "The school of Rabbi Ishmael taught: '[The word of God is] like a hammer that breaks a rock in pieces' (Jeremiah 23:29). Just as a hammer [striking a rock] divides into many sparks, so,

too, every word emanating from the mouth of the Holy One, blessed be He, divides into seventy interpretations (Shabbos 88b)."[10]

Christian allegorists employed the same methods as their Jewish counterparts but arrived at different conclusions. Zockler has provided five divisions for analysis of the Christian allegorists. These are (1) mystico-spiritual, (2) mystico-doctrinal, (3) mystico-historical, (4) mystico-chronological, and (5) mystico-mariological. Mystico-spiritual interpreters view the Song as an insight into the intimate union of Christ and the believer effected by regeneration. In the mystico-doctrinal perspective Shulamith represents the church, the bride of Christ, and Solomon typifies Christ. The majority of Christian interpreters adopt this position, though they differ radically in specific details. Mystico-historical advocates follow the view of the Targum, seeing in the Song a history of the theocracy of the Old Testament, whereas mystico-chronologists adapt the historical motif to the church and see the Song as a history of the church. Still more farfetched were the mystico-mariological interpreters, who by some allegorical sleight of hand found that the Shulamite was really Mary, the mother of God.

DRAMATIC INTERPRETATION

As early as the fourth and fifth centuries the Song was construed as a drama. That view has also found currency in modern exegesis. Generally two different approaches can be noted. Some, like Delitzsch, divide the Song into acts and scenes, assigning major parts to Solomon and his rural lover, Shulamith, and a minor role to a chorus of virgins. Other dramatic interpreters detect three major characters: the beautiful country girl, her shepherd lover, and the amorous and worldly King Solomon, who tries to woo the shepherdess into his harem. These inter-

10. Meir Zlotowitz and Nosson Scherman, *Shir HaShirim* (New York: Mesorah, 1977), p. xii, xiii.
11. Zockler, pp. 28–35.

preters see the Song as an apology for chastity and monogamy and a polemic against polygamy.

WEDDING SONG INTERPRETATION

Proponents of this view, observing that the Song has been used extensively in Jewish nuptial celebrations, suspect that this indicates that the Song was originally a series of descriptive poems, called *wasfs*, extolling the bride's virtues and sung to her over the period of a week.

LITURGICAL OR CULTIC INTERPRETATION

Espoused by the majority of modern liberal scholars, the liturgical or cultic approach views the Song as the surviving form of ancient Hebrew New Year liturgies that depicted the still more ancient myths of the fertility cults of Mesopotamia. Marvin Pope and Theophile Meek cite passages from Ugaritic, Babylonian, and Indian literature that employ phraseology similar to the Song. This suggests to many writers that the Hebrews borrowed substantive elements from these religions and gradually deleted the more objectionable, less ethical, dimensions. For these inter- preters the Song of Solomon is not really a word from God but a fascinating story of evolving history and developing religion.

SECULAR LOVE SONG INTERPRETATION

Theodore of Mopsuestia (A.D. 360–429) was perhaps the first to view Canticles as a collection of secular love songs. Robert Gordis has written a more recent analysis of the Song in which he advocates the same position with some modifications.[12] Most exponents of this theory argue that the early association of Solomon's name with the book caused its canonization.

12. Robert Gordis, *The Song of Songs and Lamentations* (New York: KTAV, 1954).

LITERAL INTERPRETATIONS

Dillow and Glickman are characteristic of modern interpreters who admit that the Song is a love song but differ sharply with those who have questions about its place in the canon. These literalists see no hidden theological agenda in the Song. They stress that the canon would have been incomplete without a work dignifying human love, for that, too, is a part of God's creation. The Song of Solomon demonstrates a godly approach to sexual and marital concerns.

LITERAL-ANALOGOUS INTERPRETATION

This approach to the Song of Solomon is a variation and expansion of the previous interpretation. It recognizes that the Song of Solomon is literally about human love and appropriately included in the canon even if that were its only dimension. But it also acknowledges that the Bible abounds in domestic analogies. In the Old Testament, for example, Israel is the wife of Yahweh. Israel's unfaithfulness to her husband, Jehovah, is the subject of both Hosea's prophecy and Ezekiel's parable of the two sisters (Ezek. 23). Again, the church is presented in the New Testament as the bride of Christ eagerly awaiting the coming of her bridegroom. Even though the New Testament imagery shifts away from strictly conjugal relationships, the domestic analogy is perpetuated in the concept that believers are the children of God the Father and brothers and sisters in Christ.

These analogies are useful in two ways. First, they utilize something from life that has been experienced and understood, at least to some degree, to express relationships existing in the higher or spiritual realm. Second, they tend to establish the idea of intimacy and permanence in the divine-human relationship, confirming the sanctity of the relationships that exist in the human family. Therefore the physical love expressed in Song of Solomon is not only noble and sanctified, it also illustrates the nature and permanency of the relationships existing between the saint and his Savior and between the church and her Lord.

It is crucial to distinguish this method from allegory. In allegories details are pressed into service for esoteric meanings never intended by the author, and there is no correspondence between the interpretation and the literal meaning of the words. The literal-analogous method, on the other hand, maintains this correspondence, even though it, too, extends beyond the author's recognized purpose, for it is unlikely that Solomon was aware of later possible analogies. But in the wisdom of the Holy Spirit the Song not only demonstrates God's blessings on monogamous love, including its most intimate expressions, but also suggests the greater spiritual intimacies and devotion that exist between Yahweh and Israel, and Christ and His church.

Embarking upon such a program of interpretation involves rejection of the other methods mentioned above, particularly the allegorical method, though it has been prominent even among evangelical theologians. Reasons for discarding this method need to be stated. First, although Theophile Meek was premature in announcing the demise of the allegorical interpretation of *Shîr HaShirîm*, his own critique is on target: "The allegorical interpretation could make the book mean anything that the fertile imagination of the expositor was able to devise, and in the end its very extravagancies were its undoing, so that it has now all but disappeared."[13] Meek is correct in asserting that a major reason for rejecting the allegorical interpretation is the inability of its advocates to reach a consensus. As Delitzsch observes, "The synagogal and church interpretation, in spite of two thousand years; labour, has yet brought to light no sure results, but only numberless absurdities, especially where the Song describes the lovers according to their members from head to foot and from foot to head."[14]

The second reason for abandoning the allegorical approach derives naturally from the first. In the absence of consensus eisegesis (the reading of one's own thoughts into the text) has

13. Meek, p. 93.
14. Delitzsch, p. 3.

prevailed. As a result, allegorical interpretations have ranged from the barely conceivable to the clearly preposterous. One may appreciate the profound piety and devotion evident in most of the allegorists and also recognize that imagination and emotion dictated their interpretation to the degree that the real message of the Song has often been completely obscured.

Finally, the historical milieu of the Song is forfeited. Much of the opportunity to glean insight into the life of the tenth century B.C. is missed. Worse, by hurdling the natural meaning of the text, one of the sublimest apologies for the sanctity and normalcy of human love is reduced to a mysterious ballad whose enigma remains unresolved after three millennia of earnest effort.

The dramatic approach, commendable in that it recognizes in the Song literature belonging essentially to the Solomonic era, is also rejected. Henry Green's critique of this view is telling. Assessing the efforts of both Delitzsch and Zockler, he concludes,

> They are both captivated with the idea, which we are persuaded is fallacious, of finding a regularly unfolded plot, and in their eagerness to make out continuity and progress they have obtruded upon this sacred poem what finds no warrant in its text, and marred the artless simplicity of its structure by needless complications.[15]

Additionally, drama was foreign to Jewish orthodoxy, characters are difficult to identify with certainty, and the book is more monologue than dialogue, all of which make the dramatic interpretation highly unlikely.

Advocates of the wedding song theory are guilty of reading later Judaism and the practices of other Semitic people back into the tenth century B.C. Although it is possible to view the Song of Solomon as an epithalamium written in anticipation or memory of nuptial events, one factor in the Song prevents this approach from being adequate. The epithalamium was almost always a

15. W. Henry Green, tr., "The Song of Solomon," in *Lange's Commentary on the Holy Scriptures* (Grand Rapids: Zondervan, 1969), p. 23.

song in honor of the bride and her virtues. Even though the Song of Solomon includes such praise, the king, or groom, is the subject of praise just as profuse as that of the bride. Therefore, Canticles is sufficiently distinct from other examples of epithalamia to render this interpretation untenable.

If the wedding song theory is untenable, the liturgical or cultic interpretation is unthinkable. Unquestionably similarities to the language and approach of the Song can be documented in the cultic poetry of Babylon, Assyria, and even India, for cross-cultural pollination of ideas and art forms was inevitable. Consequently, that the genre of cultic literature with its frequent depiction of sexual themes occasionally parallels the Song of Solomon comes as no surprise. But the involved and tedious attempts of scholars to establish certain influences and sure connections between these cultic hymns and the simple idyll of Solomon are useless. The tastefulness and beauty of the presentation of the intimate themes in the Song is in stark contrast to the blatant licentiousness of the cultic hymns. Furthermore, it has not been demonstrated that the Hebrews hallowed a cultic song by deleting the more objectionable elements. For where is the textual evidence of such purging? Or why must one assume that the Song is not substantially preserved as it was originally conceived?

The advocates of the liturgical or cultic view have advanced a fascinating theory almost completely lacking in historical, linguistic, and stylistic support. Authors such as Marvin Pope have provided superb analyses of the nature and decadence of the religious rites of the ancient world, but they have failed to provide compelling evidence to show that the Song of Solomon belonged in any sense to that genre of literature or to the general purposes of cultic worship. One can only conclude that the Song of Songs is precisely what it appears to be: a lovely song of love and devotion.

Does this mean that the fifth interpretation is correct? Should the Song be construed as a secular love song void of religious or theological significance? In a sense this view is the exact opposite of the liturgical view. Yet either approach would result logically in the exclusion of the Song from the canon of Scripture. In the case of the liturgical view exclusion is the only possibility because the nature and purpose of the Song would fail to meet the high moral and spiritual standards of the other canonical books. The secular love song theory has the same result because it is widely acknowledged that the Bible is a book of faith and theology, and there is no place in the canon for atheological literature.

However, the absence of the word *God* is not a conclusive argument for the secularity of the Song, for the very context from which it is derived makes the Song religious. Israel's genesis and continued existence constitute a theological milieu. And like the book of Esther in which God's name is also absent, the context of the Song and its use in Judaism is that of faith. Also, the extensive treatment of such themes as marriage, cohabitation, relationships, and the populating of the earth are established religious themes from the earliest chapters of Genesis. The Song of Solomon is not merely secular.

The literal approaches of Dillow, Glickman, and others are much more faithful to the intent of the book. The limitations of these strictly literal approaches are the tendency to see sexuality as a more prominent feature of the Song than is justified by the text and the propensity to overreact to the absurdities of the allegorical method to the extent of missing justifiable analogy.

Therefore, the most satisfying approach is the seventh, which views the Song of Solomon as a love song of Solomon and Shulamith. It derives its religious significance and its place in the canon in two ways. First, God is the creator of man, his sexuality, and all other facets of his being. How man uses God-given abilities is frequently the most basic distinction between sin and righteousness. In the Song of Solomon the lovers are on holy ground, demonstrating, as will be shown in the commentary, that love is more than selfish satisfaction. Second, the invigorating relationship of devotion between the lovers is analogous to the devotion and tenderness that ideally exists between Christ and His church.

J. Sidlow Baxter takes a similar approach. He views the book as an *idyll*, a short, pictorial love poem couched in pastoral rather than epic, heroic, or dramatic scenes. Further, he identifies Psalm 45 as an example of the same type of literature and suggests that the psalm may owe its origin to the period and events that produced the Song of Solomon. Pointing to the use of Psalm 45:6–7 in Hebrews 1:8–9, Baxter discovers a messianic analogy applicable to the Song.[16]

There is no question about the similarity of Psalm 45 and the Song of Solomon. Neither can the messianic nature of Psalm 45:6–7 be questioned, for the passage is so interpreted in Hebrews. The only difficulty in Baxter's approach is the lack of specific use of the Song in similar interpretive passages in the New Testament. Although this presents no major problem to understanding the Song as a love poem analogously depicting the relationship between Jesus and the church, it does limit the extent of the analogy and excludes the pressing of details. The analogy should be interpreted broadly.

The sense in which the sacredness of physical love is religious has been expressed succinctly by Robert Gordis.

> When the Song of Songs is studied without preconceived notions, it emerges as a superb lyrical anthology, containing songs of love and nature, of courtship and marriage, all of which revel in the physical aspects of love and reveal its spiritual character. The two Greek terms, *eros*, "carnal love," and *agape, "caritas*, spiritual love," reflect a dichotomy that has entered into classical Christian theology. The classical Hebrew outlook, on the contrary, finds it entirely proper to apply the same root, *'ahabah*, to all aspects of love. The ideal relationship of man to God, "You shall love the Lord your God" (Deut. 6:5), the love of one's fellow man, "You shall love your neighbor as yourself" (Lev. 19:18),

16. J. Sidlow Baxter, *Explore the Book*, vol. 3 (Grand Rapids: Zondervan, 1962), pp. 173–81.

"You shall love him (the stranger) as yourself" (Lev. 19:34), and the love of man and woman. "How fair and how pleasant you are, O love, with its delights!" (Song of Songs 7:7)—all are expressed in the Bible by the same Hebrew word.[17]

Certainly this is the major significance of the Song of Solomon. It is an idyll of love that focuses upon companionship, loyalty, joy, peace, devotion, forgiveness, chastity, tenderness, and sexual union as the plan and purpose of God in marriage. Such a marriage, with all of its finest attributes, is one of the primary pictures used in both Old and New Testaments to explain the union of God and His people.

The Song of Songs is profitable, then, for those who seek to inculcate the plan of God in their own marriages. From it emerge attitudes and perceptions that are both righteous and foundational for happiness and fruitfulness in marriage and the home. Furthermore, the scope is ever widening. Relationships of parent-child, brother-sister, and the larger family unit are impacted. Indeed, as the interpreter comprehends the message of the Song and applies it to his own family relationships, he will inevitably be drawn to the conclusion that the godly attitudes and perspectives portrayed in this book are also characteristic of those that should exist in his relationship to God.

CANONICITY

The place of the Song of Solomon in the canon has been vigorously debated. Rabbi Shammai and Theodore of Mopsuestia were surely wrong in their assessments that the Song should be excluded. Rabbi Hillel and many Christian exegetes were also in error in viewing the Song as the apex of all revelation. Rather, the Song of Songs is an essential part of biblical revelation, extolling the wonder and joy of the most intimate human commitment. Such a book is needed in the Bible.

17. Gordis, p. x.

In the final analysis the only reasons marshalled for its exclusion are (1) the absence of the name of God; (2) the presence of frank language regarding physical intimacies; and (3) the difficulty of interpretations. The first objection fails to understand that what makes a book religious or theological is not bound up exclusively in the presence or absence of God's name. Besides, there is evidence that the personal name for God may, in fact, appear in 8:6. The second objection fails to understand the sacredness of marriage, including its physical aspect. The third objection was answered by J. Hudson Taylor, far-famed missionary to China, in a small monograph first published in 1914.

> Like other portions of the Word of God, this book has its difficulties. But so have all the works of God. Is not the fact that they surpass our unaided powers of comprehension and research a "sign-manual" of divinity? Can feeble man expect to grasp divine power, or to understand and interpret the works or the providences of the All-wise? And if not, is it surprising that His Word also needs superhuman wisdom for its interpretation? Thanks be to God, the illumination of the Holy Ghost is promised to all who seek for it: what more can we desire?[18]

OUTLINE

The difficulties of interpreting the Song of Solomon extend to the outlining of the book. Efforts to outline are essentially designed to determine a book's structure. The Song yields itself to numerous possible divisions, none of which can be exclusively substantiated. I have chosen to include the outline that I prepared for the *Criswell Study Bible*[19]:

I. The Setting of the Wedding: A Time for Mutual Expressions of Love (1:1–2:7).

    A. The Anticipation of Preparation for the Wedding Festivities in the Palace (1:1–8).

18. J. Hudson Taylor, *Union and Communion* (London: China Inland Mission, 1914), p. 2.
19. W. A. Criswell, ed., *Criswell Study Bible* (Nashville: Thomas Nelson, 1979).

B. The Sharing of Praise at the Banquet Table (1:9–14).

C. The Excitement of Fulfillment in the Bridal Chamber (1:15–2:7).

II. The Time of Courtship: A Time for Mutual Delight in Love (2:8–3:5).

A. The Invitation to Commitment for Lovers (2:8–14).

B. The Challenge of Lovers in Facing Problems (2:15–17).

C. The Attack on Lovers by Doubts and Jealousies (3:1–5).

III. The Wedding Procession and Ceremony: A Time for Mutual Praise (3:6–5:1).

A. The Splendor of the Bridal Procession (3:6–11).

B. The Ecstasy of the Wedding Night (4:1–5:1).

IV. The Marriage: A Time for Mutual Adjustment (5:2–8:4).

A. Mutual Desire (5:2–8).

B. Mutual Admiration (5:9–8:4).

1. The Shulamite's description of the king (5:9–6:3).

2. King Solomon's description of the Shulamite (6:4–8:4).

V. The Conclusion: The Love Covenant Between Solomon and the Shulamite (8:5–14).

1

THE ANTICIPATION OF LOVE

The initial segment of the Song of Songs captures the emotions, confidences, and in some cases the reticence of the shepherd girl known to us as Shulamith. (Actually Shulamith is a reference to the geographical area from which she came. In this book the designation will be used as a substitute for her name, which is unknown.) The initial verses express her burgeoning desire for love, her natural timidity when faced with the aristocracy of the court, and her adoration for the one who had become her royal lover.

1:1. The legitimate title of the book is the "Song of Songs" (Hebrew, *Shîr HaShirîm*). The expression is like other intensives found in the Old Testament, such as "Holy of holies," the reference to the inner sanctum of the tabernacle, or "vanity of vanities," the expression so prevalent in Ecclesiastes. According to 1 Kings 4:32 Solomon was prolific in his production of both proverbs and songs, numbered at 3,000 and 1,005 respectively. Obviously, the majority of these have not been preserved for us in any of Solomon's writings (Proverbs, Song of Solomon, Ecclesiastes). The declaration, however, that this is the song of songs emphasizes that it was the zenith of his songwriting labor.

The text identifies the Song as having been written by Solomon, but considerable question exists concerning this first verse. Some think it constitutes a title for the book added later, perhaps during the post-exilic period, in which case the actual song begins with verse 2. If that is the case, verse 1 bears eloquent testimony to the early unanimity regarding the Solomonic authorship of the book and should be given its fair value by those who allege that the book is a compilation of love songs from multiple sources. If, on the other hand, the title was written by the author of the Song, he either has misled us or is indeed Solomon as declared. In either case, inasmuch as deception on the part of the writer is unlikely, the remaining choices leave powerful evidence for the hand of Solomon, the king who reigned from 971/70 to 931 B.C.

Obviously all of the songs penned by Solomon were not of the same genre as this one. Many were songs of worship and praise. Certain psalms (such as 72, 127, and perhaps 45) have been credited to Solomon. Assuming that these were indeed written by him, it may seem strange that this particular song would be considered his ultimate accomplishment. One reason for assigning such an important place to the Song of Songs lies in the fact that it stands in isolation among the books of the Bible as an expression of the rightness and righteousness of conjugal love. Further, as indicated in the introduction, by analogy the book suggests the sweetness and intimacy of the love of Christ for His people.

1:2. Marking a major distinction between the Song of Songs and the love ballads of other cultures, Shulamith not only spoke more frequently than Solomon but also initiated the idyll with an expression of desire for her royal lover. That desire was specifically a longing for "the kisses of his mouth," a universal symbol of tender affection. Especially is the kiss the appropriate yet chaste initiatory expression of warm affection and intent on the part of a man for a woman. It is worth noting that Shulamith did not see herself in an aggressive role but rather awaited Solomon's overture. The reason for her desire was that Solomon's love was "better than wine." In most modern cultures interpret-

ers would find it difficult to appreciate the significance of that
statement. But in the culture of the tenth century B.C. wine
constituted almost the total fare for drinking other than water.
Only in modernity do we have such a variety of drinks to choose
from. Consequently, wine was not merely another liquid; it was
highly treasured. And the best wine was carefully preserved for
the most important social occasions (see Esther 7:2). However,
for the Shulamith there was no social occasion, whatever the
accompanying pleasure and joy, to equal the tender expressions
of Solomon's love for which she longed. Although Zockler
argues that what is in view here is not so much the intoxicating
power of wine as its sweetness, the context of other Solomonic
writings suggests the possibility that both may be in view. In
Proverbs 5:19, for example, a man is cautioned to be "ravished
always" with the love of the wife of his youth. "Ravished"
(Hebrew, *tishgeh*) means "to be drunken" or "inebriated."

"Your love" is a translation of the Hebrew word *dôd*. Unlike
'ahăbâ, which is a broad term for love, *dôd* indicates a physical
expression. Its association with the kiss in verse 2 leaves little
doubt that this was the author's intent.

1:3. Not only was the tender physical expression of love
valued, but also the Shulamith's affection for the name of her
lover was expressed. Names were of far greater significance in
antiquity, especially in the cultures of the Middle East, than in
the modern world. Names were bestowed on children for various
reasons. Sometimes the anticipated character of the child was
involved, such as when Joseph was instructed by the angel to
call the name of Mary's child Jesus ("Yahweh is salvation")
because He would save His people from their sins. Occasionally
a child was naméd as an expression of the parents' particular
feeling at the time of the birth. A poignant case of this is
Benjamin's birth to Rachel at Bethlehem on the way to Ephrath
(Gen. 35:18). Rachel named her child Benoni, meaning "son of
my sorrow," apparently because she recognized that her life was
ebbing away. However, Jacob changed his name to Benjamin,

meaning "son of my right hand," thereby indicating that though
he sorrowed for Rachel, he viewed Benjamin as a special asset.
In another instance Sarah named her son Isaac, or "laughter,"
perhaps a reference to her elation at giving birth to a child in her
old age (Gen. 21:5–6). Sometimes the parent would name the
child to reflect his desire in regard to the child's future. Nevertheless, in most cases the name of the child was significant and
came to be a reflection of his character and purpose.

Those who advocate the shepherd-lover hypothesis face their
first serious interpretative difficulty in this verse. For though the
name of a shepherd-lover might be especially significant to
Shulamith, it could scarcely be said of all the virgins that they
loved him. Such a statement would be applicable only to a major
public figure who was universally known in the kingdom. Properly the verse argues strongly for the view that Solomon was
Shulamith's lover.

Shulamith extolled Solomon as one whose name was like a
pungent ointment that has been "poured forth" or "wafted
about" the room. (Seeing the name as a fragrant unguent is a
theme found elsewhere in the Scriptures; see Eccles. 7:1). As a
consequence of the pleasurable sensation created by the mere
mention of his name, the virgins are said to love him also.
"Virgins" (Hebrew, *'ălāmôt*) is one of the two words (the other
is *bᵉtûlâ*) that may be properly rendered "virgin." It has been
argued that only *bᵉtûlâ* truly bears this meaning. However, of the
seven instances in which *'almâ* appears in the Scripture (Gen.
24:43; Ex. 2:8; Ps. 68:25; Prov. 30:19; and Song 1:3 and 6:8)
the word seems always to denote a virgin and not merely a
young woman of marriageable age. In Isaiah 7:14 the Jewish
translators of the Septuagint so understood it and thus rendered
'almâ as *parthenos* or virgin. In the case before us the word may
suggest either the presence in Solomon's court of numerous
unmarried females who remained virgins while performing their
various functions in the royal household or virgins in general, a
reference to the fact that all the young ladies of the kingdom
would have been honored, as was Shulamith, to have been the

object of Solomon's affections. From the expression itself no case can be made to indicate that these women constituted a harem.

This praise of Solomon's name is also important because it reflects a theme that will reappear with some frequency in the Song, namely, that the intimacy of sexual love is predicated on other commitments and perceptions. In this case Shulamith's admiration for Solomon, her glorying in the mention of his name, portrays an almost worshipful adoration of him. Her perception provided the kind of relationship in which sexual love can receive its most profound meaning.

1:4. The frequent use of the first personal plural pronoun "we" may indicate that verse 4 is the response of the chorus. There are places where an unseen and actually nonexistent chorus seems to chime into the narrative. Such a case is clearly found in verse 8 of this chapter. Whether verse 4 is a continuation of the statement of Shulamith or the refrain of the chorus, however, makes no difference in its ultimate interpretation because the initial words are "draw me." Still, it may be better to see the verse as a continued appeal for Shulamith.

The rich tones of the word "draw" (Hebrew, *māshak*) have to do with the intimacies of love to be experienced only between two persons. The word might well be translated "tenderly beckon me to follow" and is associated elsewhere in Scripture with the compelling power of Yahweh's love for His people. This points the reader to an important analogy. In Jeremiah 31:3 Yahweh says, "The Lord hath appeared of old unto me, saying, Yea, I have loved thee with an everlasting love: therefore with lovingkindness have I drawn thee." Again in Hosea 11:4 He says, "I drew them with cords of a man, with bands of love: and I was to them as they that take off the yoke on their jaws, and I laid meat unto them."

Shulamith not only expressed her desire for Solomon to draw her, she promised to run after him when he did, exalting in the fact that the king has brought her into his chambers. The king's chambers could be the royal palace; more probably they are Solomon's private chambers. Understandably, this is a cause of gladness and rejoicing for Shulamith, who again promised to remember Solomon's love more than the tasty wine of a feast.

The concluding phrase declares that all who love Solomon do so justly. The phrase may mean that those who love him do so sincerely or from a right heart. Interestingly, the word for "love" is not *dôd* used for Shulamith's physical relationship with Solomon as before (v. 2), but *'ahăbâ*, i.e., a love that could function without physical ramifications of any kind.

1:5. Contemplating her surprising transfer to the king's private chambers within the royal palace, Shalamith allowed herself an introspective moment to reminisce about her origins and present circumstances. Certain important facts are revealed in verses 5 and 6. Shulamith noted that she was "black, but comely." She further called on the "daughters of Jerusalem," apparently a reference to the other women of the court, to note that she was like "the tents of Kedar" and "the curtains of Solomon."

As Delitzsch says, "These words express humility without abjectness."[1] He further notes that "black" (Hebrew, *sheḥôrâ*) is not intended to note "soot blackness" but a developing darkness brought about, as the text later declares, by the tanning of the sun. Shulamith compared her blackness to the tents of Kedar. Kedar is apparently a reference to an ancient Ishmaelite tribe of whom Pliny spoke. The black, goat-hair tents were part of the Bedouin culture that has been perpetuated from the tenth century B.C. until the present day. These tents are especially adaptable to the Bedouin way of life and were not only readily observable to a country girl but perhaps constituted Shulamith's dwelling place at times.

Shulamith tastefully admitted to a certain natural comeliness. The word "comely" (Hebrew, *nā'wâ*) is one of two words

1. Delitzsch, p. 25.

translated "beauty" in the Song. The word *yapâ*, used in 6:4 and 7:1 implies not only physical beauty but internal suitableness also, whereas *nā'wâ* seems primarily to reflect physical beauty. Shulamith compared her comeliness to the curtains of Solomon. Whether the reference is to the richer and more lustrously colored tents that Solomon might employ in the field or to the tapestries of the palace is not certain. In either case the point is clear that whereas Shulamith was dark or swarthy from exposure to the sun, she was nonetheless possessed of a certain natural beauty that the keenly observant Solomon had noted at first sight.

1:6. Shulamith continued with an explanation of her swarthiness. Cautioning the daughters of Jerusalem not to stare at her because of her blackness, she explained that the sun had "looked upon" her. This transpired as a result of the rather harsh treatment of her brothers, who in anger thrust her into the vineyards as a vinedresser. The constant outdoor labor exposed her to the rays of the baking sun.

Some authors understand the phrase "my mother's children" to mean that those who had thrust her into the vineyards were either halfbrothers or stepbrothers with little interest in Shulamith, possibly viewing her as competition. Such a conclusion, however, is not warranted, for the Scriptures frequently refer to siblings with similar expressions (see Gen. 27:29; Deut. 13:6; and Ps. 50:20 where the expression "mother's sons" seems to mean "brothers"). What probably can be legitimately deduced from this passage is that Shulamith's father had died when she was very young. The vineyards that the family kept were passed along to the brothers, and the entire family had to work. Perhaps there were other sisters (at least one may be mentioned in 8:8) who labored in the tasks around the home. Shulamith, failing to find favor with her brothers, was placed in the vineyards.

In the concluding comparison, Shulamith contrasted her own body to the vineyards that she tended. Because she was forced to labor in her brothers' vineyards, she lamented that her own vineyard had not been kept. Observation of the daughters of Jerusalem, the ladies of the court, had doubtless reminded her that natural beauty was all she possessed. She had not had available to her the luxurious baths and toiletries or fashionable clothing of the court. There had been no opportunity for her to take care of her hair, skin, or hands according to the obvious courtly style.

1:7. Solomon had ferried Shulamith from her country home to his own chambers (v. 4). It now becomes apparent, however, that her expression of longing for him in the early verses of chapter 1 was brought about by his temporary absence from the palace. Solomon was away either checking his possessions or directing the affairs of state. Shulamith's statement suggests the former, but Zockler does not think it constitutes an actual reference to Solomon's pastoral activities. Instead it is an indication that Shulamith knew nothing of the responsibilities of the king and interpreted his absence in the only milieu that she did know, that of following the flocks. But there is indication in Ecclesiastes 2:7 that Solomon possessed flocks, and though he was a king abundantly endowed with wealth, it is also probable that the pastoral activities of his own father, David, had left Solomon with intense interest in such pursuits. The shrewdness of his observations of animal and insect life, seen not only in the Song but also in Proverbs, bears eloquent testimony to the frequency with which Solomon must have been in the field.

Shulamith's plaintive request to be told the precise location of the feeding and resting places of Solomon's flocks may be understood as the desire to leave the palace and go to him in the fields. Not only would she feel more at home there, but that was also where they had enjoyed fellowship together. Shulamith certainly longs for the personal, physical expression of Solomon's love, but more than that she simply wants to be with him. This may be seen in her use of the word "loveth" (Hebrew, (*'ahăbâ*), which expresses a kind of love that is void of selfish-

ness and desires and wants only the opportunity to meet the
needs of the object of its affections.

The concluding phrase of the verse has been the subject of
considerable debate. The problem concerns the Hebrew word
translated "turneth aside." The term k^e'$\hat{o}t^ey\hat{a}$ is thought by some to
derive from '$\bar{a}t\hat{a}$, meaning "to cover." Hence, Shulamith's
statement reads, "Why should I be as one who is veiled [the
mark of an unscrupulous woman of licentious intent] by the
flocks of thy companions [i.e., for all to see]?" But this sense is
alien to the passage. The Syriac version and the Targums favor
the rendering "wandering" or "straying," which also better fits
the context. In short, Shulamith asked about Solomon's location
to save her (his beloved) from wandering about and searching
for him among the flocks of his companions.

1:8. The chorus, which, one must remember, merely reflected
the poetic nature of the Song, responded to her request in a
rather condescending way. They acknowledged Shulamith as the
fairest among women but taunted that if she did not know the
whereabouts of her lover and was not willing to wait in the
palace for his return, then she should take her little goats and be
content to feed them beside the shepherd's tents. Delitzsch is
probably right in supposing that this was an ironic response
designed to remind Shulamith that if she could not "apprehend
the position of Solomon, she may just remain what she is."[2] The
saying was designed to hurt and to repulse.

1:9. Verses 9 to 11 constitute Solomon's first praise of
Shulamith. The initial comparison, which may be strange to
Western ears, was high praise indeed from an oriental monarch.
Solomon compared Shulamith to "a company of horses in
Pharoah's chariots." Archdeacon Aglen has noted that "an Arab
chief would not hesitate to prefer the points of his horse to the

2. Ibid., p. 32.

charms of his mistress.''[3] If Aglen's comment is overdrawn, it is
not by much. Actually the Hebrew text reads ''my mare'' rather
than ''company of horses.'' Solomon was providing a favorable
comparison between the beauty of his beloved and the stately,
sleek beauty of his favorite mare—a horse apparently bred in
Egypt for service with Pharaoh's chariots. Solomon's infatuation
with horses is noted in 2 Chronicles 9:28, where it is recorded
that he imported horses from Egypt and other countries, as well
as in 1 Kings 10:26, where it is said 12,000 horsemen and more
than 1,400 war chariots made up his entourage. Such a comparison was not at all unusual in ancient literature. Theocritus, for
example, compared ''the rose complexioned Helen'' to a
''Thessalian steed.'' For Solomon the horse was more a cher-
ished companion than a beast of burden. His praise of Shulamith
recognized her beauty and her graceful movements.

1:10. The beauty of Shulamith's cheeks accentuated with
''rows of jewels'' (Hebrew, *tôrîm*) that either dangled on both
sides of her head from a headband or possibly were interwoven
in the braids of her hair, was the subject of his next observation.
The stateliness of her neck was appropriately draped with glistening chains of gold.

1:11. The oriental delight in jewelry was characteristic of
Shulamith also and was carefully noted by Solomon, who pledged
to add to Shulamith's collection by providing her with further
ornaments of gold studded or pointed with silver. ''Borders'' is
the same word translated ''rows'' in verse 10.

1:12. Verses 12 and 13 suggest that the king had returned
from the royal pursuits of the day. It is not stated whether
Shulamith succeeded in her efforts to locate him. The success of
that mission, however, becomes unimportant because the scene

3. Charles John Ellicott, *Commentary on the Whole Bible* (Grand Rapids:
Zondervan, 1981), p. 388.

has shifted to the evening banquet table. The king's mind has focused on the evening ahead.

Shulamith had carefully prepared herself for her presentation to the king. It is noted that her "spikenard," or perfume, sent forth its inviting fragrance. Spikenard, or nard, was the extract of a plant grown in northern India and imported to the Middle East. The aromatic oil was used in much the same way that modern women use perfume. The pungency of this plant is substantiated by the narratives of Mark 14:3 and John 12:3 where Mary of Bethany poured an alabaster box of the expensive ointment on Jesus' head, resulting in the filling of the entire house with its fragrance. A small amount skillfully placed on the body of Shulamith was certain to reach the nostrils of her royal lover.

1:13. In anticipation of the intimacies that lay ahead. Shulamith described her well-beloved as a "bundle of myrrh." Myrrh, like frankincense, belongs to a family of aromatic leaves and flowers that are grown in Palestine. It was often specially prepared and tied together in a small repository that dangled from the neck of a woman, falling between her breasts. The suggestion here is metaphorical. It is not that Shulamith wore such a bundle on this occasion but rather that Solomon himself constituted such a sweet fragrance between her breasts. The picture that evolves is one of sweet intimacy that did not exhaust itself in coitus but continued through the night hours in fond and restful embrace.

1:14. The four concluding verses of the chapter revert to Solomon's adoration of Shulamith. Solomon compared her to a "cluster of camphire in the vineyards of Engedi." Camphire is to be identified with henna, a plant providing both a perfume and a paste used extensively in Palestine until this day. The henna is a small shrub reaching a maximum of ten feet in height with pale green foliage cratering clusters of white and yellow blossoms. The fragrance is powerful, and a paste made from the dried leaves is used for the dyeing of the palms of the hands and sometimes the soles of the feet. Although apparently not native to Palestine, it was transplanted and grew for awhile in abundance at Engedi.

Engedi, meaning "the well of the goat," often figures into the biblical narrative. It may be visited even today on the West bank of the Dead Sea between Qumran and Masada. A beautiful oasis, Engedi spawned by a waterfall that runs year around from high in the Judean highlands, down a rocky gorge, and into the Dead Sea. Trees and shrubs grow plentifully on all sides of the river, and the rocks above are inhabited by wild goats known as ibex. Visitors today may observe rather large herds of these graceful mountain goats and occasionally spot one of the numerous leopards now returning in strength to the area.

Engedi is mentioned in the prophecy of Ezekiel as one of the borders of an enormous fishing village that will exist during the Millennium, when the Dead Sea brings forth fish abundantly (Ezek. 47:10). It was the place to which David frequently repaired when pursued by King Saul. In fact, it was here that he had the opportunity to take Saul's life, choosing instead to leave the king to the judgment of God (1 Sam. 24:1–6). Beautiful pools of water and cool caves surrounded the area otherwise baked by the tropical heat. Henna was the most pungent of all the plants grown in the vineyards of Engedi. As Solomon looked across the table at Shulamith and caught the scent of her perfume, he was reminded of the sweet smelling henna of Engedi.

1:15. Solomon continued to observe his beloved. He noted that she was "fair." Overwhelmed with her beauty, he repeated the avowal again. Each time the Hebrew word is *yāpâ*, indicating a beauty that was far more extensive than mere shapeliness and physical attraction. He noted particularly her eyes, which intrigued him enough to merit mention again in 4:9, where he observed that, with just one look of her eye, she ravished his heart. Her eyes were compared to a dove's, apparently an indication of the softness, purity, gentleness, and simplicity of Shulamith's gaze.

1:16. Shulamith's fairness was noted a third time, suggesting the degree to which Solomon had become captivated by the simple beauty of this rustic maiden. The word "pleasant" (Hebrew, *nā'îm*), a general term for "good" or "loveliness," is used to describe the taste of bread in Proverbs 9:17, the music of a lyre in Psalm 81:2, and the name of God in Psalm 135:3, which records: "Sing praises unto his name; for it is pleasant."

The concluding phrase of the verse comments that the bed or couch shared by the couple is green. Some would understand this as a reference to the bed of Solomon within the palace, which, according to this view, is described in verse 17. This would not mean that Solomon's bed was painted green or draped with green silks but rather that the expressions of love on that bed were fresh and alive. However, in 3:7 Solomon's bed is referred to by a different Hebrew word. Even though the reference there is not to the bed in Solomon's palace, it still seems unlikely that *'ereś* (the word used here) refers to the bed in Solomon's chamber. It is more likely that Solomon's thoughts had reverted to the pleasant circumstance under which he first noticed Shulamith. There is evidence that their initial contacts were the product of a chance meeting in the meadows of Galilee (7:11–12 and 8:5). The reference to a bed of green, therefore, would not describe the bed of sexual intimacies found in chapter 3 but the joy and happiness of the open-air meeting in the verdant meadows.

1:17. Although the cedar house beams with fir tree rafters are conceivable descriptions of the Solomonic palace (see 1 Kings 6:9), it seems more probable that they also refer to the idyllic scene that was the location of the couple's initial rendezvous. Lying or sitting on the ground, they talked and imagined that the cedar and fir trees overhead comprised the beams and rafters of their temporary domicile. Cedars were grown extensively in Lebanon, and they were not unknown in the boundaries of Israel, especially in northern Galilee where Shulamith resided.

In all, the language of verses 16 and 17 emphasizes the pleasantness of the physical surroundings resulting from the joy of fellowship between Solomon and his beloved.

For Further Study

1. In a good concordance trace the significance of the "kiss."
2. Read an article in a standard encyclopedia such as *Britannica* on the "Bedouin." See if you can determine the extent of the uses made of the black goat.
3. In verse 3 the "good name" is mentioned. What else do you find in Scripture about the importance of names?

2

COMMITMENT AND CHALLENGE

This chapter is divided logically into two portions. The first seven verses introduce the reader to the lovers' continued accolades for one another together with their progression in the intimacies of love. Verses 8–17 are cast in a rural setting in the spring of the year where the awakening of the flowers and the signs of the gentle birds of the field are the occasion for renewed romance between the two lovers.

PRAISE AND FULFILLMENT (1-7)

½2:1. Shulamith's first words may appear boastful. However, Solomon's bride did not intend them to be personal reflections of admiration for her own beauty but rather her recognition of the prominent position to which she has been elevated by virtue of the identity of her lover. Therefore Shulamith said, "I am a rose of the plain of Sharon."

At least three different possibilities are suggested for the location of Sharon. Delitzsch argues that the intended location is the district between Mt. Tabor and the Sea of Galilee because Shulamith is a Galilean.[1] There is also a Transjordanic Sharon

1. Delitzsch, p. 40.

mentioned in 1 Chronicles 5:16. But the most famous location by that name is the broad plain which covers the Mediterranean coast from Joppa, or modern Tel Aviv, to the region around Caesarea Maritima. Precisely which of these locations is intended it is not possible to say, though the probabilities lie with the latter due to its almost universal fame. "Rose" (Hebrew, *ḥăba'elet*) is either the lily, narcissus, or meadow saffron, a flower with poisonous bulbous roots that mixes shades of violet and white together. William Wilson suggests that etymologically the word comes from *hames*, meaning "acid" or "acrid," and *besel*, meaning "bulb." This would confirm that the meadow saffron is the correct identification.[2] Whichever flower is intended, however, the English reader should not visualize a rose but rather a wild autumn flower of the valley.

Next, Shulamith described herself as a "lily of the valleys." "Lily" (Hebrew, *shôshannâ*), which may be masculine or feminine in Hebrew, is feminine here. It refers to a lovely white blossom with six leaves and six petals. Occasionally the plant grows to four or more feet in height, and it is strikingly delicate in form. The lily was especially prominent as a decorative carving in the pillars of the temple and on the molten sea furnishing of the temple (1 Kings 7:19, 22, and 26). This flower was especially associated with nuptial occasions and perhaps even gave its name to wedding festivities. A possible case of this occurs in Psalm 45, mentioned earlier. That song is said to be for "the chief musician upon Shoshannim" (apparently the plural, "lilies"), thus referring to the use of these beautiful valley lilies in such weddings. In effect Shulamith has referred to herself as a wild flower in the meadow, her beauty being like that of wild vegetation rather than that of the carefully manicured flowers of the palace garden. The affirmation corresponds to her earlier observation in 1:5 that though she was black, she had a natural beauty.

2. William Wilson, *Old Testament Word Studies* (Grand Rapids: Kregel, 1978), p. 361.

2:2. Solomon responded to her affirmation as though to say, "Wild flower, indeed, my love, but a beautiful wild flower who appears like a flower among thorns when compared with all the other daughters of men." In the passage, "daughters" is equivalent to all other women in the world and is high praise indeed from one who daily observed the lovely women of the king's court.

The word used by Shulamith to identify Solomon has principally been *dōdî*, translated "my beloved" as in 1:13. Solomon here spoke of Shulamith as "my love" (Hebrew, *ra'yātî*) for the second time, the first being in 1:9. Delitzsch maintains that the word (derived from *rā'â*) means "to guard, care for, tend," or "ethically to delight in something particularly."[3] It appears to be the word that Solomon will favor to express his special delight with Shulamith. Compared to her, all of the other women assume the look of thorns. Solomon does not purpose here to be derogatory toward other women, only to be profuse in his praise of the superior virtues of Shulamith.

2:3. Shulamith replied to Solomon's panegyric with a eulogy of her own. She compared her beloved to "the apple tree among the trees of the wood." The precise nature of this apple tree (Hebrew, *tappûaḥ*) is in question. Some contend that the apples mentioned in Scripture are actually quinces—golden, fragrant, and delicious. That would explain the reference in Proverbs 25:11 to "apples of gold." Others think the citron is more probably the tree intended, for that tree not only has golden-colored apples but also is characterized by its refreshing scent. Because of its size, greenness, and beauty the citron tree could be noticed almost immediately in any arbor. Shulamith thought of Solomon as having the strength of the apple tree whose beauty was unique among all the trees of the woods. That the comparison of Solomon to an apple tree was intended to indicate strength is revealed by the protective dependent metaphor

3. Delitzsch, p. 32.

that Shulamith continues. Literally, the text reads, "In his shadow I delighted and I sat down." The seated posture is always one of rest and security. The extent of the dependence and trust displayed by Shulamith may be observed in the Hebrew verb *himmadtî*, for the piel stem intensifies its normal meaning. The translation might therefore read, "In his shadow I *greatly delighted* and I sat down."

Furthermore, Shulamith noted that "his fruit was sweet to my taste." "Sweet" (Hebrew, *matôq*) means "to smack the lips with delight."[4] Precisely what was in Shulamith's mind cannot be absolutely determined, but the expression certainly encompasses the physical intimacies they enjoyed. Probably, however, more is intended, for the passage obviously deals with attributes transcending physical intimacies. "Sweet fruit" is to serve later as a foundation for the expression of coitus. Sexual love, to be all that God intended, must be built upon such qualities as sincere admiration (1:3), absolute trust, and dependence.

2:4. To genuine admiration and trust Shulamith added a third foundational quality to godly love, namely, possession. She recounted that she was brought into Solomon's banqueting house and that his banner over her was love. As a wild flower of Sharon, transferred out of her native environment to the banqueting house of the king, she understandably would find herself ill at ease. However, her lover unfurled over her a banner of protective love. Noting the unfamiliarity of such a metaphor today, Gordis correctly observes that it is "a bold and striking figure."[5] It is conceivable that the comparison is either to a protective covering marked with the ownership of Solomon or to a battle standard placed on the wall of a city, identifying its allegiance and guaranteeing its protection. It is clear, however, that the banner of verse 4 is not a material banner but refers instead to the

4. Francis Brown, S. R. Driver, and C. A. Briggs, *A Hebrew and English Lexicon of the Old Testament* (Oxford: Clarendon, 1962), p. 608.
5. Gordis, p. 81.

abiding presence of Solomon's love (Hebrew, *'ahăbâ*). The
assurance of Solomon's devoted affection provided Shulamith
with the security so essential to happy marital relations. Seeing
herself as Solomon's possession did not suggest servility but
trust. Eventually this trust proved to be ill advised, for Solomon
attempted in later years to encompass other women under his
banner, but at this point in the relationship he had earned her
trust, and she was confident in his love.

2:5. The country girl's advancement to the court of the king
and her ardent desire for Solomon's love overwhelmed her. The
sickness described in this verse was not a physical malady; it
was the sense of being swept along uncontrollably. Nevertheless, the weakness experienced was very real. Shulamith's plea
was for sustenance, therefore, as suggested in the two Hebrew
verbs *sāmak*, meaning "to support" and translated "stay me,"
and *rāpad*, translated "comfort" and originally meaning "to
spread" but often "to spread about" in the sense of protecting
or guarding. Gradually the latter word evolved also to mean
"sustain." The original sense of "guard" is kept in the translation as "comfort me." However, the idea of comfort here is
clearly that of strengthening.

"Flagons" (Hebrew, *'ăshîshôt*) refers to dried fruit cakes,
perhaps raisin cakes, which were often the accompaniment of
romantic encounters in the ancient world. Apples, too (perhaps
again the quince or citron), were viewed as having almost
the quality of an aphrodisiac. The question is whether Shulamith
was using these requests metaphorically, denoting Solomon's
embrace, or literally, referring to physical sustenance. Either
understanding is possible. The solution depends on the connection of verse 5. Viewed in relation with the presence of Shulamith
at the banquet in the preceding section (1:12 and 2:4), the
requests are no doubt literal. Taken with the following verse
(2:6), however, the flagons or raisin cakes and apples are probably symbols of love. Perhaps the latter is the better solution, for
there is a rather abrupt break between verses 5 and 6 otherwise.

2:6. The verse indicates that the couple was reclining with Solomon slightly to the left of Shulamith. His left hand beneath her head holds her and supports her. With his right hand he embraces her. The Hebrew verb *ḥābaq* means "to clasp" or "to fold one's arms as in idleness." The name of the prophet Habakkuk, meaning "the embracer," is evidently derived from the same root. The verb, therefore, might be rightly understood to include Solomon's tender embrace of Shulamith, but it could imply more extensive physical expression. In any case the tenderness that Shulamith obviously sensed in his embrace answered the call for sustenance and comfort in verse 5. The success of these intimacies demonstrates the difference between the tenderness of the godly, holy love expressed throughout this book and the rather brutal roughness of many of the intimacies advocated in modern society.

2:7. Two basic possibilities exist for understanding the nature of the oath invoked by Shulamith in verse 7. Zockler and others find in the verse a strict ethical passage adjuring the daughters of Jerusalem to join Shulamith in not inducing love's pleasures by artificial means, either by actual physical stimulation or fantasying, until it was appropriate. If the verse is taken this way, it provides a caution against premarital sexual involvement and places limits on behavior designed to arouse sexual passions.

The second perspective understands the verse to be the contented reflection of the rural maiden. Enjoying the king's embrace, she did not want him to be prematurely interrupted or awakened from the slumber of love in order to attend to the affairs of state. As much as one might like to follow the sentiments of the first view, both the language and position of the verse in the poem favor the second. In the first place, the word "love" employed in this verse is *'ahăbâ* rather than *dôd*. As noted in 1:2 *dôd* is used to describe sexual intimacy, whereas *'ahăbâ* is a broader term more nearly the equivalent of the New Testament *agape*. In the second place, the embrace of 2:6 seems to picture the initiation of passionate love, which logically extends into verse 7. On the other hand, the Hebrew verb translated "stir not up" may be translated "to wake" or "to arouse to action and attention." It is less likely to be used of sexual titillation than of the cessation of one activity in order to pursue another. The sense of the verse, then, would be that Shulamith instructed the daughters of Jerusalem not to interrupt the profoundly satisfying embrace of the couple.

"Charge" (Hebrew, *shāba*ʻ) is normally translated "to swear." The word comes from the Hebrew word for seven, a sacred number and therefore the number by which oaths are confirmed. Deuteronomy 6:13 allows for the invoking of the name of God in oath. Apparently appealing by oath to various aspects of God's creation was also permissible. In this particular case the oath is by the roes and hinds of the field. "Roes" (Hebrew, *ṣebî*) is the antelope that once roamed the Judean and Galilean hillsides in great number. They were prized by the orientals for their elegance even when running at great speeds. "Hind" refers simply to the female deer, again noted for its grace and charm. Shulamith here invoked adjuration, swearing by these graceful and tender animals as most appropriate for an oath relating to her desires.

RENEWED ROMANCE (8–17)

2:8. The scene has changed from the banqueting house of Solomon to the blossoming verdancy of the countryside in spring. It is not clear if the location was near Jerusalem or to the north in the tribal precincts of Issachar near Shunem. But whether the description recorded a visit of Solomon to the queen's chambers, inviting her out into the countryside he knew she loved, or the return of Shulamith to Shunem to be with her family for a while and there to be visited by the shepherd-king, the theme for the scene is the blossoming of love and romance in the spring of the year. Shulamith was the speaker for the entire passage.

The joy engendered merely by the hearing of the loved one's voice is suggested not only in verse 8 but also in verse 14. One need only think of the joy infused in his or her own heart on such an occasion to sense something of the elation of Shulamith. There is a reminder of Elisabeth's response to Mary when she exclaimed, "As soon as the voice of thy salutation sounded in mine ears, the babe leaped in my womb for joy" (Luke 1:44). In this case the voice is pictured as approaching the dwelling of Shulamith by leaping on the mountains and skipping across the hills. Instead of using *'ahăbâ* to describe the lover, *dôd* is employed, once again bringing distinctively passionate expectations to the narrative. The mention of mountains and hills accords as well with the topography of Jerusalem as that of Shunem, but it perhaps better represents the path along which Solomon would have come from Jerusalem, through the mountains of Samaria and into the hills of southern Galilee, making his way to Shunem. Solomon's approach was compared to that of an energetic young man with the vivification of spring coursing through his body. Apparently Shulamith detected his coming by the sound of his voice while he was still some distance away.

2:9. Solomon's arrival reminded Shulamith of a gazelle or young stag, strongly beautiful, and bold, yet cautious, approaching with a shyness born of uncertainty. The description points to the relatively youthful years of Solomon rather than later when all such reticence had probably vanished. The analogy captures the marks of inexperience, i.e., boldness mixed with shyness, but also suggests the epitomy of strength and beauty. Standing behind the wall, Solomon looked in through the small windows (Hebrew, *ḥallōnôt*), showing himself playfully through them. He quickly disappeared and moved along the wall. Suddenly he showed his full form through the latticework (Hebrew, *harakkîm*).

2:10. Finally, Solomon spoke to his lover. Calling her by his favorite term of endearment, he also complimented her beauty and invited her to join him in the fields.

2:11. The rationale for Solomon's invitation was first that "winter is past and the rain is over and gone." Winter rains in Palestine often create havoc. The valleys become soggy with the rainfall, and travel is rendered difficult at best. Rain and melting snow cascade down the mountainous topography as the water races through the wadis toward the rivers and seas. Even today it is not unusual to be stranded in Palestine due to the washing out of roads and bridges. Once winter rainfall ceases, however, there is normally very little precipitation in Palestine during the late spring, summer, and early fall, although snow is found on the top of Mt. Hermon usually the year round and frequently falls in the mountains of Judea and the higher regions of Galilee.

2:12. Throughout the winter the Judean hillsides had been parched, brown, and presumably incapable of producing vegetation. Corresponding to the advent of spring, however, flowers were beginning to appear, and birds were winging their way across the land. Solomon knew the voice of the "turtle" could be heard. "Turtle" (Hebrew, *tôr*) refers to the turtledove, a migratory bird whose advent marks the return of spring (Ps. 74:19; Jer. 8:7). The turtledove, as a harbinger of the season, was employed by Solomon to impress on Shulamith that the time had come for them to be outdoors again.

2:13. Solomon also referred to the fig tree's productivity and the pleasant aroma of the tender grapevines. The Hebrew word *paggêha*, translated "her green figs," refers to the figs that remained on the tree through the winter and ripened in the early spring. "Putteth forth" is not a reference to the initial development of these figs, which, as already indicated, were on the tree through the winter, but rather is a translation of *hānaṭ*, meaning "to spice" or "to perfume"; hence, the sense of the aroma of springtime is present in both the reference to the figs and to the vines. In the case of the vines, their "tender grapes" (Hebrew, *ṣᵉmādār*), which would be better translated "vine blossoms," also provided a pleasant fragrance. These combined indicators of spring, the cessation of the rains, the appearance of flowers and migratory birds, and the fragrance of the blossoming trees, all provided evidence that the time had come for Solomon's love to arise and accompany him to the meadows.

2:14. Shulamith's reaction was to compare Solomon to a dove or rock pigeon. The rock pigeon (Hebrew, *yônâ*) is noted for its propensity to build its nest in the towering craggy places of the rocks far from the habitats of men. Shulamith noticed the reticence of Solomon and compared him to these rock pigeons who made their homes in "secret places." Actually, the term "secret places" is the noun form of a verb that means "to hide." The modern traveler who views from a distance the ascent to the waterfall at Engedi or the various high places at Petra gains the impression that there is no way up. However, on closer examination rocky stairs become visible. These hidden stairs constitute the perfect resting place for the rock pigeon. Like that shy bird, to Shulamith Solomon seemed circumscribed in his approach. Such shyness was unnecessary, however. Shulamith longed to hear his voice, "for," she said, "sweet is thy voice." This was the second mention of Shulamith's exuberance at the sound of Solomon's voice. "Sweet" is a different word from the one used in 2:3 to describe the fruit of Solomon as sweet to her taste. There the word was *mātôk*, meaning "sweet to the taste." The word used here (Hebrew, *'ārēb*) means "agreeable or pleasant." Furthermore, his countenance was "comely." The term for countenance included his entire form and not his face alone. That is, having observed his face through the window and latticework, she desired to see his entire countenance because he was "comely" (Hebrew, *nā'weh*), meaning simply "becoming" or "graceful." This word differs from *yāpâ*, which Solomon tended to use to describe Shulamith's beauty.

2:15. Considerable difference of opinion exists about the nature of the "little foxes" that spoil the vines. Some view them as other potential paramours who would steal away the affections of Shulamith. Those who maintain the shepherd-lover hypothesis take the words to refer to Solomon and his efforts to spoil the shepherd-lover's chaste love for the country maiden. A third possibility would be to equate the foxes metaphorically with those troublesome aspects of marriage that inevitably accompany any long-term relationship. As Delitzsch puts it, there are "great and little enemies and adverse circumstances which threaten to gnaw and destroy love in the blossom, ere it has reached the ripeness of full enjoyment."[6]

"Take us" (Hebrew, 'ehezû) literally means "to grasp" or "to catch or apprehend." "Foxes" (Hebrew, shū'alîm, a word that may also include the jackal), which abounded in Palestine, were the animals caught in great numbers by Samson (Judg. 15:4), tied together by the tails, ignited, and loosed in the fields of the Philistines. They were especially destructive of the various fruit crops and particularly the grapes, whose vines would be especially susceptible when they were beginning to blossom.

The possibility that other potential paramours were here envisioned and that Shulamith was making a plea that her chastity be protected is highly unlikely. Not only is there no mention of other lovers in the context, but also her almost total preoccupation with the virtues of Solomon seems to preclude this possibility. Equally unlikely is the theory that "the little foxes" refers to Solomon and that the plea is addressed to her shepherd-lover. Doubtlessly they picture the troublesome concerns and hurtful attitudes that may spoil the continued idyllic nature of romance. These minor matters compare to the actions of a fox at night, stealthily and harmfully rummaging through the fresh grape crop. Therefore, Shulamith urged Solomon to lay hold of such attitudes and interruptions before they could do any harm. The destructiveness of attitudes is a frequent theme of the Scriptures. For example, in Hebrews 12:15 bitterness is said to be like a root springing up in a man's life, at first almost unnoticed but in the end defiling many. Shulamith was concerned with bringing

6. Delitzsch, p. 54.

into captivity all minor issues that might spoil the happiness of this romance.

2:16. Reciprocity and mutual ownership were the themes of Shulamith's affirmation that her lover belonged to her and she to him. This sense of mutual possession is a critical feature for any happy marriage. One might have expected this oriental maiden to stress the king's claim on her exclusively. What is unusual in the text is that she clearly understood that Solomon also belonged to her.

The same mutuality was expressed by Paul in 1 Corinthians 7:3–4 where the husband is told to render ''due benevolence'' unto his wife, and the wife is instructed to treat her husband similarly. Furthermore, Paul indicated that the wife does not have authority over her own body; rather the husband exercises that authority—such a state would be thoroughly anticipated in a first century context. Surprisingly, however, the apostle also declared that the husband does not have authority over his own body, but rather the wife exercises that authority.

This reciprocity and mutuality are exemplified in a dramatic fashion in the third chapter of the book of Hosea. Gomer, Hosea's wife of harlotries, had been placed on the auction block, and Hosea purchased her for fifteen pieces of silver and a homer and a half of barley. The purchase complete, Hosea understandably said to Gomer, ''Thou shalt abide for me many days; thou shalt not play the harlot, and thou shalt not be for another man'' (Hos. 3:3). These words from Hosea could almost have been anticipated. The astonishing part of the verse is its concluding phrase of commitment from Hosea. Even though Hosea had not been the one at fault in the unfaithfulness, he said, ''so will I also be for thee.'' This willingness both to possess and to be possessed, to enmesh one's life thoroughly in the life of the spouse, is surely something of what was intended in God's original design for marriage given in Genesis 2:24, ''Therefore shall a man leave his father and his mother, and shall cleave unto his wife.''

The poetic figures that Shulamith used to describe herself are terms such as "vineyard" (1:6), "garden" (4:16), or "lily" (2:1). In this verse Shulamith's observation that Solomon was feeding among the lilies probably extends the concept of mutual possession to include the pleasant enjoyment that he was experiencing with the Shulamith.

2:17. Solomon was invited to experience the joys of feeding among the lilies "until the day break and the shadows flee away." The problem in verse 17 is to determine whether the time being discussed is the morning, with the corresponding loss of darkness, or the late afternoon, when the shadows grow longer and finally vanish. Good interpreters support both positions, indicating that the language itself is not precise. "Break" (Hebrew, *pûaḥ*) literally means "to blow" or "to breathe," but again it is not certain whether the reference is to the blowing in of the new day or the blowing out of the old. "Shadows" is probably the best translation of the Hebrew *ṣeᵉlālîm* (see Ezek. 31:3), which may also mean "dark" or "obscure" or even "shelter," as in Genesis 19:8 and Isaiah 18:1. Because shadows would hardly be thought of as belonging to the night, the time must be late afternoon. Accordingly Shulamith was urging her princely lover to return from his pursuits in the late afternoon before the day was completely over and the shadows had fled into darkness.

Once again, Solomon was urged to be like the gazelle or young deer or perhaps the stag on the mountains of Bether. The admonition was apparently a desire for his quick or sudden appearing. Deer, with the remarkable ability to blend into their surroundings, may reveal themselves with a startling suddenness. Just so, Solomon was not expected to return from his foray into the countryside until after dark. Shulamith expressed her desire that he would come sooner and thus surprise her.

"Mountains of Bether" has been the object of considerable discussion. Some writers have supposed that the reference is to Bithron, a mountain ravine east of the Jordan mentioned in

2 Samuel 2:29. Favoring that identification is the added fact that Mahanaim is mentioned in the same verse in 2 Samuel and apparently again in Song of Solomon 6:13. The latter passage reads "as it were the company of two armies," but the better translation seems to be "as at the dance of Mahanaim." Others interpret "Bether" to mean a "severed portion" and thus translate "in the severed portions of the mountains" or "in the cleft of the mountains." Following that translation but relating it especially to the love story unfolding, a third group of interpreters find a metaphorical description of Shulamith's perfumed breasts. The latter interpretation is highly unlikely, for explicit language is employed in chapter 7 as well as elsewhere in the Song. There is no hesitancy on the part of the writer to speak openly of Shulamith's physical virtues. The best solution is probably to understand Bether as referring to the cleft in the mountains where the deer suddenly appears.

For Further Study

1. How do you explain the apparently boastful language of Shulamith in the early verses of this chapter?
2. Verse 8 mentions the "voice of my beloved" and ascribes to the voice the ability to "skip" along the hills. Can you discover other places in the Bible where the voice is given remarkable abilities?
3. List ten "little foxes" that can destroy a marriage.

3

DOUBT, JEALOUSY, AND SPLENDOR

Two distinct scenes are described in this chapter. The first encompasses verses 1–5 and the second verses 6–11. The first ode is considered by most interpreters to be Shulamith's dream, the content of which is presented poetically. However, there is nothing in the text to suggest that the incident described did not actually take place. Again most interpreters understand Jerusalem to be the setting for this scene, though the statement in verse 4 that Shulamith brought her lover into the house of her mother suggests that it reflects the journey of the couple to the bride's Galilean home in Shunem instead. The likelihood that either Solomon or Shulamith would be out walking at night in the large capital city of Jerusalem is much less likely than that the stroll happened in Shunem.

The last part of the chapter, beginning with verse 6, apparently describes the formal wedding party. Some interpreters understand Solomon to be the one ferried by his swordsmen, others understand the passenger to be Shulamith, and still others suppose that both lovers were present. The description of the palanquin itself accords more nearly to one prepared for the queen. The description "coming up out of the wilderness" fits the topography of Jerusalem. Perhaps, therefore, the wedding party here envisioned is the procession of Solomon's men bringing Shulamith up to Jerusalem for the official wedding.

SHULAMITH'S ANXIETY (1–5)

3:1. The experience of loneliness is universally dreaded. Shulamith recorded that she awakened in the midst of the night on her bed seeking Solomon, but she did not find him. Because the order of the various stanzas of the Song is not necessarily chronological, this particular sonnet may reflect a time after the official marriage. Or it may be that the marriage took place in Shunem, and the latter part of the chapter details the magnificent procession that brought the bride from Shunem to Jerusalem. In any case, it is clear that Shulamith expected to find Solomon beside her in bed but did not. "Bed" (Hebrew, *mishkāb*) occurs infrequently in the Old Testament. *Mishkāb* is used to specify a place of sleeping (Job 33:15), a place for sexual activity (Isa. 57:7–8 and Prov. 7:17), and occasionally a coffin (2 Chron. 16:14). It differs from the bed described in 1:16. The latter term, normally a bed covered with a hanging curtain, was probably employed because the trees surrounding the place where the couple was lying made the setting seem like a bed with hanging curtains. Later in 3:7 and 3:9 still different words for bed (translated "chariot") are employed.

The search must not have taken long, but the word "sought" betrays the intensity of Shulamith's longing and the poignancy of her disappointment on discovering Solomon's absence. The one she sought was described as "him whom my soul loveth." "Soul (Hebrew, *nepesh*), which according to Bruce Waltke occurs 755 times in the Old Testament and originally meant "to breathe," may be translated in a number of ways, though basically it is best rendered "life," "soul," or "person."[1] One of the major emphases of the word is desire or craving—for

1. R. Laird Harris, Gleason L. Archer, Jr., and Bruce K. Waltke, *Theological Wordbook of the Old Testament,* vol. 2 (Chicago: Moody, 1980), p. 590.

food, sex (it is translated "pleasure" in Jer. 2:24), ambition (e.g., David's desire to be king described in 2 Sam. 3:21), etc. *Nepesh* also frequently occurs with verbs denoting yearning or longing for someone or some thing, and this is the way it is used here. Shulamith expressed her profound longing for Solomon, whom she was unable to find.

3:2. Having failed to locate her lover where she anticipated he would be, Shulamith found that sleep was not possible. Therefore, she arose and went about the city looking for Solomon, but she still did not find him. Apparently she sought him also outside the walls of the city in the broad or expansive places.

3:3. In the process of Shulamith's diligent search, she encountered the watchmen who guarded the city by night. It may be objected that if Shunem was the location of this particular incident, it was probably not large enough to merit watchmen by night. But any city concerned about the safety of its premises would have provided such watchmen. In Shulamith's query she did not identify her lover. That was unnecessary. She was known and recognized (something that would not necessarily have been the case in the larger city of Jerusalem), and King Solomon ws certainly known. So she simply asked, "Saw ye him whom my soul loveth?"

3:4. Shulamith continued to comb the streets of the darkened village, and it was only a short while after departing from the watchmen that she found the object of her affections. This strophe makes no attempt to explain why the king has absented himself from the bedchamber or what pursuit it was that took him out into the night. Yet explanation would have been extraneous to the point. The sonnet is intended to emphasize the closeness that had developed between Solomon and Shulamith, a closeness demonstrated in physical intimacy but more profound than that, the binding of soul to soul.

Although there is no indication that Solomon's absence was a cause of alarm to Shulamith, the extent of her adoration of him was apparent. Finding him, she reminisced that "I held him, and would not let him go." The Hebrew term '*āḥaz* (translated "held") is a vivid expression meaning "to grasp or take possession of." For example, in Job 16:12 the word (translated "taken") is used to describe God's seizing a man in wrath and in Psalm 73:23 of taking hold graciously. In the further avowal that she would not let him go, there is allusion to the strength of the word.

Shulamith prevailed on her lover to return to her mother's house and chamber. *Ḥeder* usually refers to a private chamber, such as a bedroom, and sometimes even a bridal chamber. Genesis 24:67 records a similar event when Isaac first met Rebekah. He took her into his mother Sarah's tent, made her his wife, loved her, and "was comforted after his mother's death." Such an action emphasized the unity of the family that was so profoundly valued in the oriental culture. Furthermore, taking Solomon to her mother's bedroom, where apparently two decades or so before she herself had been conceived, was especially meaningful to Shulamith. It is as if that particular bed and room was hallowed as the matrix from which life had sprung. In that place Solomon and Shulamith express their love to one another, emphasizing the sanctity of the physical relationship that accompanies genuine love. As the author of Hebrews said, "Marriage is honourable in all, and the bed undefiled: but whoremongers and adulterers God will judge" (Heb. 13:4).

3:5. Shulamith returned to the refrain she introduced in 2:7 and will employ again in 8:4. The ushering of her princely lover into the bedchamber of her mother presupposed that coitus would take place. Afterward, as the two lay together in blissful harmony of spirit, Shulamith wished to avoid any disruption of that tranquil moment. Consequently, she charged the "daughters of Jerusalem," a phrase intended to encompass anyone who might

interrupt, not to intervene or awaken the king from his tranquil
slumber until he himself desired to arise.

THE WEDDING PROCESSION (6–11)

3:6. The scene has changed with the new strophe in verse 6.
However, the chronology of chapter 3 may be consistent. After a
period of time in Shunem, the king may have returned to Jerusalem to make preparations for the formal processional that would
bring his bride to Jerusalem.

The section begins with a question, "Who is this that cometh
out of the wilderness?" "Cometh" (Hebrew, *'ola*) literally means
"ascending or coming up." There were numerous routes from
Galilee in the north to the capital city of Jerusalem, but two
major ones were generally taken. The route through the Samari-
tan mountains was circuitous, difficult, and hazardous due to
robbers. Consequently, many took the Jordan Valley road, which
is also the one most frequently chosen today. Therefore, leaving
Shunem in the land of Issachar near Mt. Gilboa, the bridal
procession doubtlessly made its way through Bethshean slightly
to the east and turned south along the Jordan River road until it
arrived at the wilderness oasis of Jericho just north of the Dead
Sea. Turning west the party ascended from the lowest depression
on the surface of the earth, fourteen hundred feet below sea level,
to the top of the Judean mountains in a distance of only about
eighteen miles. On days when the haze caused by the evapora-
tion of water from the Dead Sea is blown away, one may stand
at Jericho and clearly observe Jerusualem perched like a crown
on the top of the Judean mountains.

The one who ascended from the wilderness was accompanied
by "pillars of smoke perfumed with myrrh and frankincense."
"Pillars of smoke" is not to be understood as swirling dust
stirred up by the horses and foot soldiers accompanying the
procession. Rather, the pillars were the result of the burning of
incense accompanying the official procession. Although not to
be identified with the pillar of cloud that preceded and protected

the children of Israel in their wilderness wanderings, something of the same idea was intended. Just as God's presence was symbolized by a pillar of fire at night and a pillar of cloud by day, so the presence of royalty in the procession was signified by the columnar smoke that wound its way heavenward. This identification is verified by the expression "perfumed with myrrh and frankincense." Frankincense (Hebrew, *lᵉbônâ*) is a gum extracted from a shrub in Arabia. It was noted for its strong and bright flame and was constantly employed in the temple service as an emblem of prayer. The burning mixture of myrrh and frankincense could first be seen in the pillars of smoke, and afterwards it made itself known by its aroma. "Powder" (Hebrew, *'abqat*) is different from the other words used in Hebrew to describe dust or powder; it has the distinct meaning "aromatic powder." The powder was prepared by the traveling spice merchants common in that day.

3:7. The central exhibit of the royal parade was Solomon's bed flanked by sixty valiant men which represents one-tenth of the royal bodyguards spoken of in 1 Samuel 27:2 and 30:9. *Mittâ* is the word for "bed" most frequently employed throughout the Old Testament. The word translated "chariot" in verse 9 is a reference to the same bed but is more descriptive, designating precisely what kind of bed was involved. *Mittâ* merely specifies that it was portable.

3:8. Each of the sixty warriors held a sword and was thoroughly instructed in battle. The terminology suggests both training and experience. Each man's sword was girded on his thigh because of "fear in the night." "Fear" (Hebrew, *pāḥad*) better rendered "apprehension" or "dread," is not likely to describe the royal guard; rather, so that Shulamith would have no fear or apprehension in the night, the guard was present to comfort her as she was brought to Jerusalem.

3:9. Further information is now provided concerning the bed mentioned in verse 7. The text indicates that Solomon made a "chariot" from the wood of Lebanon. The word used here (Hebrew, *'appiryôn*) is unusual. It is also a *hapax legomenon*, occasioning extensive discussion as to its exact meaning. Apparently we are to understand a palanquin. In fact, there are some who suggest that its origin lies with the Sanskrit *paryanka*, which may have given rise to that term. Others object, insisting that the word is of Greek origin (Greek, *phoreion*; one can readily hear the similarity between *phoreiaon* and *'appiryôn*) and refers to that which is borne along. Regardless of the etymology of the word, however, the description provided is sufficient to make it clear that this was an enclosed litter perhaps pulled by animals but more likely borne by a portion of the royal guard. The palanquin was constructed of wood from Lebanon, whose ample forests also provided wood for the temples and palaces of Jerusalem.

3:10. The four pillars that held the roof of the palanquin were made of silver. The base on which they rested was gold. The expression "the covering of it of purple" utilizes the Hebrew word *merkāb*, which means "seat" or "saddle" (cf. Lev. 15:9 and 1 Kings 4:26), so it is clear that the writer of the Song intended to communicate that the place for reclining or sitting was purple. According to Pope "purple" (Hebrew *'argāmān*), a word of Anatolian origin, designates cloth dyed with a reddish purple dye extracted from the murex shellfish. The dye was very expensive and early became an emblem of royalty.[2]

The concluding phrase describing Solomon's palanquin has been the occasion for difficulty in interpretation. It is generally agreed that the text should read "by" rather than "for the daughters of Jerusalem." However, regarding the further statement that the interior of the palanquin was "paved" (Hebrew, *rāṣap*; literally, "to arrange stones artificially as in a pave-

2. Pope, p. 444.

ment," "tessellated") not with stones but with "love," three different possibilities have been suggested by interpreters. First, the interior of the palanquin was made bright by the presence of a lovely girl, that is, Shulamith. Second, the interior of the palanquin had been the object of as much concerted effort as the outside, thus making it a lovely piece of work. Third, there has been a transcriptional mistake. Rather than *'ahăbâ*, or "love," the text should read *hobnîm*, meaning "ebony," or even, as Driver and Meeks suggest, the heteronym of "love," which means "leather." Because evidence is lacking for textual variance, however, this third explanation must be rejected. Of the remaining alternatives, the best view is to suppose that the daughters of Jerusalem, lacking the craftsmanship necessary to prepare the exterior of the palanquin, nevertheless skillfully modeled its interior into a delightful place for the shepherdess to ride as she approached her moment of destiny in Jerusalem.

3:11. The phrase "daughters of Jerusalem" is exchanged for "daughters of Zion." "Zion," a synonym for Jerusalem, originally denoted the mountain in the city's midst held by the Jebusites prior to its conquest by David (2 Sam. 5:6–9). The daughters of Zion were invited to go forth and behold Solomon, the son of Bathsheba, who was still alive and had personally fashioned a crown for his espousal. Crowns, usually wreaths of flowers rather than royal crowns, were frequently worn by the nuptial couple in wedding festivities. The mention of the daughters of Zion going forth to behold Solomon suggests that the procession was drawing near to Jerusalem and that Solomon, who had previously ridden out to meet it, was now returning to the city with the royal entourage. "Espousal" (Hebrew, *hatunnâ*) is another *hapax legomenon*. It seems to mean "marriage" or "wedding" rather than "espousal." This makes better sense in the context and establishes that Bathsheba's crown was made for Solomon's wedding day, that is, "the day of the gladness of his heart." That concluding expression is important to an understanding of the nature of happiness in the home. Often in weddings the bride is said to be happy, but here it is Solomon who is identified as possessing gladness in his heart. The joy Shulamith's coming brought to him met every desire and hope of the king.

For Further Study

1. What aspects of love and devotion are stressed in Shulamith's search for Solomon in the first five verses?
2. Reference is made to Solomon's "valiant men" in verse seven. Can you locate the names of any of the mighty men of Solomon's father, David?
3. Can you discover the usual meaning of "espoused" in verse eleven?

4

THE ECSTASY OF GOD'S DESIGN

This chapter contains two odes sung by the bridegroom and an invitation by Shulamith for Solomon to make overtures of love. The first ode is comprised of verses 1–7 and the second of verses 8–15. Verse 16 is the response of the maiden. The initial sonnet consists of high praise for the variegated beauties of the bride. The second strophe is a further description of the bride referring to her origin, faithfulness, and delightfulness.

4:1. Solomon repeated his recognition of Shulamith's beauty. The double enunciation has the effect of the English expression *exquisitely beautiful*. His listing of her particular charms began with the notice of her "dove's" eyes, a reference to the softness, twinkling energy, and insight reflected in them. Her eyes were further described as "within thy locks," but the word translated "locks" (Hebrew, *ṣammâ*) is a rare word employed only twice in the Hebrew canon. The word means "veil" and refers to the fact that the veil that covered Shulamith's face called special attention to her dove-like eyes.

The hair of the rustic maiden flowed about her shoulders, reminding the poet of a flock of goats such as those that might appear on Mt. Gilead. The exact meaning of the word translated "appear" has been debated by interpreters. Some prefer to translate it "recline," others "ascending." But whichever is correct, the poet has in mind a long observed Palestinian scene, namely, the large flocks of black goats grazing on the sides of the mountains. For centuries these black goats have served both Bedouins and resident farmers alike as the most strategic of domestic animals. Though devastating to the vegetation of the land and thus considered by some a nuisance, goats were nonetheless profoundly valued by most of the ancients. The first and more important product of the goat was its milk and cheese. The meat was eaten, but normally this was only true of the younger animals. Goatskins were used to make water bottles, and goathair, then as now, was unsurpassed for making the water-repellent tents used by Bedouin wanderers. Almost certainly Abraham's tents were at least in part made from this goathair.

"Gilead" refers in general to the mountainous region of Transjordan bordered on the south by the Arnon River and on the north by the Yamuk River. This region, reaching more than 3,300 feet above sea level, provides a magnificent view of the Sea of Galilee below. The slopes of Gilead that border the Jordan River receive greater amounts of rainfall than the mountain slopes on the western banks of the Jordan valley and consequently have beautiful vegetation.

4:2. Solomon's description continued, using metaphors that were likely to be appealing to his rural lover: "Thy teeth are like a flock of sheep that are even shorn, which came up from the washing." Shearing removes the outer growth of the sheep's wool, which through constant exposure to the elements and the environment becomes dirty. Washing is not only for the sake of cleaning but also for protection. The description served to focus on the glistening whiteness of Shulamith's teeth as well as the moistness of her mouth. The concluding expression reminds the reader that the sheep in Solomon's Palestine typically bore two lambs at a time. These twin lambs looked so much alike that only the most observant shepherd would be readily able to distinguish them. The poet, who was still talking about his lover's teeth, meant to indicate that there was a perfect symmetry about his lover's teeth with the two rows appropriately corresponding to each other, thus creating a genuinely beautiful face.

4:3. Observation of Shulamith's teeth made notice of her lips inevitable. Solomon likened them to "a thread of scarlet." Though Shulamith was dark from the sun, her general health was suggested by the redness of her inviting lips. Furthermore, her speech had a comeliness or beauty. The mention of this fact, occurring as it does in the midst of a description of Shulamith's physical attributes, indicates that love is far more than physical attraction or intimate involvement. Although not shunned anywhere in the Bible and addressed at some length in the Song of Songs, it is nonetheless true that for a marriage to be what it ought to be, physical attraction must be complimented by genuine love. Shulamith's speech profoundly appealed to Solomon and enhanced her physical beauty.

Next Solomon remarked that her "temples are like a piece of pomegranate." "Temples" (Hebrew, *raqqa*) refers to the upper cheeks. Interpreters are divided over the precise analogy of this comparison. Some argue that the exterior of the pomegranate is intended, but Delitzsch insists that the inner side is in view.[1] When severed, the pomegranate presents an abundance of small seeds ranging in color from ruby red to a subdued or translucent white. It was the subdued white of Shulamith's flesh punctuated by the redness of her cheeks that caught Solomon's attention. Once again "locks" (ṣammâ) means "veil."

4:4. The poet stated that the bride's neck was like "the tower of David" built for an armory on which hung "a thousand bucklers, all shields of mighty men." This is not a comparison of size but of stateliness and more especially of adornment.

1. Delitzsch, p. 73.

Numerous towers have been suggested as the one to which Solomon referred. However, it is doubtful that he had any particular one in mind; he was simply suggesting that Shulamith's neck was like a tower. "Buckler" (Hebrew, *māgēn*) is a general word meaning "shield." The word translated "shield" (Hebrew, *shelet*) refers more often than not to ornamental shields less intended for battle than for display. The phrase in its entirety probably refers to an armory. In it were a thousand shields of mighty men. Ornamental shields were also hung in splendor. And just as those towers were richly ornamented, even so Shulamith's stately neck was beautiful both naturally and also because of the embellishments she employed.

4:5. As the poet's eyes surveyed the fullness of Shulamith's lovely form, he noted that her breasts were like two young roes or fawns, the twins of a gazelle. The word "gazelle," though omitted from the King James Version, is present in the Hebrew text. The gazelle had long been a symbol of feminine grace, beauty, and softness, and Shulamith's breasts reminded Solomon of gazelles feeding among the lilies in the field.

4:6. Expressions previously used by Shulamith (1:13; 2:17) were repeated by Solomon. He determined to go to the "mountain of myrrh" and to the "hill of frankincense" until the day literally blew or broke, and the shadows fled away. Two possibilities exist for the meaning of the verse, depending entirely on the identity of the speaker. Some suggest that Shulamith spoke these words and once again referred to her love of the outdoors. She desired for Solomon to take her into the mountains of myrrh and hills of frankincense that he had planted in the gardens of Engedi (perhaps elsewhere also). Both trees were imported from the East Indies by Solomon's mercantile fleet (Eccles. 2:5). However, a major problem exists with such an interpretation. There is no indication of a change in speaker, leading one to believe that the words belong to Solomon. Obviously, he is the speaker in the following verse, and it therefore seems that verse

6 is a part of the entire sonnet. Another problem is that this interpretation creates a break in the flow of the sonnet, rendering it very unlikely.

The second possibility is that the mountain of myrrh and the hill of frankincense constitute a restatement of verse 5, reflecting the ardor and desire stirring within Solomon as he observed the beauty of his bride. If so, the words must be construed as a tasteful yet specific statement of intent to consummate his love physically.

4:7. Once again the beauty of Shulamith is extolled. The phrase "my love" (*ra'yātî*) demonstrates that the statement was Solomon's. His final declaration was that Shulamith is without spot. "Spot" (Hebrew, *mûm*) may refer to any blemish on the body. Perhaps it could be argued that no one is void of all blemishes, but as Solomon views his bride, he is convinced that she could not have been more perfect.

4:8. Advocates of the shepherd hypothesis—that a third character, the real shepherd-lover of Shulamith, is involved in the narrative—regard verse 8 as his intervention and invitation to Shulamith to come away with him back to their mountain home. However, verses 8–15 are better understood to be a continuation of the ode of Solomon, in which he reminds his bride of their encounter in the north country in the area of Mt. Hermon.

Solomon invited Shulamith to come with him from Lebanon and to look down from the lofty prominences of Amana, Shenir, and Hermon. The location of these three peaks may be established with a fair degree of accuracy. Mt. Hermon, located at the southern spur of the Anti-Lebanon chain of mountains, is the highest peak in Palestine. It rises to a height of about nine thousand two hundred feet above sea level and is often snowcapped the year round. Today three countries—Syria, Lebanon, and Israel—meet on its slopes.

According to Pope, Amana is the modern mountain known as Jebel Zebedani, the source of the Abana River, which was men-

tioned by Naaman in 2 Kings 5:12 as one of the rivers that flow
through Damascus.[2] The modern name of the river is Barada.
Deuteronomy 3:9 identifies Shenir as the Amorite designation of
Mt. Hermon, but in 1 Chronicles 5:23 the two mountains are
not the same. In any case Shenir is part of the Hermon or
Anti-Lebanon range. These mountains were the dwelling place
of abundant wildlife, much of which can still be observed there.
The lions mentioned in verse 8 are gone, but leopards are
returning and exist in some number both in the national forest at
Engedi and in the Lebanon mountains.

For the first time, Solomon referred to Shulamith as "spouse"
(Hebrew, *kallâ*). According to Holladay, the word sometimes
means "bride" as in Isaiah 49:18 or even "daughter-in-law" as
in Genesis 11:31.[3] Here it means "bride" or "spouse" for the
wedding had taken place. Though he will still call his beloved
ra'yātî, as in 5:2, he nevertheless began to frequently use *kallâ*
as a term of endearment.

4:9. Solomon proclaimed that his spouse had "ravished" his
heart, once again emphasizing the totality of Shulamith's impact
upon him. "Ravished," occurring twice, is a denominative
verb derived from the noun "heart" (Hebrew, *lēb*) and means
"to unhearten" or "to take away the heart." The translation
might well read, "You have taken away my heart, my sister,
[my] spouse; you have taken away my heart with one glance of
your eyes." The sense in which the expression was intended is
not that of Hosea 4:11 where "whoredom . . . and new wine
take away the heart," but rather the sense of captivation. Nor
was it necessary for Solomon's lover to expend great energies in
order to entice him. He noted that with just one of her eyes she
had worked her enchantment. The reference is to a single glance
in which Solomon saw the reflection of her love. He also noted
the additional effect of her jewel-clad neck. The order is signifi-

2. Pope, p. 475.
3. William L. Holladay, *A Concise Hebrew and Aramaic Lexicon of the Old
Testament* (Grand Rapids: Eerdmans, 1974), p. 158.

cant. Efforts to entice and inspire by means of adornment alone
are of limited value and success, but where the personality of the
individual gleams from the eye, accentuated by whatever skillful
ornamentation may be added, the created impression is of lasting
significance.

One additional appellation is added to the growing list of
names by which the king identifies his beloved. She is called
"sister" (Hebrew, *'aḥôt*), which may seem to be a strange title
for a wife, but the Hebrew word is used in two distinct senses.
On the one hand, there is its strictly technical use, referring to a
female sibling. Other times, however, the word is used in a
more general way to mean a female with whom one has a very
close relationship, sometimes even an intimate relationship. In
this verse the word is used in the latter sense.

4:10. Shulamith has been described as fair or beautiful. This
time, however, Solomon referred to the physical intimacies of
love (*dôd*) by employing the word that Shulamith used regularly.
He spoke of her love—her various physical expressions of love—as
being "better than wine." Spurgeon explained the meaning of
that phrase. First, her love was superior because it could be
enjoyed without question. Second, her love, unlike wine, would
never turn sour. Third, also unlike wine, Shulamith's love never
produced ill effects. And finally, Shulamith's love produced a
sacred exhilaration.[4] The smell of her ointments is of greater
delight to him than that of all spices. The references here may be
to the particular unguents or perfumes that the bride has employed, but Delitzsch thinks it is to her personality, "as it were,
her soul," which he imbibes along with the perfumes.[5]

4:11. Interpreters differ sharply over the significance of the
dropping of honeycomb from the lips of Shulamith and the
honey and milk found under her tongue. Dillow and others are

4. Spurgeon, pp. 2–6.
5. Delitzsch, p. 83.

certain that the reference is to the passionate kissing that would accompany foreplay and sexual intimacy.[6] Pope acknowledges the probability of that meaning also.[7] Other commentators refer to Proverbs 16:24 where pleasant words are said to be like honeycomb and to Psalm 140:3 where slanderous words are poisonous. Psalm 10:7 also speaks of the storing of curses in the mouth and mischief under the tongue. Proponents of this theory suggest that passionate kissing is not the subject of the verse. Rather, the reference is to the sweetness and comfort of Shulamith's words. Either interpretation is plausible, but the word for love in verse 10 supports the former interpretation. Hence, it is probably better to understand that the sweetness of the passionate kiss is in view. Two different Hebrew words for "honey" are employed. The first is *nōpet*, which means a sprinkling or dropping of pure honey directly from the combs; whereas the second word, *dᵉbash*, refers to palm honey or honey made from the juice of boiled-down grapes. Two different sweetnesses therefore describe the enjoyment of the kiss. Kissing remains even today a common greeting in the ancient Near East, especially among good friends and loved ones. However, the greeting kiss is distinct from the passionate kiss described here, a rather unique expression of affection that is only appropriate between husband and wife and only in a private setting. The natural result of such kissing would be to arouse further desires for more extended intimacies, which seems to be part of the rationale behind it.

Solomon compared the smell of Shulamith's garments, scented with aromatic perfumes as was the custom of the East, to the smell of Lebanon. Lebanon, with its mountainous recesses, crisp and fresh mountain air, and odoriferous cedars, always provided a pleasant aroma.

4:12. Shulamith is said to be a "garden enclosed," "a spring shut up, a fountain sealed." Archdeacon Aglen explains, "The

6. Dillow, p. 80.
7. Pope, p. 486.

closed or walled garden and the sealed fountain appear to have been established metaphors for the pure and chaste wife."[8] That verse 12 is, in fact, a reference to the virginity of Shulamith at the time of her marriage and further testimony of her faithfulness to her princely lover is indicated by the usage of the garden metaphor in verse 16 and in 5:1. Furthermore, the Shulamith had already described herself by a similar metaphor in 1:6, where she said that her brothers made her keeper of the vineyards "but mine own vineyard have I not kept." The reference of her vineyard is a reference to her body. "Enclosed" is the same word translated "shut up" here.

The bride was described as a garden, a spring, and a fountain. A garden suggests a delightful, relaxing setting in nature. A spring and a fountain suggest both satisfaction of thirst and refreshment. Ideally, human sexuality is designed by God to provide exactly those features. The *Criswell Study Bible* notes five distinct purposes of sexual intimacy: (1) knowledge (Gen. 4:1), (2) unity (Gen. 2:24), (3) comfort (Gen. 24:67), (4) procreation (Gen. 1:28), (5) relaxation and play (Song of Sol. 2:8–17, 4:1–16), and (6) avoidance of temptation (1 Cor. 7:2–5). Specific responsibilities seem to be delineated for the husband in the sexual experience. He is to experience satisfaction (Prov. 5:19), delight, and joy (Prov. 5:19; Eccles. 9:9) while exhibiting tenderness (Prov. 30:19) and unique sensitivity to feminine needs (Deut. 24:5).[9] The restfulness of the garden and the refreshing and satisfying nature of springs and fountains provide the insight that human sexuality was intended to be far more than merely a procreative drive.

The terms "enclosed" and "shut up" indicate limitation of access. Clearly Shulamith's garden and spring was accessible only to the one who had the key. By the same token the sealed fountain was a token of ownership and identity. Shulamith belonged to Solomon alone. The verse as a whole provides a

8. Ellicott, p. 395.
9. Criswell, p. 773.

startlingly clear argument for monogamy and for the absolute faithfulness of the marriage partners.

4:13. Discussion of the Shulamith's garden led Solomon to extol the satisfying qualities found therein. He did so in terms of various fruits, spices, and perfumes that might be a part of a carefully tended garden. "Plant" (Hebrew, *shelaḥ*) means "a shoot" or "a sprout." The reference is probably to Shulamith's various charms, which were like an orchard of pomegranates and other pleasant fruits. "Pleasant" (Hebrew, *meged*) refers generally to costly or precious gifts. Reference here may be to the excellency of the fruits in the garden. "Camphire" refers to the "henna" mentioned in 1:14. This was a shrub with bunches of flowers that grew to about ten feet in height. "Spikenard" is discussed in 1:12 and refers to nard, a plant grown in India.

4:14. "Saffron" is probably the yellow Indian crocus. "Calamus" is a reed that grows in the marshland of India and Arabia. When powdered, it makes a very special perfume. "Cinnamon" is made from the bark of an East Indian tree that grows to a height of as much as thirty feet. After the bark is dried, the cinnamon is extracted. "Frankincense," which is mentioned in 3:6, is a gum that exudes from a shrub found in Arabia. "Myrrh," discussed in the notes on 1:13, was taken from an Arabian tree on which the myrrh distilled like tears. It made an exquisite incense and was also gargled by some to produce sweetness of breath. "Aloes" referrs to the wood of an Indian aromatic tree. The concluding expression incorporating all other chief spices is meant to be inclusive of all the delights of Shulamith's garden. Dillow is right when he speaks of Solomon's description of Shulamith's garden as containing the finest spices. "He means it is as rare and as much to be valued as the most precious of aromatic herbs." Dillow further points out that perfume was used to scent the breath (7:8); clothing was perfumed (Ps. 45:8;

Song 3:6; 4:11), and couches and beds were also sprinkled with appealing scents (Prov. 7:17).[10]

4:15. The description continued with references to some of the metaphors employed in verse 12. Shulamith is "a fountain of gardens, a well of living waters, and streams of Lebanon." A similar expression occurs in Proverbs 5:15–18 where sexual intercourse is described in terms of "fountains dispersed abroad" and emphasis is placed on engaging in it only with "the wife of thy youth." These activities are to be "only thine own, and not strangers' with thee." The fountain of the gardens and the cascading waters are compared to streams from Lebanon. Reference is to the rivers flowing with the crisp, cool, and refreshing water of melted snow from high in the Anti-Lebanon range of mountains.

4:16. Desire had been fully awakened in Shulamith. North and south winds are invited to blow upon her garden. The east wind is frequently a hot and arid wind, whereas the west wind often brings storm clouds from the seas. Consequently, either would be inappropriate to the desired imagery. North and south winds are refreshing, however. Therefore Shulamith employed that imagery to speak of the dispersing of those spices that were a part of her body's response to sexual stimulus. Solomon the beloved was invited to "come into his garden, and eat his pleasant fruits." Two things are of interest here. First, this constituted an invitation to Solomon to consummate the marital relationship and to enjoy sexual union with her availing himself of all her charms. Second, Shulamith requested that the north and south winds blow on "my garden" but promptly spoke of that garden as "his." This reminds us not only of the law articulated by Paul in 1 Corinthians 7:4 but also of the one-flesh union authorized by God in Genesis 2:24. The union has not taken place in verse 16, but the invitation has been made.

10. Dillow, p. 83.

For Further Study

1. In what respects is genuine love preferable to wine?
2. The expression "a garden enclosed is my sister" suggests monogamous marriage as an ideal. How do you explain Solomon's later practice of polygamy?
3. What is the significance of the listing of the spices when speaking of Shulamith's "garden"?

5

LOVE'S DISRUPTION

Three divisions should be made in chapter 5. The first verse properly belongs with chapter 4. It is Solomon's response to Shulamith's invitation in 4:16. The chapter division was placed a verse too soon. Verses 2–8 reveal Shulamith's dream, in which both the lovers exhibit unthoughtful and selfish perspectives and face corresponding consequences. Verses 9–16 provide the most extensive physical description of any character—in this case Solomon—in the Old Testament. Although it is poetic and thus deserving of some allowance for poetic license, the essentials of the description are accurate.

5:1. In the concluding verses of chapter 4 the king had praised his spouse. In response Shulamith had invited her beloved to enter his garden and partake of its pleasant fruits, almost certainly an expression of her openness to Solomon's sexual advances. A testimony of Solomon's response to that invitation is the content of verse 1. The unity of the two lovers was recognized by Solomon. He spoke of her as "my garden." Clearly he meant Shulamith, for he referred to her as "my sister" and "my spouse."

Three affirmations are made concerning Solomon's activities.

First, he gathered his myrrh. Second, he ate his honeycomb and honey, and third, he drank his wine and milk. All of these metaphors express the fully satisfying nature of the sexual encounter. The gathering of myrrh and spices is certain to have a fragrant and enriching result; the eating of honey and honeycomb suggests the sweetness of the relationship; and the drinking of wine and milk focuses on the satisfaction derived from the relationship and the slaking of the sexual thirst and appetites of the two lovers. Delitzsch has a perceptive remark regarding the thrust of the entire passage.

> The road by which Solomon reached this full and entire possession was not short, and especially for his longing it was a lengthened one. He now triumphs in the final enjoyment which his ardent desire had found. A pleasant enjoyment which is reached in the way and within the limits of the divine order, and which therefore leaves no bitter fruits of self-reproach, is pleasant even in retrospect.[1]

The absence of what Delitzsch refers to as "bitter fruits of self-reproach" is the especially gratifying aspect of a chaste sexual involvement, that is of a couple's loving one another according to the canons and dictates of the Lord.

Whereas this is sexual fulfillment as it ought to be, tragically much human sexual experience is only temporarily gratifying, leaving on its completion a residue of guilt and sorrow that can scarcely be estimated. The results of the relationship described here between Solomon and Shulamith were all happy ones. Like the gathering of the spices, the experience left only pleasant memories. Like the eating of honey and honeycomb, it was perpetually sweet. Like the drinking of wine and milk, it was totally satisfying.

The Bible also clearly pictures what happens when men indulge their sexual appetites outside of the expressed purposes of

1. Delitzsch, p. 88.

God. This may be observed in the sordid affair of Amnon's lust for his half-sister Tamar (2 Sam. 13). Following the ungodly advice of Jonadab, Amnon devised an opportunity to lie carnally with his sister. No sooner had the act been consummated, however, than the Bible records that "Amnon hated her exceedingly; so that the hatred wherewith he hated her was greater than the love wherewith he had loved her. And Amnon said unto her, Arise, be gone" (2 Sam. 13:15).

But Amnon's selfish deed had other far-reaching consequences. Tamar was broken and crushed. She put ashes on her head to symbolize her humiliation and walked through the streets crying (2 Sam. 13:19). Tamar's full brother, Absalom, was infuriated. He carefully nursed the bitterness of his soul for two full years and then slew Amnon, becoming a murderer. Amnon therefore further paid for his selfish and licentiously undisciplined behavior by forfeiting his young life. Finally, the sorrow that came even to David is apparent in 2 Samuel 13:31.

A similar experience with another Tamar focuses on the humiliation of Judah, who cohabited with her, thinking that he was satisfying his sexual yearning with a common harlot (Gen. 38). The vivid description of the "strange woman" in Proverbs 5 is a further warning of the disastrous complications that result from licentious sexual behavior. Though the strange woman's mouth is smoother than oil, her ending will be "bitter as wormwood" (Prov. 5:4); her steps "take hold on hell" (Prov. 5:5). She will be constantly on the move, and no one will know her ways (Prov. 5:6). When one goes in to her, he gives his honor to others and his years to the cruel (Prov. 5:9). Sooner or later he finds his own body consumed (Prov. 5:11). Further, the wayward man must deal with the Lord, for the ways of a man are always before the eyes of the Lord, who carefully ponders all of his goings (Prov. 5:21). Therefore the sinner will be held with the cords of his own sins (Prov. 5:22). All of the above is in stark contrast to the deep and abiding satisfaction produced as a result of the chaste love of Solomon and Shulamith.

Interpreters differ sharply over the speaker of the final sentence in verse 1. Some see the voice as a refrain of approval on the union of the two lovers from the daughters of Jerusalem. Others view the words as those of either Solomon or Shulamith speaking to the wedding guests who are in attendance at the wedding feast. The ancient custom of the prolonged wedding celebration extending as much as seven days may be in view here, with the words of either Solomon or Shulamith inviting the guests on the second day to join in the celebration of the consummation of their marriage (Gen. 29:28; Judg. 14:12). Other interpreters imagine that the speaker can only be the Lord, voicing His approval of the sanctified activity of the couple. The second explanation seems to be the best one, although none do violence to the text. The fact that *dôd* is used for the ''loved one'' might suggest that it is the daughters of Jerusalem who addressed the loving couple, urging them to celebrate their happy commitment together. Two different words for ''drink'' are used in the verse. The first is *shātâ*, which means ''to drink with the notion of enjoyment,'' while the second, *shākar*, carries the sense of drinking deeply or fully even to the point of hilarity. The clear indication of the concluding sentence is that the love that Solomon and Shulamith enjoy may be shared to its fullest without fear of disapproval by God or men.

5:2. The second section of this chapter (vv. 2–8) begins with what is probably a dream. It is a dream, however, that corresponds to reality. The thoughtlessness often exhibited by husband and wife for the one each holds dearest is a thoughtlessness that, in a sense, is born out of confidence and faith. Having pledged his or her deepest love and having been observed by the object of that affection over a period of time, one tends to feel that it is unnecessary to be quite as careful in the expression of love. The lover can be trusted to understand. In almost every marriage, therefore, circumstances like those depicted in these verses arise.

Shulamith began by saying that she is asleep, but her heart is awake, probably an indication that she was asleep but dreaming. In her dream she heard the voice of her beloved. He was knocking at the door of her chamber, requesting that she open the door. His speech betrayed his adoration for Shulamith and the purpose for which he had come. The profusion of the epithets were not insincere flattery but an earnest description of how he felt about Shulamith. Two of the four expressions have been used before. "Sister" indicates an established relationship. "Love" (*ra'yātî*) is Solomon's favorite word to describe his lover. He also calls her "dove" and "perfect one." "Dove" alludes to her gentleness and is in rather astonishing contrast to the type of behavior that was forthcoming. "Perfect one" (Hebrew, *tam*) basically means "without blemish" or "undefiled," though it may also imply "simplicity, sincerity, and the absence of guile or evil intention." Perhaps the word is principally intended in this latter sense here, for Shulamith's response indicated that the confidence placed in her was not altogether deserved.

Solomon further indicated that he has been out in the night, perhaps returning from an affair of state. Conceivably his thoughts in the latter part of the journey had turned increasingly toward Shulamith. His head was "filled with dew." The expression is understandable in light of 5:11, where we learn that Solomon was well favored with bushy curls. Consequently, the curls had soaked up the heavy dews of the night. The lateness of the hour, perhaps well past midnight, is indicated by the fact that the dew had begun to fall. The incident of Gideon's fleece in Judges 6 and other indications, such as in 2 Samuel 17:12, demonstrate the phenomenon of heavy dewfall in Palestine at certain times of the year. Drenched with the dew of the night, Solomon knocked at the door of Shulamith's chamber.

5:3. Shulamith was sleeping, perhaps deeply. Her response was, therefore, predictable. She had put off her coat and she did not intend to put it on again. She had washed her feet and did not wish to defile them. "Coat" (Hebrew, *kūtōnet*) refers to a tunic or a piece of clothing worn next to the skin. It is mentioned as the basic clothing of the priests and the Levites (Ex. 28:4; 29:5). Shulamith had shed this undergarment and lay unclothed beneath the covers in the cool of the night. Washing the feet before retiring for the night or reclining at a meal was an Oriental custom. Indeed, prior to the advent of paved roads and modern means of transportation, when feet were shod primarily with sandals, one might be spotlessly clean, fresh from the bath, walk only a few yards and have defiled feet. Provision was doubtless made in the court of the king for the feet to be cleansed prior to retiring. But for Shulamith to get up and walk across the floor to open the door to Solomon would have meant the necessity of washing her feet once again.

Two remarks should be made about the behavior of the lovers. First, Solomon did not choose the best time to make an overture of romance. In this he failed to exhibit the great wisdom credited to him. Second, Shulamith, wise in the ways of the outdoors, demonstrated an almost total insensitivity to the fragility of the male ego in the matter of sexual rejection. In effect, Shulamith's reply to Solomon was, "I know what you want, but the time is inappropriate."

5:4. The initial rebuff may have discouraged the king, but it did not turn him away. He found another way to manifest his desire and press the issue. His precise action is difficult to interpret due to our lack of knowledge about the construction of the queen's chamber. Some writers suggest that the hole through which the king placed his hand was latticework, such as that mentioned in 2:9. But the Hebrew word *hôr*, translated "hole," probably refers to an opening in the door that permitted access to the crossbar that held the door closed. Because the queen's chamber was probably in Solomon's palace, it is doubtful that Solomon anticipated that the door would not only be barred but also locked. Perhaps he felt that by reaching through the opening he could lift off the crossbar and open the door. That way, Shulamith's excuses would be successfully countered, for she would not have to defile her feet by leaving the bed, and, of course, in Solomon's present mood he was more than content for her not to have to put on her *kūtōnet*.

Having observed his determination to enter and his ardent desire to be with her, Shulamith, fully awakened, began to have a very different response. She found that her "bowels were moved for him." "Bowels" does not refer to the gastrointestinal tract but rather to the innermost feelings that were awakened. "Moved" (Hebrew, *hāmâ*) literally means "to make a great noise" or "a commotion." This agitation of spirit is attested in other passages, such as Isaiah 63:15 and Jeremiah 31:20. Shulamith suddenly found herself profoundly drawn to Solomon.

5:5. Having experienced conviction of soul about her temporary rejection of Solomon's overture of love, Shulamith dreamed that she rose from her bed to open the door to her beloved. She remembered that her hands were dripping with myrrh and that it distilled from her fingers on the "handles of the lock." "Lock" (Hebrew, *man'ûl*) signifies a bolt or bar for a gate or enclosure (Neh. 3:3). The only question regarding the interpretation of verse 5 is whether the dripping of the myrrh and its distillation on the handles of the bolt is to be viewed literally or poetically. If literally, the phrase suggests that Shulamith applied perfume prior to opening the door to her lover. This view has in its favor that it explains why, on opening the door in verse 6, she discovered that Solomon was gone. The time involved in preparing herself for the king's entrance perhaps became a discouragement to him, for he could not have known that she was making such preparation.

If the passage is to be construed poetically, then Shulamith is expressing the degree of passion that belatedly was aroused in her. The rejection of a few moments before was transformed into desire for her lover. It was as though perfume was dripping from her fingers and distilling on the bolt of the door. Inasmuch as the occurrence is a dream, it should not be pressed for details, such as how long it was before Shulamith got the door open or what she did in the intervening moments.

The first interpretation has value from a practical viewpoint. It is apparent here and elsewhere in the Song that Shulamith exercised wisdom in preparing herself for the physical aspects of marriage. But whereas a foolish woman may give careful attention to the feeding of her family, the cleanliness of the house, and other activities, she neglects to prepare or plan for the most intimate expression of her life. The foolish woman believes it is enough to be available for her husband. She never realizes that something as deeply profound and personal as sexual interchange demands, if anything, more careful preparation, planning, and variety than other more mundane tasks of life.

5:6. Whatever the cause for Shulamith's delay in opening the door, her lover was not there. In discouragement he had "withdrawn." The text preserves the poignancy of that term (Hebrew, *hāmaq*), which means "to put or place oneself elsewhere." This discovery, Shulamith recalled, caused her soul to fail. "Fail" (Hebrew, *yāṣā'*) means "to go out" or "to go forth." What is suggested is that on opening the door and finding that Solomon has departed, the significance of his request dawned fully on the reticent bride. They became like daggers to her soul, and she experienced the combined emotions of sorrow for her mistake, panic at the hurt caused to Solomon, and confusion as to how to respond next.

As is often the case, one mistake leads to another. Shulamith went into the night through the streets of the city seeking Solomon, but she could not find him. She called (Hebrew, *kārā'*; literally, "to cry out") to him, but he gave no answer. She could not be faulted for her diligence but only for her failure to be sensitive to her princely lover.

Frequently the male ego is exceedingly fragile. A considerable portion of male boasting and threatening is often subconsciously designed to bolster a sagging self-confidence. Solomon was hardly a weak character—all that we know of his reign would suggest that he was a decisive and able monarch. Yet, being human, there were certainly times when he suffered serious questions about his own worth and value. Especially would that be true concerning the one to whom he had revealed more of himself that to any other. For her to reject him on this particular occasion was doubtless an experience of far greater pain than if there had been some sort of political reversal in the kingdom. Therefore the king turned away to rest himself elsewhere and to attempt to recover his confidence.

5:7. As Shulamith wandered about the city in her dream, the watchmen found her. Apparently thinking her to be a woman of the night, perhaps on the way home from her escapades, they seized the opportunity to make her life as difficult as possible. The location for these events is not Shunem, where Shulamith first encountered the watchmen (3:3), but Jerusalem. It might be objected that the watchmen of that city would neither fail to recognize Shulamith as the king's bride nor treat her in such a reckless fashion. But it must be remembered that those who watched the streets at night would have had little opportunity to observe the female members of the king's household. Thus they might not recognize her. Furthermore, the record is a dream and bears no necessary correspondence to reality. In the dream the watchmen wounded Shulamith, and those who kept the walls took away her veil (Hebrew, *rādîd*). This is not the same as the coat mentioned in 5:3, which was a sheer undergarment. Rather, this garment refers to an upper robe, a plaid-like overgarment thrown over the shoulders to keep the upper parts of the body warm. Shulamith fled, forfeiting the garment to her captors in much the same way that Joseph left his outer garment with Potiphar's wife (Gen. 39:12) in order to escape an intolerable situation.

5:8. The conclusion of the dream consists of a mandate given to the daughters of Jerusalem. They were put under oath once again to become messengers or emissaries of Shulamith. If they encountered her beloved, they were required to tell him that she was "sick of love." The translation could suggest that the thought of physical love was repulsive to her. The opposite is meant, and a better translation would be "sick with the need for love." The phrase suggests that she was in a weakened state in terms of her ability to pursue any other activity. She had not the mental strength to contemplate other assignments. Her thoughts were of her beloved.

A practical lesson may be derived from Shulamith's wisdom. Having discovered her hurtful mistake, she loved Solomon enough to rectify the situation. Messengers were employed, and their words would suggest to Solomon the intensity of the sorrow that Shulamith felt for her failure to receive him. Furthermore, Shulamith sought to rebuild Solomon's sense of masculinity by letting him know that she greatly desired him and was lovesick because of his absence. Such a message would have to have been exceptionally gratifying to Solomon, doubtlessly overcoming the hurt and rejection experienced the night before. Apparently no time was lost in transmitting this message. The cruciality of every moment was recognized by the wise shepherdess.

5:9. Verses 9–16 probably belong to Shulamith's dream also. If so, the importance of the passage is not diminished, for it provides an extensive portrayal of King Solomon. Because exaggeration was frequent in antiquity it could be alleged that the only value to the description is its idyllic charm. Yet it is scarcely imaginable that Shulamith's description had no correspondence to reality, especially considering that the author of the Song was Solomon. One may, therefore, assume that Shulamith's description is trustworthy, constituting the clearest picture of an Old Testament character available.

Having been placed under oath by Shulamith, the daughters of Jerusalem responded by inquiring why she believed her lover to be superior to other lovers. A modern rendering of the phrase might be, "How is your sweetheart superior to any other sweetheart?" The query seems to be the product of Shulamith's effort to enlist them in her service to take a message to her beloved. It reflected a certain reticence on their part to be drawn into the search. Therefore, somewhat tauntingly, they asked why their involvement was required. The following description was Shulamith's reply.

5:10. The opening phrase is at first sight contradictory. Shulamith described her beloved as "white and ruddy." "Ruddy" (Hebrew, *'ādōm*) means "red." It belongs to the same root as the word used to describe Esau's sons, the Edomites. Esau himself was ruddy, or red, at birth. Moreover, Solomon's father, David, is described similarly in 1 Samuel 16:12, providing further evidence that Shulamith's description is essentially accurate. The problem is to explain how Solomon could be at once white and red. The answer lies in the word translated "white," for the Hebrew word *ṣaḥ* is better understood as "dazzling." Hence, the Shulamith actually said that her lover was "dazzling to look on." Having noted the reddish tinge to his flesh, she proceeded to speak of him as "the chiefest of ten thousand." "Chiefest" (Hebrew, *dāgal*) is a passive participle from a root meaning "to carry a standard." Shulamith therefore declared that he was "distinguished" or "conspicuous" among ten thousand.

5:11. The comparison of Solomon's head to "the most fine gold" was not designed to be a statement of color but rather an affirmation of stateliness and kingly bearing. It may also hint at his wisdom. Some of the interpreters who understood the comparison as a statement of color think the previous description might indicate the general whiteness of Solomon's flesh accentuated by reddened cheeks. If so, the red involved is not rose but a color more nearly approaching bronze. Therefore, the general look of his face was like fine gold. The remainder of the description refers to Solomon's hair. "Locks" is an obscure word in Hebrew but probably suggests curls. The term "black" is the one used by Shulamith to describe herself in 1:5–6, but here the comparison "black as a raven" indicates more than swarthiness. Apparently Solomon's hair was kinky or curly, worn fairly long, and as black as a raven.

5:12. Brightness and alertness, manifestations of the intelligence of Solomon, were displayed in his eyes, which were "like doves by the rivers of waters." The explanation "washed with milk" probably refers to the white of the eye contrasted with the dark pupil. The expression "and fitly set" might be more accurately rendered "sitting upon fullness." The Hebrew word is *millē't*, which may be semantically related to the famous "Millo" mentioned in 2 Samuel 5:9 and 1 Kings 9:15 and 24. For years scholars have attempted to ascertain the precise nature of Millo, which was built and later repaired. Only recently in the archaeological investigations of the city of David and the ancient Jebusite city has there been a probable identification. Millo was apparently a filled-in or terraced section of the wall. The verbal root means "to fill in" or "to make full." Therefore the reference to Solomon's eyes suggests that they were like doves by rivers of waters that run with abundance and fullness.

5:13. Solomon's cheeks were "like a bed of balsam, banks [Hebrew, *migdᵉlôt*, from *gidal* "to grow"] of sweet-scented herbs" (NASB). The latter phrase suggests that Solomon wore a beard, for *gidal* refers to the growth of hair (Num. 6:5) as well as plants. Delitzsch suggests that his beard may have been sown with some sort of aromatic plants, but that is not obvious. Aromatic herbs, "sweet flowers" in the King James text, are mentioned, and it is possible that Solomon used perfume much as men today use cologne. But it may also be possible that Shulamith was referring poetically to the enjoyment she experienced contemplating his bearded face. His lips were "like lilies," that is, crimson rather than white. They dropped sweet smelling or flowing myrrh. Once again the reference was either to his speech or to the satisfaction derived by Shulamith from his kiss.

5:14. Solomon's hands were like "gold rings set with the beryl." "Ring" (Hebrew, *gālîl*; "roll or turning") is an unusual word. Some have rendered it by the expression "rod," i.e., "his hands are like rods of gold," highlighting Solomon's well-rounded fingers bronzed by the sun. The "beryl" is the Tarshish stone. Interpreters differ emphatically over whether it refers to the onyx, a stone similar to our modern turquoise, or the chrysolite, a precious stone that is apparently to be identified with the topaz. In either case the figure alludes to Solomon's rings.

Tarshish stones were not mined at Timnah or any other of the royal mines in Palestine. In 1 Kings 10:22 and 2 Chronicles 9:20–21 the historians record that Solomon had a fleet anchored at Ezion Geber that went to Tarshish every three years and returned with treasures and exotic animals for the king's court. If Tarshish is the Spanish town of Tartessus, an identification that has been long advocated but never proved, it is difficult to determine why the trip was made so infrequently and also why Solomon's fleet did not use a Mediterranean seaport for such a journey. Possibly, therefore, Tarshish stones were brought from much further than has been originally imagined, conceivably even from the new world.

With the next phrase Shulamith's description became more intimate and private. Solomon's belly, translating a Hebrew word that means "the bowels"—in this case, the lower portion of his torso—was described as "bright ivory overlaid with sapphires." "Bright" (*'eshet*) means "wrought" or "perfectly carved" ivory. She noted that there was no flaw in his muscular midsection. The phrase "overlaid with sapphires" has been the cause of interpretive difficulty. Delitzsch concludes that it refers to "nothing else than the blanching blue veins under the white skin."[2] However, other writers think that such an interpretation is odd and hardly contributes to a picture of the beauty of the king. They favor an allusion to the royal blue clothing worn to cover the king's midsection. "Overlaid with" could very well mean "clothed," although this is not the basic meaning of the term.

5:15. The description of Solomon's legs "as pillars of marble" was obviously intended to reflect strength, the muscular and

2. Delitzsch, p. 105.

athletic contouring of his thighs and calves. "Sockets" or bases "of fine gold" referred to his feet. In the ancient Near East, because most people traveled by foot, the feet assumed greater significance than is true today. This can be seen in Romans 10:15 where Paul quotes Isaiah 52:7, which says, "How beautiful upon the mountains are the feet of him that bringeth good tidings, that publisheth peace; that bringeth good tidings of good, that publisheth salvation; that saith unto Zion, Thy God reigneth!"

In the final phrase Shulamith returned to the general beauty of Solomon's countenance. Those who have had the privilege of traveling through the two mountain ranges of Lebanon are accustomed to its beauty, especially that observed in the stately and symmetrical cedars. Like the Lebanon mountains Solomon possessed a rugged beauty, and like the cedars of Lebanon his countenance was stately and well proportioned.

5:16. The lively debate as to whether the sweetness of Solomon's mouth referred to his kisses or his speech surfaces again with the phrase "His mouth is most sweet." In this passage speech was intended. Had Solomon's kisses been meant, it is probable that the description would have occurred earlier in connection with verses 11–13. Its appearance after the concluding general description of verse 15, however, suggests that the word "mouth" (Hebrew, *ḥek*, "palate") is used as an organ of speech as it is in Job 6:30, 31:30, Proverbs 5:3 and 8:7 and therefore indicates Solomon's ability with words. By thus combining both his physical desirability and poetic prowess. Shulamith demonstrated that he was altogether lovely.

For the benefit of the daughters of Jerusalem two final avowals were added, namely, that Solomon was her "beloved" (Hebrew, *dôd*) and her "friend" (Hebrew, *rê'î*). In the first Shulamith affirmed that Solomon belonged to her as the object of her affections. Because he was the king, she must share him in some ways with the daughters of Jerusalem and the rest of the populace. But as a lover, he was hers alone. Shulamith may also have meant that all of the other things previously enumerated, though important, were of less significance to her than that he was her lover.

The second avowal used a word that basically means "to take delight or pleasure in" and may be translated "paramour" or "lover" as in Hosea 3:1 or "friend" as in Genesis 26:26. The breadth of the term suggests that in any successful marriage, there is genuine friendship as well as romance. For Shulamith and Solomon, for example, in addition to their intimate expressions of affection there was also the desire simply to be together. Each doubtless had other friends, yet their most important friendship was that between themselves.

For Further Study

1. Contrast the euphoric attitude of Solomon in verse one with the sorrow created by the Amnon and Tamar incident in 2 Samuel 13.
2. In what ways could both Solomon and Shulamith have demonstrated greater sensitivity to each other's needs?
3. In verse 16 Shulamith called Solomon her "friend." Why is it important for a spouse to be a friend?

6

MUTUAL ADJUSTMENT

As though convinced by Shulamith of the superiority of Solomon over ten thousand others, the daughters of Jersualem, who had inquired of the shepherdess concerning what made Solomon so special, now respond to her entreaty to assist in the search for her lover. This chapter continues her dream and supposes that the king has been located. Once again her virtues are described in verses 4 through 10. Verses 11 and 12 recount Shulamith's pilgrimage from obscurity to prominence. Verse 13 is the call of the daughters of Jersualem, or perhaps of Solomon himself, requesting the return of Shulamith.

6:1. Having been convinced that they should join the search for Solomon, the daughters of Jerusalem requested information concerning the king's likeliest whereabouts. The expression "turned aside" suggests the possibility that he had gone to a favorite place of repose rather than to some place of diligent activity.

6:2. Shulamith replied that her beloved had "gone down into his garden, to the beds of spices." According to Ecclesiastes 2:5 Solomon was a lover of gardens: "I made me gardens and orchards, and I planted trees in them of all kinds of fruits.'' That these should have been planted and never visited is unlikely. Obviously Solomon, who was a lover of beauty, found release walking among nature's verdure, and Shulamith suspected that he had repaired to such a place. Unlike many of the ''spices'' described in the rest of the Song, *bōsém* depicts a plant that was commonly grown in Palestine (cf. 5:13).

6:3. The very thought of Solomon's wandering among the lilies again occasioned Shulamith's expression of the unique bond that existed between them. The mutuality of belonging is emphasized precisely as it is predicated upon God's ideal for a man to leave his father and mother and ''cleave unto his wife'' (Gen. 2:24).

6:4. Shulamith's beauty was compared to the beauty of Tirzah and her comeliness to that of Jerusalem. In the introduction it was mentioned that the appearance of both Tirzah and Jerusalem in a parallel statement indicates that the Song of Solomon was written before the time of the divided kingdom. Tirzah was the capital of the Northern Kingdom until the reign of Omri. The city's precise location has not been established, but it is clearly in the territory of Issachar not far from Shunem. Jeroboam originally selected Shechem as his capital but later moved it to Penuel in Transjordan and finally to Tirzah near Shunem (Josh. 12:24 and 1 Kings 12:25, 14:17, 15:21).

In Solomon's day Tirzah, located in the Galilean hills, was a rural and principally agricultural city, whereas Jerusalem was the center of the affairs of state. Accordingly, *yāpâ*, ''beautiful,'' refers to ''the quality of completeness'' and *nā'wâ*, or ''comeliness,'' to ''that which is well becoming or pleasing.'' In other words, Shulamith was intrinsically beautiful like Tirzah and as well pleasing to the king as Jerusalem.

The last phrase of the verse, ''terrible as an army with banners,'' is another panagyric puzzling to Western ears. Moreover, the expression does not actually include the words ''an army.''

Literally, the text reads "as terrible as banners," although clearly banners are associated with a marching army. "Terrible" (Hebrew, *'āyōm*) may also mean "formidable" and that is the sense here. Shulamith's beauty exercised a formidable influence over the king. Although this is precisely the influence that a "help-meet" ought to have, it must be exercised with responsibility. The ill effects of its abuse may be observed in Scripture in the stories of Ahab and Jezebel, Herod and Salome, and even Solomon, whose wives eventually turned his heart from the Lord.

6:5. Shulamith's power over Solomon was evident in the effect of her eyes. "Turn away thine eyes from me" Solomon requested, "for they have overcome me." The word translated "overcome" (Hebrew, *rāhab*; "to be high spirited or full of courage, to press greatly the attack") is used in Psalm 138:3 to express God's strengthening of the psalmist in an hour of trial and in Proverbs 6:3 to speak of making sure a friend. In all three uses one thing is common, namely, the exercise of influence or strength. Whatever defense Solomon might have against logic or physical prowess, he melted before Shulamith's gentle and adoring gaze.

Certain tributes previously offered in chapter 4 are repeated in this section. Shulamith's hair, for example, is described as a flock of goats that appear from Mt. Gilead. As before, "appear" indicates the spread of the herd of black goats along the sides of the mountain like the falling of Shulamith's dark hair around her shoulders.

6:6. The comparison of Shulamith's teeth to a flock of sheep is also repeated. Though the shearing of the sheep is not mentioned as before, it is assumed by the text, which describes them as fresh from the washing, a practice that would not be attempted until the sheep were shorn. It is declared, however, that the "flock of sheep" seem every one to bear twins, another indication of the symmetry of Shulamith's teeth. The washing alludes to their gleaming whiteness.

6:7. Shulamith's temples or cheeks were once again compared to a pomegranate. The mention of "a piece of pomegranate" is evidence that the interior, not the exterior, of the pomegranate was in view. Shulamith's radiant temples were set as in a frame with the locks of her hair.

6:8. At first the statement that there were sixty queens, eighty concubines, and numberless virgins seems to be completely out of place in the text. However, this is actually the same kind of comparison that Shulamith made in 5:10 where she compared her lover to the ten thousand. Solomon compared Shulamith to the entire harem, composed as it was of queens, concubines, and virgins, the latter perhaps being the princesses or daughters who had been born in the house of the king. Solomon suggested that among them all there was not one to compare with Shulamith.

There are two potential problems to be addressed in this verse. The first is the apparent contradiction that exists between the numbering of the members of Solomon's harem in 6:8 and the greatly increased numbers provided in the 1 Kings 11:3 description, which recorded seven hundred wives and princesses and three hundred concubines. There are two possible explanations for this apparent contradiction. First, if, as has been argued in this volume, Canticles was written in the early years of the reign of King Solomon, between 960 and 955 B.C., then it is understandable that his personal harem would have been much smaller in the earlier years. The statement in the book of 1 Kings was reckoning the harem at the zenith of Solomon's power, showing the extent to which he indulged himself and catered to his own desires in later years.

There is, however, a second and even more appealing possibility. If, as has been also argued in this commentary, the relationship of Solomon and Shulamith was monogamous at the outset, then the "queen's concubines and virgins without num-

ber'' must refer to those attached to the court of the king but not
a part of his personal harem. At his death many members of
David's harem survived him. Among them was Abishag the
Shunammite, whom Adonijah sought to wed on the advice of
Joab and Abiathar in order to seize the kingdom (1 Kings 1:3–8).
As suggested earlier, Abishag is possibly to be identified with
Shulamith of the Song, for Shulamith is obviously not a personal
name but a designation of the part of the country from which she
came. This would explain Solomon's rather severe reaction to
the plot of Adonijah and also partially explain the women of the
court listed in 6:8 without the necessity of understanding them to
have been actual consorts of Solomon. The mention of ''virgins'' (*'ălāmôt*) is a further indication that the verse should not
be understood as Solomon's personal harem. Solomon only
referred to the women of the court as the acknowledged beauties
of the kingdom, yet none of them was as fair as Shulamith.

6:9. ''My dove'' appears first in this verse, but the Hebrew
sentence begins with the term *'ahat* or ''one.'' Literally the text
reads, ''She is one,'' followed by the further description of
Shulamith as ''dove,'' the undefined or perfect one. The em-
phatic position of *'ahat* gives further credence to the proposal
that the relationship was, at the time of the writing of the Song,
a monogamous one and that 6:8 has no reference to Solomon's
personal harem. Not only was Shulamith ''one,'' that is, his only
love, but also she was again called by the names of endearment,
''dove'' and ''perfect'' or ''undefiled one,'' that is, one without
blemish. Solomon further stated that Shulamith was ''one'' to
her mother. The word ''only,'' which does not occur in the
Hebrew text, implies that Shulamith was the only daughter born
to her mother. Some consider this to be in direct contradiction to
8:8, which may be interpreted to declare that Shulamith had at
least one younger sister. But there is no confusion in the under-
lying text, which specifies that she was ''one'' to her mother
because she was her mother's choice. Solomon probably did not
mean to indicate favoritism on the part of Shulamith's mother.

Instead, he simply implied that Shulamith was the obvious choice among all those born to her mother when it came to internal and external beauty. This superiority was recognized by the daughters who blessed her and the queens and concubines who praised her. The term "blessed" (Hebrew, *'āshar*) originally meant "to walk straight" and, hence, "to be happy or blessed because of the certain end of one's direction." If the daughters, the queens, and the concubines represented the coterie of Solomon's personal harem, it is doubtful that they would have joined in the praise and blessing of the Shulamith. But if they were women otherwise attached to the court of Solomon, then that praise is understandable.

6:10. No certainty can be achieved as to whether verse 10 constitutes the conclusion of Solomon's tribute or the beginning of Shulamith's testimony. Commentators have understood it in different ways. The view that sees it as the concluding word of Solomon, perhaps even representing the combined judgment of Solomon and the ladies of the court, is less problematic, however. Solomon asked, "Who is this that looks forth as the dawn or the morning?" "Looks forth" is literally "to bend forward" and, hence, "to look down," like the rays of the sun that look down on the earth in the early hours of the day. The reference was to Shulamith's radiance. She was also said to be as "fair as the moon" and as "clear" or pure "as the sun." Again, the awesomeness or formidableness of Shulamith was included in the description.

6:11. Shulamith went into the garden of nuts or nut trees. "Nut trees" (Hebrew, *'ĕgôz*), refers to a walnut grove, but in this particular text it may well include other nuts, spices, and fruits. This is borne out by the subsequent mention of the fruits of the valley, the vines, and the budding pomegranates. The verse suggests that Shulamith had not yet found Solomon and that the preceding description was a rehearsal in her dream of the praise and adoration received in chapter 4. In her loneliness she

went into the valley grove, seeking the things with which she
had been familiar in her youth.

6:12. Verses 12 and 13 are fraught with translation difficulties. The first four words of the Hebrew text are clear. Shulamith
declared that she had not anticipated ("Or ever I was aware")
the turn of events. Before she could understand what was happening, her soul had been exalted "like the chariots of
Amminadib." Determining the exact nature of that state is problematic. "Chariots" (Hebrew, *markabôt*) may refer either to
chariots of war or carriages of state. The latter is more probable.

"Amminadib" may be a proper name (Ex. 6:23; Num. 1:7;
Ruth 4:19; and 1 Chron. 2:10). However, evidence seems to
point away from this. No significance known to commentators is
attached to the name. More probably, two words are involved—
'ammî, meaning "my people," and *nâdîb*, meaning "princely"
or "noble." Hence, the affirmation is that before Shulamith was
able to reckon with the full significance of what had happened,
her soul or life was placed in the carriages of state belonging to
her princely or noble people. The statement is an expression of
amazement at the exaltation that had taken place.

6:13. In this verse the word "Shulamith" appears for the first
time in the text. The fourfold repetition of *shûb* ("return")
indicated the urgency and necessity of Shulamith's return.
Whether the words were spoken by Solomon alone or in concert
with the women of the court and the daughters of Jerusalem is
impossible to determine. The "we" used later in the verse might
render the latter view more probable. The request for Shulamith's
return was based on the desire to "look upon" her. The Hebrew
word implies the desire to contemplate and observe. It is as
much a plea for fellowship as a remark of admiration. And
Shulamith asked what it was they wished to observe in her.

The last phrase, "As it were the company of two armies,"
has been subject to almost every conceivable interpretation.
"Company" (Hebrew, *meḥôlâ*), in its thirteen other Old Testa-

ment uses, refers to dancing of some kind. It is hardly conceivable that it means anything else in this verse. One possible explanation of "two armies" (Hebrew, *mahănāyim*) is that it derives from the Hebrew *ḥānâ*, which means "to decline, bend down or encamp." The idea of a hostile encampment may have given rise to the translation "two armies." However, more probably a geographical reference to Mahanaim (cf. Gen. 32:2; Josh. 13:26, and 1 Kings 4:14) is intended. The city of Mahanaim was located in Transjordan just south of the Jabbok River near Penuel. It was named by Jacob after he left his father-in-law, Laban, and met God's angels on the way back to Canaan. Literally, it means "the two companies." The city was located on the border between Gad and Manasseh and became one of the Transjordan cities of refuge (Josh. 21:38) and a levitical city (1 Chron. 6:80). David made Mahanaim his headquarters temporarily when Absalom attempted his coup. According to 1 Kings 4:14 Mahanaim was also the seat of Ahinadab, who was one of Solomon's twelve officers.

The concluding expression of verse 13 may, therefore, mean "the dance of the two companies" or simply "the dance of Mahanaim." This dance may have been performed by Shulamith in response to the coaxing of Solomon that she return to him so that he might gaze on her. Perhaps it was a dance associated particularly with the inhabitants of Mahanaim, although it has been noted that Mahanaim also became a name for angels at a later time. In any case the Shulamith is urgently invited to return. When she asked what anyone saw in her, she seemed to have raised a rhetorical question. She answered with her own presentation of this "dance of Mahanaim." Apparently, however, the dance was performed only for the benefit of her husband.

For Further Study

1. Analyze the events that transpired in Genesis 32 with Jacob, and see if you can relate them to verse thirteen.
2. To refer to one's tooth as "a flock of sheep" does not seem particularly complimentary. How is the sense of beauty affected by one's own culture?

7

RECONCILIATION

Assuming that the difficult concluding verse of chapter 6 refers to the dance of Mahanaim, this was in some form presented by Shulamith in the presence of Solomon alone. The first nine verses of chapter 7 constitutes an adoring description of the elegant charms of Solomon's enchantress. Verses 10–13 once again focus on Shulamith's desire to depart from Jerusalem in the company of Solomon and to seek solitude in the villages of her native southern Galilee.

7:1. The description appropriately began with her feet and "shoes" (Hebrew, *n^e'alîm*, referring to a covering of the feet that is latched or tied on, sandals). "Feet" translates a word meaning "steps" and yields itself to the possibility that Solomon did not intend the beauty of the feet per se but the gracefulness of the steps and the movements involved in the dance of Mahanaim. To understand Solomon as admiring Shulamith's feet would certainly not be contrary to Scripture. The beautiful feet of a messenger are mentioned by Isaiah (52:7) and Paul (Rom. 10:15). However, in those verses the focus is not on their physical form but on the beauty of their function. The feet by themselves are seldom considered in descriptions of beauty. On the other hand, gracefully adorned and esthetically employed as in Shulamith's dance, even the feet become beautiful.

A new appellation was provided by Solomon when he called his lover a "prince's daughter." The designation has nothing to do with her origins, which were humble. Rather, by linking her life with Solomon the king, she held the position of a prince's daughter.

Continuing the description of Shulamith's charms, Solomon noted the joints of her thighs. "Joints" is clearly misleading, for the Hebrew word *hammûk* literally refers to that which is circular. A better translation would be "the curvatures of your thighs are like jewels, the work of the hands of a cunning workman." It was the soft and appealing roundness of her feminine figure that the king extolled. It seemed to him as though her legs had been crafted with the tedious art of the jeweler.

7:2. Shulamith's navel was compared to a round goblet or bowl sparkling with mixed wine; her belly or abdomen to "a heap of wheat set about with lilies." The tastefulness of the description is notable. Although the king did not hesitate to describe each portion of the body frankly, it is noteworthy that not even here, where the description is the most explicit in the book, is the genital area per se specifically mentioned. That mention of such is certainly included in Solomon's mind cannot be doubted from the description, but once again Solomon's sense of public responsibility as well as the very purpose of the poem itself is indicated in the careful description provided.

Traveling through the wheat fields of Samaria, the bread basket of Israel, south of Jerusalem on the way to Beersheba, at certain times of the year one cannot help noticing the winnowing of wheat on threshing floors all along the way. Piles or heaps of wheat (to which Solomon referred) may be observed. From a short distance away they appear incredibly smooth, sparkling, and perfectly rounded. Like these heaps of wheat by the threshing floors in the midst of the lilies of the field, so Shulamith's virtues caught the eye of Solomon. As the king watched the dance of Mahanaim, he was impressed with the smooth roundness and sparkling whiteness of her lower torso. The comparison of Shulamith's navel to a bowl full of wine was a reference to the appealing prospect suggested to Solomon as he watched.

7:3. The female breast is a symbol of fertility and motherhood in almost every culture. Some societies, such as our own become preoccupied with its erotic significance. However, there are few if any major civilizations where the beauty and sexual attractiveness of the feminine breast has not been noted. Solomon evidenced his keen awareness of the appealing beauty of Shulamith's breasts by mentioning them in all three descriptions of her charms. Here a previous figure is repeated. Shulamith's breasts reminded him of twin fawns. That is, their symmetry was identical, and they possessed the freshness and softness of the fawn.

7:4. Shulamith's neck was like a tower of ivory, straight, stately, and smooth. Solomon altered his previous description of her eyes, comparing them to the fishpools by the gate of Bath-rabbim in Heshbon. Heshbon was located about fifty miles east of Jerusalem near the present town of Madaba. According to Numbers 21:25–30 the city originally belonged to the Moabites but was captured by Sihon, king of the Amorites, who made it his capital. The Israelites took the city and placed it within the territory assigned to the tribe to Reuben (Num. 32:37). Later it fell again into the hands of the Moabites, and its coming judgment is mentioned several times in prophetic literature. Not far from the top of the hill where Roman ruins lie, there is a large broken reservoir that may well have been one of several pools located in the area. The translation ''fishpools'' follows the Latin Vulgate reading *piscinae*, meaning ''pools for fish,'' but there is no actual indication in the Hebrew text that the pools were thus employed. These pools are said to be located by the gate of Bath-rabbim, an expression which literally means ''the daughter

of multitudes.'' Brown, Driver and Briggs understand this to be
an appellation for the popular city of Heshbon, or perhaps the
gates of that city where multitudes regularly assembled.[1]

Shulamith's nose was compared to the tower of Lebanon
facing Damascus. The reference is to defense towers placed in
the mountain range through which troops from the east would
have to advance toward Solomon's kingdom. Their mention may
be another indication that the Song was composed in the early
years of Solomon's reign. It is known that his kingdom eventually extended as far as Tadmor, which, according to the chroni-
cler, Solomon built in the wilderness (2 Chron. 8:4). Tadmor,
later called Palmyra, is located about half way between Damascus and the Euphrates River, approximately three hours east of
Damascus by automobile. Apparently it was an outpost city for
the Solomonic empire but would not have been so used until the
zenith of the Solomonic kingdom. Hence, the lookout towers of
Lebanon are here in view, and their stateliness and straightness
were brought to the mind of Solomon as he considered the
appearance of Shulamith's nose.

7:5. Having described her neck, eyes, and nose, Shulamith's
entire head is encompassed in the comparison with Carmel. Mt.
Carmel, the scene of Elijah's confrontation with the prophets of
Baal, is a rather long ridge, extending from near the Mediterranean Sea at the modern city of Haifa all the way to the outpost
city of Yoq'neam close to Megiddo. It was always considered to
be one of the most beautiful mountain ranges in Palestine, rich
with verdant growth and beautiful from every direction. As
Solomon viewed the head of his beloved, he saw the beauty and
uniqueness of Carmel.

Shulamith's hair was described differently than before. Instead of comparing it with the grazing black goats on the hillsides, this time her hair was said to be ''like purple'' (Hebrew,

1. Brown, Driver and Briggs, p. 123.

'*argāmān*), referring to a dark crimson or purple color. The image is an attempt to capture the sun's effect upon Shulamith's glossy black hair, causing it to sparkle almost like purple. Solomon confessed that he was so captivated by the shepherdess's hair that he was "held in the galleries." "Held" (Hebrew, '*āsur*) literally means "to tie, to bind, or to fetter" and is frequently employed of the binding of prisoners. "Galleries" is a misleading translation of *rahat*, which refers to a trough for the watering of cattle and, hence, for running or flowing water. The word is used only here in the Old Testament. Apparently it referred to the tresses of Shulamith's hair, which flowed from her head down around her shoulders as though in troughs of running water. Consequently, the king confessed that he was held captive by the tresses of her hair. Some commentators speculate that he referred to lying beside Shulamith intertwined with her hair. It is more likely, however, that in the dance of Mahanaim the tresses flowed back and forth around her shoulders, captivating the king and rendering him unable to take his eyes from his fair one.

7:6. Once again, as in 1:15 and elsewhere, Solomon returned to the beauty and pleasantness of Shulamith's "delights." As Zockler well says, "Solomon does not mean by it vulgar, carnal pleasures, but the sweet joys of connubial intercourse as he now experiences them anew in embracing Shulamith."[2] The Hebrew word *ta'ănûg* refers not to the caresses themselves but to the delightful sensations experienced as a result. The exclamation of verse 6 was Solomon's mental response as he beheld the lovely Shulamith in the dance of Mahanaim. It is apparent that she was scantily clad at best, and the king found himself so captivated by her beauty and the sweet memory of previous intimacies that he was moved to desire her.

2. Zockler, p. 118.

7:7. "Stature" (Hebrew, *qômâ*) means "slim or slender." Solomon compared Shulamith's figure to the slender palm tree and her breasts to clusters of grapes at the top. The metaphor appears to be mixed, for it is the date palm that develops large clusters of juicy sweet fruit near the summit or crown. However, the plump roundness and softness of the grape clusters is more in keeping with the female breasts and is doubtless why Solomon altered the metaphor. It is as though he imagined that in the summit of the date palm somehow clusters of grapes have grown. The idea is continued in verse 8.

7:8. The unusual expression "I said, I will go up to the palm tree" is an indication that Solomon had watched as long as he could. Thoroughly stimulated and aglow with adoration of both the spiritual and physical beauties of Shulamith, he determined to approach this lovely, slender date palm and become enmeshed within its boughs. He also determined to take hold of the boughs. "Boughs" (Hebrew, *sansinnîm*) refers to the shoots or branches of the palm tree on which hang the clusters of its fruit. Solomon's intent was apparently to take hold of Shulamith's arms and caress her breasts, which will please him like clusters of the vine. Further, he noted that the smell of her nose, that is, of her breath, is like the pleasant scent of apples.

7:9. The closing observation of verse 8, referring to Shulamith's scented breath, coupled with the observation of verse 9 makes it clear that Solomon was describing the pleasant sensation of her kiss. The roof of her mouth, or palate, was like wine. The intrinsic value of wine, flavored liquid, in the society of the tenth century B.C. has been mentioned. Solomon observed that Shulamith's kiss was like experiencing the very best wine as it passed across the taste buds, through the throat, and into the stomach. "Sweetly" (Hebrew, *mêshār*) basically means "evenness or equity" and probably in this case "smoothly." The good wine to which Solomon referred is so pleasant to the taste that it is easily consumed like the kisses of Shulamith. The wine's effect was to cause "the lips of those that are asleep to speak." Some interpreters, following the text, see this as a reference to the intoxicating effects of wine, which may cause a person talk in his sleep. Others attempt at a more literal rendering of the Hebrew and point out that the expression *dābab*, translated "to sleep," means "to glide or move gently." Therefore, the reference is not to the effects of wine at all but to the tender kisses that belong to those relaxing moments immediately following coitus. At that time kisses tend to decrease in intensity and increase in tenderness while the couple lie together in relaxed intimacy. Whichever is the case with the rather difficult phrase, one thing emerges as certain: Shulamith's kisses have an intoxicating effect on Solomon. However, there were no ill side effects, and Solomon could enjoy this "wine" continually.

7:10. The dance of Mahanaim resulted in the intimate caresses of Solomon followed by the relaxing euphoria that should always be the aftermath of godly sexual intimacies. The scene changed, and Shulamith spoke. The experience has had the appropriate effect on Shulamith. Whereas the male is more motivated by the intensity of his sexual passions, the female is more concerned about belonging and the assurances that provide both confidence and security for her. This is not to suggest that sexual passions are prominent for the male only but rather to insist that for human sexual experience to be all that God intended, there must be more than the mere release of those passions.

That Solomon was an excellent lover who remarkably succeeded was the eloquent testimony of Shulamith in verse 10. First, she again declared herself the property of her beloved. Far from being the objectionable condition alleged by many women today, Shulamith obviously basked in her position of subordination. This does not suggest that her personality had been dissolved in Solomon's like a drop of honey in the ocean or that she considered herself mere chattel. That is apparent from her self-assertiveness documented in 5:3. However, it does suggest that she found in her position sustaining comfort. Second, she remarked that Solomon's desire was toward her. This declaration holds special interest because "desire" (Hebrew, *t^eshûkâ*) is the same word used in Genesis 3:16 to describe a result of the fall, but in Genesis 3:16 it is the woman whose desire shall be "to" or "for" her husband. Whereas normalcy dictates that the woman's constant desire is for the loving approval and adoration of her husband, an approval that is too often absent, in this case it is Solomon whose earnest desire was the loving approval of his wife. Where a holy love exists, the effects of the fall will, in fact, be minimized, and such conditions will come to exist.

7:11. Shulamith continued with the request that her beloved take her out into the field where they could lodge at night in the villages. No doubt Shulamith made the necessary adjustments to social life in the city of Jerusalem, but her preference remained for the quiet of the rustic countryside with its plethora of flora and fauna. "Villages" (Hebrew, *k^epārîm*) denotes the small unwalled villages that dotted the countryside. This Hebrew word is conserved in such place names as "Capernaum" (the village of Nahum).

7:12. Activities that were to be pursued included rising up early in the morning to visit the vineyards to see if the vines were flourishing, the new grapes were appearing, and the pomegranates were blossoming. Conceivably the proposed visit was to the vineyards and gardens of Solomon, in effect mixing business with pleasure. Shulamith promised that there she would give him her "loves" (*dôd*). Obviously these "loves" have not been withheld from the king, but Shulamith understood her husband. She knew that however great had been his satisfaction in the past, she must continue to meet his needs and satisfy his desires. She promised that if he would take her on this journey the love they had enjoyed the night before would be multiplied in a setting even more delightful than the capital.

7:13. As though coquettishly to woo Solomon and to encourage their swift departure to the countryside, Shulamith mentioned that the mandrakes were giving a pleasant scent and that all kinds of pleasant fruits new and old were laid up for Solomon at the gates. "Mandrakes" is a reference to a wild plant common to Palestine, particularly in Galilee. They have small whitish blossoms that in May or June become small yellow apples about the size of the nutmeg. They have a very distinct and agreeable odor. The fruit and roots were used as an aphrodisiac. Among the Arabs it was called both "the servant of love" and the *tuffah eshaitain* or "Satan's apples." Leah's son found some of these mandrakes (Gen. 30:14). All through the Song Shulamith had spoken of her "beloved" (*dôd*) and "mandrakes" (Hebrew, *dudā' im*) is probably a play on words.

The mention of "pleasant fruits, new and old" is thought by most commentators to be a reference to Shulamith's anticipation that the stores of annual fruits kept near her parental home in Shunem would be made available to them. However, surely Solomon would already have been conscious of that, and in a love poem it is improbable that such an insignificant factor would have been mentioned. More likely, the pleasant fruits that she promised to bestow on Solomon were once again the fruits of love available in Shulamith's "garden." "Pleasant" (*meged*) means "costly or precious," and the word "fruits" is absent from the original text. Therefore pleasantries, the costly delicacies that Shulamith offered to give to her beloved, having carefully laid them up for him alone, surely referred to her own personal affections. "Laid up" (Hebrew, *ṣāpan*) means "to hide or to conceal."

ᵣ Two aspects of Shulamith's love were identified. First, the intimate affections promised to Solomon have been hidden, chastely preserved only for him. In the early days of their marriage she had not yet bestowed upon Solomon all that was within her power to give. In other words, she intended to marshall continuing creativity in the expression of their lovemaking so that sameness would not intrude on their relationship.

This does not suppose any sort of aberrancy, merely the creativity born of interest and concern. Second, there was an emphasis on the costliness of these fruits. Sex without cost invariably results in sorrow, disappointment, guilt, and frustration. Only when a man gives himself to his beloved and the two of them sacrifice all to one another, do the sexual intimacies mean what God intended them to mean. Solomon had paid the price. He would therefore enjoy the fruit of Shulamith.

For Further Study

1. "Beautiful feet" are mentioned in verse 1. Can you discover other places in the Bible where this part of the anatomy is honored?
2. The language of verses 1 to 9 is both picturesque and frank. How do you justify this explicit language in a holy book?
3. What advantages does Shulamith see in the villages and vineyards?

8

A COVENANT OF LOVE

The concluding chapter of Shîr HaShirîm contains in verses 6 and 7 one of the most profound statements concerning the lasting qualities of love that was ever penned in any language. Leading up to that avowal, verses 1–4 contain the voice of Shulamith as she attempted to give expression to the growing relationship that she felt with her beloved. Verse 5 is the response of Solomon, detailing what apparently constituted the initial spark of love in their relationship. Verses 6–7, alluded to already, are probably the words of Solomon but could also be construed as the words of Shulamith, analyzing the lasting significance of love. Verses 8–12 are apparently a flashback to the youth of Shulamith and her preparation for marriage, whereas the concluding two verses are a summary of the love songs that make up Canticles.

8:1. It was noted earlier (4:9) that the tendency in oriental literature to refer to one's spouse as a brother or sister is strange to Western ears. To the Oriental, however, the unquestioned loyalty and intensity of the relationship among siblings was a strategic part of the fabric of life. Consequently, for a lover to be compared to a sibling constituted no insult; rather, it was high praise and indicated the permanence of the relationship. Whereas Solomon had early called Shulamith his sister, it is only here that Shulamith expressed her desire to treat Solomon as though he were her brother. If she and Solomon had been nursed by the same mother, Shulamith explained, then finding him "without" she could kiss him and "not be despised" (literally "condemned," denoting open contempt or mockery). The allusion may be to the protocol of state and, indeed, of polite society, which prohibited the public expression of affection among lovers but not expressions of endearment among brothers and sisters. For Shulamith to find Solomon in public and openly display her affection for him would be to run the risk of public disapproval and perhaps even mockery. She wished that were not the case.

8:2. Continuing the fantasy of Solomon as a brother, Shulamith declared that she would lead him and bring him into her mother's house to be instructed (literally, "you would instruct me"). Advocates of the shepherd-lover theory face exceedingly great difficulties in interpreting this phrase. With great humility Shulamith acknowledged that she had much to learn. Already the wisdom of Solomon was widely known and sought (1 Kings 4:29–34). If the supposed shepherd-lover were here in view, it is questionable whether Shulamith would have felt herself so inferior in wisdom. Clearly Solomon is intended.

In response to Solomon's presence and instruction she would care for providing spiced wine and the juice of the promegranate. The words "I would cause thee to drink" have the same Hebrew consonants that occur in the expression in verse 1, "I would kiss you." Some authors think this is not coincidental but that the association of wine with the soft kisses of the mouth (as found in 7:9, for example) was continued. The fact that Shulamith spoke of the juice of "my pomegranate" tends to support this conclusion. In other words, she would depend on Solomon for instruction and enthusiastically return the physical intimacies he enjoyed.

8:3. Further evidence for the previous interpretation is provided by this verse, which indicates a reclining posture on the part of both the king and his bride. Solomon's left hand supported Shulamith while his right hand embraced her. "Embrace" means "to enfold with the arms" but may include other activities of sexual stimulation (cf. 2:6). Shulamith anticipated those enjoyable moments together with Solomon.

8:4. For the third time Shulamith called on the daughters of Jerusalem—and by implication all others—not to stir or awaken her lover until he was full of love and ready to cease temporarily.

8:5. The speaker in this verse was Solomon. He asked, "Who is this that cometh from the wilderness, leaning upon her beloved?" The question is rhetorical, for by now all know that it is Shulamith. The leaning posture does not suggest weakness or exhaustion on her part but rather dependence and the desire to be close to her beloved.

The incident reminded Solomon of the meeting, perhaps their first, in which love was initially awakened in Shulamith. That occurred under or near an apple tree already significant to Shulamith. "Raised" does not mean "to awaken out of sleep" but refers to the awakening of love and passion (Prov. 10:12; Zech. 9:13). The text could suggest that Shulamith was born under an apple tree, but that is not necessary. Conceivably, the apple tree marked the boundary of Shulamith's homestead. Accordingly, at the place of her birth she had also experienced the first sparks of love.

8:6. Commentators debate whether the words of 8:6 and 8:7 are Solomon's or Shulamith's. In a sense, of course, they are Solomon's either way, for he is the author of the Song. Also, the thought of the verse is more like the philosophical musings of a wise king than the simple affirmations of a rustic shepherdess, but the words certainly could be Shulamith's. The initial expression of the verse lends itself more to that understanding. In either case, the speaker asked to be set as a seal on the heart and arm of the lover.

According to Delitzsch the signet ring (Hebrew, *kaḥôtām*) was either worn on the hand (Gen. 41:42; Esth. 3:12; and Jer. 22:24) or in some other way, such as on a string around the neck (Gen. 38:18).[1] The speaker asked to be set as a signet ring on the heart or breast of the lover and on the right hand or arm. Because the seal was a mark of ownership and authority, this expression probably is more in keeping with the previous affirmations of Shulamith than with those of Solomon.

The remainder of verses 6 and 7 contain five affirmations about the nature of love that contain glimmers of the same lofty doctrine propounded by Paul in 1 Corinthians 13. First, it is said that love is as strong as death; second, that jealousy is as hard as Sheol; and third, that the coals of love are eventually fanned into a raging fire. The point of the first comparison is that love is as irresistible as death. The strength of death is the universal witness of all humanity, interdicted only by the resurrection of Christ and the promised resurrection of the saints. And just as death cannot be subdued, so love is also invincible and cannot be repressed. This strategic truth must be relearned by our present generation. Counselors frequently hear, "I used to love her, but not any more." Yet the crime that supposedly destroyed that love is often minor compared to that of the wayward boy who has become a hardened criminal awaiting execution. Nevertheless his mother pleads with tears of unbroken love for a stay in his execution. And the love between Solomon and Shulamith, the kind of love that God intended in a marriage, also cannot be broken by circumstances.

The second affirmation is that "jealousy is cruel as the grave." "Cruel" (Hebrew, *qāsā*) is almost inevitably translated "hard." Jealousy, therefore, is as hard or unyielding as the grave. "Jealousy" (the Hebrew word means "to be inflamed" or "to have violent affection of the mind either for or against someone or

1. Delitzsch, p. 144.

some thing'') may be attributed to God (Ex. 20:5), who is sometimes moved with hot indignation when robbed of His honor (Deut. 4:24). Therefore, the concept before us is not that of a carnal and baseless jealousy but of a righteous concern and protective care that is the inevitable posterity of genuine love. The precise etymology of "grave" (Hebrew, sh^e'ôl) is uncertain. It only occurs once outside the Old Testament, in the Jewish Elephantine Papyri. The word is translated "grave" thirty-one times in the King James Version, "hell" thirty-one times, and "pit" three times. Both righteous and unrighteous men are said to go there at death (Gen. 37:35; Num. 16:30). Sheol seems to be simply the "grave," the place where the bodies of the dead are placed. In this passage the meaning is grave or death, and the affirmation is that in godly love a righteous jealousy is a hard or inevitable as the grave.

The third affirmation is that the coals of love are like coals of fire that produce a most vehement flame. "Coals" (Hebrew, *resep*) means "flames" or even "lightning" (Hab. 3:5). This is reflected in the translation which fails to reckon with a most unusual occurrence in this verse. The word "flames" is suffixed by the Hebrew *ya(h)*, which many commentators believe constitutes an occurrence of the personal name for God in its abbreviated form (*Yahweh* is the form in which it usually occurs; see Ex. 6:3). If the occurrence of this suffix is, in fact, a mention of the name God, then considerable theological significance is added to the Song. The declaration would be that the flames of love generated in the heart of a man are inspired of God. This would not be true of expressions of love outside the bounds that God has established; but within those bounds the flame of love belongs to the inspiration of the Lord.

8:7. Two more affirmations about the qualities of love are added to the three of verse 6. First, building on the metaphor of the flame of love in the previous verse, the author suggested that an abundance of water is not able to quench its fire. Indeed, rivers or floods of water are not able to overflow or drown love.

Second the concluding affirmation about love was that its worth is beyond any purchase price. Were a man to give all of his substance to purchase love, he would be despised. ("Condemned" is the translation of a word that means "to despise with mockery" or "subject to contempt"). That is, the world knows that love is too precious and costly to be purchased at any price; hence, a man making such an effort would be subject to public mockery.

8:8. This verse begins a new section that includes all but the last two verses of the chapter. It recalls Shulamith's childhood prior to the onset of puberty. The words of verses 8 and 9 are those of her brothers previously mentioned in 1:6. Referring to their little sister, they identify her as a child of eleven or twelve by specifying that her breasts had not developed (developed breasts were a criterion of virgin maturity; see Ezek. 16:7). Anticipating a day when a suitor would speak for their sister, seeking her hand in marriage, the brothers wondered what they should do to protect and ensure her chastity until then. If Shulamith did not develop proper attitudes and responses, promiscuity might bring reproach on the family and hinder her opportunity to have a wholesome life of her own. Counselors report frequently that promiscuity often leads to just such dire consequences.

8:9. Two possibilities for Shulamith were considered by her brothers utilizing the imagery of a wall and a door. A wall is impregnable and therefore represents moral resistance to sexual temptation, whereas a door may be opened and closed at will and hence represents moral weakness in this case. The brothers recognized that as Shulamith developed into a woman she could choose to be a wall and resist the immoral approaches of her suitors or a door and open to those approaches, compromising her chastity and initiating a life of promiscuity.

If she chose to be a wall—chaste, noble, trusting in God for the appropriate time of her pleasure—then her brothers concluded they would build on her a palace or a pinnacle of silver (see Isa. 54:12). "Palace" (Hebrew, *tîrâ*) may refer to any tower or palace that is enclosed by a wall. The significance seems to be that the brothers would decorate Shulamith with honor, freedom, and responsibility like the pinnacle of a city decorated with silver. If, on the other hand, she seemed open to illicit overtures of love, then they promised to be her careful attendants, as it were, enclosing her with boards of thick cedar to protect her in those areas in which she was too immature to protect herself.

Although Shulamith's brothers are described, her entire family was in view. There is some evidence in the early portion of the book that Shulamith's father may have died early. Her brothers were called the sons of her mother, and whereas her mother was mentioned several times, her father was never mentioned. Perhaps the brother acted in effect as the father for Shulamith. In any case, the verse is a thorough apology for responsible behavior, particularly on the part of parents and older siblings, to protect the character and judgment of the developing child and regulate his or her activities until maturation of judgment is achieved. Failure of parents in any era to accept that responsibility will be the cause of agony both to them and to their children.

8:10. Shulamith testified of her own virginity and careful preparation for Solomon alone. She declared simply, "I am a wall." Of the two options depicted above—the wall or the door—she had exercised the maturity of judgment that her family desired and kept herself from any sexual intimacies, awaiting the day when God would bring into her life one who would become her husband. Her testimony was given at a time when she was fully prepared for marriage, as indicated by the expression, "My breasts are like towers." She had blossomed into full sexual maturity and was radiantly appealing. She had also kept herself in chastity. The result was, "Then was I in his eyes as one that found favor." The antecedent of "his" is not completely clear. However, if the reference was to the brothers, the text should have read, "in their eyes I found favor." Instead, it read "his eyes." Apparently the one of whom she spoke was Solomon. There is further evidence to this end in the word "favor" (Hebrew, *shalôm*, meaning "peace"). "Shalom" is the common greeting among the people of Israel even to this day. It does not depict so much the absence of conflict as its successful negotiation due to one's relationship to God. In all probability its use here involves a play on words. The very first word of the English text in verse 11 is "Solomon." "Peace" is *shalôm*, whereas "Solomon" is *sh^elōmōh*, a word built on the same root as *shalôm*. In Solomon's eyes she found peace or favor, and her peace was Solomon himself.

8:11. Two possibilities exist for understanding verses 11 and 12. Some interpreters have viewed the vineyard at Baal-hamon as a literal vineyard that Solomon farmed out to keepers who received a portion of the profit. However, the fact that verse 12 finds Shulamith speaking of her vineyard, which must be the same kind of language employed when she spoke of "my garden" (4:16), is evidence that the vineyard at Baal-hamon was none other than Shulamith herself. Furthermore, verse 11 ties directly into the passage immediately before and specifically to the responsibility that the brothers had taken in the rearing and protection of Shulamith. Therefore the brothers apparently were the keepers to whom Solomon let out his vineyard (even though, of course, the king was blissfully unaware that he was doing this), and the result was that it made him a profit amounting to a thousand pieces of silver (compare with the palace or pinnacle of silver that was to be built on Shulamith if she were a wall; 8:9).

No one seems to be able to identify for certain the location of Baal-hamon. Balamon, which was located not far from Shunem close to Dothan, is mentioned in the apocryphal book of Judith (8:3). Although this may be the location intended, the terminology may also be in a broader sense to denote the general area in which Shulamith grew up.

8:12. Shulamith suggested that Solomon would receive the full benefit of his vineyard. Again the language is metaphorical.

Solomon's "thousand" shekels was designed to suggest that Shulamith was going to meet his every need. Such profit, however, was due to the excellent work of her brothers. It was therefore suggested that Solomon should reward them for their part in protecting and preparing her for her marriage. Her devotion nobly is first to Solomon, but in that devotion she does not forget her family and their contribution to her rearing.

8:13. The concluding verses of *Shîr HaShirîm* are the words of Shulamith. She spoke of the one who dwelt in the gardens, suggested that the companions were listening for his voice, and added that she wanted to hear that voice herself. Others rejoiced in his voice, but she had a special interest.

8:14 "Make haste" is an excellent translation of *b*ᵉ*rah*. Though this word is often translated "flee," here it simply means to hasten from one place to another. Shulamith's desire was that her beloved would move with the swiftness of a gazelle or a young deer and that like the stag on the mountains of spices he would come quickly to her. Many separations might of necessity occur, but Shulamith was separated for only a moment from her lover before she longed for him with passionate devotion.

For Further Study

1. Compare the characterstics of love in 1 Corinthians 13 with those of Song 8:6–7.
2. Why do you believe that premarital chastity is advocated by verses 8–10?
3. Read the article on "Shalom" in a Bible dictionary such as *Zondervan's Pictorial Bible Dictionary*.
4. Having read the Song of Songs, distinguish the major themes that you discern.
5. Which of the traditional approaches to the Song seems to you most probable?

6. Read the article on "Solomon" in a good Bible encyclopedia such as *Zondervan's Pictorial Bible Encyclopedia*.

7. How does the Song differ from the books of poetry in the Old Testament?

BIBLIOGRAPHY

Baxter, J. Sidlow. *Explore the Book*, vol. 3. Grand Rapids: Zondervan, 1962.

Brown, Francis; Driver, S. R.; and Briggs, C. A. *A Hebrew and English Lexicon of the Old Testament*. Oxford: Clarendon, 1962.

Criswell, W. A., ed. *Criswell Study Bible*. Nashville: Thomas Nelson, 1979.

Delitzsch, Franz. *Commentary on the Song of Songs and Ecclesiastes*. Grand Rapids: Eerdmans, 1950.

Dillow, Joseph C. *Solomon on Sex*. Nashville: Thomas Nelson, 1977.

Ellicott, Charles John. *Commentary on the Whole Bible*. Grand Rapids: Zondervan, 1981.

Glickman, Craig. *A Song for Lovers*. Downers Grove, Ill.: InterVarsity, 1976.

Gordis, Robert. *The Song of Songs and Lamentations*. New York: KTAV, 1954.

Green, W. Henry, tr. "The Song of Solomon," in *Lange's Commentary on the Holy Scriptures*. Grand Rapids: Zondervan, 1969.

Harris, R. Laird; Archer, Gleason L. Jr.; and Waltke, **Bruce K.**, eds. *Theological Wordbook of the Old Testament,* vol. 2. Chicago: Moody, 1980.

Holladay, William. *A Concise Hebrew and Aramaic Lexicon of the Old Testament.* Grand Rapids: Eerdmans, 1974.

Meek, Theophile. *The Interpreter's Bible,* vol. 5. Nashville: Abingdon, 1956.

Pope, Marvin. *Song of Songs,* in The Anchor Bible. New York: Doubleday, 1982.

Spurgeon, Charles Haddon. *The Most Holy Place.* Pasadena: Pilgrim, 1974.

Taylor, J. Hudson. *Union and Communion.* London: China Inland Mission, 1914.

Wilson, William. *Old Testament Word Studies.* Grand Rapids: Kregel, 1978.

Zlotowitz, Meir, and Scherman, Nosson. *Shir HaShirim.* New York: Mesorah, 1977.

Zockler, Otto. "The Song of Solomon," in *Lange's Commentary on the Holy Scriptures.* Grand Rapids: Zondervan, 1969.

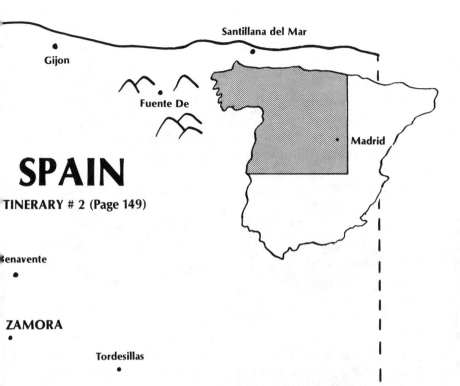

Santillana del Mar

Gijon

Fuente De

Madrid

SPAIN

TINERARY # 2 (Page 149)

Benavente

ZAMORA

Tordesillas

SEGOVIA

AVILA

Gredos

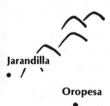
Jarandilla

Oropesa

TOLEDO

MADRID

Country Inns in Spain

Most of the accommodations in this book are inns owned and operated by the Spanish Ministry of Information and Tourism. These are known as "paradores," where it is possible to stay for an unlimited time.

These are not youth hostels or humble wayside accommodations. They have been established in old palaces of historic significance, stately homes, ancient castles, convents, and monasteries. Some are modern in design. These have been carefully restored with a maximum respect for their heritage, and fortunately for all travelers in Spain, they have been fitted with modern conveniences. Each bedroom has twin beds and a sumptuously furnished private bathroom.

There are almost a hundred of these truly remarkable accommodations scattered throughout Spain, and they present the best face of Spain today. To stay in them is to return to the glories of a Spain of the past, while at the same time enjoying the conveniences of the present.

Each parador offers breakfast with the cost of the accommodation. Lunch and dinner are also available.

Reservations at Paradores

I strongly advise that reservations be made in advance during all seasons for the Spanish paradores. This can be done through Marketing Ahead, New York City, 212-686-9213. They can also arrange for your reservations at Portuguese "pousadas."

Car Rentals

Don't hesitate to travel anywhere in Spain by automobile. The main roads are excellent and even the secondary and tertiary routes are well maintained. Advance reservations may be made before leaving North America for an AutoEurope car to be picked up, not only in Madrid and Lisbon, but in many other cities on the Iberian Peninsula. For full information about AutoEurope, see the introduction of this book.

Spanish Menus

Each of the paradores offers regional dishes featuring local specialties, and their menus consist almost entirely of Spanish food. For example, paradores on the Costa del Sol offer a great variety of delectable fish dishes, including pickled tuna and bonito, shellfish cocktails, and sardines, which are cooked both on a spit and in a frying pan. Frying fish is an art in Andalusia. This region is also well known for gazpacho in many varieties. Other possibilities on the menu could be octopus served in many forms, ham and beans, or the famous Sacromonte omelets from Granada. There are cookies from Antequera and egg-yolk candies from Ronda.

Each parador has two menus, a table d'hote and an à la carte. On the table d'hote, for one price there are several choices within each of the four courses. The first course usually has a choice of hors d'oeuvres or soup; the second course might include poached eggs, noodles, or other light dishes; the third is the main course and offers dishes such as hake, (a Spanish fish) tuna, roast chicken, stewed oxtails, or York ham and salad. The last course is dessert.

The à la carte menu allows the guest to choose at random when eating all four courses seems too heavy.

Except under unusual circumstances I did not take many lunches in the Spanish paradores. I found it very satisfactory to stop at the small grocery stores that can be found in every Spanish town. They provide fruit, bread, cheese, and mineral water for a roadside picnic. I also took a few light lunches at snack bars and smaller restaurants.

Everyone should have at least one meal of the famous paella de mariscos o pollo. This is rice cooked with garlic and spices, combined with countless tasty ingredients from the sea or farmlands, and infused with the spirit of something Spanish that goes beyond my comprehension. For centuries, paella has been served in Spain for family and visitors. It is sometimes the result of individual experimentation and each version can be a whole new experience for both the one who prepares it and the one who partakes. Its spiciness and flavor can vary from region to region.

Itineraries in Spain

This book contains my adventures on three separate trips to Spain. The first is a circle tour of Andalusia (southwestern Spain) that begins and ends in Málaga. It includes the famed Costa del Sol, Granada, the nearby Sierra Nevada mountains, the rolling plains and olive groves, Cordoba, and the fortified towns of western Spain, as well as Seville and Cadiz.

The second itinerary begins in Madrid and proceeds south a short distance beyond Toledo and then veers into the mountains northward to Avila, Zamora, Verín, and on to Galicia, including Santiago de Compostela. The route continues across Asturias, the northern coast to Santander, and the caves of Altamira. It turns south through the peaks of Europe to Burgos and Segovia, and returns to Madrid.

The third itinerary, entirely separate, includes a trip to several of the Canary Islands.

Introduction to Spain

There are several references in this book to the emergence of Spain, and to the "old" Spain and the "new" Spain. Perhaps nowhere in Spain were the changes more obvious to me than in the Madrid airport. When I first came here in 1975, the airport was in tremendous confusion and there were even several leaks in the roof. It was necessary to take buses between airports, and in general I was bewildered. Today, the Madrid airport is a model of efficiency and everything is under control.

Buses leave from the airport, although it is possible to rent an AutoEurope or other car to be picked up there if it is more convenient. I don't advise anybody to drive in Madrid, or for that matter, Lisbon,

London, Paris, Rome, or any other major European city if it can possibly be avoided.

The airport bus arrives at the Plaza de Colon, marked by very impressive fountains, which commemorates the feats of Christopher Columbus. This is one of the great intersections of Madrid, where at least six major roads all come together. The traffic is capably handled by rather attractive senoritas wearing blue coats, blue hats, and blowing vigorous whistles.

One of the broad streets that lead to the bus terminal is the absolutely magnificent Paseo Castellana, the "Champs Elysées" of Madrid. I enjoyed several invigorating walks along this avenue as it was within walking distance of the hotel where I was staying. It was early May and the trees were beginning to come into leaf and the sun provided a foretaste of warmer things to come. This is a perfect time for tourists because it's not too warm, or too cold, or too anything. The men of Madrid wear suits and jackets and the women wear dresses and light coats. In a few weeks hence the streets would be even more beautiful, enhanced by the blossoming trees.

There are occasional small cafés along this route and in one of them, instead of sitting around tables, the patrons enjoyed their refreshments on porch swings, rocking gently back and forth. They sell a complete comida (lunch). I ordered a drink whose name is totally international: Coca-Cola. These little restaurants are called kiosco.

Of course, there are literally hundreds, even thousands, of things of interest to the tourist in Madrid, and I submit to one and all that the Michelin Green Guide is a good place to start.

Before I share some of my observations about a few hotels in Madrid, I might point out if you look at Madrid on a map of Spain, you realize that it really is the hub of the country, and the main roads feeding into it are packed with traffic every morning and night. In my case it was necessary for me to come off of one main road, go into the middle of the town, and go back out another main road in order to leave my car at the airport upon my departure from Spain. Instead of trying to cope with the complexities of traffic and routes, I repeated the solution I had used in Rome: I hired a taxicab to lead me across the town's shortcuts. This will work almost anywhere.

HOTEL LUZ PALACIO, Madrid

This is a very nice hotel on a lovely street and is central to most of the things that would interest a tourist in Madrid. It's a sort of half-business and half-tourist hotel, and the prices are average for a four- and five-star establishment. As is the case in other hotels in Europe, the incoming guest checks in at the desk at the reception area and from then on does his business with the *conserjeria,* who arranges for transportation, tours, keeps the keys, collects the mail, and does a hundred-and-one other things that add up to service.

The hotel menu has a fixed-price dinner with eight or nine international items but, as in the case of other Spanish hotels, there's also an à la carte menu. In order to accommodate the many tourists who come to this hotel, the lunch or dinner hours have been moved back, because ordinarily the Spanish eat lunch at 2:30 and dinner at 9:30, and director Senor Alvarez explained that his visitors from North America simply couldn't wait that long for those two meals.

I enjoyed the Hotel Luz Palacio. I'm glad that I stayed there.

HOTEL LUZ PALACIO, Paseo de la Castellana 57, Madrid. Tel.: 442-51-00; Telex 27 207. A 182-room luxury hotel on one of Madrid's most pleasant avenues. In a city that has scores of such hotels, I found the Luz Palacio to be very pleasant and accommodating. Rates: See Index.

HOTEL RITZ, Madrid

Almost every major city in the world has a hotel called "The Ritz." As a matter of fact, the term has been used since the 1920s to indicate a sort of high style of living as popularized in a song of that time titled, "Puttin' on the Ritz." During the 1930s when the small city hotel was much more common than today, almost every town in the United States had a Ritz Hotel.

Well, the Ritz in Madrid is very ritzy—it has five stars for everything. The *Michelin Red Book* gives it top billing. It's across the street from the Prado.

On the day of my unexpected visit, I was able to browse about in the reception area and an adjacent room, but when I tried to go through the glass doors into the public parlor, I was restrained by a young, white-jacketed junior high school-aged staff member who explained that I would have to have a jacket and tie to continue my tour.

Just a few steps from the front door of the Ritz was a small kiosk selling ice cream. Both the strawberry and the mocha were excellent and made a good short lunch. It was amusing to see some of the children coming out of the Ritz Hotel and dragging their parents over to get the ice cream before stepping into their Mercedes-Benzes.

HOTEL RITZ, Plaza de la Lealtad 5, Madrid. Tel.: 221-28-57. The Michelin Red Guide lists two hotels with five stars in Madrid. The other is the Villa Nagna. I would suggest checking with your travel agent or Marketing Ahead, a reservation service in Manhattan, for full details. Rates: See Index.

❉ ❉ ❉ ❉

El Prado

I'll have to admit that art treasures of the world remained fairly obscure for me until I took the freshman course in art appreciation, given by Blanchard Gummo at Bucknell University in Lewisburg, Pennsylvania.

As they did for many other people, the slides in the darkened lecture hall of my first college course opened my imagination and widened my horizons. I only wish I had paid better attention.

I certainly paid rapt attention during my afternoon at the Prado, one of the supreme art museums of Europe. I have no intention of doing a review of the masterpieces by Goya, El Greco, Velasquez, Titian, Van Dyck, Rubens, and a host of others. To see the originals in the perspective of other inspired paintings lifts the spirit and makes the travel experience far more meaningful.

HOTEL ABEBA, Madrid

I particularly sought out another hotel to recommend in Madrid and this one is in another section of the city. Should the reader be looking for it, tell the taxicab to go to Plaza Diego de Leon.

This is a small, unpretentious, three-star hotel that is very cozy. I saw one twin-bedded room that was plain but comfortable and had a view of the roofs of Madrid. It had television, a telephone, and a good, small, but quite adequate, bathroom. Public rooms are decorated in Art Deco and Spanish modern.

HOTEL ABEBA, Alcantara 63, Madrid. Tel.: 401-16-50. This is a "comfortable hotel" (Michelin rating) of 90 rooms. The only way to reach it is by cab unless the reader is well acquainted with Madrid. I've included it because it is typical of dozens of hotels in Madrid that are more moderately priced. Rates: See Index.

An Andalusian Idyll

I made a circle tour of southwestern Spain in a counterclockwise direction, starting from Málaga and visiting Granada, Jaén, Cordoba, Seville, Cadiz, and Algeciras. There were also side trips to Ciudad Real, Zafra, Merida, and Huelva.

PARADOR GIBRALFARO, Málaga

In retrospect I realize that Parador Gibralfaro was a most fortunate choice as my first country inn in Spain. It is located a few steps below the Moorish fortress through which I had been wandering during the late afternoon.

Originally, the building was a most impressive home that now has been carefully restored and enlarged to accommodate travelers. The most memorable thing about it, of course, is the view of the harbor and the city below. However, even in another less spectacular location it would still be an outstanding experience.

The setting, so high above the tumult of the city, creates a total atmosphere of peace and tranquility. In redesigning the building to meet the needs of travelers, the architects made every possible use of the magnificent view; hence, most of the lodging rooms share the spectacle along with the second-floor outdoor terrace. I found that many Malaguenans are fond of having their midday meal or dinner at this parador.

As in all paradores there was a very comfortably furnished parlor with a fireplace, where guests frequently gathered at the end of the day. Lots of books and magazines made the place more homelike.

At most paradores the bedrooms and sitting rooms follow a carefully chosen individual decorating theme. At Gibralfaro the colors and textures were in harmony with the closeness of sea, sky, and sun, with many beige tones as well as brown and accenting touches of green. My bedroom was basically designed around the large double doors leading to the balcony.

That evening, after dinner, I walked out on the veranda to look at the lights of Málaga below. The balcony apartments of the city were small pools of yellow light in an otherwise velvety blackness. The moon over the Mediterranean created silvery paths along the crescent shores. The boulevard circling the waterfront had quite a few automobiles. The lights of the cruise ships anchored for the night continued to intrigue me. My eyes kept going back to them and wondering what activity was taking place within these floating palaces that reminded me of the cruise ships in the harbor in St. Thomas, Virgin Islands.

PARADOR GIBRALFARO, Málaga (Málaga). Tel.: Málaga 22-19-02. A most comfortable former home on the heights overlooking Málaga, 556 km. from Madrid. RR., airport. Rates: See Index.

The Alcazaba in Málaga

Here I was at last. My first castle in Spain. I had climbed to the very top of the highest tower in the Moorish fortifications known as the Alcazaba above the city of Málaga.

Beneath me lay the city of Málaga stretched out in a gorgeous crescent beside the Mediterranean. The sandy beaches extended up and down the coast as far as I could see. I leaned out over the parapet and looked down into the town. I felt like the captain general of all I surveyed—the commander, nay the sultan or king! My domain was the Costa del Sol—the coast of the sun. How the lush hills, valleys, and warm beaches must have beckoned those Moorish invaders in the eighth century who eventually overcame all of Spain. They held it in their grip for 700 years until Ferdinand and Isabella climaxed many years of war with a final victory at Granada in 1492 and began a new period in Spain's history.

Looking down from the tower into the ruins of this castle, preserved and reconstructed in many places, I could see the evidences of the Moorish influence, an influence I was to see throughout Spain. The walls and crenelated towers were of Moorish design. The Moorish arch, now an integral part of Spanish architecture, was restated in the galleries, balconies, and staircases, and the courtyards were paved with small black and white stones, repeating an intriguing, symbolic Moorish design.

I wondered how many soldiers on watch had walked these parapets, looking out over the sea, feeling not quite sure what foe there would be to repel or indeed if there would be any. How many times had a lone guard stamped his feet against the chill night air and then turned to look back at the silhouette of the saw-toothed ring of mountains around Málaga—mountains that had been here long before the Moors, Phoenicians, Greeks, and Romans? Had he, indeed, looked as I was looking now at the houses of the city, where perhaps a young lady with dark, laughing eyes awaited his return?

Church bells pealing from the city below broke my reverie and I climbed down from the top of the tower to a dungeonlike room on the lower level, where there were accumulated graffiti from perhaps a thousand or more years. It was probably a guardhouse where soldiers could warm themselves or escape from the heat of midsummer sun. Or could it have been a dungeon out here on the far reaches of the battlements from which escape was all but impossible? I gingerly leaned over the wall to trace out a possible escape route down the smooth walls to the moat below. There was none.

Now I could hear voices approaching. Soon six people in a gay, holiday mood joined me. They seemed to be bubbling over with enthusiasm and identified themselves as being from the nearby city of Marbella. One of the two men was an artist who introduced me to the others. There were also two small children who were running along the parapets playing games: We could have all been standing on the walls of Fort Ticonderoga on Lake Champlain in New York State or at the fortifications that I had visited in St. Croix in the Virgin Islands. Communication was no problem, even though I spoke practically no Spanish and they spoke halting English. People of good will can always communicate. I learned that they were on a short holiday that began in the nearby mountain town of Ronda and was continuing in Málaga. They had visited some of the historic buildings in the city and were planning to have dinner at the parador. These were the first people that I had had a chance to really talk with in Spain, and I loved it. I bade them goodbye with a promise possibly to rejoin them after dinner.

I found a very narrow staircase about three feet wide that twisted and turned downward for three levels. I imagined how difficult it would have been during an alarm for the soldiers to negotiate these stairs with their weapons and armor. I could see where one man strategically placed could stand off a small army. At one point, as I descended the staircase, I was totally in the dark, feeling my way along with a hand on each side. Finally, I could see a spot of light below me and hurried down to be in the late afternoon sunshine once again.

I left the Alcazaba through a small gate and a bird struck up an evensong. Others in the gardens joined him. I stopped for just a moment to listen to this happy warbler whose joyous song matched my own spirits as I was about to embark on a great adventure in Spain.

Miguel and Málaga

This is an excellent time to tell you about Miguel. Miguel Rodriguez Guitierrez was not only my driver for two weeks in Spain, but he became my interpreter, adviser, historian, sociologist, and friend. He lives with his wife and two children in Málaga. I found him to be modest, generous, well informed, considerate, and gentlemanly. He provided a wealth of information about all of Spain; a great deal of the additional factual material herein, as well as an insight into the Spanish people and culture, comes as a result of our conversations and exchanges of ideas. We conversed in English but with an additional amount of Spanish each day. At the start he told me that by the end of two weeks I would be able to get along in Spain very well. He was correct. Before I left I was able to comprehend conversations in rapid Spanish. On our trip we worked on my Spanish pronunciation by my reciting the names of towns and villages on the road signs. We had many laughs over my stumbling attempts to pronounce "j" like "h" and "z" like "th." It is an intriguing language, and I found that once I really got started, I moved along rather well.

The Parador Gibralfaro was at the top of the heights overlooking Málaga, so after following the circuitous road down the mountain we arrived at the bottom of the hill and found ourselves immediately involved in the activities of a Monday morning in a Spanish city. There were just a few tourists, but the number would increase considerably during the following Holy Week.

It was about ten o'clock and a number of people were having a second cup of coffee in some of the sidewalk cafés overlooking the plaza. The one-way traffic around the plaza was about seven cars wide, but most of the cars were small. The pace was rapid but not harrowing. There were quite a few motorbikes, and here and there a horse-drawn cart for tourists. Buses came by frequently and more and more shoppers poured into the center of one of Spain's major cities.

Málaga is blessed, as is most of the Costa del Sol, with a very even climate. In the summertime the breezes from the Mediterranean make the entire coast most desirable, and this section of the coast from Algeciras to Almeria is one of the most popular summer resorts in Europe.

The Road to Nerja

This section of the Costa del Sol is very popular during the summer season. It occurred to me that April and May would be an excellent time to visit southern Spain because the traffic is much lighter and the weather is mild. There is more room on the beaches and it is much easier to shop than during the summer months of June, July, and August.

We traveled from the suburbs out to the countryside and it was on this road that I first saw a Moorish tower. Some of these were built by the Arabs over 1,000 years ago as lookout points and communication centers. Miguel explained that since the coast was subject to raids from North Africa, throughout southern Spain there was a network of these towers which were used to summon aid quickly by heliograph when the coast was threatened with invasion. It was

fascinating to realize that some of these towers, which are in surprisingly good repair, were built before the year A.D. 1000. I found that almost every sizable village in Andalusia has some type of Moorish fortification or castle left over from the centuries of occupation. The Phoenicians, Romans, and Greeks also occupied this section of Spain, and on the road to Nerja, Miguel pointed out the remains of the Roman viaduct.

As we approached Nerja the terrain became more mountainous as it skirted the sea, and in many respects it reminded me of the coast of northern California. There were many marvelous overlooks, some of them 150 feet above the ocean. Then the road would drop down almost beside the sea for a few kilometers and suddenly twist its way back up to the cliffs. On this beautiful day the sun bathed the landscape, bringing vigor to the olive and almond trees, warmth to the sea, and life and beauty to everything that it touched.

PARADOR NERJA, Nerja (Málaga)

"In the popular summer months it is necessary to have reservations here for at least a year in advance." I was sitting on the terrace of this beautiful seaside parador in Nerja, talking with the parador director. We could see the beach stretching out in both directions and I could well understand why guests from so many countries find this inn an attractive place for a vacation.

The village of Nerja is one of the jewels of the Costa del Sol. It is a picturesque town on a cliff in the foothills of southern Spain's mountains and is famous for sea and mountain views. Besides being a resort community, it is also a fishing district and sometimes bathers share the beach with fishermen and their nets. There is sailing, motor boating, and sport fishing here as well.

The director had already given me an excellent tour of this inn, which is contemporary in architecture. It is built around a hollow square with a modest swimming pool and a beautiful reflecting pool. The gardens, already beginning to bloom, are exquisite.

The inn, situated on a cliff, seventy-five feet above the seashore, provides an elevator to transport inn guests to and from the beach. "Of course, the beach is one of our great features," he said. "Many of our guests have been returning year after year to get a beautiful Costa del Sol tan."

Miguel told me, as we began our journey to Granada, that

because of its nearness to the sea and the great beauty of the flowers, the Parador Nerja is one of the most popular in all of Spain.

PARADOR NERJA, Nerja (Málaga). Tel.: Nerja 52-00-50. A contemporary seaside parador, 51 km. from Málaga, 559 from Madrid. Aquatic sports, beach, swimming pool. Rates: See Index.

From Nerja to Granada

"Now," said Miguel, "we are on the road to Granada." We had departed from Nerja approximately an hour and a half earlier and were now on a road that passed through a group of small fishing villages. The panorama reminded me of traveling south from Carmel, California, on the Pacific Coast Highway. We passed through the village of Almuñécar and were now in the province of Granada. Along the coast the Moorish towers continued, each in sight of the other; most of them still in excellent repair. There was one small village after another clinging precariously to the sides of these hills by the sea.

At Motril, we turned north toward Granada. Twilight was beginning to set in and I kept looking out the rear window of the car for my last look at the blue Mediterranean for almost two weeks. There were groves of almond trees on each side. In most of the communities the people had gathered at the town square for an hour or so. It is a time for socializing and talking about the day's activities. This is a custom of the country and one that I found quite appealing. Children were playing and young people were strolling about in pairs. Dinner is not served in the average Spanish household until after eight or eight-thirty, so there is plenty of time in the early evening for the lighter things of life. I saw this scene repeated on many evenings in Spain.

We sped toward the mountains of Granada. The valleys became more steep and the road narrowed considerably at some places. I caught my first glimpse of snowcapped mountains which were still dramatically lighted by the setting sun.

Now, the oranges, greens, purples, and reds of twilight were almost entirely replaced by the blue-black of night. My watch said 9:15, but Miguel assured me that we would be in Granada well in time for a late Spanish dinner.

Granada: home of the Alhambra and one of the fairest cities in Andalusia. I wondered what surprises were in store for me tomorrow.

117

The Sounds of Granada

Granada.

Say the word one hundred times and it has a hundred different shadings and meanings. Visit Granada one hundred times and each visit will be a new experience. Granada...Granada. It can be dreamy and reflective, or it can be demanding and provocative. Trill the "r" and you'll feel like a real Spaniard.

Granada is the home of the Alhambra, the palatial city of the Moors spread grandly across the hill bearing its name and protected by a network of walls and towers. Volumes have been written about it. Washington Irving immortalized it in his Tales of the Alhambra *and Columbus must have spent quite a few days there waiting anxiously for an audience with Queen Isabella. It's been photographed from every angle, and the gardens and palaces are one of the most exquisite experiences in the world. Incidentally, I found that the best time to visit it is after three in the afternoon, when most of the tours have been completed, and the Alhambra can be enjoyed for all of its beauty and tranquility.*

Granada is a city of monuments—the guidebooks list fifty-three. It has museums, galleries, churches, palatial homes and sections of simple Moorish houses that date back to A.D. 1000. I have heard it said that Granada, rather than being a product of the culture of the Moorish civilization of Spain, was the shaper and builder of that

culture. When the Moors came to Spain, they had spent centuries on the desert and were essentially a warlike, nomadic people. Seven hundred years later, when Ferdinand and Isabella reconquered the city, they found a sensual, refined, dreaming race whose chief delights were in art and nature.

Over the entrance gate of the watch tower in the Alcazaba, there is a famous poem by Francisco de Icaza which reads:

> Give him alms, woman,
> For there is nothing in life, nothing,
> So sad as to be blind in Granada.

True, perhaps, but I found the sounds of Granada to be utterly fascinating, and I am sure any sightless person visiting this unique city would find depth and meaning in its sounds far beyond those of us who are sighted.

Some of the most marvelous sounds come from the market section. This is where people come together to shop, gossip, bargain, or to have a midmorning cup of coffee. Since I was anxious to mingle with the people of Granada, Miguel gave me explicit directions on how to reach the market area and then told me that almost anyone there could direct me to the Plaza Nueva where he would meet me at noon.

The first plaza was the center of the flower market and on all sides there were small stalls bursting with hundreds of blooms. The fragrance was intoxicating. The colors were brilliant. There were more kinds of flowers than I could possibly identify. The experience of standing in this small plaza, listening to the flower sellers call out their offerings is still clear in my mind. I am happy to report that business was very good. Everyone was buying flowers. I was delighted to see people carrying flowers along with food and other essentials.

Next, I walked through a narrow street into a plaza where almost everything seemed to be available. One store had bicycles hanging just out of reach—all sizes, colors, and types. Another store was selling grain from open jute sacks on the sidewalk in front. On either side of me were small stalls where fruit, vegetables, and clothing were sold.

I finally succumbed to the lure of the many pastry stalls and purchased a piece of flat sweet bread with raw sugar spread on top. I couldn't resist. It was about the size of a Frisbee and I broke off small pieces as I walked through the plaza. The place was lively and bustling and put me in good spirits.

The next plaza was filled with stalls of meat and fish. Apparently there were separate stalls for poultry, pork, lamb, and beef. The plucked chickens hung by their feet, looking quite chilly without their feathers. A housewife, carrying her basket, would stop and point to one or two birds which would be weighed, and a discussion would follow about the price. Then it would be wrapped and she would leave for the next stall to select some fish.

I found that fish is a mainstay of the Spanish diet. The fish market was one of the busiest places I have ever visited. Part of it was inside a public market building and there were many stalls where people in white smocks continually extolled the virtues of their wares. I have never seen so many different varieties of fish before—not even in the Fulton Fish Market in New York. There were eels, octopi, hake, bonita, sardines, tuna, and dozens and dozens of varieties beyond my comprehension.

I turned for one more look back into the market area. I was tempted to walk through once again to see the things that I had missed, but the hour was almost twelve and the Plaza Nueva was at least ten blocks away. Yes, Granada has the Alhambra, the Generalife, the Alcazaba, gorgeous monuments and magnificent buildings, but I shall be eager to return to the sounds of the marketplace.

PARADOR SAN FRANCISCO, Granada

"Sometimes when people ask whether it's noisy in the morning I tell them that when they wake up they will hear the beautiful singing of birds." I was seeing this beautiful parador, on the grounds of the Alhambra, through the eyes of the assistant director.

This parador is one of the most famous in all of Spain. Originally an Arab palace, it was used as a Franciscan monastery under Ferdinand and Isabella, and has been a parador since 1945. The original buildings have been preserved and new additions have been made to provide twenty-six lodging rooms all in the style of the original architecture. Great care has been taken to be sure that the texture and the color of the brick used is as close to the original as possible.

"Queen Isabella was entombed in this monastery from the time of her death in Granada in 1504 until 1521," he explained. We were in a secluded courtyard, looking at a marker indicating her burial place, and I, too, felt a sense of quiet respect for this woman who played such an important role in the history of the world.

Parador San Francisco is enhanced with many fountains. I learned from the assistant director that each of the fountains in the Alhambra has a different musical tone. "The Moors," he said, "developed a feeling for peace and tranquility and believed that fountains were one way to achieve it. We have many fountains in the parador." At this particular moment we were standing in a courtyard that had four fountains, each with a different musical pitch. There were tall cypress trees swaying in the wind and birds flitting from tree to tree.

We concluded our tour at the terrace, where we walked to a point overlooking the Alhambra, just a few steps away. We could see the old quarter of the city and the Generalife Gardens, across the river. The roses, which would be in such profusion in a few weeks, were just beginning to bud, and in the distance I could see the always snowcapped Sierra Nevada Mountains.

PARADOR SAN FRANCISCO, Granada (Granada). Tel.: 22-14-62. Originally an Arab palace on the grounds of the Alhambra, 429 km. from Madrid. RR., airport. Rates: See Index.

The Road to Parador Sierra Nevada

After a most enjoyable lunch at the Parador San Francisco, Miguel and I were leaving Granada on our way to Sierra Nevada. There were two reasons to visit this spectacular mountain area—to see a parador located above the snow line, and to visit this particular section of Spain, a popular winter resort area, with skiing that attracts people from all over the world. It is possible to ski at 8,000 feet from November to May, and even year around at higher altitudes. The road that we were on, the Granada-Veleta highway, is the highest in Europe.

We passed through a valley filled with poplar trees and started our ascent. Miguel had taken precautions to put high-test gasoline in the car rather than regular. He said that this would be much easier on the engine. At 770 meters, we were still going up and passed through villages built along one side of the valley, which was now closing in on us. Many of the hillsides had been terraced in order to preserve the soil for farming. We passed through both grape and olive country.

At 1,000 meters we were able to look back and see a great deal of the city of Granada. There was a blue sky overhead with a few fluffy clouds.

The car, still in third gear, brought us to a closer view of the white-clad giants and I could see the road winding through the mountains ahead of us. We passed out of the agricultural section and arrived at an altitude where the only vegetation was low bushes with goldenrod-colored flowers. Miguel explained that they belonged to the mimosa family. Here and there I saw a few groves of olive trees, but they were becoming more scarce. We then proceeded to a point where we were equal in height to the mountains across the valley.

Now we were so high that we could see all of Granada and beyond. Miguel remarked that there are some days when it is possible to see the Mediterranean as well.

PARADOR SIERRA NEVADA, Monachil (Granada)

Spain is a land of contrasts. Just twenty-four hours ago I had been in a parador on the seacoast at Nerja where it was necessary to reserve a year in advance during the months of July and August. Here, perhaps no more than ninety kilometers distant, I was in a parador above the snow line where reservations for December through March have to be made three or four months in advance. I could, if I wanted to, ski here in the morning and drive to Motril for a swim in the Mediterranean in the afternoon.

The design of this parador has been created to conform with the contour of the mountains. The dining rooms and parlors have white plaster walls and natural wood ceilings with a high glossy finish. Lodging rooms, many in duplex style, overlook the snow-filled valley in front and the mountains in back.

I walked through the impressive dining room up to a balcony where there was a small fire laid in an open fireplace. As I settled back in one of the comfortable chairs and put my feet up on the hearth, a group of school children in ski outfits trooped in with a look of hunger on their well-tanned faces.

"Oh, it's excellent. We think it is the best skiing in Europe," said one. "We're on a holiday and our parents bring us here every year. One year we couldn't get reservations here at the parador, so we stayed at the ski village just below."

I asked them how the weather had been and they told me it had been sunny all week and that the conditions for spring skiing were perfect.

"It's pretty fast in the morning but along about noon, when the sun warms up the snow, it slows down and that's when we generally stop and come back here for lunch."

I decided to ask all of them where they lived and where they went to school and I had a chorus of answers in many languages and locations. They said they were going to ski the next day and asked me if I could join them. Regretfully, I said no. Tomorrow I would be in Jaen and Ubeda. They asked me why I was in Spain and I explained that I was writing a book about the country inns in Europe and they all thought that was "real cool."

I do myself.

PARADOR SIERRA NEVADA, Monachil (Granada). Tel.: Granada 42-02-00. A contemporary mountain parador, 35 km. from Granada, 464 from Madrid. Rates: See Index.

The Neptune Gardens

I am in love with Rosarillo. The only problem is that Rosarillo is not in love with me. In fact, she wouldn't be in love with anyone who didn't pronounce her name correctly—Rosa-reo. Rosarillo is a flamenco dancer who appears almost nightly at the Neptune Gardens Nightclub in Granada.

Every visitor to Spain should see and hear the flamenco dancing of the country. There are clubs everywhere in the major cities. For the purist, it may be painful to see the traditional dances of Cadiz, Granada, and northern Spain, occasionally accompanied by a modern orchestra. I can only speak for the Neptune Gardens and for the one performance I saw. It was an exciting and sensuous show. A large portion of it was performed to the accompaniment of flamenco guitarists and singers. There were several different regional dances performed with all of the fire, disdain, pride, and real excitement that has belonged to this dance for centuries.

The women with their imperious eyes, stately carriages, and marvelous control are terrific. That's where I first saw Rosarillo. As I have seen so many times at Jacob's Pillow in the Berkshire hills, the first one or two offerings are quiet and sedate, the movements delicate and controlled. Rosarillo did not catch my eye until about the third number when the dances became more wild and untameable. She was wearing a traditional royal blue costume that looked as if it had to be sewn on her for every performance. Her eyes seemed to

generate more fire than the other women, and her movements were more talented.

Meanwhile, the male dancers were lithe, quick, and chauvinistic. Altogether it is Spanish pride and tradition portrayed in the national dance.

The show was divided into two parts and most of the first part was more or less pure flamenco. However, for ten minutes a full orchestra came on stage and presented a concert version of the song "Granada." Even though I am certain it is played every night and twice on some nights, there is something electric and convincing about this production number done in a small nightclub in Granada that brings a fresh quality to each performance. The bravura solo trumpet with its final great triumphant note hanging in the air brings down the house.

The audience was international, to say the least. There were groups from Germany, France, England, and of course many Spanish tourists as well. I took several flash photographs, as did many other members of the audience.

The second half was a bit more on the "show biz" side and after all the dancers had done their solo, duet, and trio turns, the entire company returned for a challenge dance finale that is about as moving as can be seen on a stage anywhere.

Part of the music was Khachaturian's "Sabre Dance," done with a furious flamenco rhythm. The dancers were exhorting and challenging one another to do better as each took a turn amidst the clapping hands, the singing of the dancers, and the marvelous great brassy tones of the orchestra. The crescendos kept building from one level to another with all of the members of the audience getting into the swing of things, shouting "olé." At the end, with the lights flashing and the cymbals clanging and the trumpets blaring, it was one tremendous final chord. I leaped into the air, shouting "olé" at the top of my lungs. My staid New England conservatism was once and for all put to rest.

Rosarillo, wherever you are, wait for me, I'm coming back— back to the sounds of Granada.

The High Road to Jaén

"There is the parador we're going to visit," Miguel said, with a twinkle in his eye. He pointed in the distance to the towers and walls of an ancient castle at the top of a steep, rugged mountain dominating

125

the town below. "You mean that's it, on top of that mountain?" I asked. "Yes, that's it," he replied, "if you remember, I promised you something different from anything we have seen so far."

We had driven up the high road from Granada to Jaén, passing first through the orchard country with small farms and beautiful homes, then through the low hills, and, finally, up into the mountain country. It was here that I entered the land of the Spanish olive tree. The olive tree is green and shapely, a tree of beauty and grace that is also of tremendous importance to the economy of Spain. On this road the olive groves alternated with cork oak trees.

The road threaded its way between high mountains and precipitous canyons. Occasionally, I saw shepherds with their sheep or goats. We passed through tunnels and zoomed alongside tumbling mountain brooks. In many respects the terrain resembled northern New England, except that the highlands here are not used as pasture, but cultivated for groves of olive trees extending almost to the mountain tops.

The city of Jaén proved to be a surprise because I didn't expect to see such a large, sophisticated town in this mountainous area. The road directing us to the parador passed immediately in front of one of the most beautiful cathedrals in Spain, a masterpiece of Gothic, Renaissance, and baroque architecture that took over 300 years to complete. We stopped long enough for a quick look.

Following the parador signs we found our way through the city and up the side of the mountain, the road twisting and turning as we approached the summit. Always in view, first on the right and then on the left, were the massive stone walls and tower. We passed through an old archway. We had arrived at the Parador Castillo de Santa Catalina.

PARADOR CASTILLO DE SANTA CATALINA, Jaén

My first feeling upon seeing this parador was complete awe of the building, with its massive Spanish Renaissance interior and tremendous, inspiring, mind-boggling view.

Originally, it was built by an Arab king who must have keenly appreciated its strategic military situation in the mountains. Ferdinand III laid siege and captured it from the Moors in 1266 on St. Catalina's Day, afterwards reconstructing it. About twenty years ago it was converted into a parador and during recent years has undergone extensive restoration.

The first thing I saw when I walked through the massive doors of the main entrance was a three-story-high hallway. To my left was a great hall with two handsome Spanish fireplaces and cathedral windows providing a panoramic view of the mountains and the valley. Each of the bedrooms has its own balcony, which creates the sensation of being in an eagle's aerie. I had the most curious feeling that I could actually fly out over the rows of olive trees and the houses of Jaén at the base of the mountains. The cathedral that I had just visited a few moments earlier looked like a miniature from this great height. Overhead the blue skies of morning were being replaced by cloud banks and the wind was beginning to rise causing thousands of olive trees to sway in the breeze.

In a country where castles have been converted into marvelous hotels, Parador Castillo de Santa Catalina is exceptional.

PARADOR CASTILLO DE SANTA CATALINA, Jaén. Tel.: Jaén 23-22-87. A most impressive castle parador at 97 km. from Granada, 335 from Madrid. Rates: See Index.

PARADOR CONDESTABLE DAVALOS, Ubeda (Jaén)

I was singing in the shower at a Renaissance palace. The bathroom was princely, to say the least. In remodeling this stately mansion, which would be very much in place in Florence, the architect provided the most comfortable of accommodations for two people. There were even twin washbowls.

127

I stepped out of the shower and wrapped myself in one of those incredible towels that go twice around. Even the most noble families who had previously lived in this palace were not nearly as well accommodated as the parador guest of today.

The bedroom/sitting room had a two-story ceiling and windows and shutters. The customary twin beds were supplemented with some interesting Spanish antiques, including a handsome carved

wardrobe. At the moment the most useful piece of furniture was an unobtrusive small refrigerator, from which I obtained a welcome bottle of lime soda.

About an hour earlier I had been greeted by the director of this parador, a most accommodating and effusive man. After being registered by the concierge, he was kind enough to give me a tour of the entire inn.

We began with the winery in the cellar of this four-hundred-year-old building, and now used as a dining room for special occasions. We sat for a moment at a table in the low-ceilinged room and talked about the history of the house, whose inhabitants were very important figures in the history of Spain.

We returned to the first floor and I observed that the inn is built around a glass-roofed courtyard with guest rooms on the second and third floor. There are a great many antiques, including suits of armor worn by ancient Spanish knights. The director proudly showed me the library of the parador, which is not only beautifully furnished and decorated, but has some very good books and magazines for the guests of the house. Like most of the paradors I visited, this one also has a television room.

At dinner that evening I met two retired American ladies, Mrs. Harriet Smith and Mrs. Ann Ulrich both from the state of Washington, who were driving through Spain, and having a wonderful time. When I learned that they did not speak Spanish, I asked them how they were managing. Mrs. Smith said, "Oh, we are doing wonderfully. With a combination of sign language, maps, and lots of laughs, we have been kept on the right track by these wonderful people. I just can't say enough about the generosity and manners of everyone we have met in Spain."

PARADOR CONDESTABLE DAVALOS, Ubeda (Jaén). Tel.: Ubeda 75-03-45. An extremely comfortable mansion at 55 km. from Jaén, 338 from Madrid. Rates: See Index.

PARADOR DEL ADELANTADO, Cazorla (Jaén)

I was having breakfast high in the Sierra de Cazorla with the Davenports—Jenifer and Clark, and their four children, Sara, Jad, Lisa, and Sam. They were Americans who were living in Spain for three years.

"We've been at this parador for three days," said Jenifer, passing a plate of rolls to Sam, "and we've had an absolutely marvelous time."

"And we've seen lots of wild animals, including an ibex. Have you ever seen an ibex?" This came from Lisa, who has very blonde hair and blue eyes. I had to confess that I had never seen an ibex, which by definition is a wild goat with large, backward-curving horns.

"Well, we saw one," she said proudly, "and we also saw some mountain goats and deer."

This parador is a very cozy hunting lodge. The furnishings and decor reflect the wildlife of the region. There are mounted heads of wild boar, deer, bear and mountain sheep. There are also some excellent black and white and full-color photographs of the region showing some of the huge rocky mountains and crags and steep dells.

After breakfast we all walked into the living room, where a welcome fire was blazing away in a huge fireplace. We made ourselves comfortable in the deep leather chairs, and I asked them if they were enjoying their holiday.

"Oh, yes, this is really our kind of place," said Clark Davenport. "And I must say that we never expected to find an intimate little inn like this so high in the mountains."

"Yes, and you should see our rooms," said Sara. "They have a wonderful view of the valley. When I wake up in the morning I can see the sun coming through the trees."

"I hope the rain stops today," said Jad, "because we have one more walking trip we want to make. Dad says that if it doesn't stop raining we'll take the road that leads back up into the mountains and is the source of the river that passes through Cordoba and Seville." Clark later confirmed that that was the Guadalquivir, which rises in the Sierra Cazorla.

Incidentally, I have one memento of the trip to Cazorla that I treasure very much. As I was leaving, Lisa Davenport presented me with a crayon drawing of an ibex.

PARADOR DEL ADELANTADO, Cazorla (Jaén). Tel.: Cazorla 295. A cozy hunting lodge at 27 km. from Cazorla, 137 from Jaén, 417 from Madrid. Mountain scenery, golf, hunting and fishing. Rates: See Index.

Don Quixote's La Mancha

When I ventured north from the province of Jaén into the province of Ciudad Real, I came into the land of Don Quixote and his creator, Miguel Cervantes. I was on the edge of the countryside that is known traditionally as La Mancha. Don Quixote, Cervantes' great book, and the recent musical version of it, The Man of La Mancha, have brought this touching and moving story into homes all over the world.

While I was waiting to enjoy a midday meal in the albergue at Manzanares, I made the acquaintance of an Englishman who told me some very interesting things about this area.

"It is possible," he said, "to trace the course of Don Quixote's journeys throughout La Mancha. There are towns and villages in the region to which Cervantes made several references."

PARADOR ALMAGRO (Ciudad Real)

While visiting the parador in Cazorla I heard about one in Almagro, reputed to be one of the most outstanding paradores in all of Spain.

There was nothing to do but to head north to have a look at it. The road leading to Almagro was unusual, because instead of being blacktop it was constructed of brick and looked as though it had been there for many, many years. The countryside was flat with many fields of early-ripening grain. The houses and the villages were quite different from what I had become accustomed to in southern Spain—these had sort of a squarish look. The second-floor balconies had intricate iron grilles and many had red, green, and blue flower-filled pots hanging from them.

Almagro is a middle-sized village and a short visit to the tourist office proved to be most helpful with some literature of the area, some of it in English. Among other things, I learned that there is a 13th-century theatre here, the Corral de Comedias, the only one of its kind left in Spain.

The parador was once a 16th-century convent, and it has all of the graceful architectural features that have been incorporated into the newly constructed paradores throughout Spain—graceful Moorish arches, tiled courtyards, and many musical fountains. As I found throughout Spain, a great deal of care has been taken to blend the old and the new.

PARADOR ALMAGRO, Almagro. Tel.: 86-01-00. A 65-guestroom inn in a former 16th-century convent. Swimming pool, air-conditioning (very important). It is 189 km. from Madrid, 23 km. from Ciudad Real, 230 km. from Cordoba. Rates: See Index.

Directions: Almagro is south of Madrid on C-415 between Ciudad Real and Valdepenas.

Cordoba—City of Flowers

Cordoba is a city of flowers. There are flowers everywhere—on the plazas, the bridges, the squares and on almost every corner. There are some streets with flowers in all of the windows and potted flowers hanging from balconies.

One of the most engaging plazas in this city is called La Plaza del Potro (Plaza of the Young Horse). At one end there is a 16th-century fountain dominated by a colt with its front hoofs raised, holding

the shield of the city. Also in this plaza stands an inn that existed before the 14th century. Miguel Cervantes lived for some time in a neighboring street with an uncle who was a saddlemaker. He mentions the inn several times in his writings.

Cordoba has many other engaging features. It is not as large a city as Granada or Seville and is somewhat more modest in its demeanor. It has an impressive mosque, excellent museums, and ancient ruins from a romantic past.

I was also fascinated by the Roman bridge that crosses the Quadalquivir River. Cordoba has a very lengthy history and this bridge was probably built during the time of Julius Caesar. Over the years it has undergone numerous alterations and has been the victim of wars and revolutions. It is somewhat ironic that of the sixteen arches now supporting the bridge, not one is Roman—most of them date from the Moorish period.

I paid a short visit to the mosque on a sunny morning and the *inside was a bit spooky by contrast. There was a series of repeated arches that seemed to stretch out of sight. In the middle of the mosque is a Christian church, illustrating the merging of Christian and Moorish cultures in Spain.*

In the area immediately adjacent to the mosque there were several small shops with curios and gifts of good quality. Once again, it was quite common to see mothers and daughters walking along the street with their arms intertwined. The horse-drawn, open tourist carriages were driven by men wearing the traditional flat-topped hats.

PARADOR LA ARRUZAFA, Cordoba

I will always remember the Parador La Arruzafa as the place where I had my first experience with Spanish hors d'oeuvres. It was at the midday meal *(comida)*. We had arrived late the previous evening, and I had slept beyond my usual hour in the morning. Miguel had dropped me off at the mosque and I also took the opportunity to walk through the Old Quarter and up into the main square and shopping district.

I returned to the parador and was taken on a complete tour by the courteous parador director. We visited rooms on every floor and toured the kitchen, the gardens, and the recreation area with a swimming pool. We stopped to enjoy some refreshments and the sunshine on the terrace. It had been a very busy morning and I felt unusually hungry, so I ordered the hors d'oeuvres for my first course.

Well, the dishes began to arrive. There were at least fifteen and they included delicious small clams and many varieties of small fish, very salty and extremely tasty. There were small dishes containing varieties of vegetables, small chunks of liver, and quite a few other items from the truck farm that I was unable to identify. This was only the first course.

After I finished sampling everything, I felt that I had had sufficient luncheon! But I did try the spinach omelet, one of the favorite dishes in Spain, and a light carmel custard for dessert.

The Parador La Arruzafa has all the conveniences of a four-star hotel in Spain, but the general atmosphere is far more relaxed. It is six or seven stories high, and all of the rooms have balconies facing the broad plain on which Cordoba is located. The gardens, hedges, flowers, lemon and orange trees add to the atmosphere. There is even a play area for children. Quite a few suites are available and some of them have parlors and dressing rooms.

PARADOR LA ARRUZAFA, Cordoba. Tel.: 27-59-00. This is a somewhat larger than average parador (56 guestrooms) in the northwest suburbs of the city. There are beautiful gardens, tennis courts, and a swimming pool. Cordoba is 400 km. from Madrid, 172 from Granada, 176 from Málaga, and 138 from Seville. Rates: See Index.

Land of the Skyline

Someday, I am going to return to the village of Fuenteovejuna. If I have to wait until I can pronounce it properly, I may never go back! However, I found that by taking it syllable by syllable and changing the pronunciation to read Fuento-be-huna *that I could get it approximately right.*

It's not the name alone that has such memorable qualities. Fuenteovejuna is halfway between Cordoba and Zafra in some of the most beautiful farming country (campo) that I saw during my trip. I call it "the land of the skyline" because at almost every point there was something to be seen on the horizon. In fact, I found that in Spain the skyline almost always seems to offer an exciting new vista. It might be the silhouettes of hilltop trees lined up like an army marching single file. It might be a ring of saw-toothed mountains, or a castle towering over the crest of a hill. On this particular route there always seemed to be two or three Spanish villages in the distance, nestled against the hillside, each with its own church, surrounding fields, and frequently with its own guardian Moorish tower.

I began to notice the name Fuenteovejuna in the road signs as soon as we left Cordoba because it was the next large village. At first the winding and twisting road was bordered by trees shaped like stylized umbrellas.

The villages usually have a church, a school, and a group of one-story houses, many with doorways opening directly on the road. Because it was a holiday many people were out walking along the road and in the fields. As usual there were several young couples arm-in-arm.

As we continued, there were fewer villages and long stretches of rolling countryside. Here and there I saw a cemetery. Countryside cemeteries in Spain are enclosed by white walls and surrounded by many tall, green cypress trees.

About an hour and a half after we left Cordoba, a village ap-

peared in the distance. Like so many others, it was situated on a hill, with a church steeple reigning over all below. It intrigued me that there was a wall around the entire village, and the main road did not go through the village but circled it. We decided to take a look inside the walls, so we turned and drove between the sycamore trees and passed through the gate.

I was immediately reminded of Alice stepping through the Looking Glass. It was very quiet and I attributed part of this to the fact that trucks and automobiles do not ordinarily go through this village. The main streets were just wide enough for two automobiles abreast and most of the side streets could accommodate only one car at a time. I stopped to take photographs of people sitting on chairs in front of their houses, asking their permission in my stumbling Spanish. They always granted it with a smile. I was using a Polaroid camera and gave one old gentleman a picture I took of him.

The doors of the church were open and I could see the statues inside placed on the platform in readiness for the Holy Week procession through the steep streets of the village a little later. We were lucky enough to find one store open and bought some delicious Spanish almonds to ward off hunger until we reached Zafra for dinner about ten o'clock that night. Because there were practically no autos on the narrow streets, and very few reminders of today's electronic and mechanized world, it was like walking through a village of about seventy-five years ago.

Oh, Fuenteovejuna, I may never be able to pronounce you, but I will certainly never forget you.

PARADOR HERNAN CORTES, Zafra (Badajoz)

In Spain even the expected can be unexpected. Miguel told me that the parador in Zafra was located in a castle, but even with this knowledge I was positively bowled over by the Parador Hernan Cortes.

Unlike most fortresses in Spain, this was not built by the Moors, but by the Christian rulers of the region. It has been named for the Spanish explorer of the New World, Hernan Cortes, who was a protégé of the original owners of the castle.

The adaptation of this old-world castle to meet the needs of today's travelers has been most subtle. Additions have been constructed in the same architectural style to increase the number of accommodations. Many of the rooms look out over courtyards or

gardens and, of course, they are equipped with the modern conveniences, including heating and air conditioning. The parador even has its own restored chapel.

Furniture for the public rooms and guest rooms was chosen to harmonize with the dignified formality of the castle. There are quite a few large carved tables and chairs and numerous tapestries and oil paintings. Guests enjoy walking up to the tower above the third floor to enjoy the view.

This is a very popular parador and, as in all cases, reservations should be made well in advance. On the night we arrived, there was a line of people at 9 p.m. hoping that some guests would not be there in time to claim their reservation.

Hernan Cortes was famous for his conquest of Mexico, but to a growing number of aficionados his name is now synonymous with a most beautiful parador in Spain.

PARADOR HERNAN CORTES, Zafra (Badajoz). Tel.: Zafra 55-02-00. This is also a very popular stopping-off place, not only for going to the south coast, but also for the road to Portugal, 403 km. from Madrid, 85 from Badajoz, 147 from Seville. Swimming pool. Rates: See Index.

PARADOR VIA DE LA PLATA, Merida (Badajoz)

When we drove into the little square at Merida, among the first things I noticed were the storks nesting in the chimneys of the inn. (There is something very comforting about birds nesting in or near a home.) The entrance to the inn was through a gardenlike plaza filled with countless blooming flowers, whose colors were dramatically heightened by the austere white walls of the parador. Although the building had been put to a variety of uses through the years (at one time it was a prison), the most recent and longest use was as a convent. It was modified and enlarged about fifteen years ago and I was told that the furniture and decor in the lounges, parlors, and guest rooms were typical of this region of Spain.

In spite of the many centuries of Moorish occupation and subsequent reconquest by the Christians, the city has retained strong Roman influences. It was established during the height of the Roman Empire. The name of the parador, Via de la Plata, is a combination of Latin and Spanish—it was the name of an old Roman road in Merida.

Reflecting the various cultural and architectural influences, the interior of the parador has quiet corners with single Roman columns and a profusion of intricate Moorish iron work and decoration. The chairs, tables, and other furnishings suggest the later Christian influence.

Because of the location of this parador in Merida, it is very popular with travelers en route to and from Portugal.

A special surprise awaits the traveler stopping here. Besides the appealing plaza at the entrance, the inn has its own private gardens in the rear with carefully trained hedges about twelve feet high forming a series of Moorish arches around a fountain bedecked with pots of carnations.

PARADOR VIA DE LA PLATA, Merida (Badajoz). Tel.: Merida 30-15-40. A former convent, now reflecting regional influence in decor, at 61 km. from Badajoz, 343 from Madrid. RR. Rates: See Index.

PARADOR COSTA DE LA LUZ, Ayamonte (Huelva)

"Right now we are looking down on a place where history has been made for thousands of years." I was standing on the terrace of a beautiful parador, located at the estuary of the Guadiana River that separates southern Spain and Portugal. My host, the director of the parador, was discussing the history of the region.

"First, the Phoenicians came here and then the Romans," he continued. "This area was taken over by the kings of Portugal, who then gave it to the Spanish knightly Order of Santiago. On two occasions it was the dowry of Spanish princesses who were to become the queens of Portugal. In fact, we might say that Ayamonte is a link between the two nations of the Iberian Peninsula.

"For a short time it was the capital of Spain during the Napoleonic Wars," he added. "But with all of the conflicts in Europe, this particular place has never known the ravages of an invading army."

We watched the ferry boat crossing the river to Portugal. We were within sight of about three small villages on the other side of the river, and I could see the long rows of olive trees and rich green fields.

We went back inside and passed through the lobby, where there was an art exhibition featuring the work of local painters. The director explained that the combination of bright sunlight plus the water and the landscape made this a very popular location for artists. The parador was especially designed for this site, and each room overlooks either the town or the estuary. The long hallway was accented with huge pots of ivy whose green tendrils reached to the floor. It is a single-story building designed to blend with the skyline.

As we turned toward the dining room, the director explained that because of the proximity to the sea the typical Ayamonte cuisine tends to center around fish and crustaceans. "We have a continual change of specialties," he said. "Sometimes we have marine stews and now and then we have fresh sardines, which are caught at dawn. There are lobsters, prawns, crayfish, and clams available, and we try to keep our menu exciting by having as many of these regional specialties as possible."

The village of Ayamonte has received numerous national and provincial prizes in recent years for the beauty and cleanliness of its streets, gardens, and parks. After visiting this attractive fishing port, I can certainly see why.

PARADOR COSTA DE LA LUZ, Ayamonte (Huelva). Tel.: Huelva

32-07-00. A beautiful parador on the Guadiana River near the border of Portugal. At 60 km. from Huelva, 696 from Madrid. RR., swimming pool. Rates: See Index.

Paying Attention to Terminal Vowels in Spanish

Miguel and I had now spent at least two weeks together and I was getting pretty proud of my touristic Spanish. In fact, I was becoming positively sophisticated.

As we drove up to the lovely parador in southwest Spain, I suggested that we go in and I would address the conserje and ask for information, including a brochure. Miguel would remain in the background and we would see how I did. Please remember that he had done all the talking up to this point, so I was having my first adventure.

I strode purposefully toward the desk where the conserje held forth and said to him in what I considered to be faultless Spanish, "Por favor" (the polite way to precede a question in Spanish). Pressing on intrepidly, I then said in Spanish, "May I please have a copy of your foyetta?" The man looked puzzled, then he started laughing; then a woman who was in the booth with him also started laughing; then a few other Spaniards who were in the vicinity politely snickered. I looked back at Miguel, but he just stood there with a twinkle in his eye that said, "Okay, you got yourself into this, now get yourself out."

I finally put the same question to the conserje, using the word "brochure" instead of "foyetta." "Ah," he said in almost faultless English. "You must be very careful about the endings of Spanish nouns. Let me explain. One of the words for booklet, or brochure, in Spanish is foyetto. You asked me for a foyetta." I braced myself for what I was sure was going to be the punch line of all time.

"Here is a foyetto," he said, handing me a brochure. "A foyetta is one of the words that describes a woman of the evening!"

Boy, am I careful of my terminal vowels in Spanish now.

PARADOR CRISTOBAL COLON, Mazagon (Huelva)

I visited this parador on a stormy day and it still looked beautiful. It is located on the Costa de la Luz, south of the city of Huelva, overlooking the Gulf of Cadiz.

I toured the grounds after borrowing an umbrella from the

concierge. From the cliffs, where the parador is located, I could see the whitecaps tossing about in the Gulf. This is one of the older paradores, especially constructed by the Ministry of Tourism for the purpose of accommodating travelers and holiday-seekers. There is a swimming pool and a beach, both of which are very popular during the summer months. In fact, the concierge informed me that reservations for the warm-weather months must be made a year in advance.

The interior design reflected the colors of the landscape and sea, with a great many yellows, light greens, blues, and light browns. The dining room had picture windows with a fantastic view of the gardens, cliffs, and the ocean beyond. As far as I could see, every room had its own patio, overlooking either the garden or the ocean.

As we were leaving this parador, the sun was breaking through and the afternoon promised to answer the wishes of all of those children and their parents who were hoping for the good weather. I, too, would have liked to remain for two or three days at this delightful parador on the Costa de la Luz.

PARADOR CRISTOBAL COLON, Mazagon (Huelva). Tel.: 37-60-00. A beachside parador, 42 km. from Huelva, 640 from Madrid. Beach, swimming pool. Rates: See Index.

PARADOR DEL ALCAZAR DEL REY DON PEDRO, Carmona (Seville)

We were on the road from Seville to the mountain village of Carmona, a distance of only thirty-five kilometers. The torrential rain that had drenched the city and cancelled the Holy Week procession the night before was now replaced by brilliant Andalusian sunshine. Even from some distance we could see the white village and the Alcazar on top of a precipitous hill.

Upon our arrival we stopped for a few moments to do some shopping and then proceeded through a huge stone gate to another world—the world of Don Pedro the Cruel, for this magnificent parador was once his castle.

The completely walled courtyard was big enough for six football fields. In one corner, the unrestored crumbling remnants of the castle still stood as mute reminders of another epoch. Before going through the front door of the inn we turned aside and walked through a colonnade of Moorish arches to a precipice overlooking the countryside. The vista was idyllic. It was Spain in springtime. Stretched

out farther than the eye could see was a series of small farms whose tilled grounds were bursting forth into life in the warm sun. It was a panorama of countless shades of green gathering new strength every day.

We passed through a large, two-story living room with walls decorated with armor and swords. These bellicose artifacts were balanced by the serenity of the open courtyard, where the fountains sent melodious sounds into the atmosphere. The sun was now shining directly overhead into this gentle haven and I appreciated once again the Moorish affinity for the musical sounds of water.

We walked through still another handsome living room and out onto a terraza, which I understand is the correct term for the outside larger balcony. Here we had another view of the countryside, including the swimming pool of the parador, a blue oval shape directly below us.

We were joined briefly by the assistant director, who had some interesting news for us. "Our King, Juan Carlos, was here just two weeks ago," he announced.

Since we had a short wait, he suggested that we might enjoy a tour of some of the lodging rooms of the inn. We walked through a courtyard with a fountain and up two flights of stairs to the top floor. An elevator was also available.

He ushered us into an attractively designed bedroom and explained that all of the rooms had balconies. As is true in most of the paradores, the bedspreads, curtains and rugs have designs that are identified with the local region.

"It took six years to build this parador," he explained. As I stepped out onto the balcony I leaned over to look at the walls below, and I could see that restoration of this magnificent building was an engineering feat. Some of the skilled workmen must have been able to fly.

Other interior touches were handsome carved doors and carefully designed windows with multicolored panes.

As we returned to the main floor, I asked him about the swords hanging on the walls and he explained that these were copies of weapons belonging to Don Pedro and his brother, Henrique. "They had a duel," he said. "Henrique killed Don Pedro and became king. That was long ago."

PARADOR DEL ALCAZAR DEL REY DON PEDRO, Carmona (Seville). Tel.: 25-32-60. A magnificent castle-parador high on a hill, 35 km. from Seville. Rates: See Index.

PARADOR CASA DEL CORREGIDOR, Arcos de la Frontera (Cadiz)

Arcos de la Frontera is one of the white villages of Spain. This particular group of villages is located on the peninsula with the Costa de la Luz on one side and the Costa del Sol on the other. Some of these highly picturesque villages are on one of the coasts, and others, like Arcos de la Frontera, are in the highlands that lie midway between the two coasts. The "de la Frontera" portion of the name was bestowed on the town by a Spanish king as the result of noble achievements by the townspeople. "Frontera" refers to the Spanish-Moorish frontier of the 14th century.

Arcos de la Frontera is a community that commands the traveler's attention. Sitting high on a promontory above the Guadelete River, the white walls of its houses and the gay colors of its patios have been likened to a staircase of light that compels the visitor to scale the heights. Many of the houses hang precariously over the edge of a ravine.

The road through the village to the plaza at the top led through narrow streets where there seemed to be barely enough room for a single car.

However, the crest is a prize well worth the effort of negotiating the narrow streets because the beautiful church, the exceptional parador, and the plaza, all share a vista that reminded me of the beautiful panorama at Carmona.

The parador is built in a restored stately home with all of the guest rooms and dining rooms sharing the impressive view. The comparative austerity of the white-walled exterior calls attention to the Gothic facade of the church.

Each of the twin-bedded rooms has attractive furniture and the entire atmosphere would encourage me to remain for a long visit.

The director of the parador was a most pleasant and accommodating man. We sat on the terraza and talked of innkeeping in

Spain and America. "One of the things I enjoy most about being here is that many people return each year because they find it such a restful and inspiring experience," he said.

Even as we were talking, a schoolteacher from Connecticut, who was on a year's sabbatical in Spain, introduced himself and said that he had visited this parador three times during the past two years. "I have been to many," he said, "but this is by far my favorite."

PARADOR CASA DEL CORREGIDOR, Arcos de La Frontera (Cadiz). Tel.: Arcos 362. A restored stately home, at 85 km. from Cadiz, 666 from Madrid. Rates: See Index.

HOTEL DOS MARES, Tarifa (Cadiz)

Miguel and I were on the road from Cadiz to Algeciras, driving along next to the ocean, when I saw a sign for "Hotel dos Mares." It directed us through a grove of trees to a group of buildings on the beach.

That's how I met Robbert Jan Van Looy, the innkeeper and owner of the Hotel of the Two Seas. Robbert (two b's are correct) and I hit it off immediately. He is a Dutchman in his mid-forties, who has

had wide experience in the hotel business in various parts of Europe. We settled down for a chat in the lounge of the inn, which enjoys a most impressive view of the ocean.

"We call this the Hotel dos Mares because we are at the point where the Atlantic Ocean and the Mediterranean Sea almost come together," he said.

Robbert suggested a tour of the inn, so we started out by walking downstairs by way of a circular staircase that sweeps into a dining room overlooking the sea. The atmosphere was bright and gay with blue tablecloths and nautical decorations. We walked out through the adjoining stone-arched terrace to a grassy part of the beach, and I looked at some of the little bungalows in which most of the lodgings are located. The cottages are separated by sufficient distance to give a feeling of privacy, and all of them overlook the dunes and the rolling surf. The rooms have twin beds and are very clean, but somewhat austere.

We returned to the inn and talked about the food. "Our menu is international because our guests come from all over the world. Of course, we always have Spanish dishes as part of the choice, but a typical dinner menu has a choice of four first courses and two middle courses. Generally, we have a choice of either ice cream or fresh fruit for dessert."

I was very glad to find this intimate little fourteen-room inn on the water. From now on I will always follow my intuition.

HOTEL DOS MARES, Apartado ao Tarifa (Cadiz). Tel.: (9) 56-684035. A 14-guestroom privately owned seaside inn, 25 km. from Algeciras. Open April 1-November 1. It is necessary to reserve well in advance. Send first night's room charge as deposit. Rates: See Index.

Jimena de la Frontera

Miguel wanted to show me one of his favorite villages, and we drove on a back road northeast of Linea heading into the hills. The road followed a small river lined with many trees and springtime flowers. After a stop at a clean little country store, we continued our journey and soon came to this ancient fortified village, built on the side of a steep hill and topped by a great, round tower. The houses, built centuries ago, were all huddled together near the base of the fortress. At the top of the village the ancient crumbling walls still loomed overhead. I walked to the top through an arch that must have been part of a wall around the village, but now had grass and nesting birds in its crevices. Crumbling blocks of stone were all that remained; however, the threatening presence of the tower, commanding the valley in three directions, still dominated the entire hilltop. Just below, a caretaker serenely tended an orchard and a small vegetable and flower garden.

Some Iberian Observations

Spain and Portugal are not the same, and Spanish words frequently are not the same as Portuguese words. Anyone making a trip to both countries would be well advised to purchase both a Portuguese-English and Spanish-English dictionary. Make certain that the food sections of these dictionaries are adequate, because this is an area that causes the most puzzlement.

Basically, the night and day porters (concierges) (conserjes) at paradors and pousadas do not have any English at all. In such cases, it would be well to have one or two such phrases available as the translation for "I have a reservation for tonight" or "Have you a room for tonight?" It is well to recheck the following night's reservation, which will be done by the concierge and for which there will be a slight charge. Be certain that the concierge understands whether you are confirming a previous reservation or want a completely new reservation.

Breakfast at individual pousadas and paradors can vary widely, and in some cases they are extra. Completo breakfast consists of simple buns or rolls and coffee. A good trick is to wander through the dining room and see what is being served. The alternative is to go to the nearest bar-restaurant for take-out coffee and to the grocery store for a picnic breakfast. I had a picnic at lunch about every day.

Paradors do not supply Kleenex, but this, like practically anything else that the American or British traveler would find essential, can be purchased in stores throughout Spain and Portugal. The trick is to know how to ask for the proper item. In this case, it might be "paper handkerchiefs." Remember, if all else fails, sign language will reign supreme.

The simple courtesies of life are necessary in both Spanish and Portuguese, including, "please," "thank you," and "I beg your pardon."

Ronda, the Delightful and Unexpected

The road from San Pedro on the coast to Ronda in the mountains is unbelievable. It is one of the most twisting, turning, exciting scenic roads I have ever been on in my life. It is a steady climb for forty of the fifty-four kilometers, with views of the mountains, whose beauty is in their starkness. There is a moonscape quality about everything, with different strata of rock revealing surprisingly brilliant streaks of color. Sometimes on the distant ridges, I could see a cluster of houses clinging precariously to the sides of the mountains.

There were sweeping views of valleys and range after range of mountains, some of them snowcapped. As we neared the end of the trip, the terrain softened somewhat, and there were pine and oak trees and flocks of sheep and goats being tended by a lone shepherd.

I never expected to find a town of such dimensions at the end of this narrow, twisty road. The biggest surprise about Ronda is that this small city has an extraordinary setting of almost unequaled grandeur on the lip of a gorge, which the guidebook says is 1,000 feet deep. Ronda makes a wonderful side trip.

PARADOR DEL GOLF, Torremolinos (Málaga)

I must confess that when I left New York I never expected to be playing golf at a country inn in Spain, but here I was at the Parador Del Golf in Torremolinos playing nine holes.

I had heard about the Parador Del Golf from Marilyn and Dan

Sullivan, who live almost next door to me in the Berkshires. She and Dan are enthusiastic golfers and travelers, and it so happened that they went to Spain about three weeks ahead of me. They stayed ten days at this parador. In her letter to me from Spain, these are some of the things she had to say about her stay at this inn in Torremolinos:

"I know you will like it here. The beach is only about 100 steps away. We spend most of our time walking on the beach or on the golf course or enjoying the swimming pool built in the center of a three-sided square that is formed by the buildings of the inn. Our room is lovely with walls of pine board and drapes and bedspreads of a finished burlap material with a Spanish design. And I have never seen such beautiful, enormous bathrooms.

"The golf course is great. You know how Dan is—it has to be just right to please him, and he is ready to come back to Spain anytime. One thing we can't get over is the food. I think we could put on ten pounds apiece if we aren't careful.

"Be sure you visit Marbella, it's an attractive seacoast town—there are many Americans who have condominiums there. I am enclosing a postcard showing all of the sailboats. I have to go now because Dan says we are teeing off in about three minutes. By the way, you can rent golf clubs here, so don't bother to bring yours."

Well, Marilyn, thank you so much. I think we have seen the Parador Del Golf from your eyes. The only thing you didn't send me were instructions on how to correct my American hook while in Spain.

PARADOR DEL GOLF, Torremolinos (Málaga). Tel.: 38-12-55. This parador is on the road between Torremolinos and Málaga. It is modern in design, with the beach nearby, a swimming pool, and a Robert Trent Jones golf course. Convenient to airport. Rates: See Index.

Itinerary Number Two

As I mentioned in an earlier section, this itinerary starts from Madrid, goes south to Toledo and then turns northwest to Galicia, across the top of Spain to Santander, and then swings south to Burgos, Segovia, and Madrid.

Toledo

"Seventy kilometers from Madrid, the city of Toledo rises heavenwards, immersed in an atmosphere of violent light. It sprawls over an enormous crag that seems to be challenging space, while the fast-flowing River Tagus on its way to Portugal surrounds the city in a tight curve as though the ancient walls were anchored in this natural moat. The silhouette of the city stands out in sharp relief against a background formed by the crest of the encircling hills and the more distant ranges of hills and mountains.

"Toledo is the city which presents the most complete and characteristic ensemble of all that the genuinely Spanish land and civilization have ever been. It is the most perfect epitome, the most brilliant and evocative summary, of Spain's history. So, a traveler who can only spend a single day in Spain ought, without hesitation, to spend it seeing Toledo." I wish I could say that I was the first person to write those impressive words, but somebody else wrote them first. They are from the brochure published by the Spanish Tourist office.

Toledo—the Michelin Green Guide gives six-and-a-half pages to its churches, ancient palaces and houses, cobbled alleys, beautiful courtyards, lovely cloisters, synagogues, hidden chapels, museums, bridges, and the numerous excursions into the nearby countryside where Miguel Cervantes wandered and Don Quixote rode. It is a land of windmills and silhouettes of castles against blue skies.

El Greco, one of the great figures in Spanish painting, made his home in Toledo and bequeathed his best works to the city. His finest paintings are still in the city and its province, which have become a virtual museum for his works. Very near to the spot where the painter

actually lived, there stands the El Greco House and Museum housing an important collection of his canvases, particularly the "View of Toledo."

There are so many periods of history involving Toledo that I shall suggest the reader turn to Michelin and other guidebooks for a more substantial account.

PARADOR CONDE DE ORGAZ, Toledo

In the waning sun of a Saturday afternoon, I arrived for what I thought would be perhaps a two- or three-hour stay in Toledo. Following the signs for the parador on the road around the walled city, I realized that this would be more than a mere hasty visit.

There are only eighteen rooms at this parador, so I hope the traveler will reserve with Marketing Ahead in New York City well in advance. However, if you can't be booked there, the Hotel Alfonso VII has a creditable rating in Michelin, and arrangements should be made for an overnight stay.

Guest rooms have balconies and the public rooms are decorated with gorgeous ceramic tiles and crafts typical of the region.

Conde de Orgaz has the most desirable view of this jewellike city, both day and night, and this view is eminently paintable—the earth colors of ocher and terra cotta are thrilling in their harmonious blending. As I stood admiring this panorama, the bells of Toledo began to toll the faithful to an early evening mass.

PARADOR CONDE DE ORGAZ, Toledo. Tel.: 22-18-50. A very pleasant well-designed inn with an exceptional view of the city of Toledo. Seventy km. from Madrid; 106 km. from Oropesa. Rates: See Index.

Directions: From Madrid N-401 leads directly to Toledo.

PARADOR DEL VIRREY TOLEDO, Oropesa (Toledo)

Even though this 15th-century castle-cum-palace is auspiciously situated in the Alcazar of Oropesa, one of the things I remember most vividly is the huge stork's nest on the top of the town clock, in itself worth several photographs. The clock tower is on the top of an arch that provides a passageway for automobiles. Storks' nests are considered good luck in all of Europe.

Oropesa stands in the eastern foothills of the Sierra de Gredos and is one of those little Castilian towns that have somehow managed to preserve not only their character throughout the centuries, but also the historical and artistic traditions that testify to their past splendors.

On the crest of a small hill crowning the town is the castle that was once the palatial home of various dukes and other notables of Castile. In spite of wars and rumors of wars, the fortress was kept in a magnificent state of repair until the arrival of Napoleon's armies, who destroyed it.

The incredible thing about so many of these castles is that they are so *ancient!* The famed Isabella of Spain figures prominently in the history of this one, which was already old in her time.

Well, enough of history, except to say that the various owners would certainly be pleased to see what has happened to their little home in the country, because in 1930 it was converted into a national parador, and that makes it one of the earlist in Spain.

Basically, it is built around three sides of a square; the fourth side is made up of some ancient ruins and a rather well-restored keep or tower.

The view stretches across the plains to the snowcapped mountains that seem to rise suddenly from the floor of the plain. With the

sun on the peaks, they looked as if they were moving closer and closer all the time. In fact, I would be moving towards them in a few days.

The inner balconies had been hung with dozens and dozens of plants, all in beautiful flowery profusion during my visit. The feeling is truly of old Spain and everything has been done in the tradition of the paradors.

The guest rooms are a tribute to the late King Alfonso, who initiated the construction of the paradors, and the bathrooms are a symphony of tile and convenience. Wandering from one end of the castle to the other, one cannot help but be impressed with the collection of old furniture and tapestries.

The Parador Del Virrey Toledo in Oropesa is at or near important crossroads for the traveler in Spain. If he chooses, he can go north into the mountains to Jarandilla and Avila, or east to Lisbon by way of Merida, Badajoz, and then to Estremoz in Portugal.

PARADOR DEL VIRREY TOLEDO, Oropesa (Toledo). Tel.: 21-172. A 47-guestroom hotel in an elegantly restored feudal castle, within a short distance of the mountains. Rates: See Index.

Directions: There are two Oropesas in Spain. This one is in the province of Toledo about 148 km. from Madrid. The other is by the sea about 440 km. from Madrid. This is on the N-V (E-4), one of the main roads west and southwest from Madrid. Parador signs lead through the village and to the castle on the top of the hill.

PARADOR CARLOS V, Jarandilla de la Vera (Cáceres)

It had been an interesting day, mixing the old Spain with the new, and now on the well-worn steps of this 15th-century castle here on the slopes of the Sierra de Jarandilla Mountains, the mix was becoming rather cacophonous.

A traveling carnival had set up shop just a few hundred yards from the parador. The portable Ferris wheel with its bright lights and the other rides that delight children of all ages were in full operation, accompanied by a public address system playing rock and roll. Apparently, carnivals are the same in all parts of the world.

I couldn't help but wonder what Carlos V would have thought of all of this activity. In 1555, he gave up his life as the reigning monarch and began the construction of a monastery at Yuste, about eight miles southwest of Jarandilla, where he spent the last two years of his life in quiet and solitude.

Carlos lived here at this castle for a few months while the monastery was being completed, and it appears to be much the same as it was during his time. There is a large courtyard, many towers and ramparts, and even a drawbridge. It was verily an almost impenetrable fortress.

The interior looks like a castle—stone walls, winding stairs, and tapestries. The guest rooms, combining old and new, are impeccably designed and the bathrooms are a joy. This is the case in all the Spanish paradors.

Eventually, even the Ferris wheel and the public adress system grew weary and the carnival packed up, leaving Jarandilla to its four-hundred centuries of quiet and Carlos V could sleep in peace. However, I'm only kidding because, although this is a mountain town, it is really quite modern and there are many new buildings being built—quite in the spirit of what I found was going on throughout Spain.

PARADOR CARLOS V, Jarandilla de la Vera (Cáceres). Tel.: 56-01-17. A 16-guestroom hotel in an impressive feudal castle in the Sierra de Gredos mountains. The village itself is well worth the visit and the Yuste Monastery is nearby. Rates: See Index.

Directions: For the traveler between Madrid and Portugal on N-V (E-4), there is a choice of staying overnight at the parador in Oropesa or driving another 60 km. into the mountains to Jarandilla. Either could be an excellent choice. Jarandilla is on C-501 between Plasencia and Arenas de San Pedro. Curiously enough, C-501 actually starts on the outskirts of Madrid and I would suggest using this country road from Madrid to Jarandilla, instead of following the motorways. See map for verification.

PARADOR DE GREDOS, Gredos (Avila)

Now, here's one I almost missed and I'm certainly glad I didn't.

Having departed the parador at Jarandilla, I was traveling on a lovely mountain road (C-501) through several colorful villages, which even though remote all had modern facilities. The ever-ascending road winds around mountains and finally emerges above the treeline. It's just the kind of road I enjoy the most.

About thirty kilometers from Arenas de San Pedro, I saw a

parador sign pointing to the left. Consulting my watch and realizing that I was already two hours behind schedule, I felt I might as well go the whole way. This road led up into the mountains about ten kilometers, arriving at what I later learned was the first of the Spanish paradores. Alfonso XIII was responsible for creating these wonderful Spanish national inns and he attended the opening of this one in 1928. It is located at an altitude of 6,200 feet and the entire aspect is one of complete mountain remoteness, although the parador is furnished with modern conveniences throughout.

I enjoyed a very good lunch and a short conversation with one or two of the other patrons. This would be a wonderful place to spend a few days on a quiet holiday. It might even be a good place to work on a travel book.

PARADOR DE GREDOS, Gredos (Avila). Tel.: 34-00-48. A 79-guest-room mountain hotel, especially noted for its quiet atmosphere. Spectacular views of the Sierra de Gredos. Rates: See Index.

Directions: Gredos is on C-500 between El Barco de Avila (N-110) and C-501. It is about 57 km. from Avila.

PARADOR RAIMUNDO DE BORGONA, Avila

To someone who has never seen a completely walled city, Avila gives the impression of something fantastic and unreal—it is like a giant stage set for the Middle Ages. The walls of Avila, the oldest and best preserved in Spain, if not in all of Europe, are of a most impressive size, forming a rectangle with a perimeter of 7,500 feet. Access to the city is through nine entrance gates.

When the sun shines on the towers and battlements, it gives the golden stones a coral blush, making the sight of this martial and monastic city even more dreamlike.

The history of Avila goes back to 2,000 B.C., and there are still many sculptures representing bulls and pigs that bear witness to the existence of an ancient Iberian civilization that continued into the first century A.D. when the city was Christianized. Avila has seen Visigoths and Moors, as well as the great reconquest under Ferdinand and Isabella. All of this and much more, including the pervading influence of Santa Teresa, can be found in the palaces, museums, cathedrals, churches, and convents of this city. I would suggest contacting the Spanish Tourist Office in a major city in North America

for a small booklet entitled *Avila*, available in English, that gives a wonderful background.

All of this doesn't leave very much space for me to discuss the parador, which has the full complement of amenities found in all the government-owned inns and is reached by walking through a very handsome garden. Fortunately, if this parador is fully booked, the *Michelin Red Book* for Spain and Portugal shows a 73-room luxury hotel, as well as two others that are rated "comfortable," in Avila.

Avila is 108 kilometers from Madrid and is also at a crossroads for the traveler who may be headed for either northern or northwestern Spain. Plan on spending the best part of the day, and enjoy lunch at the parador. Just seeing the walls of the city makes it a memorable experience.

PARADOR RAIMUNDO DE BORGONA, Avila. Tel.: 21-13- 40. A 27-guestroom hotel in one of the most impressive walled cities of Spain, 108 km. from Madrid, 65 km. from Segovia. Rates: See Index.

Directions: Avila is on N-501 between Madrid and Salamanca. Circle the walls of the city and follow the parador signs.

PARADOR TORDESILLAS, Tordesillas (Valladolid)

Not every Spanish parador is in an ancient castle, convent, monastery, or palatial mansion. Many of them have been newly built and provide excellent accommodations. This one is a rather sprawling edifice with modern appointments. The dining room has a very impressive tapestry showing the adventures of Christopher Colum-

bus. The guest rooms all have the usual admirable amenities and are decorated in a contemporary mode.

The parador is located in a very quiet section of the city in an almost parklike atmosphere. It is one of the few in this section of Spain with a swimming pool.

Tordesillas is just a few kilometers to the southwest of Valladolid, a much larger city with several attractions for the architecture and history buff. Among other historical events, the marriage of Ferdinand and Isabella took place here in 1469.

Valladolid contains some excellent examples of the Isabelline style of architecture, as well as the Renaissance and the Herreran influence. The house where Miguel Cervantes spent the last years of his life is little changed, and it was my understanding that some of the present furnishings were belongings of this eminent Spanish author. The house where Christopher Columbus passed on is also in Valladolid. The church of Santiago has three works by Goya.

PARADOR TORDESILLAS, Tordesillas (Valladolid). Tel.: 77-02-51. A 73-guestroom modern hotel tastefully decorated and located in a small city, 180 km. from Madrid and 30 km. from Valladolid. Rates: See Index.

Directions: Tordesillas is located on N-VI, northwest of Madrid.

PARADOR CONDES DE ALBA Y ALISTE, Zamora

I went to Zamora from Tordesillas because I noticed on my excellent *Michelin* map of Spain (990) that a parador was located there, and it turned out to be a very pleasant Spanish city of about

50,000 people. Although there are no great tourist attractions, Zamora has a most natural and comfortable feeling.

I arrived to find people from the offices and stores filling the streets at noontime, and I was delighted to join the happy jostling crowd.

The parador is a rather austere 15th-century palace, with a well in the middle of the courtyard and double-decked galleries on both floors, as well as some rather intricate stonework decorating the pillars.

There is an impressive and majestic staircase to the second-floor gallery, off of which is the dining room. Overlooking the courtyard are excellent visitors' lounges with comfortable sofas and walls decorated with traditional Spanish prints.

Literature from the Zamora office of the Tourist Bureau indicated that the cuisine of the province has its own individual character. Included are some veal *presas* and other succulent roasts. There's also cod a *la tranca*, octopus a *la Sanabresa*, spiced with strong, tasty sauces, and the famous chickpeas and asparagus. Trout is well known further in the mountains.

PARADOR CONDES DE ALBA Y ALISTE, Zamora. Tel.: 51-44-97. A 19-guestroom elegant hotel in a former ancient palace. Zamora is a quiet city and this would make a pleasant overnight stop, 245 km. from Madrid. Rates: See Index.

Directions: Zamora is on N-630, which runs due north from Salamanca to Oviedo. The parador is on the Plaza de Canovas and takes a bit of persistence and patience to locate. I'd suggest hiring and following a taxi, since the distance is not too far.

PARADOR REY FERNANDO II DE LEON, Benavente (Zamora)

The main road from Madrid to northwestern Spain is the N-VI and the traveler is likely to share it with heavy traffic, including quite a few trucks. I looked in vain at my excellent map of Spain and Portugal (990) for secondary parallel roads, but unfortunately N-VI seems to be the only way.

However, the Parador Rey Fernando II de Leon is well worth the trip and is one of the most attractive accommodations in all of Spain.

This is another case of the Spanish government recognizing that one of the most attractive ways to present Spain in the best light is to create a blend of the old and the new. Jan Lindstrom's drawing of this

parador shows clearly the tower of this castle-palace, all that remained after the soldiers of Napoleon devastated it. An enlarged
photograph taken in 1880 is on display in the foyer of the castle and
it underscores the remarkable restoration.

Two massive wooden doors form the entryway, and the new part
of the parador has been designed around the old tower. A stairway of
modern design leads up to the first level where the beautifully designed dining room with graceful arched windows looks out over the
countryside.

A very handsome lounge on the second floor extends to two-
and-a-half stories with a balcony and a beautiful handpainted, vaulted ceiling. Adorned with impressive tapestries and some painted
cloth, it is one of the most memorable rooms of this nature that I have
seen in a parador. The textures of the fabrics combined ideally with
the rough walls and beautifully finished wood.

The guest rooms, too, were most inviting, many of which had
their own private balconies with rocking chairs—invitations for quiet
contemplation or reading.

159

I enjoyed a very pleasant luncheon at this parador with the attractive woman director who spoke no English, and although I do very poorly at Spanish, each of us managed to make ourselves understood. She even took me on a tour of the kitchen. We laughed a great deal.

It's obvious that much of the stone rubble of the main portion of the castle had been used to construct the parador, and someone with an eye toward contemporary art has blended old pieces with new in a way that enhances each.

PARADOR REY FERNANDO II DE LEON, Benavente (Zamora). Tel.: 63-03-00. A 30-guestroom hotel in an impressively restored fortress, 259 km. from Madrid, 242 km. from Orense. Rates: See Index.

Directions: Benavente is located at the junction of several different main roads leading north or northwest. From Madrid take N-VI. From Oviedo, Leon, and other points north take N-630. The parador is on N-VI, northwest of the city.

PARADOR MONTERREY, Verín (Orense)

The road (N-525) from Benavente to Verín now assumed a character that was more to my liking. Apparently, a great deal of the truck traffic on N-VI continues north, and N-525 leads northwest through some very high mountains. I saw snowcapped peaks in the distance. A great deal of this road reminded me of northern New Hampshire.

Verín was the first stop in the northwest section of Spain, called Galicia. Many rivers filled with salmon flow through fruitful valleys. The courses of the rivers widen progressively until they lose themselves in the immensity of the Atlantic through *rias,* or estuaries. However, Verín has none of this bucolic, agricultural euphoria. Its location at some distance from the sea makes it a sort of country cousin to the rest of the province.

From the south, the first glimpse of the Castillo Monterrey with its high walls and turrets is impressive. Coming closer, I followed the parador signs, winding around the hill.

The panorama from both the parador and from the nearby Castillo Monterrey is magnificent. The parador is set on a high hill and has a very arresting view of the castle, which played an important part during the Spanish-Portuguese wars. Within the castle walls had

been a town with a monastery and a hospital. It was abandoned during the 19th century; however, it is maintained by the government today and is open to travelers. I spent at least two hours wandering around the walls and old buildings and it reminded me very much of a hotel located in a castle-fortress at Trigance in the Alpes-Maritimes of France.

The parador is a modern building, tastefully decorated with furniture and decorations that fit in well with the design of the building. It has a swimming pool that would make it very pleasant for warm weather visiting. Some guest rooms are small but comfortable.

It was here that I was introduced to a number of Galician dishes on the parador menu, which were fortunately translated into English.

A good reason to stay overnight or even longer at Verín is the opportunity to sit quietly for hours and look out over the truly magnificent panorama and to spend some time within the walls of the ancient castle. Even on a cloudy day you can see into Portugal.

PARADOR DE MONTERREY, Verín (Orense). Tel.: 41-00-75. A 23-guestroom mountaintop hotel, 6 km. from a most impressive preserved ancient castle. Swimming pool on grounds; 430 km. from Madrid. Rates: See Index.

Directions: Verín is at the junction of N-525 and C-532,17 km. from border of Spain and .Portugal. It is on the road between Benavente and Orense.

PARADOR DE SAN TELMO, Tuy (Pontevedra)

There are actually two ways to go from Verín to Tuy. One is to follow N-525, the main road (colored red on the 990 *Michelin* map of Spain) to Orense, and then left on N-120 and proceed to the Galician coast.

The road I took through the mountains (colored yellow) was C-531 from Ginzo de Limia. (I almost always prefer the yellow roads to the red ones because they are less-traveled.) Most of the mountains were covered with heather, and as far as the eye could see there were carpets of flowers stretching out to the horizon. The villages are rather remote and some of the old ways still persist. One can see women working in the fields and carrying bundles of grass on their heads. There are many burros.

A few kilometers beyond the turnoff, at the northern end of Ginzo, I came to the town of Celanova, certainly one of the bright spots of the trip. It was very clean and the central square was extremely attractive. Because it was not on the main road, it had a relaxed and natural feeling about it. It's just a few miles from the Portuguese border.

Tuy was a bit of a surprise. It is one of the oldest and most characteristic cities in Galicia, lying on the Mino River opposite the Portuguese city of Valenca. The *Michelin Green Book* lists a cathedral, the San Telmo chapel, and the San Bartolome Church, as well as some gardens.

The Parador San Telmo was laid out along almost the same lines as the more modern hotel in Verín, the big difference being that this is next to the river, rather than on top of a mountain. It has a very pleasant aspect with a swimming pool and a garden, and from the parador you can look across the hill to the cathedral-fortress. There is a bridge across the river, making Tuy one of the gateways to Portugal.

PARADOR SAN TELMO, Avenue de Portugal, Tuy (Pontevedra). Tel.: 60-03-11. A 16-guestroom hotel of relatively modern design in a town on the Spanish-Portuguese border, 606 km. from Madrid. Swimming pool on grounds. Rates: See Index.

Directions: Locate Tuy, south of Vigo. It is accessible from the Portuguese coastal road N-13.

❖   ❖   ❖   ❖

PARADOR DEL ALBARINO, Cambados (Pontevedra)

The town of Cambados is located geographically almost in the middle of one of the great series of estuaries on the Galician west coast, called Rias Bajas. Coming by way of the sea, it is but a short distance from Bayona and the city of Pontevedra; however, great care should be taken to avoid going to the other seaside city of Vigo, particularly during the morning and afternoon heavy traffic hours. There are alternate roads available.

Of particular interest in Cambados is the magnificent square. In a country where every village, hamlet, town, and city has a plaza, this one stands out.

I was particularly taken with this parador and impressed by the fact that this one was likely to be more quiet at night than the one in Pontevedra. It is located off the main street, almost directly on the tidal basin and set in a grove of swaying sycamore trees. Oddly enough, even though Cambados is in northwestern Spain, some distance from the Mediterranean, the basic foliage is semitropical because of the sun and presence of the Gulf Stream.

The tide was out during my visit and there were several fishing boats propped upright between posts on the wet sand.

The parador is in a contemporary building, apparently built for that purpose at least twenty years ago. The brilliant spring sunshine flooded the inner courtyard, where I enjoyed an early morning cup of hot chocolate and carried on an animated conversation with the parador director who had no English and was as amiable a fellow as one could hope to find. Even with my very inadequate Spanish, we were able to have a very pleasant conversation.

It occurs to me that while no mention of Santiago de Compostela has been made thus far in this book (to be discussed in some detail in the following pages), many of these Galician paradors would be excellent places to stay while on a visit to that unusual city. Besides those that I visited, there are other paradors at La Coruna and Puertomarin. These would all be suitable for day visits to Santiago.

PARADOR DEL ALBARINO, Cambados (Pontevedra). Tel.: 50-13-57. A 63-guestroom hotel in a relatively modern building on a river estuary and tidal basin. It is the only hotel listed in Cambados; 640 km. from Madrid, 53 km. from Santiago. Rates: See Index.

Directions: From Pontevedra take C-550, which leads out into a small peninsula and is about 1 hr. from Cambados. From Santiago follow N-550 to Puentecesures and then C-550 to Cambados.

PARADOR CONDE DE GONDOMAR, Bayona (Pontevedra)

With my arrival in Bayona, a relatively short distance from Tuy, I realized that I was experiencing the typical terrain of Galicia. Bayona was the first of the towns and villages on the estuaries of several rivers that I would visit in Northwest Spain.

It was to Bayona that the *Pinta* returned in 1493 with the exciting information that Columbus had indeed discovered the New World. Bayona was also the port to which many ships returned during the next few centuries with precious jewels and gold from the Spanish colonies in the New World.

By far the most impressive edifice in this part of Spain is the fortress Monte Real, within whose ramparts is located the spacious Parador Conde de Gondomar, with its 128 guest rooms, swimming pool, tennis courts, and beautiful gardens.

This is a luxurious hotel of a contemporary design. The furnishings, including beautiful carpets, tapestries, watercolors, oils, sketches, and a courtyard fountain, are in themselves worth a visit. In one room I saw what I'm sure is one of the world's most immense oil paintings. It portrayed sailors pulling away from a foundering ship during a storm. Of course, the guest rooms overlooking the sea are particularly desirable.

An exciting diversion is a walk on the walls, which extend for more than three kilometers to a point where the water from the

Atlantic comes boiling in and crashing up against the rocks. The sound of the surf can be deafening. At the farthest point stands an old watchtower and a couple of old canons pointing out to sea. One could sit here for hours imagining the stories that Monte Real could tell of the invasions of the Romans, Visigoths, Saracens, and even of John of Gaunt, the Duke of Lancaster, who lived here for a short time. Drake tried unsuccessfully to land in 1585, and Napoleon succeeded in holding this fortress for only a month.

PARADOR CONDE DE GONDOMAR, Bayona (Pontevedra). Tel.: 35-50-00. A 128-guestroom hotel in a reproduction of a typical stately palace from Spain's romantic past, within the ramparts of a famous fortress. Tennis, swimming pool; 618 km. from Madrid. A little too far to commute to Santiago. Rates: See Index.

Directions: Bayona is on the northwest coast of Spain between the Portuguese border and the city of Vigo, which should be avoided because of traffic problems. Bayona is a long drive from Madrid. I would suggest staying overnight at the parador at Benavente or the other at Verín, and then proceeding to N-120, and turning off at Ginzo de Limia on C-531 via Celanova.

PARADOR CASA DEL BARON, Pontevedra

This is an in-town parador in one of the busiest towns in Northest Spain. In fact, Pontevedra and the city of La Coruna have the highest population density in Spain.

In a former palatial mansion, this parador, in its interior design and decoration, still looks much like the very expensive house of a nobleman or a merchant prince. The entrance and reception hall, with its broad, carved baronial staircase, would make an ideal setting for one of Shakespeare's plays. It would be excellent for romantic interludes and exciting swordplay.

The parador menu is well supplied from both the countryside and the sea. Salmon, trout, eels, hake, scallops, octopus, bass, and other fish grace the menu, as well as excellent oysters, crabs, clams, lobsters, king crabs, and others.

Be sure and order sardines *(redenidas)* and potatoes boiled in their jackets with spiced oil. Galician cuisine can be found in all the regional paradors, but I would encourage many adventurous forays into small local restaurants, especially for the lobsters.

The handicrafts of the area include laces, pottery, ceramics, basket jars, vases, platters, wicker work, gold, wood and stone carving, necklaces, small boxes made from tiny shells, wooden pails and buckets. The wooden shoes are most interesting, and some are small enough to be carried back home.

The celebration of festivals and pilgrimages is accompanied by ancient melodies played on the bagpipe and tambourines. A fascinating project might be to trace the arrival and influence of the Celts on the Iberian Peninsula.

PARADOR CASA DEL BARON, Pontevedra. Tel.: 85-58-00. A 47-guestroom hotel in an ancient stately home. Suitable for commuting to Santiago; 607 km. from Madrid, 57 km. from Santiago. Rates: See Index.

Directions: If you are driving from Madrid, I would suggest an overnight stay at the parador at Benavente or Verín, both situated on N-VI and N-525. Pontevedra is located on N-550 between Santiago and Vigo on the northwest Spanish coast.

Santiago de Compostela

Had it not been for the apostolic zeal of James the Greater, the small city of Santiago de Compostela would never have become a powerful center of ecumenical faith, history, and culture, nor the great spiritual springboard that made possible the reconquest of Iberia from the Moors.

Built on legend, faith, and some astounding history during the Middle Ages, Santiago has attracted pilgrims from all parts of Europe, and today is one of the most sought-out tourist objectives in the world.

The legend begins with the Apostle James, who came to Spain to convert the inhabitants to Christianity. He is said to have landed at Padron in the estuary of the Ulla River, a few kilometers north of Cambados.

According to history and legend, after the remains of James were brought back to Spain they were lost in the course of invasions by the barbarians and Arabs. However, early in the 9th century a star is believed to have pointed out the grave to some Spanish shepherds and the remains were then taken to Santiago.

In the reconquest of 844, during an attack on the Moors, a knight in armor, mounted on a charger and bearing a white standard with a red cross on it, is said to have appeared on the battlefield. As he beat back the infidels, the Christians recognized Saint James, who then gained the appellation, Matamore, or "slayer of the Moors," in addition to an earlier title, "The Thunderer," given for his temper.

To add even further to the legend and mystery regarding the region, there is a story about a man who, fleeing from the Moors, swam across one of the estuaries and emerged from the water covered with seashells. Shells, which now can be seen in many forms, even in the exterior decorations of buildings, are to be found throughout Galicia. They even appear in an English nursery rhyme about "silver bells and cockleshells" dating from the mid-16th century and the marriage of Queen Mary of England to Spain's King Philip. The wearing of the shells was a sign that one had made the pilgrimage to Santiago de Compostela.

These relics of Saint James, discovered earlier in the 9th century, became the object of pilgrimages, and in the centuries to come, a journey to Santiago ranked equally with one to Rome or Jerusalem. Germans, Italians, Scandinavians, and Britons made the long pilgrimage, traveling for the most part through France along the routes organized to a considerable degree by the Benedictines and Cistercians. The route led across northern Spain, where hospices were built to take care of the sick and weary.

The first "tourist guide" ever written, a "Pilgrim Guide" of 1130, describes the inhabitants, climate, customs of the different countries, and the most interesting sites along the way.

With the passage of time, the faith that stirred people to set out on pilgrimages began to diminish. Under threat of attack by Drake, the remains of James were removed from the cathedral and were again lost for 300 years! In 1879 they were found once more and the pilgrimages were resumed.

The pilgrimages to Santiago brought the peoples of all of Europe together and laid foundations for future intercommunication. These pilgrimages had important repercussions on medieval thought, literature, art, sociology, and economy, and without them it's very possible the western world would be quite different today.

The view of Santiago from a distance is most striking, and as evening draws on, the towers, churches, hospitals, monasteries, and palaces, with the light of the setting sun on their roofs, look like an immense stone bonfire ablaze in the midst of the lush, delicate, and varied greens of the woods, meadows, and cultivated fields.

Santiago is not just a city of monuments; the city itself is a monument. Its grace and charm can be appreciated at any time or in

any weather. At night it is particularly enchanting when the silence (except during the feast days) is broken only by the church bells.

The Santiago pilgrimages culminated at the cathedral, which has acquired its present appearance over the course of many centuries. Without my going into architectural details, I should note it is dominantly Romanesque with many Gothic overtones.

Today, Santiago contains many places of great architectural interest, particularly in the Old Town with its buildings of great antiquity. I personally found the tourists and travelers who filled the streets to be of even greater interest, and I enjoyed the shops and stores that were filled with all manner of attractive items.

HOTEL DE LOS REYES CATÓLICOS, Santiago de Compostela

The *Michelin Red Guide to Spain* lists this hotel and about a half dozen more that would be basically suitable for one or two nights in Santiago. There are several paradors within pleasant drives of the city, making them also very suitable for overnight accommodations.

Originally, the building in which this hotel is located was founded by Isabel and Ferdinand as a pilgrim inn and hospital and is located on one side of the great square that also contains the present cathedral. It is built in the form of a cross, with a hollowed square that has four patios. Even if one is not a guest, it is possible to visit the public rooms between 10 a.m. and 2 p.m. and between 4 p.m. and 7 p.m. by applying at the hotel reception desk.

This 157-room, five-star hotel, palatial in the true sense of the word, is also part of the parador network in Spain, and reservations may be made through Marketing Ahead in New York City. I suggest requesting a room that does not face the plaza—rooms 101-105 and 205-209, for example, are on the noisy side.

It is like staying in a ducal palace, and all of the guest rooms have high ceilings and highly ornamented furniture. The public rooms are equally ornately appointed. The sophisticated menu and service are as close to Paris as is possible in a small city in northwestern Spain.

I skipped breakfast at the hotel and found a side-street bakery shop where I enjoyed a warm croissant and a cup of hot chocolate, while sitting in one of the smaller, more quiet squares of the town.

Where one stays when visiting Santiago, or *whether* one stays overnight is not important, since there are other accommodations available in nearby towns and villages. The important thing is to go.

HOTEL DE LOS REYES CATÓLICOS, Santiago de Compostela. Tel.: 58-22-00. A 157-guestroom palatial hotel, originally built in the 16th century, on the square with the famous cathedral and several other imposing and historic buildings. This is one of the showplaces of Spain. However, Santiago may be visited on day trips from several paradors within a short drive. There are six other hotels in Santiago according to the Michelin Red Guide; *610 km. from Madrid. Rates: See Index.*

Directions: All roads in Northwest Spain lead to Santiago. There is also a major airport. The hotel is immediately adjacent to the cathedral, which dominates the entire town and is easy to find. Parking for hotel patrons is in the plaza directly in front. This can be explained to the policeman who will attempt to divert you to another street.

PARADOR CONDES DE VILLALBA, Villalba (Lugo)

I arrived in Villalba and found the 14th-century tower I had heard about—it's located in the middle of the town. Amazingly, it has actually been standing all these years. In a conversation with the parador director, I learned that it might even be of Moorish origin, possibly dating back to the 11th century.

The entrance is over a drawbridge and then into a three-story-high reception hall, adorned with fascinating paintings, murals, tapestries, and medieval artifacts. There is a big fireplace and a stairway leading to the floors above.

A very pleasant young man, the *conserje,* took me all the way to the top floor and I saw most of the six guest rooms that had recently been redecorated. There were two rooms on the top floor and then one more flight up took us outside to the very top of the tower, where I looked out over the crenelated ramparts to the roofs of the town.

The narrow windows that had once accommodated crossbow-men were in walls nine feet thick. The staircase and the chimney that ran through the tower were modern additions.

The restaurant is on a floor actually below ground level and also has a vaulted ceiling with rafters and overhead beams. It looked very comfortable. The menu, with many Galician entrées, was printed in three languages.

PARADOR CONDES DE VILLALBA, Villalba (Lugo). Tel.: 51-00-11. A 6-guestroom rather attractive inn situated in an ancient medieval castle, 60 km. from Santiago; 60 km. from Ribadeo on the northern coast. Rates: See Index.

Directions: Locate Lugo on Michelin map 990. Villalba is due north on N-634, one of the principal roads from Santiago to Ribadeo.

Cantabrica Cornisa

The Cantabrian Corniche stretches from the easternmost borders of Spain to the Ribadeo River in the province of Lugo. The whole shoreline is washed by the Cantabrian Sea and is broken by the Cantabrian Mountains that parallel the sea. The northern part of Spain is characterized by two geographic features: the sea and the mountains. The atmosphere of this region includes fertile meadows, rich pastures, and solitary steep-cliffed beaches. Behind the coast, the line of the mountains rises to the colossal heights of the Picos de Europa, a mountain mass impressive for the height of its peaks and for the magic labyrinth of valleys and incredible gorges carved in the rock by the rivers that cut through it.

However, not all of this area is bucolic in nature. Corunna, El Ferrol, Gíjon, Oviedo, Santander, Bilbao, San Sebastian, and other cities are heavily populated and industrially oriented. The traveler should have patience until the return to the countryside. This northern shore is linked by coastal highways that for the most part are printed in red on the Michelin map (660) of Spain and Portugal.

PARADOR RIBADEO, Ribadeo (Lugo)

I was now at the top of Spain on the imaginary border line between Galicia and Asturias. Like a few other paradors that I would be visiting in the next two or three days, this one provides a respite for travelers along the road leading from west to east into France, Germany, and Britain, as well as for those visitors from northern countries who are enjoying an excursion into Spain. In fact, there was a bus tour from Germany having lunch at this parador during my visit.

Overlooking a river leading to the Cantabrian Sea, each of this parador's rooms has a balcony from which to enjoy the bustling river traffic, the cultivated fields across the river, and several small villages that are also visible. The dining terrace also partakes of this excellent and interesting view.

Below the terrace, indeed a very pleasant place, I discovered a small, welcome, swimming pool.

The big living room is one of the most comfortable that I've seen yet, with a fireplace almost within a fireplace. There was a big reproduction of King Alfonso, the original of which I should imagine was painted in the 1920s. He's the man who started the parador movement and all of us who love Spain owe him a deep debt of gratitude.

PARADOR RIBADEO, Ribadeo (Lugo). Tel.: 11-08-25. A 47-guest-room seaside inn with a very pleasant view of the river estuary; 592 km. from Madrid; 350 from Santander; 158 sometimes difficult km. from Gijon. Rates: See Index.

Directions: Ribadeo is on the principal east-west road across the top of Spain (N-632).

PARADOR EL MOLINO VIEJO, Gijón (Oviedo)

Because I'm an early riser, once again I literally was up with the birds. However, at this small six-room parador in a delightful park near the northeastern edge of Gijón, I was convinced some of the birds never had gone to sleep. Early morning joggers (ubiquitous lot, these joggers) passed by, raising a hand in greeting, and the ducks were already foraging for an early morning meal.

I reflected that this might also be called the parador of the ducks because there were so many ducks here in the park and on the millstream that runs under the hotel.

The previous afternoon's drive was one of the most interesting and rewarding in Spain. Often along the seashore and sometimes through beautiful ravines with towering mountains and terraced hillsides, it is a main road that requires much patience should the traveler get behind a truck. It alternately hugs the sides of the mountains, cresting at the top, and then plunges down into the river valleys below. Because it was spring, the fruit trees were beautifully in blossom and there were hues of green in the haying pastures. I'm sure that only a team of oxen could be used to plow such precipitous fields.

This is not the Spain of the south, although women work in the fields here and the wash is hung out to dry every day. There aren't as many castles on the skylines, and there's a brisk air of industry, even among the small farms. This is the area where there are barns and houses *(horreo)* built in a rather picturesque fashion on stilts, creating a somewhat Japanese effect. Also, this is one of the few areas in Spain where I ran across bagpipes, and if the traveler is lucky enough to be in a small village during one of the feast or celebration days, he's bound to have the experience of seeing native dancers being urged on by pipers.

Until I made this trip to northern Spain, I wasn't quite aware of the wide Celtic influences and these are, so I'm told, the same Celts that Caesar called Gauls who also lived in northern England, Scotland, and Ireland. Perhaps this is an explanation for the bagpipes.

My morning walk over, I returned to my very pleasant room and began to pack. The windows opened out onto the park and I was tempted to linger for a few extra minutes to enjoy the songs of the birds.

The previous evening I enjoyed a very good meal of baked pork and a good mixed salad. There were several dishes on the menu that indicated some originality in the kitchen. Dessert was oranges served in kirsch.

This little parador is listed as a restaurant with six bedrooms, all located on the second floor off a bright, white-washed hallway, where the polished wood is an interesting contrast.

PARADOR EL MOLINO VIEJO, Gijón (Oviedo). Tel.: 37-05-11. A simple 6-guestroom inn adjacent to Parque de Isabel in a quieter part of a surprisingly large city; 465 km. from Madrid; 292 from Bilbao, 322 km. to La Coruña. Rates: See Index.

Directions: Traveling from west to east following N-632, take the motorway bypass from Avilés (A-68) to Gijón. Proceed east through the heavy traffic of the town, making inquiries for the Plaza de Toros. Then make inquiries for the Parque de Isabel. The parador is on the edge of the park. Coming west, be certain that you take N-632, a yellow line on Michelin 660, and once near Gijón inquire for Plaza de Toros.

PARADOR GIL BLAS, Santillana del Mar (Santander)

There are twenty-four bedrooms in this parador, and I hope that every one of our readers who is planning a trip to Spain will reserve sufficiently in advance to be able to stay overnight in one of them. There are really two reasons to be here. First is the village itself, rich in history and literature, and the second is the nearby Caves of Altamira, where gifted artists who lived in this region 15,000 years ago painted bison, wild boar, deer, and horses on the ceilings and walls.

Right from the start I could feel that this village and its parador were different. It was off the beaten track, but still attracted tourist trade that seems to be kept in control. There is an absence of the usual hurly-burly.

The placing of a parador here was a true inspiration, because both the parador and the village belong together. There's a very pleasant air of accommodation about both of them. The parador is one of the main stops on a journey across the top of Spain and the clientele is quite sophisticated, with many French, Americans, Germans, and Britons filling the rooms almost every night.

The parador is an ancient mansion of the family Barreda, and its name is a sentimental reminder of that notorious rogue, Gil Blas, who was the protagonist of Lesage's famous picaresque novel.

I wandered through the square in front of the parador on a sunny Sunday morning. A few of the housewives were straightening out the flower pots on many of the sun-drenched balconies, and even on a Sunday the ever-present laundry was on the line. The wonderful

173

beige tint in the old stone buildings could have been acquired only by centuries of sun and weather.

Even as I wandered about the town on that morning, I began once again to feel the two contrasts of Spain. For example, I passed a music bar, where the night before I had heard the pervasive sounds of electronic instruments raising the patrons to a high-decibel Saturday-night fever. Certainly, the night belonged to the Spain of today, but with the sun on the ancient buildings, grass growing out of the tiled roofs, birds flying from gallery to gallery, and the tolling of the church bells, this morning belonged to the past.

PARADOR GIL BLAS, Santillana del Mar (Santander). Tel.: 81-80-00.
A 24-guestroom inn pleasantly in an ancient stately home near the
Caves of Altamira; 392 km. from Madrid; 130 km. from Bilbao; 30
km. from Santander. Rates: See Index.

Directions: Santillana del Mar is on a road that cuts off a portion of
the main road west of Santander. It is noted as C-6316 on the map.

The Caves of Altamira

The caves themselves are not accessible to the public; but it is
possible for a limited number of people to sit in an informal theater
and, leaning back in the seat, look overhead to see colored photo-
graphic reproductions of the paintings projected on the ceiling. Even
in this somewhat restricted manner this is really an impressive experience, and I think it's most interesting because the prehistoric artists
who lived in this section so many thousands of years earlier were the
predecessors of the talented and sensitive artists, designers, and
architects among the Romans, the Visigoths, and, of course, the
Moors who were to follow.

These unknown cave dwellers expressed a freedom of spirit that
is found in the works of such great Spanish painters as Goya, Velaz-
quez, Gris, Miro, Picasso, and Dali. The simple statements on the
walls of the Caves of Altamira are no less eloquent than the paintings
on the walls of the Prado in Madrid.

Bookings can be made through the Tourist Office in Santillana
del Mar. There are other caves open to the public not far from
Santillana.

PARADOR DEL RIO DEVA, Fuente De (Santander)

This parador was a surprise. It has seventy rooms furnished in a
contemporary style. Its truly magnificent views are rivaled possibly
only by the Parador Sierra Nevada near Granada in southern Spain.

The basic structure is stone, quarried locally; but in profile it
looks like a European Alpine hotel. Built especially to accommodate
the large numbers of Spaniards and other visitors who enjoy the
wonderful mountain atmosphere, it is very popular over Easter,
during Holy Week, and in July and August when it's quite warm
elsewhere in Spain.

PARADOR DEL RIO DEVA, Fuente De (Santander). Tel.: 73-00-01. A
78-guestroom modern hotel high in the Picos de Europa, with striking

views of valleys and mountains, immediately adjacent to an aerial tramway that ascends even higher; 426 km. from Madrid; 140 km. from Santander. Rates: See Index.

Directions: Locate Santander on the map at the top of Spain, and then look for N-621, which goes south from N-634 at Unquera. Follow this wonderful mountain road approx. 40 km. to Potes. N-621 proceeds even higher into the mountains and ends at Fuente De. From Madrid and points south, take N-611 north and turn west on unmarked yellow road on map between Aguilar and Cervera. Then follow C-627 to Potes and follow above directions. The Michelin Green Guide shows several itineraries among these mountains that have many gorges, defiles, passes, and caves.

The Peaks of Europe

I was asleep in the sunshine on the Picos de Europa. It was a pleasant Saturday afternoon and after following N-261 from Unquera to La Hermida and Potes, I had enjoyed an over-sumptuous lunch at Parador del Rio Deva and decided to take the cable car trip to the high mountains that tower behind it.

Even in mid-May there were snow fields on the very top and my feeling of intimacy with the high peaks grew with every moment. As I leaned back against some smooth rocks and closed my eyes, I felt that the 8,000-foot peaks were closing in on me. I awakened to the sound of laughter from a group of junior high school students who were pelting their teachers with snowballs. There was much shouting and horseplay, and one of the snowballs glanced off a rock near me. They drifted away and for a moment all was quiet again.

The road from the sea to the mountains was unquestionably the most spectacular I had experienced in Spain. Winding its way upward alongside a river in a deep gorge, with massive rocks towering at least a thousand feet on each side, it passed through several small villages and settlements, one S curve following another. The higher I climbed, the more the air seemed to clear, leaving the sea mist below. Behind me and ahead of me was a continual parade of vistas and panoramas, and above all, the almost tortured statement made by the great bare cliffs.

The jagged outline of the peaks was somber against the sky, and at one point, I could actually see blue sky through windows in the rocks. Sometimes the river was green and placid, and other times it rushed down the falls between boulders in a white, frothy torrent. Where the soil had held, some farms clung to the precipitous hillsides.

The town of Potes was a very thriving mountain community, a sort of jumping-off place for skiers and travelers en route; somewhat reminiscent of Stowe and Aspen. It was obvious that it would be bent and stretched out of shape by the large number of international visitors who would come both in the summer and the winter. Today, on a Saturday in May, it was delightful.

Segovia

It was 7:30 a.m. at the Parador de la Granja in Segovia. I surveyed the commanding view, not only of the small jewellike city of Segovia with its cathedral, Alcazar, and magnificent Roman

177

aqueduct, but also of the snowcapped mountains that form a crescent of protection around the city.

This was my last morning on this trip in Spain and I mentally reviewed the previous day's events. Leaving Santillana on the northern coast in the morning, I had followed N-611 to Reinosa and C-6318 to N-623. North to Burgos, the road leads through an area of most impressive natural beauty. Over millions of years the river, similar to the Colorado in the Grand Canyon and the Genesee in western New York State, has carved its way through the earth creating a tortuous and twisting course and fashioning marvelous caves, rock cairns, and castles of limestone. I stopped for a brief midday picnic

by the side of the road overlooking the canyon and the river, and watched four or five of the ever-present, ever-watchful eagles as they circled higher and higher in the sky, caught by the up-draft.

South of Burgos, I took the wrong turn for a "shortcut" and spent at least an hour and a half wandering around on real Spanish country roads, stopping at every village to get new directions for Segovia. It was at the same time both irritating and humorous; however, I found all of my informants cheerful, willing, and certainly verbal. Never had so many things been said to me that I didn't understand. How-

ever, basically, I was able to get the picture and I had the opportunity to see rural Spain, which I would have otherwise missed.

Each of the little villages has its own stores and shops and is really set apart from the others. From high places on the road it was possible to see three or four villages at the same time. What I really desperately needed was a compass. After some false starts and some retracing, I did find the way to Segovia and to this unusual parador.

PARADOR DE LA GRANJA, Segovia

This must be the flagship of the fleet, because it is very modern and yet retains a distinctive old Spanish flavor. This is more of the "new Spain" that is conscientioulsy clinging to the best part of the past in terms of textures, materials, designs, and colors. The public rooms, dining room, lounges, and numerous sitting areas have all been done in a tasteful but highly contemporary manner. Very careful attention has been taken to provide every lodging room with a contemporary Spanish flavor.

Every room has a view of the city and the mountains. From the balconies I could look out over the countryside and see several small villages, as well as many herds of sheep being tended by the traditional sheepherders.

Late in the afternoon and early evening, I visited the great cathedral and the fortress, but the most impressive thing to me about Segovia was the marvelous Roman aqueduct running right across the center of the city. With 118 arches it rises to the height of 96 feet. The exact date of its construction is not known, although modern research places it in the second half of the first century. It is a colossal piece of engineering and is an eloquent testimony to the architectural genius of Rome. It still carries water as it did when it was first built.

Oddly enough, as I was driving through Segovia to return to Madrid, once again I witnessed a meeting of the old and new Spain—a herd of sheep was being driven under the aqueduct through the middle of the town, and the police held up all the traffic as the animals came through.

Segovia, like Granada, Toledo, Merida, Fuenteovejuna, and the Alcazaba in Málaga, I shall never forget you.

PARADOR DE LA GRANJA, Segovia. Tel.: 41-50-90. With more than 50 guestrooms and a 3,000-foot altitude, this is one of the newest paradors in Spain. Swimming pool, nearby skiing, excellent sight-

seeing in a rather quiet city. Spectacular views of the mountains; 91 km. to Madrid; 199 km. to Burgos; 860 km. to Santander. Rates: See Index.

Directions: Segovia is a relatively short distance from Madrid, the most difficult task being to find one's way out of the Madrid traffic and north on the N-VI. It leads through some dramatic mountain passes with snowcapped peaks.

THE CANARY ISLANDS

What and Where Are the Canary Islands?

The Canary Archipelago, actually a part of Spain, is composed of seven islands and various islets. It is in the Atlantic off the coast of Africa just four degrees north of the Tropic of Cancer, on the same parallel as Havana. The Canaries are subtropical in appearance, but have a spring climate all year around. Their position in the Atlantic makes them a port of call on almost all sea routes between Europe, the Middle East, Africa, and the Americas.

Each of the islands has its own peculiar and distinctive beauty. Volcanic in nature, they present every kind of scene from towering even snowcapped peaks and lofty ranges to out-of-the-way secluded valleys, sandy deserts, rugged crags, perfect craters, and lovely woodlands. Each island is a true continent in miniature with scenes recalling, in some way, beauty-spots from every corner of the globe. Pine, palm, and chestnut trees are as likely to be found on the various islands as that ubiquitous desert plant, the cactus.

The Canaries, incidentally named after wild dogs that formerly overran them, have large sophisticated cities such as Santa Cruz de Tenerife, Puerto de la Cruz, and Las Palmas, as well as dozens of small towns and villages that are natural and appealing. The warm sunshine, beautiful beaches, and easy accessibility by jet from Europe have made the islands very popular as vacation and holiday objectives. The result is an abundance of high-rise buildings in some cities near the beaches.

How To Get There

From North America, Iberia Airlines has flights directly to Las Palmas International Airport. The other Canary Islands are served by domestic airlines. Travel among these and other islands is also possible by ship.

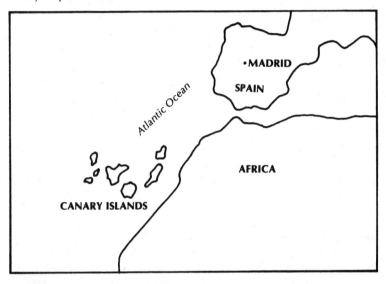

Country Inns in the Canary Islands

I visited four different islands and stayed at the four paradores maintained by the Spanish Ministry of Information and Tourism. Just as on mainland Spain, these quiet country inns are definitely Spanish in character and cuisine, and differ greatly from the towering hotels in the larger cities.

Reservations

Reservations for the paradores in the Canary Islands can also be made with Marketing Ahead in New York City, 212-686-9213.

Canary Island Menus

The traveler will have an ample opportunity to enjoy typical Canary Islands cuisine at the paradores, and also at the many, many small restaurants in villages throughout the islands. The fish is marvelous. It is generally served with the celebrated "wrinkled" potatoes and an especially piquant sauce called mojo picon. Other Canary

Island dishes are potage de berros, *a soup made from watercress and herbs,* sancocho canario, *a salt fish, also with a special sauce. Bananas and tomatoes, as well as alligator-pear and papaws, appear on island menus, also gofio—flour made from wheat, corn, or barley, toasted before milling, and eaten in the form of gruel or dumplings, instead of bread. Some islands have their own specialties. By all means, eat at these small village restaurants. They are unlike anything we have in the United States and they are a new experience in good food.*

Renting a Car

Most people visiting the Canary Islands pick one spot, preferably near a beach, and stay put. However, these are such strange and wonderful places that auto tours should be a part of every visit. Arrangements can be made at the two principal airports and most of the other smaller airports as well. Most of the islands have good bus service.

Maps and Guides

The best maps and guides are available through each of the paradores. An overall brochure of the islands is available from any Spanish National Tourist Office, but the more specific folders are obtainable only on each individual island.

My Itinerary in the Canary Islands

From Madrid I flew to Las Palmas Airport on Gran Canaria Island where I remained for a few days. Then I took a plane to Fuerteventura for a 24-hour visit. Another flight took me to the island of Tenerife for a two-day stay, and still another, to the island of La Palma. I returned to Madrid by way of Las Palmas Airport on Gran Canaria. I rented cars on Gran Canaria and Tenerife and used taxis and buses on Fuerteventura and La Palma.

CRUZ DE TEJEDA RESTAURANT, Tejeda, Gran Canaria Island

I was seated on the terrace at this restaurant enjoying the sunshine. Behind me I could hear the singing of the girls as they washed the floors and prepared the dining room for the noon meal. The manager was whistling as he sorted out the mail and took care of the accounts.

On the terrace, I made the acquaintance of Elizabeth and Walter Lillie from England, and spent the best part of the day with them touring the mountains. More about that later.

The restaurant is a white building with a traditional red tile roof and an informal garden in the front. Many pine trees grow on and near the grounds, and there are flower beds and potted flowers everywhere.

The village of Tejeda is in the heart of the island. Nearby, the majestic Roque Nublo, a jagged spike of basalt, reaches to the sky, and almond groves, truck gardens, and rugged peaks look out over the splendid panorama.

After the Lillies and I spent a day of sightseeing, we returned for dinner and we all sampled each other's courses. I had some of the famous salted fish with the hot and tasty Canary Island sauce. For dessert there was a combination of fruits served in an almond sauce with ice cream.

Most visitors to Gran Canaria stay at hotels in the city of Las Palmas and do not really experience the heart of the island. For this, it is necessary to drive up into the mountains into the "green belt," where the country people live and where it is not tourist-oriented. Here I found people walking on the road wearing straw hats and gathering flowers and herbs from the roadside. They are polite, and happy to be living in such mountainous splendor. The air is clean and clear and everything is green and fresh, a marked change from the

seashore. This is the soul of Gran Canaria, and the Cruz de Tejeda is right in the middle of these mountains with a marvelous view across the straits to the high mountains on Tenerife Island.

CRUZ DE TEJEDA RESTAURANT, Tejeda, Gran Canaria, Canary Islands. Tel.: 65-80-50. A mountaintop restaurant approx. 1 hr. to the city of Las Palmas and 1 hr. to Las Palmas Airport. Within 1 hr. of the Gran Canaria beaches, and very short drives to unbelievable mountain scenery and villages. Breakfast, lunch, and dinner served daily to travelers.

Directions: Rent a car at the Las Palmas Airport and proceed, following the map, through the towns of Telde and San Mateo to Tejeda.

An Afternoon with Walter and Elizabeth Lillie

The Lillies were ideal sightseeing companions. They were wonderfully informed about the flora of the island and kept exclaiming joyfully at new discoveries. There was a lovely purple flower along the road that Walter told me was called a "wallflower." He identified quite a few varieties of small field daisies and red and purple poppies.

We stopped off at the village of Artenara to have tea at the Restaurant La Silla, reached through an ancient arched cave that emerges onto a terrace carved out of the rock overlooking a splendid

valley. Below us were groups of villages and we could see the roads twisting around among the terraces. It was a moody kind of day with moving clouds and bars of sunshine alternately highlighting the skyline of trees that looked like horsemen climbing to the top of the hill. We were at an altitude of 6,000 feet, enthralled by a panorama of differing textures and shades. As Elizabeth remarked, "This is a land of foregrounds and backgrounds."

Walter ordered tea, which we enjoyed in the glass-enclosed section of the terrace as the wind was getting a bit chilly.

Continuing on, we stopped for some photographs at one of the village laundromats—Canary Island style. This is an open wash-house with water rushing through a trough in the middle; there, the women, wearing straw and knitted hats, stand on both sides pounding away on their clothes and carrying on animated conversations. I'm sure the village gossip was quickly going the rounds.

Drying takes place very quickly as the clothing is spread out on the ground. There were a great many jeans and brown panty-hose.

After our tour, I bade the Lillies farewell, and I look forward to seeing them at their home in England within the next year.

PARADOR DE FUERTEVENTURA, Puerto del Rosario, Fuerteventura Island

I slipped between the sheets of my sleigh bed—yes, that's right, a sleigh bed in this Canary Islands parador on the island of Fuerteventura.

I had arrived by Iberia in midafternoon and was most gratified to find such a modern and attractive parador located on the ocean with a very welcome swimming pool. From the air Puerto del Rosario, the principal city of the island, seemed quite small in comparison with Las Palmas.

I enjoyed dinner that evening with two Dutch businessmen who gave me an indication of things to come. They were interested in buying land for future development and told me that a great many Dutch people feel that this island is very suitable for vacations in the sun. They told me about the broad, white sand beaches on the north end, and beautiful beaches in some places where there were as yet no roads. "However, we would put in the roads, if necessary."

Dinner with my two acquaintances from the Netherlands was marked by my first taste of fried squid, one of the parador specialties, along with grouper fish, caught on the waters off the island and served in various ways. The waitresses were in island costumes.

The parador was furnished with the same taste that I had seen in many of the paradores on the mainland of Spain. One wall of my lodging room was of sliding glass overlooking the sea. The bathroom with its big parador towels was a joy.

The other furnishings and decorations included some excellent reproductions of full-color prints done in an Art-Nouveau style depicting Greek legends.

In many ways I felt that I had discovered something quite special on this rather remote island. The people were friendly; it was not crowded as yet; and I saw enough to feel glad that I had gotten there among the first. It may be relatively undiscovered now, but it is only a matter of time.

PARADOR FUERTEVENTURA, Puerto del Rosario, Fuerteventura, Canary Islands. Tel.: (928) 85-1150. A 24-guestroom seaside parador on a quiet Canary Island. Swimming pool and beach within a few steps. Rates: See Index.

Directions: The best way is to take a taxi from the airport, about 2 km. It is another 3 km. into the small city of Puerto del Rosario.

PARADOR DE LAS CANADAS DEL TEIDE, Las Canadas, Tenerife Island

I have found country inns in many different places but I never expected to find one in the crater of a volcano! This parador is completely removed from the sights and sounds of the remainder of the highly touristic island of Tenerife. It is over 6,000 feet in altitude and sits in the middle of the crater of the now-extinct volcano of del Teide, the cone of which at 12,162 feet is the highest in Spain. The area immediately adjacent to the inn reminded me a great deal of Arizona and New Mexico, although the vegetation is much more varied and in some cases heavier. It consists of bushes with long pine needles, and sometimes when the sun is right it looks like acres and acres of porcupines!

Immediately in front of the parador are pinnacle rocks that appear to be precariously balanced on uncertain feet getting weak at the ankles. Footpaths have been carved into some of them and it is great fun to climb to the top.

Fortunately, a few years ago a good blacktop road was completed to the mountain, bringing the beaches of Tenerife and the tourist areas within an hour's drive of each other. It is possible to lodge at this parador and drive to the beaches or wander around the island and be back well in time for the evening meal. The wonderful, fresh, cool mountain air is most conducive to good sleeping. While I was there not a cloud was to be seen at this height, although each day, driving down to the beaches, I had to drive through an encircling blanket to reach the seashore.

The parador is delightful. I became acquainted easily with the conserje, the staff, and the director, who has excellent English. The building is constructed of white plaster, and inside there are columns of green granite with additional decorative wood panels. My bedroom overlooked the uppermost section of the volcano's cone, which is always snowcapped. The twin beds were attractively carved, and there was the usual superb parador bathroom.

I understand this parador is very popular with the inhabitants of the island, who frequently come here for dinner as well as for short vacations.

Most of the visitors to Tenerife find the beaches and large seaside cities a great attraction. As in Gran Canaria, a very few find their way up the imposing slopes of del Teide to the dry, desert country—the entirely different world—up above.

PARADOR DE LAS CANADAS DEL TEIDE, Tenerife, La Orotava, Canary Islands. Tel.: 33-23-04. A 27-guestroom inn 6,000 feet high in the crater of a volcano. Swimming pool. Nature walks. Approx. 1 hr. drive to most beaches. Breakfast, lunch, and dinner served daily. Rates: See Index.

Directions: Rent a car at the Tenerife Airport (you'll need it). Parador is 1 hr. from airport on a road straight up the mountain. Follow the signs that say Las Canadas. The trip from sea level to the parador includes some positively gorgeous pine forests and the scenic vistas are remarkable.

PARADOR DE LA PALMA, Santa Cruz de la Palma, La Palma Island

"In this part of the world," said Harry Evermann, "the idea is to find an island that is at least comparatively undiscovered. I think we've done it." Harry and his wife, Anne, and I were enjoying breakfast at the Parador de la Palma, overlooking the sea in this beautiful city.

This was a farewell meal. The final chapter of an adventure that had started more than thirty-six hours earlier when I deplaned at La Palma Airport and Harry retrieved my wide-brimmed coconut straw hat. When he handed it to me I discovered that he spoke English.

In the short time we were awaiting a taxi at the airport I learned that Harry was a purser for Lufthansa Airlines, that he and Anne were looking for property for a vacation home in La Palma, and that they were not acquainted with the parador where I would be stopping.

I persuaded them to come and see it for themselves and everything worked out beautifully. There was a double room available for them, and they were kind enough to invite me to share the cost of a rented car to see the sights of the island.

We started early the next morning, driving across the island for a visit to one of the most amazing national parks anywhere in the world—Caldera de Taburiente. Inside a volcanic crater there is an observation point in the park where the peaks seem close enough to touch on every side. It has exceptional beauty and awesome scenery.

We continued across the island, enjoying lunch at a Spanish sidewalk restaurant in a small town, and then drove north amidst views of the ocean and mountains that were really beyond description.

La Palma with its 457 square miles and only 76,000 inhabitants is an ideal green island. It has the greatest altitude in the world relative to its circumference. Most of it is covered by beautiful green vegetation and there are many farms and orchards.

After some rather exciting adventures on narrow back roads, we returned to the parador for dinner at approximately ten o'clock. Among the specialties were chicken soup, fried octopus, delicious gazpacho, rabbit, and a goat cheese, native to the island, which I liked very much.

The parador is one of the oldest in Spain and the furnishings are all in the traditional style. The very attractive main lounge has an attractive television room and a library where there were magazines and newspapers in several different languages. Almost all of the bedrooms face the sea and have their own balconies and terraces. Perhaps this parador's most beguiling feature is the fact that it is located on the main road around the harbor where modern buildings are next to old mansions with great wooden balconies and terraces.

I awakened at daybreak and sat on my terrace, overlooking the semicircular expanse of the broad harbor, and watched the sun come up out of the sea. The warm prevailing wind was delightful.

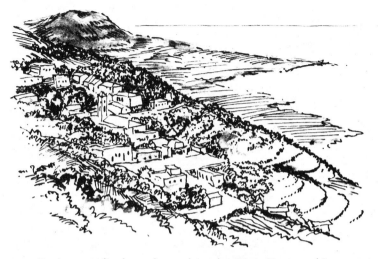

During our final meal together, the Evermanns and I were exchanging notes and addresses and promising to contact each other. We agreed that La Palma, the island, and Santa Cruz de la Palma, the city, had exceptional qualities of sunshine, tranquility, and marvelous scenery. As Anne said, "I wouldn't be at all surprised if we find our little house here, and if so, you must come visit us."

PARADOR DE LA PALMA, P.O. Apartado 48, Santa Cruz de La Palma, La Palma, Canary Islands, Tel.: 41-23-40. A 28-guestroom inn located on the Avenue Maritime overlooking the sea in downtown Santa Cruz de La Palma. Breakfast, lunch, dinner served daily to travelers. About 5 km. from nearest beach. Rates: See Index.

Directions: Take taxi from airport.

PORTUGAL

SPAIN

• Sintra
LISBON

Guincho

• Merida

• Badajoz

Estremoz • Elvas

Palmela
Setubal

Evora

Santiago do Cacem •
Serpa

São Brás de Alportel

Sagres • **FARO**
Armacao de Pera
Santa
Barbara
de Nexe

TRAVEL SUGGESTIONS FOR PORTUGAL

Pousadas, Palacios, and Other Portuguese Inns

It is possible and tempting to travel all over Portugal, spending every night in a government-owned inn, a pousada. Pousadas are similar to the paradors of Spain and are located in castles, convents, and so forth, though some have been built specifically to take advantage of a scenic spot. However, I have included other inns as they fit the criteria of good food, a friendly welcome, and providential location.

Pousadas are more than simple country inns since each deliberately reflects the style and culture of the region in which it is located. Great open fireplaces, cool verandas, mosaics, and fine original art put the traveler in the mood to appreciate more fully the history and character of the country. Accommodations are good to excellent, with modern bathrooms and comfortable beds. Pousadas accept credit cards. MasterCard and Visa are the most widely used.

191

As the pousadas have relatively few rooms, reservations are necessary, especially during the high summer season. They may be made in advance through Marketing Ahead, New York City, 212-686-9213. If you visit midweek and off-season, you can frequently find a room available, though not always the most choice. Try arriving mid-afternoon or asking your innkeeper of the night before to telephone ahead. Prices are reasonable, especially for the value received.

Pousadas serve three meals a day with a continental breakfast included in the room price. Sandwiches, beverages, and snacks are available between meals. The regular meal is generally four courses with both a fish entrée and a meat entrée, each fully garnished with potatoes and vegetable. You can ask for three courses instead of four at a twenty-five percent reduction in price. Regional dishes are served as well as English-style grills with boiled or fried potatoes. Several hundred years of British tourism have left their mark on the cookery. The influence of France is seen in other inns.

Portuguese Menus

Small or large, Portuguese restaurants are likely to be very clean and serve same-day fresh food. As you would expect in a seafaring nation, fish is very good and served in a variety of ways. Caldeirada, a fish and shellfish stew similar to French bouillabaisse, is delicious. Grilled fresh tunny (tuna) or salmonete (red mullet) and a green salad with plenty of chewy Portuguese bread and sweet butter are hard to surpass. The national dish is bacalhau (dried codfish), reshaped into an infinite number of dishes and worth sampling.

Caldo verde is a soup made with potatoes and kale that appears on many menus. Porco à alentajana is pork and clams, popular in the south-central Alentejo region, the farm belt of Portugal. Bife no frigideira is steak with mustard sauce. Desserts are often served from a cart and include almond cake, caramel custard, fruit tarts, and fresh fruit in season.

Touring

"Praia" is the sign for a beach, and there are plenty of them. As the main roads do not hug the shore, you watch for a sign, then proceed down an access road a few miles to the beach. Along the shoreline, there are spectacular cliffs with lovely golden beaches in coves as well as sweeps of open sand. Midweek, you will often have the beach to yourself, though weekends can be crowded, especially in the areas nearest Lisbon. South-facing beaches are calm and good for swimming, but those that front directly on the Atlantic have booming breakers and treacherous undertows.

The Michelin Green Tourist Guide to Portugal contains very good accounts of historic sites, buildings, churches and local history. I found it indispensable. The Michelin map for Spain and Portugal (990) also guided me well. Contact the Portuguese Tourist Office (548 Fifth Avenue, NYC 10036) for information on the areas you intend to visit.

My trip to Portugal began at Lisbon, then proceeded by rental car, first to the coastal area northwest of Lisbon, then south to the Algarve, east and north again touching the Spanish border before circling back to Lisbon. In this region I visited all the pousadas, though there are others in the north of Portugal that I will include in a future edition.

Lisbon and the Lisbon Coast

The areas just northwest of Lisbon attracted a good many of Europe's displaced monarchs a few decades ago, and so have an international style as well as many foreign visitors. The beach resorts of Estoril and Cascais are famous and crowded; the mountain town of Sintra is more of a retreat.

Sintra, one of the most beautiful and restful places in Portugal, is less than an hour's drive from the airport and an oasis of tranquility. Byron called it a "glorious Eden," and it is still a place where gardens flourish, horse-drawn carts take leisurely drives, and hiking trails lead to great vistas as well as somewhat bizarre royal residences. It is convenient for touring the beach towns, but it is not the place to stay if you want to be in the center of the action.

There are no pousadas in Sintra, though its five-star hotel was originally restored by the government. I also sampled life in a private manor house that takes bed-and-breakfast guests.

HOTEL PALACIO DOS SETEAIS, Sintra

The name translates to "Palace of the Seven Sighs" for a reason more political than romantic. When the treaty ending the Peninsular War was signed on the premises, the Portuguese correctly guessed it was not going to send the French home as soon as promised. The diplomats adjusted to the realities with sighs. It is a beautiful building set back from the road in its own park with eighteen large antique-filled guest rooms and a dining room that attracts a Lisbon as well as a local clientele.

The palace was built in the eighteenth century as a private residence by a Dutch diamond merchant, became a hotel under government supervision, and is now owned by the Tivoli chain. Service and amenities are what you would expect for five stars, that is to say, first rate. The public rooms are exceptionally beautiful with hand-painted walls and museum-quality furniture. The carpets are hand-woven, needlepoint style, from the town of Arraiolos in patterns designed especially for the hotel. There is a swimming pool and, of course, there are gardens. For all its elegance, Palacio dos Seteais is not prohibitively expensive, though reservations must often be made far in advance.

If you can't get a room, try to go for a meal or afternoon tea. It is only three kilometers outside Sintra.

PALACIO DOS SETEAIS, Sintra. Tel.: 923-3200/25/50. Telex: 14410 HOPASE. An 18-guestroom luxury hotel in a beautiful setting, with historical and cultural associations as well as a fine restaurant, gardens, and views. Open all year. Credit cards accepted. Reservations important. Rates: See Index.

Directions: From the center of Sintra (outside the Royal Palace), take the road to Monserrate, technically the Rua Barbosa du Bocage. The Palacio is 3 km. north of Sintra on your right, set well back from the road.

QUINTA DE SÃO THIAGO, Sintra

One of the latest in the government's plan to make things comfortable and authentic for travelers is the encouragement of stately homes to open their doors to overnight guests. There are now a number of these throughout Portugal, and one of the most charming is just four and a half kilometers farther than the Palacio on the Monserrate road. At least that is where the turn-off is and the sign "Quinta de São Thiago." I proceeded down a dirt road that became increasingly narrow and rocky, and just when I decided I could go no farther, I was there. The *quinta,* a noble hacienda built in 1535, is behind huge green gates in a rock wall. Parking is across the road.

This has been the home of the English Braddell family for fifty years and has been open to guests only since 1981. There are ten

rooms with private baths and two family suites with shared baths. Public rooms include sitting rooms, a library, a game room, a chapel, and a large dining room where breakfast is served at the guests' convenience and evening meals are served on request.

The grounds of the estate are well tended and lovely—flowers from the extensive gardens appear throughout the house as well. Mrs. Braddell not only gives helpful hints for touring, but will arrange for horseback riding and anything else her guests desire, including attendance at special events and *festas* generally not open to the public.

Inside the thick walls of the hacienda, you experience the way of life that has made the Sintra area so attractive to Europe's displaced royalty as well as to retired ambassadors and British merchant princes. This is country house lodging at its best.

QUINTA DE SÃO THIAGO, Sintra. Tel.: 923-2923. A 10-guestroom (private baths) privately owned 16th-century manor house on a country estate; also 2 family suites. Bed-and-breakfast rates, but evening meal available on request. Swimming pool, tennis court, gardens. Open all year. Reservations advised. Contact Mrs. R.N.L. Braddell. Discounts off-season. Rates: See Index.

Directions: Take the Monserrate road out of Sintra, past the Palacio dos Seteais (3 km.) for another 1.5 km. Turn right at the first-and-only right turn (there is a green sign indicating Quinta S. Thiago). Continue 900 m. to large green gates on left. Park across road.

ESTALAGEM MUCHAXO, Guincho

West from Sintra, down the mountainside to the coast, I went to see Cabo da Roca, the westernmost point in Europe. From this windy headland you can stare into the seemingly endless Atlantic, then, from a combination restaurant and tourist office, pick up a certificate proving forever you visited the spot.

Having done that, I turned south towards Guincho, nearby at the other end of the crescent beach. Here I stopped for dinner at the Estalagem Muchaxo, a popular inn with a large sea-water swimming pool set in the rocks. Muchaxo started out as a modest beachfront snack bar, grew into two restaurants frequented by famous political and literary figures, then added overnight accommodations as well. Although I arrived a little early for dinner, there was no problem. I was seated at a choice table overlooking the sea and presented with a dual-language menu.

The fresh lobster soup was still bubbling as it was placed before me; the turbot was fried in butter; the coconut custard pie was served with strawberries on the side. Altogether, a thoroughly satisfactory meal with very good service as I watched the sun sink into the sea.

ESTALAGEM MUCHAXO, Guincho. Tel.: 285-0221/9342. A 24-guestroom (private baths) beachfront inn with 2 restaurants. Prices vary according to the view, with the most expensive facing the sea. It is 6 km. north of Cascais, 35 km. from Lisbon.

Directions: From Cascais, take the coast road to Guincho. The Estalagem is on your left as you drive north, well marked and with ample parking.

COZINHA VELHA, Queluz

Between Lisbon and Sintra is the town of Queluz, home to a pretty pink rococo palace built in the 18th century by Pedro III for his mad queen, Maria. The palace has been used to house visiting dignitaries such as Queen Elizabeth and President Eisenhower, but I went there because it has turned its old kitchen into an unusual and remarkable restaurant, the Cozinha Velha.

Many of the original fittings are still used: giant spits, a fifteen-foot-long marble work table, and a walk-in fireplace. Waitresses wear regional costumes, and the service is both prompt and courteous. The food was excellent, too, with shellfish, veal, and fowl all well prepared and garnished with fresh vegetables. For dessert I had strawberry tart, but it was a difficult choice considering the cakes, pies, native cheeses, and fruit presented to me.

Cozinha Velha (which means Old Kitchen) attracts many diners from Lisbon. It takes one hour to tour the palace, which may be done before or after lunch, depending on whether you want to whet your appetite or walk off your meal. The formal gardens may be visited separately and convey the fairy-tale quality that I was to see again and again as I traveled about the country.

COZINHA VELHA, Queluz. Tel.: 95-02-32. This restaurant is part of the Palacio Nacional de Queluz. Entrance is through a patio and somewhat hard to find until the doors open. Luncheon is served from noon until 3 p.m.; dinner is 7:30 to 10 p.m. Open year-round and seven days a week.

Directions: From Lisbon take the 117 Motorway towards Sintra. Queluz is off the main road, but it is well marked, and you will be turning right.

A Day in Lisbon

One interesting way to solve the problem of visiting a big city without taking the car into the Centro is to leave the car at a recognizable point outside the city and take a bus into the center. In Lisbon I parked my car at the Santa Maria Hospital, checked the bus numbers that I would need to find my way back, and left the driving to the bus line.

I congratulated myself every block of the way, because Lisbon has unbelievable traffic. It is a beautiful, sophisticated city with modern apartment buildings and wide boulevards bordered by attractive mosaic sidewalks. And yet a turn of the corner can be a

journey into yesterday as one discovers the narrow, winding cobblestone streets that climb up and down the famous seven hills. But it also has heavy traffic.

I arrived in the center of the city and took bus 37, which follows a route from the downtown area (where there is always a long queue) through some of the more narrow streets of the Alfama (the old Moorish quarter) to the ruins of the Castle Saint Jorge crowning one of Lisbon's hills.

From the vantage point of the highest place on the castle grounds there is a very good view of the Tagus River and the great bridge and also of the majestic statue of Jesus. Also at the top in a little park there is the ever-present game of soccer that is a universal language here in Portugal. As soon as you have two small boys and a soccer ball, the game is on.

According to the Michelin Green Book on Portugal (don't leave home without it), the castle was constructed by the Visigoths in the 5th century and then strengthened by the Moors in the 9th century. It boasts ten towers linked by massive battlemented walls. Michelin doesn't say anything about the millions of birds nesting in the live oaks, whose calls are sometimes shrill and piercing and often times soothing.

On my way back to the bus, I saw an ancient, four-door, leather-seated, convertible Oldsmobile of 1922 vintage being used as a taxi—it was really sensational. At the bus stop outside the castle gates were old three-and four-storied buildings with people leaning out of the windows, looking down through the ubiquitous lines of laundry.

Lisbon has lots of outdoor cafes, and the passing show can be viewed also from the benches in the parks, gardens, and squares. The Portuguese version of the "Good Humor" men take their carts of ice cream up and down the cobbled hills.

Music, generally in melancholy strains, floats out from the taverns, restaurants, and houses, sometimes getting fierce competition from roosters, ducks, turkeys, and dogs. Street musicians play the lighter folk tunes.

One of Lisbon's great treats is the Gulbenkian Museum, which has one of the world's greatest private art collections, including two Rembrandts, a Rubens, and a rich collection of silver made for Catherine the Great by Thomas Germain. There are several small galleries exhibiting Roman, Greek, European, Egyptian, Mesopotamian, Islamic, and Oriental art treasures, as well as Persian tapestries, silver, ancient Greek and Egyptian pottery, jewelry, Turkish textiles, and delicately carved ivories and woodcuts from the Orient. The museum is located in an art complex that includes three auditoriums; one for music, a second is a theater, and a third for meetings. Around the corner from the entrance to the Gulbenkian, still on the property, is the Center of Modern Art. Opened in 1983, it contains over 500 works and was presented to Lisbon by the Gulbenkian Foundation.

YORK HOUSE/RESIDENCIA INGLESA, Lisbon

As soon as I stepped through the gates of York House, I left the city behind me. There are stone steps, flowering trees, a courtyard full of greenery, and a very old stone building. York House was a convent in the 16th century, restored from ruin in the 20th and converted into a pension by a Frenchwoman who only recently retired from active management. As a pension it has sheltered not only travelers, but British and American foreign service personnel awaiting permanent housing, as well as any number of famous writers who stayed for months at a time.

A few years ago, a handsome 19th-century town house, once owned by a British diplomat and located just up the street, was renovated as an annex, adding more rooms and a touch of late Victorian style. The dining room is still in the original York House,

though breakfast is served to guests either in their rooms or before the fireplace in the parlor of the Residencia Inglesa as well.

Food is prepared in a provincial French-Portuguese manner that has delicious results. There is usually a choice for the entrée, but otherwise it is a set three-course meal, both at luncheon and dinner. Lighter fare is available in the bar. York House, no longer strictly a pension, works on a bed-and-breakfast basis. In summer, however, you may be asked to take demipension; that is, one main meal either midday or evening.

Guest rooms are slightly larger in the Residencia Inglesa annex, while views are considered superior at York House, where your room will face either the courtyard or the river. All rooms are furnished with antiques and are immaculate. Although you are not in the center of town, you are on a convenient streetcar line, and the Museum of Ancient Art is close at hand. There is some limited parking next to Residencia Inglesa. Incidentally, the street name translates to "the street of the green window shutters."

YORK HOUSE/RESIDENCIA INGLESA, 32, 47 Rua das Janelas Verdes, Lisbon 1200. Tel.: 66-81-44 or 66-24-35. A 46-guestroom (27 with bath) inn in the southwestern part of the city, not far from the 25 de Abril bridge, the longest suspension bridge in Europe, and the museum attractions of Belem. Rates: See Index.

Directions: Rua das Janelas Verdes is a short length of a street that changes its name with confusing frequency. It parallels the main

CASTELO PALMELA

avenue off the Rio Tejo waterfront, Av. 24 de Julho and intersects with Av. Dom Carlos I. If you require instant directions, ask how to get to the Museu de Arte Antiga, just up the street. York House is on the north side of Janelas Verdes and Residencia Inglesa is on the south side.

POUSADA DO CASTELO PALMELA, Palmela

Here I was above the clouds in my own castle in Portugal, master of all that I surveyed—ready to send my ships to the New World and my traders to the Far East!

Sitting in the bedroom window of the Pousada de Palmela, just a few miles south of Lisbon, I was a hundred million miles away from the real world. High above the fields and the city, I was actually above the flocks of gulls that keep their constant winged vigil around the walls of this truly incredible fortress-cum-hotel.

The great walls that tower so menacingly above the countryside were built more than a thousand years ago by the Moors, as was a mosque transformed later into a church, only the ruins of which remain. Another line of fortifications was erected later, and nearby are what seem to be Roman ruins.

The pousada guest rooms, as in most cases, are modern with all the conveniences that travelers have come to appreciate, including private bathrooms, hot water, plenty of "walking around" space, and comfortable beds. This pousada should be on every traveler's Portuguese itinerary. In fact, when visiting Lisbon I would prefer to stay here or at the Pousada de São Filipe at Setubal, just a few miles away, but more about that in just a moment.

I spent at least a morning wandering about the grounds, all within the massive walls. There were millions of beautiful yellow field daisies growing up among the ruins and in the crevices of many ancient buildings.

Here was a surprise—a swimming pool on the edge of the battlements; certainly one of the very sunniest spots, and from it one could look across the countryside or down through the steep fields where goats seem to wander unattended.

The roofs of the town with their variegated patterns and planes cried out to be photographed or painted, and from that height the villagers below looked like vigorous ants busily going about the duties of the day. From the top of the walls, the view to the west is towards the mountains, and to the south there is a line of windmills. Taken all in all, it is one of the most impressive views in Portugal.

Ah, Palmela, how I wish I could press a magic button and return to your vaulted windows and exotic panorama again.

POUSADA DO CASTELO PALMELA, Palmela. Tel.: 235-1226. A 27-guestroom fortress-castle inn with large, pleasant rooms. Swimming pool. Forty km. from Lisbon, 200 km. from the Spanish border at Badajoz. Rates: See Index.

Directions: Leave the E-4 Motorway from Lisbon at Palmela Exit and follow pousada signs straight up the hill.

POUSADA DE SÃO FILIPE, Setubal

It seems unfair that there should be two such magnificent pousadas within a short distance of each other. Besides the Pousada do Palmela, standing high on the top of a commanding hill overlooking miles and miles of the Portuguese countryside, there is this magnificently placed pousada on the cliffs, overlooking the estuary of the Rio Sado River, the sea, and the Tróia Peninsula, leading to the sunny land of the Algarve. It's a joy to walk about the rocky ramparts and take in the entire panorama. Occasionally, I cast a furtive look over my left shoulder toward the walls of the other pousada, more pleasant than menacing at such a distance.

From Lisbon I had taken the second Setubal entrance from E-4 and followed the roads and signs to the Centro. From that point, the

pousada signs directed me through the main part of town and up a steep hill where there was a certain ambivalence regarding the correct road (I subsequently learned to stay on a paved road and watch for a sign indicating the castle was to the left).

Passing through an ancient archway, I was in the moat of the castle, now being used as a parking area. I went through a huge door into a cavernlike entranceway, at that time being reconstructed. To my right was a long set of stairs leading through a tunnel at the end of which I could see a light. (There may now be an elevator.) I walked to the top and found a terrace overlooking the estuary and the sea.

The terrace was furnished with many small round tables with white umbrellas, and I learned from my own experience that it is possible to sit for hours just looking out over the fascinating panorama of the seaport town with its little ferries plying the estuary and literally dozens of dory fishermen out on the water almost at first light. At night the lights of the town create a yellow crescent of pearls stretching out as far as the eye can see.

A dissonant symphony of sounds drifts up from the town—fire sirens, police car signals, barking dogs, crowing roosters, and the ubiquitous Moped.

That evening I joined the regular diners in the dining room, which also enjoys the spectacular view, and was invited to join a squadron of British Navy mine sweepers who were taking a holiday evening. We were a most jovial gathering.

The guest rooms, some of which were on the small side, were comfortable. Request a sea view.

I suggest the traveler book one night at the pousada at Palmela and the other night here at Setubal to enjoy the best of all possible pousada-castle worlds. Be sure to arrange reservations well in advance.

POUSADA DE SÃO FILIPE, Setubal. Tel.: 238-44. A 15-guestroom inn established in an ancient fortress, 50 km. from Lisbon; 200 km. from the Spanish border at Badajoz. Originally built in 1590 to subdue the inhabitants of the town below. There is a very pleasant chapel on the castle grounds. Rates: See Index.

Directions: From the center of Setubal follow pousada signs up the high hill to the castle walls.

POUSADA DE SANTIAGO, Santiago Do Cacém

I have a feeling that after having landed in Lisbon, many first-time travelers in Portugal will set out for the sunny Algarve, bent on arriving there as quickly and conveniently as possible. However, I hope that many will stop at the Pousada de Santiago, an unusually quiet and sedate pousada near the coast, about 146 kilometers from Lisbon and a little more than the same distance from Sagres. I stopped here for lunch and was sorry that I hadn't decided to spend a pleasant afternoon on the nearby beach and stay for dinner and overnight as well.

Unlike many of the pousadas in Portugal, established in former castles, historic buildings, and monasteries, this little gem is in a stately old house overlooking the town and the countryside, and is surrounded by evergreen trees that have been cut back to permit a better view.

It is set apart from the bustle of the nearby town, with a row of windmills on the top of a high hill just behind it, and a rather impressive little church nestled near the top of the hill on the opposite side of the village. The poplars and many lilies and other brilliant early summer flowers give it a gay and colorful air.

I wandered around the grounds and shared the setting with several peacocks, who seemed to be masters of the place except when their reign was threatened by the presence of a very raucous goose. I'm not at all certain that he approved of me.

On the day that I visited, the place seemed to be in charge of a rather prim and proper waitress, who showed me a few of the bedrooms, explaining that they were quite similar to all the others. I thought they were very pleasant and certainly seemed quiet.

A surprise here for me was my first menu translated into English, although I was now becoming adept at making quick translations. Among other offerings was a regional lamb stew, grilled filets of pork, curry of chicken with white rice, grilled beefsteak, and eggs and bacon and country sausage. The dining room had a very light and airy feeling and this modest pousada looked like it did a brisk luncheon business, especially with people driving to and from the Algarve.

POUSADA DE SANTIAGO, Santiago Do Cacém. Tel.: 224-59. A 7-guestroom quiet, atypical pousada on the main route south from Setubal to Sagres. A quiet setting, simple rooms, good food and a swimming pool. Good beaches nearby; 146 km. from Lisbon. Rates: See Index.

Directions: Follow the coastal road south from Setubal.

POUSADA DO INFANTE, Sagres

For many visitors to Portugal, Sagres is where the Algarve begins. The Pousada do Infante is one of two pousadas on the southern coast, the other being in São Brás de Alportel, several kilometers to the east. I did find two other modest hotels in the Algarve, described in the following pages.

The Pousada do Infante turned out to be beautifully accommodating, as are so many of the other Portuguese government-owned inns. For one thing, it's set apart from the town, which is beginning to lose its native charm and succumbing to more highly touristic interests.

One of the thrilling things for me about this inn was its location at a geographical point that is rich in history. This is the point of land around which the ancient Phoenicians sailed in their quest for further trade in the Atlantic Ocean. Here, too, the Norsemen and Vikings came from the north and swung east into the Mediterranean.

Today, ships from many nations are within sighting distance as they continue their journey to Africa around the Cape of Good Hope to the Indian Ocean, or perhaps around Cape Horn into the Pacific. The Portuguese thought so highly of it as a strategic location that they built the fortress of Prince Henry the Navigator.

Amidst all of this interesting history, I was surprised to discover that the decorative theme of the Pousada do Infante is Art Deco, which blends very well with the unusual marble in the hallways, arches, and floors. It is a two-story beige building, faintly reminiscent of the architecture of Florida in the early 1920s, before the great land boom. There is a feeling of respectability and restraint about it. Each of the bedrooms has a small balcony overlooking the patio, the cliffs, and the sea beyond.

The main lobby has a beautiful big marble fireplace with a vast semicircular couch in front of it and many, many comfortable chairs. The terrace off the main dining room is a very pleasant place to spend the afternoon. An overhead chandelier lends a sort of formal quality to the dining room.

I learned that during the high season the occupancy by American visitors was as high as sixty or seventy percent.

Instead of having dinner at the pousada, I went to a local restaurant, A Tasca, which overlooks the clear waters of the bay. Before going in I stood awhile and watched the fresh fish being unloaded in the cove and prepared for their next destination in a big, well-lighted shed. There was much shouting and singing as the men went about their work.

A Tasca's specialty is fresh fish, naturally. The catches of the day are posted on a blackboard, and everything is cooked to order. When ready for dessert, I made my selection from a refrigerated glass case where there were many cakes, tarts, and puddings, settling at last for a creamy vanilla custard and fresh berries.

POUSADA DO INFANTE, Sagres (Algarve). Tel.: 642-22. A 21-guest-room very comfortable seaside inn on the extreme western end of the Algarve, 286 km. from Lisbon. Would advise reservations as far in advance as possible. Near several of the famous Portuguese beaches. Rates: See Index.

Directions: From Lisbon follow the coastal road, which begins across the Rio Sado estuary at Setubal and continues to the southwest corner at Sagres. The pousada is well signposted.

✠   ✠   ✠   ✠

The Algarve

The Algarve is the entire southern section of Portugal, extending from Sagres at the westernmost point to the borders of Spain in the east. It is very much like the Costa del Sol in Spain and, in fact, each is an extension of the other. The word comes from the Arabic *el gharb,* which means the west of the "land beyond." Like the rest of the southern Iberian peninsula, it bears the unmistakable marks left

by 500 years of Moorish domination. Not only in place names, but in architecture and in the characteristics of the people. Historically, it has always been a very important place, and the Phoenicians and Carthaginians, as well as the Greeks, Romans, Visigoths, and, of course, the Moors have left vestiges of their tenures.

Today, it is important as an international holiday objective. The winter temperature ranges between 50° and 68° Fahrenheit, and the summer, between 68° and 86°. The Algarve boasts of having over 3,000 hours of sunshine a year (California has 1,000 to 2,000). Early spring is supposed to be one of the best times to visit, when there is an abundance of flowers and blossoms and, I might add, relatively uncrowded conditions.

In the Algarve the beach is one of the main preoccupations, and there are all kinds of beaches available. There's also lots of golf, fishing, sailing, water skiing, night life, and shopping, not only for the crafts of the region, but in the chic shops in the larger cities.

There are several large cities in the Algarve—Faro, Lagos, Portimao, Albufeira, and Tavira. It's possible to fly to Faro from any point in Europe.

There are two pousadas in the Algarve: the one at Sagres is very popular and should be booked well in advance, and the other at São Brás de Alportel is located almost midway between Spain and the Atlantic Ocean. I also found two excellent small hotels. I think it would be possible to stay at any of these and enjoy some day trips to other parts of the Algarve.

I think the Algarve would be a very happy experience between November and April. The almond trees are in glorious bloom in February.

HOTEL DO LEVANTE, Armacão de Pera (Algarve)

Oh boy, that sun felt good. I burrowed into the warm sand, cradled my head in my arms, adjusted my sunglasses and looked out towards the sea, where there were several small fishing boats and a large freighter dancing on the blue waters. Behind me and ninety steps up the cliff was the Hotel do Levante, a wonderful find for me.

I had spent the previous night in an unsatisfactory hotel in Albufeira, and because I was sure there was something along the road between Sagres and São Brás de Alportel, I doubled back on the beach road from Albufeira and stumbled into the somewhat modern village of Armacão de Pera. There were a few modern looking, designed-to-accommodate-as-many-tourists-as-possible hotels, and then I caught a glimpse of Hotel do Levante, which had obviously been built a few years ago and had the pleasant white buildings and red roof that characterize Mediterranean design.

I liked it immediately and, after introducing myself to the management, I was taken on a short tour of some of the forty-one rooms, some of which have terraces and balconies. All have telephones, music, bathrooms, heating, and a sea view. I decided to take an hour on the beach in the sun and reflect upon my adventures in the Algarve.

I passed the inviting swimming pool, made my way down the wooden steps, and soon found just the right spot. At low tide the beaches extend for miles and miles in both directions. I was treated to the sight of parading beach strollers complete with broad hats against the already sizzling sun. It was fun.

My brief tour of this very attractive small hotel also included an explanation of the menu, which, because of the international nature of the guests, was printed in several languages. There are several different plans available, including a full three meals a day, if desired.

HOTEL DO LEVANTE, Armacão de Pera (Algarve). Tel.: 32322. Telex: 18778 Levant P. A very pleasant, quiet, seaside hotel just east of Albufeira and 47 km. from the Faro airport. (Not listed in Michelin.) May be booked through a travel agent and various plans are available throughout the year with a considerable range in rates. Swimming pool, gardens, mini-golf, and quiet accommodations for children. Rates: See Index.

Directions: Armacão de Pera is just 3 km. south of Route N-125. Follow signs to the south.

HOTEL LA RESERVE, Santa Barbara de Nexe (Algarve)

Many visitors think the Algarve is endless waterfront, but there are also back roads that lead to country inns and small villages. One of these inns is La Reserve, a Swiss-managed hostelry that began as a fine French restaurant in an old manor house. Its location is northwest of Faro, almost dead center in the Algarve.

Following signs, I found myself on a back road between the villages of Santa Barbara de Nexe and Esteval. La Reserve is surrounded by citrus trees and a whitewashed wall with wrought iron gates. I announced myself, and the gates swung open so I could proceed to the hotel, a handsome white Moorish structure set in gardens around a swimming pool. There are five acres of grounds with seventeen varieties of fruit trees and a large kitchen garden that supplies the dining room.

La Reserve has twenty suites, including twelve studio-style and eight duplexes. The latter are two-bedroom, two-bath, two-veranda, and two-story. All the suites have small kitchen facilities for light meals. Breakfast is served in the room or on the veranda. Evening meals (which require firm reservations) are in the restaurant across the garden.

HOTEL LA RESERVE, Santa Barbara de Nexe (Algarve). Tel.: (089) 91474-91434. Telex: 56790 (Fuchs). An outstanding country house hotel and restaurant, 10 km. from Faro airport on a pretty back road between the coast and the foothills, not far from the Roman ruins of Milreu and the palace at Estoi or the market town of Loulé. Tennis courts, two swimming pools; horseback riding and golf can be arranged. Rates: See Index.

Directions: The main highway through the Algarve is Rte. 125. If you are driving west to east, after passing through Almancil watch for a road on your left leading north to Esteval. Turn left and follow signs to La Reserve. Coming from the airport or Faro and going east to west, the turn is at Patacão, towards Santa Barbara de Nexe. Again, there are signs to guide you all the way.

POUSADA DE SÃO BRÁS, São Brás de Alportel (Algarve)

Although Faro, the principal city of the Algarve, is only eighteen kilometers distant there is a considerable difference between the atmosphere at this countryside pousada, located in the hills of the Algarve, and the rest of this resort area. The pousada is set on a height of land with views of olive, orange, and fig groves and a hint of the coast in the distance. The bright sunshine floods the small balconies of each of the rooms facing the south and it's very pleasant to sit in the sun enjoying breakfast and occasionally gazing over the countryside.

I found this particular place very restful and at the same time within a very short drive of the beaches and also the small village of Alte, with its reputation for being one of the most picturesque villages in Portugal.

I made a short excursion to Tavira, a few kilometers to the east, and as it was during May and not the high season, there were not too many tourists in the town and it proved to be a very pleasant afternoon and evening. It's particularly pleasant along the river.

POUSADA DE SÃO BRÁS, São Brás de Alportel (Algarve). Tel.: 423-05. A 15-guestroom countryside inn somewhat removed from the remainder of the town; 283 km. from Lisbon; 19 km. from Faro. Rates: See Index.

Directions: The basic road east and west across southern Portugal is the N-125. São Brás de Alportel is on N-270, which fortunately acts as a bypass enabling the traveler to cut across the hill country and omit visiting Faro. It is approx. 44 km. from the Spanish border.

North from the Algarve

Leaving the Algarve and crossing the mountains, I found myself in the rolling farm country of Portugal. Donkeys wearing flowered hats still pull carts to market here, and the villages are crowned with centuries-old hilltop castles. It did not surprise me to find the best lodging available is in the pousadas.

POUSADA DE SÃO GENS, Serpa

The sun was setting and the shadows were getting longer as I sat on the spacious balcony of this pousada in central southeastern Portugal, about a pleasant afternoon's ride from the Algarve. Stretched out before me was a marvelously endless sea of corn and groves of cork oak. The sound of the birds singing their twilight song was reassurance that whatever else might be happening in the world, here in this portion of Portugal life was still sweet and anticipatory.

This pousada is in a building of relatively recent construction, but one that has maintained the memories of the Moorish occupation, which are found throughout the Iberian peninsula. The walls are chalk white and the balconies have the traditional elegant Moorish arches. The interior, with its elegant, spacious public rooms, high ceilings, and surprising fountains, provides a restful haven from what can be insistent sun.

Leaving São Brás de Alportel just before noon and heading north on N-2, I was delighted to find that the road ascended to considerable heights, passing through some most interesting villages and towns, including Barranco do Velho, Ameixial, and Almodóvar. This was the time of year that acres and acres of spring flowers bloomed in rampant purples and yellows across the high plains like a delightful, colored blanket. The landscape was playfully punctuated with the large umbrella cork trees that look as if they were painted in place.

Portugal has many storks and almost all of the towns and villages had steeples and roofs where they could be seen nesting.

Dinner was enlivened by the presence of the vivacious woman

director of the pousada, who made several interesting and helpful suggestions from the menu. I particularly remember a plate of sweets that she said were typical of the area.

A glance at the map would show that Serpa is on the main road from Lisbon to Seville, Spain, and would make an excellent overnight stop. I was headed north from the Algarve to the mountains of western Spain and found it made an ideal break.

POUSADA DE SÃO GENS, Serpa. Tel.: 523-27. A 17-guestroom extremely quiet and comfortable inn on the rolling plains of southeastern Portugal, approx. 221 km. from Lisbon. Characterized by splendid views of the countryside. Swimming pool under construction. Rates: See Index.

Directions: Serpa is on N-260 about 30 km. from the Spanish border at Rosal de la Frontera. The pousada signs are much in evidence.

POUSADA DOS LOIOS, Evora

It was raining in Evora, but I joined in grateful rejoicing with the inhabitants, many of whose ancestors have lived in this walled town since Roman times. In the courtyard of the Pousada dos Loios the flowers of early May were grateful for the moisture, and small birds were flitting from bush to bush shaking the droplets from the leaves. Perhaps the spirit of the morning was best expressed by two of the maids of the pousada, who were on their knees scraping, brushing, and cleaning the stone steps and offering a gratuitous duet of Portuguese songs.

I had digressed from my usual picnic lunch, partly because of the rain, and also because the dining room atmosphere with the gleaming white napery and beautiful surroundings persuaded me to enjoy an indoor lunch. It consisted of cream of pea soup, followed by two small white fish, sautéed in butter and served with fresh spinach, a slice of very tasty tomato, and three small white potatoes.

The design of the arches and the delicate coloring and tints in the dining room were in the Manueline style, characterized by delicacy of design, beauty, and accuracy of color.

This pousada is a former 15th-century monastery with 20th-century conveniences, and the bedrooms, while extremely neat and furnished with cautious good taste, are a tad on the small side. As the brochure notes, "Over the years it has been embellished and enlarged with donations and legacies without losing any of its sobriety and dignity. The monks, whose habit was as blue as the skies of Alentejo, practiced charity, offered hospitality, and studied."

The town of Evora is well worth a visit and the traveler can park the car right next to the pousada and have the pleasure of an at least three-hour tour of many churches, palaces, museums, and stately mansions. I was most fascinated by the surviving columns of a Corinthian-style Roman temple, erected in the second century. The capitals and bases were of Estremoz marble and the columns of shaft granite.

I'll confess to having never heard of Evora until I started making plans for this trip, but my visit proved most interesting and rewarding. I could see why at one time it was the preferred capital of the kings of Portugal and the center of humanism, attracting scholars, sculptors, painters, and architects.

The pousada at Estremoz and this one in Evora are only a few kilometers apart and the traveler bent on using his time wisely could stay at either one and visit the other for lunch the following day. Both pousadas and towns have much to offer by way of supplying a feeling of Portugal, both of the past and the present.

POUSADA DOS LOIOS, Evora. Tel.: 240-51. A 33-guestroom elegant pousada in a former 16th-century monastery, decorated in the grand style. See Michelin Green Guide for historic sites nearby; 142 km. from Lisbon; 108 km. from Badajoz, Spain. Rates: See Index.

Directions: From the west leave N-4 at Montemor-O-Novo and follow N-114 to Evora. From the east leave N-4 just west of Estremoz and follow N-18, an enjoyable road. The pousada is located in the center of the walled town in the historic district.

POUSADA DA RAINHA SANTA ISABEL, Estremoz

Unlike the pousadas at Setubal and Palmela, really fortifications with many characteristics of castles, the Pousada da Rainha Santa Isabel is a bona fide live-in castle that also has a keep, a tower that thrusts its way even higher into the blue Portuguese sky.

This pousada is named for a queen saint—Isabel of Aragon, the wife of King Dinis, who was known as the poet king and the farmer king, and was an enormously active person who founded the university at Coimbra and established Portuguese, a dialect from the Oporto region, as the official language.

Both the pousada and its keep are on the top of a hill that dominates not only the town of Estremoz, but the entire countryside for miles around. Going up through the very narrow streets of the town with even the smallest model of automobile involves almost scraping the rough walls of houses on both sides.

However, the effort is well rewarded, not only by the inn's fabulous view, but also the excellent accommodations, furnishings, service, and food.

The pousada was built around a central courtyard, and the hallway that traversed three sides contained mirrors, sculpture, paintings, rugs, and very impressively decorated lamps. At each turn there was a delightful surprise—an old oil painting, an arrangement of painted furniture, or a delicate piece of porcelain.

I have visited many castle-hotels in many different countries of Europe, but I have never been in one that was so *well preserved*. I am not sufficiently well acquainted with periods of Spanish furniture design to vouch for its authenticity, but I can attest to the fact that every one of the guest rooms was furnished with opulent period furniture and richly embroidered or painted decorations, many in beautiful hand-tooled leather.

The dining room had a high, vaulted ceiling with several very substantial solid marble columns and very heavy wooden chandeliers. The high-backed chairs were covered in red velours with brass nail stubs, creating a highly decorative effect.

The *Michelin Green Guide* devotes an entire page to Estremoz, pointing out its famous potteries and the rural museum. There are several churches, including the chapel with wall murals depicting the life of Queen Saint Isabel. One depicts a particularly charming legend about the king and queen called the Miracle of the Roses. I will not spoil it for you.

There is a vast square in the center of the lower town with

215

several interesting ancient buildings and a very lively Saturday market, as well.

POUSADA DA RAINHA SANTA ISABEL, Estremoz. Tel.: 226-18. A 23-guestroom luxurious hotel in a former medieval castle; 179 km. from Lisbon, 62 km. from Badajoz on the Spanish border, 46 km. to Evora. See Michelin Green Guide for historic sites nearby. Rates: See Index.

Directions: Estremoz is on the M-4. The pousada, on the top of the hill above the town, can be seen at some distance. Once in the center of the town, follow the pousada signs that lead up the hill.

POUSADA DE SANTA LUZIA, Elvas

It can be hot in Portugal in early May, particularly in the interior near the Spanish border. It was a great relief to find temporary respite from the heat when I stepped into this modest air-conditioned inn.

The German translation in the brochure of the pousada refers to it as a "Rasthaus." This is a very apt description as it is not in a resort area where the traveler might be encouraged to spend more than one night, although the town does have some historic interest. It is located on one of the main roads between Lisbon and Madrid, and has eleven very light and airy, comfortable bedrooms adorned with fresh flowers. Some had twin beds and many of them had small balconies.

The pousada brochure, translated into four languages, speaks of the town as "a white and bright city, beautiful as a bride, strong and remarkable, surrounded by a wall formed of dark stones, mortared with the blood and sweat of eternal deeds."

One of the sights worth seeing in the old town is a five-tiered aqueduct built in the 16th century on a Roman foundation. Ninety feet high, it has a formidable series of 843 arches that still support pipes that carry water into the town. Although not as large as the one in Segovia, Spain, it is nevertheless impressive.

Inside the small fortress at the top of the hill, a group of small boys played soccer in the dusty yard, many of them wearing their Sunday clothes. As I departed, the last thing I saw was the soccer ball bouncing all the way down to the bottom of the hill, having been kicked over the wall.

POUSADA DE SANTA LUZIA, Elvas. Tel.: 22194. An 11-guestroom inn with a very comfortable restaurant in a quiet setting, somewhat apart from the town, 222 km. from Lisbon and 17 km. from the Spanish border. See Michelin Green Guide *for historic sites nearby. Rates: See Index.*

Directions: Elvas is on Estrada N-4. Follow pousada signs.

SOUTHERN GERMANY

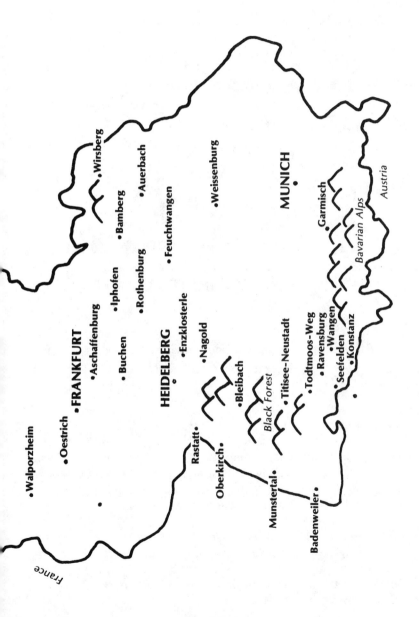

TRAVEL SUGGESTIONS FOR GERMANY

How to Get There

Pan Am and Lufthansa Airlines provide excellent service from many U.S. cities to several gateway cities in Germany. Your Eurailpass is good in Germany.

Country Inns in Germany

Innkeeping in Germany is a highly respected and traditional occupation. While visiting small hotels, I found three, four, and even five generations of family-owners, and where the ownership has passed through the wife's family, her maiden name has also been retained, linked by a hypen with her husband's name. For example: Familie Sachs-Stern.

The inn buildings are frequently rich in architectural heritage since many have been in continuous use for centuries. Dining rooms are especially attractive with many handpainted designs lovingly applied to the mellowed wall panels and chair backs. There are almost always splendid wood carvings as well.

The service is excellent and cheerful, both in the dining room and in the house, although I had to adjust to the idea of frauleins carrying my bags; there are many sons and daughters sharing the responsibilities. Almost everyone speaks English, but I found it fun to practice my German, sometimes with hilarious results.

Visiting these small family-owned hotels provided me with a rich opportunity to learn more about Germany and the Germans themselves. The experience was similar to that of visiting country inns in North America.

Reservations

Most of the accommodations I visited in Germany are members of a well-coordinated group of hotels and restaurants known as Romantik Hotels. They are found in many countries of Europe. These Romantik Hotels have a "Plan as You Go" travel plan that includes a voucher for a minimum of six overnight stays and longer. The first night's accommodation is booked in advance; the following stays can be reserved by each Romantik Hotel. You or your travel agent can book this plan by calling 800-826-0015 from North America (206-885-5805 in Washington). The address in Germany is: Romantik Hotels, D-8757, Karlstein am Main, Postfach 1144. Telephone (0 61 88) 5020, Telex 41 84214.

German Menus

What wonderful treats are in store for the visitor in Germany who loves to eat! Here are a few of the Hauptegerichte (main courses) that I enjoyed at the small hotels: Bayerischer linsentopf (Bavarian lentil casserole with smoked pork and spices); hasenlaufe in jager-rahmsauce (rabbit in a hunter-style dark cream sauce of mushrooms, shallots, white wine, and chopped parsley); several different kalb (veal) dishes, including sweetbreads poached in white wine; veal meatballs, and fricasseed veal. There are many varieties of sausage, sauerbraten (a beef pot roast that has been marinated several days in vinegar and vegetables and spice), and zigeunerschnitzel (a gypsy-style preparation of veal cutlets sautéed in tomato sauce with thin strips of pickled tongue, red peppers, mushrooms, and possibly truffles).

The Germans prefer to linger over their delicious pastries and desserts in the late afternoon during the coffee hour. In this case the konditorei *(bakery) also serves as a cafe. Two of the most important words on the dessert menu for me were* schlagrahm *(whipped cream) and* schokoladen *(chocolate). The varieties of strudels would stretch from Munich to Frankfurt.*

Car Rentals

It is possible to arrange for an automobile as part of the "Plan as You Go" program. However, for other travelers may I suggest that you see the section in the front of this book, "Renting a Car for Europe." It is possible to arrange for a car to be picked up in one country and dropped off in another.

Driving Tips

German roads are excellent; even the secondary and back roads are well marked and well constructed. The thinnest lines on the map lead through beautiful farming and mountain country with very little traffic. They may not have route numbers, but the villages are clearly shown.

The international road signs are described in the Michelin Green Guide *for Germany.*

My Itinerary in Germany

For traveling in Germany, I have provided a group of five different itineraries, starting from Frankfurt and going in many directions.

Itinerary Number One: *From Frankfurt northwest through the Rhine and Mosel River Valleys.*

These suggestions can also be used by travelers from Berlin, Switzerland, Austria, Luxemburg, Belgium, and the Netherlands. It leads through the beautiful wine country of both the Mosel and Rhine River Valleys.

HOTEL SCHWAN, Oestrich im Rheingau (Rhine)

It was a beautiful morning on the Rhine and I was faced with the problem of getting bathed, shaved, and dressed as rapidly as possible, and at the same time keeping an eye on the ever-changing

parade of river traffic. Occasionally, there would be a barge with an automobile perched on it, a popular way to take both car and driver up and down river.

The setting of the Schwan would be worthy of an operetta. Below me were the white tables and gay awnings of the terrace, with the maple trees in bloom. There were already some hotel guests wandering along the river banks, perhaps to look at the old crane that used to be operated by foot power to lift casks of wines to barges. At a table on the terrace, a young couple I had seen in the dining room were sitting close to one another, and I had a feeling they had the bridal suite. If they had cared to, they could have had breakfast in their room.

Now, something new was added as a company of local fireman came down to the river, apparently to test their hoses and pumping equipment, and soon there were three or four silvery streams of water arching into the river.

The date on this hotel is 1628, and my host, Dr. Wenckstern, remarked that things have remained the same for a great many years. "We are now, through my wife's family, in the fifth generation of innkeepers and with few exceptions it has been in the family since it was built."

We were joined by Jens Diekmann, and even though he had been here many times, he said that he was learning some things about this beautiful old hotel. We visited the historic wine cellar, where there were long rows of wine casks and dust-covered bottles of the Rhineland's most famous product.

There was one lodging room on the top floor with six windows that had an absolutely smashing view of the river in both directions, which my host said had been described by the famous travel writer, Temple Fielding, as resembling the bridge of an ocean liner. I wish I'd said it first.

The hotel will arrange a two-day "Romantik Rhine Tour." This includes wine-tasting, a drive through the Rheingau Vineyards, a boat trip on the most beautiful stretch of the Rhine, and ends with a candlelight dinner at the hotel.

Because the Schwan is within a very reasonable distance of the Frankfurt Airport, for many people it is either the first or last night Germany.

ROMANTIK HOTEL SCHWAN, 6227 Oestrich-Winkel. Tel.: 06723-3001; Telex 42146. A 60-room rambling hotel directly on the banks of the Rhine River. Breakfast, lunch, and dinner served daily. Rhine River excursions in either direction are available at hotel landing. Many beautiful drives through the wine country. Rates: See Index.

Directions: Oestrich is located on Rte. B42 between Wiesbaden and Koblenz.

RESTAURANT WEINHAUS SANKT PETER, Walporzheim/Ahr (Rhine)

I was seated under the famous chandelier of St. Peter's-wein Church. In front of me was the magnificent stained glass window showing St. Peter holding two keys in his hands, protectively taking care of all the guests.

I couldn't help but be impressed by the interior of this ancient building, which tradition says was built in 1246. The simplicity of the white plaster walls provided a dramatic background for the black wrought-iron work. The main dining room is two stories high with a small balcony traversing the upper story.

The Weinhaus St. Peter, along with a few others I visited in Germany, has a reputation for gourmet cooking. The owner, Herr

Brogsitter, told me that many of the important members of the government in Bonn hold frequent luncheon conferences here, and the restaurant guest book certainly bore him out with some very flamboyant signatures, photographs, personal business cards, and even a cartoon. The Weinhaus St. Peter has obviously played host to a considerable number of political and artistic people.

It was the Saturday midday meal (*midtag*), and for the most part the guests were families enjoying the holiday with their well-mannered children seated around the big tables, obviously enjoying, as children do everywhere, the fun of "eating out."

A light repast was all I wanted, and the headwaiter suggested a local fish enhanced by a delicious sauce. One of the young waiters

brought a gigantic board holding at least twenty-eight kinds of cheese; I chose a variety and ate them with the usual excellent German bread.

Walporzheim is a small village next to the larger walled town of Ahrweiler. It is 145 kilometers (about four hours) from Bernkastel, through the countryside west of the Rhine by way of the famous Nurburgring, the well-known race track, the scene of professional automobile and motorcycle races. This section is known as the Eifel and is a most attractive ride. The St. Peter is an excellent luncheon stop between Bernkastel and Oestrich.

225

ROMANTIK RESTAURANT WEINHAUS ST. PETER, 5483 Walporzheim/Ahr (Bad Neuenahr). Tel.: 02641-34031. A most attractive restaurant open from 11 a.m. until midnight daily. Closed for holidays and Jan. and Feb. No lodginds.

Directions: Weinhaus St. Peter is located on Rte. 266, which runs east and west from the banks of the Rhine at Linz. Walporzheim is adjacent to the larger walled town of Ahrweiler, which is on most maps.

Itinerary Number Two: *From Frankfurt south via Heidelberg to the Black Forest.*

    This itinerary includes some of the most popular vacationing sections of Germany.

Heidelberg

    Ah Heidelberg! A romantic city where the Student Prince in Lehar's operetta caroused and sang with his fellow students and fell madly in love. Michelin gives it three full pages with an extensive description of the Heidelberg Castle and the other impressive sights within the city and its environs.

    Heidelberg is the oldest university town in Germany and the university and the students play an important role in its ambience. There is a student jail (studtenkarger), used between 1788 and 1914, allowing certain too-uproarious students to cool their ardor. To be so incarcerated was considered by many of them a mark of distinction.

They have left timeless reminders of their tenure with inscriptions and drawings on the walls. It is one of the principal tourist sights in Germany, particularly with thousands of young people finding their way there with guitars and backpacks. I saw quite a few American college T-shirts, although these are sold in stores everywhere in Europe.

The pedestrian section of the old city, cordoned off from automobile traffic, is a conglomeration of stores with a blatant appeal to tourists situated cheek-by-jowl with oriental rug shops, banks, jeans stores (everywhere), ice cream stands, and motion picture theaters. It is a meeting of the old ways and the new. As one Scottish boy responded when I asked him why he came to Heidelberg: "Why mon, this is where it's at!"

HOTEL ZUM RITTER, Heidelberg

Now, Heidelberg and the Zum Ritter! It is hard to imagine Heidelberg without the Zum Ritter.

There are two most uplifting experiences at this hotel. The first is to stand on the street and to become absorbed in the truly magnificent facade. The other is to ascend to the roof garden and enjoy a leisurely view of this historic, romantic city on the River Neckar.

The hotel derives its name from the statue of a young Roman knight (*ritter*) poised on the uppermost gable of the many-storied facade. Each of the five stories is supported by carved pillars on which are depicted a variety of figures from Roman history and mythology, as well as representations of the nobility of Heidelberg in the 16th century. The intricate designs of each section could be studied for hours at a time.

The oldest part was built in 1592 by master builder Carolus Belier, and was spared the ravages of a siege 100 years later. It was the only structure in Heidelberg to survive; everything else was burned to the ground.

On the first floor there are high vaulted ceilings and rather formal dining rooms and sitting rooms that have fragments of sculpture and carvings, including a bust of the builder of the house, who is further commemorated by two large oil paintings.

On the floors above, the rooms in the original section have been furnished with traditional pieces—the honeymoon suite, for example, is positively lavish and has two alcoves overlooking the church across the street. Oddly enough, there is a cradle in the hallway in front of the door. Other traditionally furnished lodging rooms have a holiday feeling.

The innkeeper, Georg Kuchelmeister, is an avid hunter, and on the day before my arrival had been hunting in the nearby Odenwald, a beautiful forest just across the river. He explained to me that he provides some of the venison and small game that is served frequently in the hotel dining room. A specialty of the house is Heidelberg *schlossplatte*, a beef, scrambled eggs, and vegetable dish.

The view from the roof garden puts it all into perspective; I could see that the city nestles at the foot of the mountains on both sides of the Neckar. The ancient castle still towers above the city, its ruins a continual reminder of bygone centuries.

The Zum Ritter, a late Renaissance masterpiece, is one of the important sights of the city. The Church of the Holy Spirit, just across the cobblestone street; the Heidelberg Castle and gardens towering over the city; and the Philosopher's Walk are all points of interest.

Heidelberg and the Zum Ritter are, indeed, well matched.

ROMANTIK HOTEL ZUM RITTER, Hauptstrasse 178, 6900 Heidelberg. Tel.: 06221/24272 and 20203. A 36-guestroom historic hotel in the center of the old part of Heidelberg adjacent to the university, the Old Bridge, and within a short walk of the cable car to the ruins of Heidelberg Castle. Breakfast, lunch, and dinner served daily. Margarete and Georg Kuchelmeister, Owners. Rates: See Index.

Directions: Motorists should use the nearby multistory parking in Parkhaus Kornmarkt (in the direction of the Castle/Schloss). To unload luggage, drive away from the river to the parking place behind the Heiliggeist Church, just opposite the hotel. The pedestrian precinct in front of the hotel may only be used by cars up to 10 a.m.

RESTAURANT KATZENBERGER'S ADLER, Rastatt
(near Baden- Baden)

I'm finally "one up" on John Ashby Conway, the distinguished gourmet chef and owner of the Farmhouse Restaurant in Port Townsend, Washington, for I have enjoyed a meal at Rudolfh Katzenberger's restaurant in Rastatt, and John has yet to enjoy that magical experience.

Mr. Katzenberger joined me at a corner table for a few moments, and we had a lively talk, frequently interrupted by his greetings to new guests and goodbyes to those departing. During the course of this conversation I assured him I would be quite satisfied with something very light for lunch, and he assured me that he had just the answer to my needs.

Shortly thereafter, a cup of delicious soup was set before me which, he told me, is served once a year and "tells us that spring is definitely here."

This was followed by two tasty dumplings topped with two small shrimp and accompanied by three crescent-shaped pastries. One bite and I was transported. I ate everything on the plate, and then felt that it would be sensible to order a small dessert.

That's when Isolde, Mr. K's daughter, came with a large platter containing a noodle omelet and veal cutlets. When I protested that she must be at the wrong table, she replied, "Oh no, you have only just started. Besides that, you must also eat your salad."

I restricted myself to a few bites of the noodle omelet and the veal cutlet, although it took a very firm effort on my part not to consume everything on the plate. Isolde returned and I told her I was finished, but she shook her finger at me and told me I should eat more. Before she could take the plate away, Mr. K. came back and looked very upset because he thought I didn't care for the food.

I assured him that it was ambrosial. Well, so much for my eating adventures at this exceptional restaurant originated by such an exceptional man. I hope that perhaps in some way I have conveyed the inherent pride and concern that are expressed here. I would say that Rudolfh Katzenberger enjoys a reputation in Germany somewhat akin to that of a cabinet minister, and certainly his tenure has been much more enduring. Many other innkeepers told me that he was the dean of chefs in Germany and possibly Europe.

As for John Ashby Conway, I would love to introduce him to Rudolfh Katzenberger and then just sit down and listen to both of them talk.

Since that visit, Rudolfh Katzenberger has handed over his business to his children, Isolde and Paul Hagelberger. Paul has been in the kitchen of the "Adler" for over ten years and was responsible for the quality of the cuisine during Mr. Katzenberger's time. Although Mr. Katzenberger is no longer there, the Adler is still an outstanding restaurant.

ROMANTIK RESTAURANT KATZENBERGER'S ADLER, #7 Josefstrasse, 7500 Rastatt. Tel.: 07222-32103. A distinguished hotel and restaurant. Luncheon and dinner served daily except Mon. Lodging available. Rates: See Index.

       ⬚   ⬚   ⬚   ⬚

The Black Forest (Schwarzwald)

The three sections of the Black Forest contain some of the most popular resort and recreational areas of Germany. The Michelin Green Guide devotes five pages to it. I visited several Romantik Hotels in which it would be a pleasure to spend an entire vacation.

The Black Forest has beautiful lakes, high mountains, vineyards, great rivers, graceful bridges, farmhouses crouching under sloping hip roofs, and perhaps one of the continual challenges to photographers: old towns with crooked lanes.

For the active sports-minded vacationer there is downhill and cross-country skiing, horseback riding, tennis, fishing, sailing, hiking, and back roads to content the most lively heart. At various times of the year there are special festivals where traditional costumes are worn and there are many displays of arts and crafts. Black Forest hospitality has a tradition of centuries, and the cuisine in the area features venison, rabbit, and other wild game. Black Forest cake in its many variations is known the world over.

HOTEL POST, Nagold (Black Forest)

Kurt Scholl was translating from a most fascinating book written in 1841 about the various hotels in Germany. He turned to the page with information about the Hotel Post. "In former times the Hotel Post was called the Hotel Sonne. The innkeeper was also the manager of the post office. The hotel is located on the road from Stuttgart to Strasbourg. It has twelve guest rooms with very good furniture and stables for the horses. Concerning the cellar and the kitchen we recommend it as one of the best restaurants in this area. The service is very good, the bill is not too high, and it can be recommended for travelers in all walks of life."

"Nothing has changed," I said. "Except that your father is not the postmaster of Nagold." The moment was punctuated by the arrival of Kurt's father, Karl, who joined in our laughter. "You might be surprised," he said, "at the number of recipes that have been used in the kitchen since the 19th century."

"My great-great-great-grandmother was the chief cook and was known as a woman with a very strong mind. The King of Wurtemberg was having dinner here during a very hot period of the summertime and there were a great many flies. He ordered my venerable ancestor to prepare a table for the flies. Naturally, she was rather indignant, but she complied with his demands and then returned to him and said, 'Your Majesty, the table for the flies has been prepared. Please order the flies to sit down!' "

This was only one of several most amusing anecdotes that Karl told throughout the evening.

Kurt, who majored in economics in Switzerland, is very proud of the family heritage of innkeeping. He is now very much the director of the hotel and pointed out that since Nagold is so close to France, it is inevitable that there should be an emphasis on French cuisine. For example, there is a saddle of hare, marinated in juniper sauce and served with potato croquettes and a chicory salad garnished with nuts. There is also stuffed leg of lamb, cooked in a pastry jacket and served with potatoes au gratin and kidney beans.

In its role as both post office and inn, the old hotel has

flourished, and the older sections, including the paneled dining rooms, have been admirably preserved. In recent years, a more modern annex has been constructed, providing guest parking. All of the guest rooms in this section have been modernized throughout.

Besides the King of Wurtemberg, other distinguished guests of the house have been Napoleon, Otto von Hapsburg, and Prince Louis Ferdinand of Prussia.

The pride in the tradition of innkeeping expressed by this family is typical of what I found throughout Germany. I am sure that the now-unknown travel writer of 1841 would endorse the improvements that have been made, but would also agree that the really important things have remained unchanged.

I had the pleasure of entertaining Connie Scholl, Kurt's sister, during her recent tour of North America. Connie is majoring in hotel management at a prominent college and will be joining her father and brother at the Hotel Post in the very near future.

ROMANTIK HOTEL POST, Bahnhofstrasse 2, 7270 Nagold. Tel.: (07452) 4048 and 4221. A 42-guestroom city hotel at the northern border of the Black Forest. Parking available for guest cars. Breakfast, lunch, and dinner served daily. Familie Scholl, Innkeepers. Rates: See Index.

Directions: Nagold is southeast of Karlsruhe and Heidelberg and southwest of Stuttgart. The hotel is located in the Centrum.

I believe it would be of interest to our readers to know that there is a very active program of travel among the innkeepers of the Romantik Hotels in Europe and the innkeepers in Country Inns and Back Roads, North America. *Several of the North American innkeepers have made the trip to Europe on the "Plan as You Go" program and have returned with glowing praise for accommodations, food, and the spirit of cooperation they have found in these tidy little family-owned hotels.*

At the same time there have been several visits by owners of the Romantik Hotels to North America and in some cases the innkeepers have become very good friends. On one particular occasion, several owners from Romantik Hotels came to one of the many meetings of CIBR North America innkeepers, held throughout the country every year. In addition to exchanging ideas, we all had a wonderful party in which several speeches were made in English and German and the innkeeping bonds of friendship were pledged again and again.

HOTEL OBERE LINDE, Oberkirch (Black Forest)

One of my lasting impressions of this tidy hotel in the central Black Forest is that the names of all the innkeepers dating from 1659 have been painted on one of the rows of beams of its classic half-timbered construction. That means it has been an inn for over 300 years!

The hotel has two recently restored buildings connected by a small, second-floor gallery. One building houses the dining rooms and the principal public rooms, as well as a few bedrooms; the other is entirely occupied by bedrooms.

Located on the main street, a few squares from the town center, it is a popular hotel, particularly in the height of the vacation season, and it is also a very important town meeting place—for example, the Rotary Club meets here every week. The hotel dining room and gardens frequently have an interesting cross section of both visitors and town people. In the rather spacious basement there are two bowling alleys that are slightly different from the American variety. Several local bowling clubs have matches there every week.

The two attractively decorated main dining rooms have a collection of lanterns, rolling pins, ceramics, copper, and pewter ware displayed on plate rails. Also on display is a large collection of photographs of young people, children and relatives of the owners, no doubt—this practice is quite common in Germany.

I arrived at lunchtime and after looking over the extensive menu, chose a bowl of soup and a piece of delicious homemade Black Forest cake. Accompanied by an ice-cold glass of milk, this chocolaty, creamy concoction was close to divine.

Oberkirch is a small, attractive town and, because of its quite mild climate, it is a center of strawberry growing. There is a strawberry market in town, the largest in Germany, where a strawberry festival is held every year. There is also a sizable outdoor swimming pool and park. During the summertime there are frequent concerts.

A new guest house, in keeping with the old building, with four-poster beds and many other amenities, is now available. An indoor swimming pool, sauna, and solarium are in the planning stages.

In many ways, the Obere Linde in Oberkirch, Germany, reminds me of the Red Lion Inn in Stockbridge, Massachusetts. Each has definite community ties while at the same time providing warm hospitality to travelers.

ROMANTIK HOTEL OBERE LINDE, 7602 Oberkirch. Tel.: (07802)/3038. A 34-guestroom family-style inn a few squares from the center of a German town in the Black Forest. Breakfast, lunch, and dinner served daily. Closed for two wks. in Feb. Familie Dilger, Innkeepers. Rates: See Index.

Directions: Oberkirch is on Rte. 28, which runs east and west from Freudenstadt to Strasbourg.

I took a few hours to explore some of the scenic views and mountains of the Rhine Valley and even got lost. While I was leaning over the radiator of the car examining the map, a man stopped his car and asked me if he could help. He not only showed me the way on the map, but then suggested that I follow him so that I would not lose my way. I had many such instances of courtesy and consideration in Germany. I find it extremely touching.

HOTEL-RESTAURANT STOLLEN, Gutach-Bleibach (Black Forest)

I will always remember this little crossroads inn for its flowers— there were flowers at every window, on all the balconies, and throughout the dining and sitting rooms. The tasteful arrangements bespoke a lover of flowers who, I am sure, was very happy in his or her work. The blooms, many of them geraniums, were set off beautifully against the whitewashed exterior walls and, on the inside, against the traditional brown carved beams and posts, and the white walls and ceilings.

As is the custom in this part of Germany, on the first floor there is a wine room that usually accommodates guests who wish to have light refreshments or the German version of a simple snack. There were also two more formal dining rooms, one decorated in red and the other in shades of yellow. I saw the familiar corner fireplace.

The guest rooms on the second and third floors were furnished either traditionally or in a contemporary mode. They looked very comfortable and pleasant.

The innkeeper and chef, Herr Jehli, explained that the inn had been built in 1847 and had been in his wife's family for many years. "She and I are the fourth generation of innkeepers," he said. Unfortunately, his wife was not present that day and he had to excuse himself to return to the kitchen; however, he generously invited me to wander around in the hotel at will.

Bleibach is just a few kilometers north of Freiburg, one of the centers of recreation and entertainment in the Black Forest

ROMANTIK HOTEL STOLLEN, 7809 Gutach-Bleibach. Tel.: 07685/ 207. A 14-guestroom crossroads inn kept in the Black Forest tradition. Breakfast, lunch, and dinner served daily. Familie Jehli-Kiefer, Innkeepers. Rates: See Index.

Directions:; Bleibach is a few kilometers north of Freiburg on the upper road to Offenburg (look for Rte. 294).

HOTEL ADLER-POST, Titisee-Neustadt (Black Forest)

The Titisee area is one of the most popular recreational areas in the Black Forest. The main reason is a very beautiful lake that offers a considerable dimension to vacation pleasures. From its shores I could look to the tops of some of the great mountains nearby, and when I was there in April the ski lifts were still running. During the summertime there is sailing, tennis, golf, bicycling, swimming, horseback riding, and the ever-present thermal baths.

Let me explain that there are two towns. One is Titisee, located on the lake, and the other is Titisee-Neustadt, just a few kilometers distant. The "Neustadt" part means "new town" and it was founded in 1251 and has been known as the new town ever since.

Titisee-Neustadt is a business town, and bustles with the air of a prosperous Midwest American community.

Although this squarish stone building seemed rather conventional, I was surprised to find a reception area that was quite rustic in design and furnishings. The twisting staircase to the second floor, with its carved woodwork and painted decorations, reminded me of a similar staircase at the Glen Iris Hotel in Castile, New York.

There were several surprises at the Adler-Post. For one thing, on the second floor there is a small swimming pool, sauna, baths, solarium, and a few unobtrusively placed pinball machines. (Excellent for rainy day entertainment and practicing body balance.) There was also a massage parlor and I was assured by the assistant manager, who had visited Texas, that any similarity to the kind we have in America is in name only.

Guest rooms furnished in the traditional manner were quite handsome with parquet floors and hand-decorated beds. As usual, there were also a number of rooms furnished in a more contemporary manner.

The Adler-Post is another example of a good, smallish German hotel that, because of its location in a resort area, has a mixture of both vacationers and business travelers. An outstanding feature of its menu is the many different cuts and preparations of venison. "There are many way to prepare it," said my host, "and I believe our chef knows most of them."

ROMANTIK HOTEL ADLER-POST, Hauptstrasse 16, 7820 Titisee-Neustadt. Tel.: 07651/5066 and 67. A 35-guestroom in-town hotel just a few minutes from the resort town of Titisee. Indoor swimming pool, sauna, solarium, and massage available in the hotel. Breakfast, lunch, and dinner served daily. Familie Ketterer, Innkeepers. Rates: See Index.

Directions: The Titisee area is in the upper Black Forest, 28 km. to the east of Freiburg. Titisee-Neustadt is about 3 km. east of the town of Titisee on Rte. 31.

HOTEL SPIELWEG, Münstertal (Black Forest)

Bright sunshine bathed the gentle spring morning with its warming goodness. I paused for a moment to breathe the marvelous Black Forest air and look out over the brook, across the deep valley and up the steep mountain, where a little girl was leading a cow along the mountain path. The sounds of the cow bell were clearly audible.

"Is it not beautiful?" I turned to look into the blue eyes of a very lovely lady who introduced herself as the mother of the innkeeper of the Hotel Spielweg. She suggested that we have breakfast together while she told me about the history of this attractive resort hotel.

"This is a very old house," she said. "It has been here since 1650. We built the new section several years ago." (In Germany I discovered that almost all of the innkeepers refer to a hotel or inn as the *haus,* or house.) "My son, his wife, and I are trying to preserve the very best of the old ways, while at the same time making improvements and progress with new methods. For example, here in the original building we have maintained the traditionally furnished rooms with painted doorways, antique beds, chests, and other furniture. In the new building, where you are staying, each accommodation has its own balcony, or terrace, overlooking the brook and the mountains. We know that a great many of our guests relish that wonderful feeling of being close to nature, so one whole wall of every room is of glass. However, perhaps you have noticed that the ceiling in your bedroom is wood and the beds are decorated with the

237

traditonal Black Forest flowers and other designs." (I will add a footnote here that my bathroom was an absolute joy.)

"Here in this building, we've made very few changes. That's my favorite pewter displayed on the plate rail and I'm very particular about even the the smallest detail. We place fresh flowers throughout the hotel, and our waitresses wear aprons and blouses made in the same styles that were worn in the middle of the last century."

She continued, "The holiday preferences for the average European family have changed considerably during the last thirty-five years, and so we have changed with the times. I have been here for

many years, and I sometimes cling to the old ways—fortunately, my son and his wife have joined me and they have shown me that new ideas make for better innkeeping. I think that we make an ideal threesome."

"The alpine and cross-country skiing nearby bring enthusiastic families who must be provided with recreation after a day on the slopes. That's why we have the game rooms and television rooms, and why we also built an indoor swimming pool as well as one outdoors."

After a most pleasant breakfast, we parted and I went out into the clear Black Forest spring morning to my room to pack my bags and continue my travels through Germany. I am already looking forward to my return trip.

ROMANTIK HOTEL SPIELWEG, 7816 Münstertal. Tel.: 07636/618 and 1313. A 42-guestroom resort-inn in the heart of the upper Black Forest region. Indoor and outdoor swimming pool on grounds. All Black Forest sports and outdoor activities within a few minutes' drive. Breakfast, lunch, and dinner served daily. Familie Stemmle-Fuchs, Innkeepers. Rates: See Index.

Directions: Locate Freiburg on map and then move your eye carefully south to look for "Belchen"—this is one of the highest Black Forest mountains. Münstertal is just above it.

HOTEL SONNE, Badenweiler (Black Forest)

According to my friend, Jen Diekmann, Badenweiler is an ideal place to recover from everyday stress and enjoy a good vacation. "It is the spa," he said, "where knowledgeable Europeans go who wish to have a quiet, tranquil vacation along with the thermal baths."

Let me advise you in advance that you cannot park in the middle of the town. There are free parking centers on the outer edges of the town, and one takes a bus into the centrum where it is so pleasant because there is no traffic.

I was now riding the bus and enjoying a conversation with another traveler who seemed to be quite informed about this resort community. "The most popular activity is the thermal baths," he said, "although I am sure that many people who visit here never go near them, as there are other things to do. There are some beautiful shops showing the latest fashions and several restaurants and hotels." As we got closer to the centrum, I realized that Badenweiler was a very sophisticated town.

The Sonne Hotel is near the *rathaus* (town hall) and is distinguished from the other hotels and pensions because of its traditional design—the building is 200 years old. The Fischer family, fourth-generation proprietors, reflected the sophisticated spirit of the town, and were most accommodating when it came to explaining the hotel and the ambience of the area. "It is so easy to drive almost any place in the southern Black Forest within a short time," declared Frau Fischer, "and there are many bus tours that leave on a regular schedule from Badenweiler to dozens of nearby points of interest."

The Sonne Hotel appears to be very comfortable. In particular, I was impressed with the large lobby that had many, many chairs and tables arranged to encourage conversation. The main dining room was rather formal; however, the two side dining rooms were decorated in the traditional Black Forest manner, and the wooden chairs even had hearts carved in their backs.

The rooms, most of them with balconies, overlooked the garden in the rear and there was also a terrace for sunbathing. As I recall, plans were in the works for an indoor swimming pool.

The Sonne Hotel appeals basically to people who are looking for a rest and perhaps a few days in and out of the famous baths, just a few steps away. Frau Fischer explained that it is indeed a very lively place with concerts, films, theater, folk singing, and many other types of live entertainment scheduled in the town on a continuing basis.

ROMANTIK HOTEL SONNE, 7847 Badenweiler. Tel.: 07632/5053. A 42-guestroom hotel located in one of the Black Forest's famous spa areas. Breakfast, lunch, and dinner served daily. Familie Fischer, Innkeepers. Rates: See Index.

Directions; Badenweiler is located at the southwestern edge of the Black Forest. It is a short distance north of Basel (Switzerland) and is accessible from the Autobahn running next to the Rhine.

Itinerary Number Three: *Frankfurt, southeast via Aschaffenberg, Buchen, and the Romantic Road. This itinerary includes some of the most picturesque and famous old towns of Bavaria.*

HOTEL POST, Aschaffenburg (Frankfurt)

Like others in Germany, the Hotel Post has a history as a stagecoach stop, and this background has set the theme for some of the interior decorations in the inn. For example, in the main dining room where I was enjoying my first lunch in Germany with Jens Diekmann and innkeeper Karl Seubert, there are many reminders of earlier days, such as several prints and ceramic tile paintings of old coaches. One of the most striking features is the *half* (actually) of a stagecoach, built into one corner of the main dining room. As innkeeper Seubert explained, "The whole coach would take too much space, so we split it in half and put it here for everyone to see." It is possible to open the door and step up on the driver's seat.

The outstanding menu of the Post has won a gold medal, not only for the rich and unusual design, but also for the orderly and easily understandable contents, most of which are in both German and English. It has sixteen pages with a center spread of extremely intricate paintings done in the Bavarian style. The richly decorated pages are done in the manner of an illuminated medieval manuscript.

Here are a few of the menu items that caught my eye. In the hors d'oeuvre section there was corn on the cob, smoked trout, frogs' legs, smoked salmon, and caviar. International soups included Hungarian goulash, turtle soup, Russian borscht, and Indian hotchpotch. There were several different types of salads, many eggs dishes, and a variety of fish, including river trout and sole meunière. The meats included pork cutlets, rump steak (very popular in Germany), leg of lamb, and several others. There were also venison and chicken.

After my first meal in Germany we took a tour of the hotel, which included an unusual dining room dedicated to Holland, be-

cause the innkeeper and his wife had been married there. In it were Dutch wooden shoes, Delft china, and ceramic figurines. The window paintings on glass were done after the manner of Rubens, Franz Hals, and Breughel.

This hotel has still another unusual feature—an indoor swimming pool. Two of the walls had saucy murals depicting life in medieval Bavaria.

The guest rooms looked very comfortable and tidy, and somewhat contemporary in furnishing; although, as was the case everywhere I traveled in Germany, I found the traditonal goosedown-filled comforters that are covered by a sheet and changed after each guest's stay.

Recently, my friend Karl Seubert has been succeeded by Eveline and Roland Hofer as innkeepers; however, Karl is often to be seen in the hotel.

ROMANTIK HOTEL POST, 8750 Aschaffenburg. Tel.: 06021/21333. A 100-guestroom midtown hotel about a half-hour drive from the Frankfurt Airport. An excellent, quiet accommodation for Frankfurt visitors. Breakfast, lunch, and dinner served daily. Indoor swimming pool. Eveline and Roland Hofer, Innkeepers. Rates: See Index.

Directions: From Frankfurt Airport follow Autobahn east to Aschaffenberg exit.

The Romantic Road

The Romantic Road links the River Main and the Bavarian Alps by way of some extremely picturesque old medieval towns. There is a complete description of it in the Michelin Green Guide to Germany and I am certain that the German Tourist Offices in North America will be happy to supply folders in English about this area and the other tourist areas in Germany.

I have described Romantik Hotels, either on or near this road, a much-traveled highway for Europeans heading south on vacation trips.

The Romantic Road begins in the old cathedral town of Wurzburg and continues through Rothenberg, Feuchtwangen, Dinkelsbuhl, Donauworth, Augsburg, and Landsburg, finally coming to an end at Fussen in the foothills of the Bavarian Alps.

HOTEL PRINZ CARL, Buchen (Romantic Road)

I'll always remember the Prinz Carl, not only for the fact that it was where I spent my first night in Germany, but because we all had such a wonderful, laughing time together. There was Jens Diekmann, innkeepers Werner and Elizabeth Ehrhardt, and Ilse and Bettina, their two very attractive young daughters. A third sister, Waltraut, was unable to be with us. We all quickly became acquainted and they were most courteous in attempting to speak English as much as possible. I, in turn, taught them two ersatz German-American words with which they were not familiar: "schuss-boomer" and "sitzmark." Everybody though this was most hilarious.

Furthermore, I am now a member of the famous *Goldener Kanne* Club. Jens Diekmann and I were both inducted by innkeeper Ehrhardt in a very touching ceremony that took place in the main dining room, amidst the congratulations and bravos of the other assembled guests and friends. In order to supply proof of membership, I now possess a scroll on which Herr Ehrhardt has written my name, and I am officially entered in the club rolls. In addition, I have a miniature golden *kanne* (stein) with a flip top.

The Ehrhardts have kept the Prinz Carl these thirty years, and Werner is the chef. He is particularly well known for the preparation of a saddle of venison and for a range of pastries that include tarts made from sour cherries.

That evening my dinner started with a tasty duck liver paté and then followed with their famous "green wheat" soup, also a house recipe. The next course was delicious french-fried shrimp with a Béarnaise sauce in which tomatoes had been mixed. The main course was medallions of veal served with artichokes, and we finished with everybody sampling two delicious desserts: a chocolate mousse, one of my favorites, and a very scrumptious ice cream cake.

The Prinz Carl was a post station for many years. Today, it is a most interesting combination of the old and the new. The dining room and the main reception hall are furnished in a traditional manner, as are several of the lodging rooms on the second floor. However, a new section has very attractive contemporary furniture, reminiscent of the Scandinavian style. My room, Number 22, was a studio room overlooking the roofs of the town.

When I left the following morning, the entire family gathered in the center hallway to speed me on my way. I was to have many a warm welcome and companionable experience at German inns for

the next several days; however, none would exceed the enjoyable time I had at the Prinz Carl.

There have been some interesting and expected changes since my last visit. I understand that the three daughters of the house are now married and are no longer at the hotel, although Frau and Herr Ehrhardt are still continuing their loving care of *CIBR* readers!

ROMANTIK HOTEL PRINZ CARL, 6967 Buchen/Odenwald. Tel.: 06281/1877. A 26-guestroom village inn, 50 km. south of Frankfurt. Breakfast, lunch, and dinner served daily. Riding, indoor and outdoor swimming, walks through the forest, boat rides on the River Main, and many castles nearby. Familie Ehrhardt, Innkeepers. Rates: See Index.

Directions: Locate Frankfurt on the German road map and then Heidelberg about 50 km. to the south. Buchen is east on Rte. 27. From Frankfurt the road through Miltenburg and Amorbach is very scenic.

HOTEL MARKUSTURM, Rothenburg ob der Tauber (Romantic Road)

"What is *stammtisch?*" I asked Marrianne Berger, while the two of us were seated in the reception hall of the Hotel Markusturm. We had just completed a brief tour of the many different lodging and public rooms of this truly old hotel. It was just a few moments before dinner.

"*Stammtisch,* oh you will see that in just a moment. I am sure that you will like it very much."

Her husband, Otto, and her daughter, Gabriella, and son, Stephan, joined us and we stepped into a most attractively decorated dining room. The waiters wore green vests, flowery white shirts, red ties, and black trousers. Otto explained that this was the Empire style, worn to commemorate the first 700 years of the freedom of the town. "This was celebrated in 1974," he explained, "but we decided that the men would continue to wear the costumes and the waitresses would wear theirs only on special occasions. Marrianne sewed eight costumes that year and they are all very beautiful and elaborate."

The Hotel Markusturm was constructed out of the first fortified wall of the city of Rothenburg, and is located where St. Marc's Tower, built in 1204, and the Roeder Arch (1330) formed one of the romantic corners of this medieval city. It is one of the most historic buildings in the town. The hotel served as barracks for soldiers who were assigned to duty in the tower. In later years it was both a brewery and a *gasthaus.*

Our meal started off with one of the specialties of the house, called *ratsherrimspiel,* consisting of various kinds of meats, onion, sausage, bacon, and other succulent things served on a skewer with potato croquets. It was served on a special plate that is only used for this particular dish. Gabriella and Stephan, who were studying English in school, explained to me that there were many other plates designed for special menu items at the Markusturm. "We have eight cooks in our kitchen," Stephan declared very proudly.

For dessert I had a local cheese that was very strong and peppery and came wrapped in a napkin. Marrianne insisted upon my sampling some sliced apples that had been dipped in a batter of meal and beer and then dropped in hot oil. They were delicious.

It was during this meal that I learned about the German custom of the *stammtisch*. While we were discussing the history of Rothenburg, one of their friends came to the edge of the table and knocked three times. Otto and Marrianne smiled and said, "Hello," and the man sat down at the table and lit his pipe. A few minutes later, another man did the same thing. About ten minutes later, a few more men came over, knocked, and we moved a little closer together so that everybody could sit down. Each time, I was introduced briefly, and we went on with our conversation, while some of them started their own.

Marrianne looked at me with a gay smile and said, "Now you know about the *stammtisch*. It is a custom at almost every hotel in Germany that there is a table where friends and the people of the town come to sit and talk and gossip, or just to be together. Instead of everyone standing up and shaking hands, which you know all Germans love to do, the newcomer simply knocks on the table and everyone says hello and he takes his place."

Before the evening had ended we had a dentist, a factory manager, a folk singer, a bricklayer, a couple from another town (who used to live in Rothenburg), and a bookseller.

A marvelous custom is *stammtisch*.

ROMANTIK HOTEL MARKUSTURM, ob der Tauber, Rodergassel 8803, Rothenburg. Tel.: 09861/2370. A 30-guestroom village inn. Breakfast, lunch, and dinner served daily. Sauna, solarium, garage (if desired). Familie Berger-Reinwald, Innkeepers. Rates: See Index.

Directions: Rothenburg is in central Germany, south of Wurzburg and west of Nurnberg. The Markusturm is about three squares from the town hall (hallestadt).

Rothenburg ob der Tauber

Rothenburg is a walled town, and like Maastricht in the Netherlands, as the town expanded and more walls were built, a series of walled rings were created around the city. Today, so zealous are the townspeople in preserving the ancient atmosphere and quality, that any construction or remodeling in the old part of town must conform to the old architecture. No modern buildings may be built.

The town history started around A.D. 900 and continued through fire, earthquake, and wars. One of these was the Thirty Years' War (1618-1648) when the town was besieged and conquered by three different armies.

There are many yearly events celebrated in the town, including the historic Shepherds' Dances, when members of the Shepherds' Guild meet in the afternoon to perform the historic dances in front of the town hall. The performance of farces, plays by the famous 16th-century shoemaker-poet, Hans Sachs, are also presented at Whitsun-tide.

Rothenburg has gates, churches, castles, fountains, museums, and old houses—all incredibly beautiful and well preserved.

One of the unusual sights is known as the Alte Rothenburg Handwerkerhaus, a remarkably restored and preserved house of a Rothenburg tradesman built in 1270. It contains eleven rooms from the ground floor to the attic, all furnished with original medieval furniture, and shows most graphically how large families, including grandmothers and grandfathers, lived and worked a few centuries ago. The furniture, utensils, stoves, fireplaces, toys, and clothing have all been thoroughly researched by the Berger family, the owners of the Hotel Markusturm. It is truly a glimpse into life in the Middle Ages.

HOTEL GREIFEN-POST, Feuchtwangen (Romantic Road)

I was standing in one of the dining rooms of this very old hotel, and Brigitte Lorentz was explaining the meaning of one of the five murals.

"The first one shows Kaiser Karl, who was out hunting in this area around A.D. 700. He became thirsty and saw a pigeon and followed it to a fountain. He was so enchanted that he caused a Benedictine monastery to be founded on the spot. There you can see King Karl and the pigeon and the fountain."

Other important turning points in the history of the region are also depicted in the murals, and in the final scene I saw a typical 14th-century marketplace scene, when Feuchtwangen flourished as a trade and corn market.

Brigitte and Edward Lorentz are continuing in the innkeeping tradition of Edward's grandfather, who transformed this 1599 building from a brewery gasthaus to a hotel. Most of the old feeling has been retained and there are walls with many exposed half-timbers on the second and third floors.

I discovered that the Greifen-Post is two hotels with a second-floor bridge connecting the Greifen to the Post. In the Post, the rooms are furnished in the tradtional manner, whereas in the Greifen, more modern furniture has been used.

Feeling as if I were stepping back into the Middle Ages, we returned to the main hallway and reception area, where Brigitte pointed out a scroll inscribed with names of such renowned early guests as Emperor Maximilian, who stayed here; Queen Christina of Sweden, who stopped on her way to Rome (possibly disguised as a

man). The mother of Queen Victoria of England was a guest in 1844, and Jenny Lind, the famous Swedish nightingale, also stopped off for lunch during a tour. Immediately next to the scroll was a notice that the chef at this hotel had won a medal at a recent exposition for preparing what Brigitte called a "farmer's dish."

We walked into the front dining room and discussed the various regional specialties on the menu, like the homemade soups, Bavarian liver and dumplings, goulash-and-garlic creamed soup, a recipe of Edward's grandmother.

"We cook everything with butter and cream, and only use fresh things," she declared. Other regional specialties include mushrooms in cream on toast with Bavarian cheese, and Franconian sausage served with sauerkraut.

Brigitte took me to one corner of the dining room where there was a mural showing a man in the forest confronting a wild boar. She translated the German saying just above the mural: "I would rather be with the wild pig in the forest then to be at home with my scolding wife."

ROMANTIK HOTEL GREIFEN-POST, 8805 Feuchtwangen. Tel.: 09852-2002. A 50-guestroom hotel on the market plaza. Breakfast, lunch, and dinner served daily. Very convenient to Rothenburg. Elevator, swimming pool, sauna, and solarium. Rates: See Index.

Directions: Feuchtwangen is on Rte. 25, a few km. south of Rothenburg.

HOTEL ROSE, Weissenburg (Romantic Road)

If glamour is supplied by guests who are theatrical and political celebrities, then the Hotel Rose in Weissenburg certainly qualifies as being glamorous. I took a look at the rather elaborate guest book under the watchful eye of its owner, Edgar Mitschke, and on the very first page I found that Chancellor Konrad Adenauer had been a guest here in 1957. There was also a most impressive number of television, theater, and musical stars, many of whom included their photographs as well as appropriate sentiments. It reminded me of the registers of old inns from the 19th century in the United States, in which itinerant theatrical troupes took advantage of the opportunity to do a little advertising.

Although Weissenburg is not a large city, the Hotel Rose has a "big city" atmosphere with a certain air of elegance about it. Some of the bedrooms, particularly those facing the square, are rather elaborately furnished. The single and double rooms in the back of the house were somewhat austere.

The *ratskeller* in this hotel dates back to 1320, and the arched brick ceilings have been whitewashed and decorated with animal skins. The light, furnished from candles, created a romantic atmosphere, and in one corner was a small, private fireplace that could supply extra romance for four people.

Over a cup of delicious hot chocolate with whipped cream, Herr Mitschke and I sat in the main dining room and discussed his elaborate menu which, in addition to offering local German specialties, apparently caters to international tastes as well. He explained that there are certain weeks in the year when they feature a particular kind of cuisine, such as French, Hawaiian, or Swiss.

ROMANTIK HOTEL ROSE, 8832 Weissenburg/Bayern. Tel.: 09141/ 2096. A 37-guestroom midtown hotel in a very busy central Bavarian town. Breakfast, lunch, and dinner served daily. Familie Mitschke, Innkeepers. Rates: See Index.

Directions: Weissenburg is on Rte. 2 south of Nurnberg and east of Feuchtwangen via many back roads. (Bring magnifying glass for map.)

Itinerary Number Four: *From Frankfurt east through Bemburg, Wirsberg, Bayreuth, Auerbach, and Munich.*

HOTEL ZEHNTKELLER, Iphofen (Romantic Road)

I have visited inns both in North America and Europe with many unusual features, but this is the first time I have ever visited an inn where an opera was written! A well-known German composer, Hans Pfitzner, composed it while he was a guest in this hotel in 1932.

I learned all this from Henry Seufert, the innkeeper. This hotel has been owned and operated by the Seufert family since the late 19th century. Henry is a very interesting man in his early forties and is proud of the fact that he has not only vineyards, but a winery as well. I found Henry's wine in other Romantik hotels in Germany.

The entrance to the Zehntkeller from the road is through an arched gate, and in the early German spring there were pansies and daffodils growing in pots and an old wooden wheelbarrow.

Inside the massive door, I approached the reception desk, which, with wonderful practicality, is right next to the service bar.

I walked about the inn, which at noon had a distinctly bustling air. The waitresses were hurrying back and forth with platters of delicious-looking food with tantalizing aromas. There were two rather small but very attractive dining rooms, both of which had paneling halfway up to the ceiling, topped with the characteristic plate rail with pewter, silver, and ceramics.

When Henry appeared, he and I plunged into history. The old building was originally a monastery, dating back to 1250, and later was occupied by the town tax collector. At the turn of the century it was acquired by the Seufert family.

We talked about the menu, and the specialties of the house included chicken in wine, mixed grill, venison, and duck. There are also several veal dishes. For dessert at lunch, I had sliced apples lightly sautéed with flour and cinnamon. I later tried them in my own kitchen.

Henry explained that this was an excellent stopover for people from Belgium, Holland, and northern Germany, who were headed for Austria or Italy. Many guests returned several times on these trips. Most guests stayed for just a single night. Slightly off the highway, it has a very restful air about it.

In the guest book of the inn, the composer of the opera did something rather novel—he wrote a few musical notes and the legend, "Here you have what you want." I have a feeling that many people have found the restful atmosphere, good food, and warm hospitality of the Zehntkeller exactly what they want.

ROMANTIK HOTEL ZEHNTKELLER, 8715 Iphofen. Tel.: 09323-3318 and 3518. A 40-guestroom inn about 1 km. off main highway. Breakfast, lunch, and dinner served daily. Familie Seufert, Innkeepers. Rates: See Index.

Directions: About 25 km. south of Wurzburg. (Rte. 8)

ROMANTIK HOTEL WEINHAUS MESSERSCHMITT,
Bamberg (Bavaria)

Bamberg is a rather sizable, attractive city with colorful old buildings, a river running through the middle of the town, and a shortage of parking spaces. Although I wasn't certain of the location of the Messerschmitt, I took my chances and rode right into the centrum—and there it was! I joined the rest of the German drivers and parked on the sidewalk.

The hotel has a look of antiquity about it, with wood-paneled ceilings, elaborate chandeliers, substantial furniture, many plants, and gleaming white tablecloths. The menu had quite a few specialties, including different varieties of soups and fish, as well as steaks and veal dishes; among an extensive selection of French and international entrées was Mexican rump steak.

The most tempting and largest dessert menu I think I have ever seen was called "La Dolce Vita" and featured all kinds of ice cream dishes, including banana splits, and quite a variety of crêpes; also coffee with heavy cream, and chocolate. It was tantalizing to someone with a sweet tooth like mine.

Equally tantalizing are the guest rooms at this Romantik Hotel. There are special weekend packages on art and gastronomy during November to March, also a three-day cookery course.

ROMANTIK HOTEL WEINHAUS MESSERSCHMITT, Lange Strasse 41, 8600 Bamberg. Tel.: 0951-27866. A 14- guestroom hotel, restaurant, and weinhaus in the center of a small, attractive German city. Lunch and dinner served daily. Familie Pschorn, Innkeepers. Rates: See Index.

Directions: Reaching Bamberg, follow signs to center of city and ask directions.

HOTEL POST, Wirsberg (Swiss Franconia; Bavaria)

Frau Herrmann and I were seated *in* a beer barrel. She was recounting the history of this hotel, high in the Swiss Franconia resort section of Germany, just a few kilometers north of Bayreuth. "My grandfather and grandmother came here and planted the oak tree across the street in front of the church," she said. She showed me some photographs of the inn at the turn of the century and also of her father and mother, who continued in the innkeeping tradition.

"I was born in Room 2," she said, and then added with a big

smile, "why that is the room you are staying in." Room 2 overlooks the triangular-shaped plaza of the town, around which are several shops. In one corner is a church whose bells peal every quarter-hour for twenty-four hours a day; I was a bit shaken at this information, but she assured me I would not hear them after I had gone to sleep, and I did not.

The hotel is furnished with both romantic and contemporary furnishings. My bedroom, as did most, included a television, a small honor-system refrigerator, and a bathroom heater, which I made good use of on a chilly April morning.

At dinner I enjoyed sliced venison served in a gravy-laden casserole with red cabbage and apple. "We have dishes from Alsace, Yugoslavia, and Mexico," she said. "We also have special weeks when we feature unusual international dishes."

She joined me for breakfast the following morning, and we continued my education on Germany. I enjoyed her very interesting observations, expressed in a combination of English and German. She suggested that I take a walk around the village and also the gardens of the modest castle, which her family was restoring.

Now, how did we happen to be seated in a beer barrel? Because, in one of the dining rooms, a booth that accommodates at least five people has been fashioned from a beer barrel. A decorative lamp hangs from the top, and seat cushions make it very cozy and comfortable.

ROMANTIK HOTEL POST, 8655 Wirsberg. Tel.: 09227/861. A 40-guestroom village hotel in the high hills, about 20 mi. north of Bayreuth. Breakfast, lunch, and dinner served daily. Wirsberg is at a very pleasant high elevation with many narrow but excellent roads for car touring and miles and miles of walking in the forest. Indoor swimming pool; outdoor swimming pool is nearby in the hills. Familie Herrmann, Innkeepers. Rates: See Index.

Directions: Wirsberg is a few miles west of Berlin-Nurnberg Autobahn (E-6). On the map look for Bayreuth and Kulmbach; Wirsberg is just off Rte. 303.

HOTEL GOLDNER LOWE, Auerbach (Bavaria)

I was seated in the *Knappenstube* with Frau Ruder. It was like having lunch in a coal mine—overhead were rough beams and planks supported by massive posts from which the bark had been stripped. The walls were rough, raw rock with the streaks of orange iron ore plainly visible.

"We here in Auerbach are very proud of the heritage of the iron miners," said Frau Ruder. "So, we have decorated this dining room to resemble the tunnels in the mines below the city. The word *knappen* is the German word for iron miners." She pointed out the many miners' lamps and tools, and even a big cart from the mines that had been used to bring up the ore in the mine shafts. Now, it was gaily decorated with greens and Easter eggs, a reminder of the holiday just past. There were several wrought-iron lamps and candleholders. In one corner was a statue of Saint Barbara, who, I understand, is the patron saint of iron miners.

The Goldner Lowe has been in existence since 1144, and until 1898, when a disastrous fire destroyed a great deal of the town, has occupied the same building. It was rebuilt on the same site, and there are some very interesting primitive paintings in one of the dining rooms showing both the old inn and the new. The Ruder family has owned it for almost a hundred years.

In the reception hall, there are some excellent primitive wood carvings of miners, showing the great strength of those men who worked beneath the earth.

Frau Ruder translated some of the original Bavarian dishes on the menu, including salted brisket of beef served with horseradish, pigs' knuckles, fresh trout, kept in a tank in the kitchen. For a rather unpretentious hotel, there were some surprisingly sophisticated dishes on the menu; I never cease to be amazed at the versatility of many of the chefs in these middle-class hotels, who are able to prepare dishes from all over the world.

One interesting dish on the menu is called *Knappen Toast*, pork steak, horseradish, and anchovies.

Guest rooms in the Goldner Lowe are furnished in both traditional and modern styles. Several have handmade furniture from local craftsmen. There are very pleasant views of the town. Everything is clean and wholesome-appearing.

Auerbach is not far from the city of Bayreuth, the site of the famous Wagner festival, and the Goldner Lowe would make an ideal quiet place to stop for a few days.

ROMANTIK HOTEL GOLDNER LOWE, 8572 Auerbach/Oberfalz. Tel.: 09643-1765. A 28-guestroom village inn in an old Middle Ages town. Breakfast, lunch, and dinner served daily. Familie Ruder, Innkeepers. Rates: See Index.

Directions: Auerbach is a short distance south of Bayreuth, about 10 km. east of the Berlin-Nurnberg Autobahn (E-6). Exit is marked Forcheim-Amberg.

HOTEL VILLA SOLLN, Munich

This small hotel, about fifteen minutes from downtown Munich, has twenty-five guest rooms with direct-dial telephones, television sets, and an inside swimming pool as well as a sauna, garden, and an unusually good breakfast.

HOTEL VILLA SOLLN, Wilhelm-liebl str. 16, 8000 Munich 71. Tel.: 089-792092/93. All reservations to the Villa Solln Hotel should be made directly with the hotel as it is not part of the Romantik Hotel chain. Rates: See Index.

Itinerary Number Five: *Munich, south to the Bavarian Alps and east to Lake Constanz.*

This itinerary includes part of the famous Alpine Road, where the traveler may continue into Austria. It leads from Garmisch through Oberammergau, skirting the northern edge of the mountains and continuing into Vangen and Lake Constanz.

CLAUSING'S POSTHOTEL, Garmisch-Partenkirchen (Bavarian Alps)

What a beautiful, sun-drenched, blue-skies morning in Garmisch! What a remarkable contrast to the day before, when snow fell upon the Bavarian Alps in mid-April just as it does in midwinter. Certain roads had been closed and it had been necessary to arrive in Garmisch by a different route.

I was having breakfast on the heated terrace at Clausing's Posthotel, where the hot spring sun had re-exerted its customary role and was beginning to melt the ten inches of snow that had accumulated on the tabletops and chairs of the outdoor section. Visitors and townsfolk alike were following the beckoning sounds of Sunday church bells.

I joined some new friends from Iowa whom I had met the night before, who were also traveling in Europe during the off- season.

The waitress brought me tea and a basket of assorted breads, along with a plate of sausage and cheese slices and pots of honey and marmalade. She explained my egg would follow. After a week in Germany I had come to enjoy these German breakfasts very much.

Clausing's, as it is called, is a busy, well-run hotel with a sophisticated, international, yet definitely Bavarian, flavor. My room was comfortable, but probably scheduled for remodeling in the future, and I saw several others that had a similar appearance.

There were a few quixotic touches. For example, during dinner a lady came through the dining room selling flowers, and hot on her

heels was a man in a business suit, wearing a Bavarian hat, taking photographs of the guests on request.

Henry Mike Clausing, the innkeeper and a fourth-generation hotelier, explained that about 85% of all the people who came to Garmisch each year are from Germany, although there is a U.S Army rest and recreation center here. Clausing's is very popular with American service families. It isn't large enough to accommodate the bus tours, so most of the guests are in groups of two and four. There were several families in the house enjoying the unexpected bonus of a weekend of late spring skiing. On Saturday night the discotheque nightclub had been running at full capacity, and I was happy to see that cheek-to-cheek dancing was still alive and well in Garmisch.

Clausing's has been many things to many people for many years—a place for honeymooning, anniversaries, and holidays in all seasons. Best of all, I think it is fun.

ROMANTIK HOTEL CLAUSING'S POSTHOTEL, Marienplatz 12, 8100 Garmisch. Tel.: 08821/58071. A 45-guestroom in-town hotel in one of Germany's most famous resort towns. Breakfast, lunch, and dinner served daily. Familie Clausing, Innkeepers. Rates: See Index.

Directions: Garmisch is about 1½ hrs. from Munich, also about ¾ hr. from Innsbruck, Austria. The map shows a choice of several roads.

Saturday Night in Garmisch

It was six o'clock on an April evening in Garmisch. The sun, which had been hidden behind the heavy snow clouds all day, was now providing us with some marvelous shots of gold on the top of the snow-clad mountain peaks which completely surround this Bavarian Alpine town.

An unexpected heavy snowfall provided Garmisch with another full weekend of skiing, and mingling with the German families dressed in traditional Bavarian garb were American servicemen pelting each other with snowballs.

There is lots of traffic on a Saturday evening in Garmisch, including Mercedes-Benzes with Munich plates, Porsches with U.S. Army plates, local town buses, and many taxis that shuttle back and forth to the train station.

The big attraction in Garmisch is the mountain peaks, like the Zugspitze at nearly 9,000 feet, the Dreitorspitze and the Alpspitze at 7,500 feet, and the Osterfeoderkopf at 6,000 feet. All of them have

many ski lifts, tramways, and cable cars. The 1936 Winter Olympic games were held here, and since then Garmisch has been one of the ski capitals of the world. There is also bobsledding, ice skating, and extensive cross-country skiing.

In summer there are the ubiquitous climbing, walking, and excursions. During the warm weather, lakes provide swimming and boating and the famous castles Linderhof and Neuschwanstein are nearby, as is also the village of Oberammergau, where the famous Passion Play is held.

I came to Garmisch in the spring, hoping for a glimpse of summer, instead found a generous helping of winter. It was like Christmas on the 4th of July!

HOTEL ALTE POST, Wangen (Bavarian Alps)

Herr Veile is a man who loves to smile and laugh. As far as I could see he had a great many things to smile and laugh about. For one thing, he and his wife, Louisa, have been keeping this hotel for over thirty years and it apparently has been prospering under their direction. It is located in a beautiful section of Germany, well within sight of the peaks of the Bavarian Alps and only a few kilometers from Lake Constance, which has many beautiful drives, homes, castles, and churches.

After meandering through the Bavarian Alps from Garmisch on

a beautiful Sunday afternoon, I arrived in Wangen, a baroque walled town, as the bells were tolling six o'clock. The bells of Wangen are still another story. I heard them ring many times, but couldn't make any sense out of them. One seemed to toll four times every hour, and in turn found a response in another deeper-toned bell that tolled the hour correctly. As soon as this duet was finished, a soprano bell took up the message, apparently just marking time.

The Alte Post, once a post stop, is located just outside one of the town gates, which has a very impressive clock tower. After a most refreshing bath and a short rest, I found my way to the second-floor dining room where quite a few people from Wangen were enjoying dinner. The atmosphere was very pleasant.

After being shown to a table, I was joined by a German businessman and his wife, who shared the table with me. We became acquainted quite easily, and again I was pleased with the custom in middle-class European restaurants of guests sharing tables when there are no other available tables.

After a most satisfying dinner that wound up with the specialty of the house, an ice cream cake with slivered almonds, I had a long visit with Herr and Frau Veile and learned that there is an annex about a half-mile away on an elevation overlooking the town. We made an appointment to look at it in the morning, and after a short tour of the guest lounge and the hallways, where I found many extremely interesting and attractive pieces of antique furniture, I enjoyed a good night's sleep under my down comforter.

The following morning Herr Veile showed me around the remainder of the house and modestly pointed out the fact that he had received an award as a *Kuchmeister,* which meant that he was a master of the kitchen.

The Alte Post Hotel is a beautifully decorated, well-furnished accommodation. It has an interesting history that goes back to 1409, 200 years before the formation of the German postal system in 1670.

Yes, Herr Veile has much to smile about.

ROMANTIK HOTEL ALTE POST, 7988 Wangen im Allgau. Tel.: 07522/4014. A hotel with 31 guestrooms in the main building, next to one of the walls of the town, and the annex, on a slightly higher elevation. Breakfast, lunch, and dinner served daily. Familie Veile, Innkeepers. Rates: See Index.

Directions: Wangen is on Rte. 18 approx. 30 km. from Lake Constanz. It is 2 to 2½ hrs. from Munich.

259

HOTEL WALDHORN, Ravensburg (Lake Constanz)

It was Monday morning in Ravensburg. The streets were enlivened by housewives with their shopping bags, and gentlemen of commerce were busy with the affairs of the day.

In the Hotel Waldhorn, the main affairs of the day seemed to be clean, clean, clean! In the front dining room there was a young lady standing on the table dusting off the plate rail and picking up every piece of pewter and china to give it a good swish. She even opened every decorative beer stein and wiped out the inside. Fresh flowers were being arranged on every table; the sweepers were sweeping; the vacuum cleaners were vacuuming.

I was enjoying a cup of tea in one of the dining rooms when I felt someone jump on the bench next to me and wag a friendly tail. "His name is Bimbo," explained my hostess, "he is also part of the family." The family in this case includes the innkeeper and his wife, along with his son and daughter-in-law.

Frau Bouley-Dressel showed me to the second floor, where the hotel was hosting an exhibition of chocolate manufacturers from Switzerland. I have never seen such an incredible collection of fanciful chocolate. I walked around several of the tables aching to pocket many of the tantalizing morsels.

We progressed to a series of guest rooms, most of which were very pleasantly furnished, several with television sets. We returned to the ground floor and I was asked to sit and have some refreshments where I could watch the activities of the morning.

Albert, the son, joined me and we had a brief discussion about some of the specialties of the newly remodeled kitchen, a splendid example of cleanliness and good organization. He explained that one of the policies of the house was to serve only fresh vegetables. "Nothing frozen or in cans," he said. Consequently, the menu is constantly changing according to the season. One of the popular dishes is chicken Bresse, cooked in a Burgundy wine sauce and served with Gruyere cheese. There is also lamb Bretaigne and many fresh fish dishes. I sampled the homemade goose liver paté and truffles, grown in the Strasbourg region a little to the north.

I was seated at what I learned was the *stammtisch* table in the front dining room with its paneled ceilings and walls and interesting carvings and ceramics.

ROMANTIK HOTEL WALDHORN, Marienplatz 15, 7980 Ravensburg. Tel.: 0751/16021. A 20-guestroom hotel in the center of a fairly large town. Quite convenient for many excursions both to the Lake Constanz region and the Alps. Breakfast, lunch, and dinner served daily. Familie Bouley-Dressel, Innkeepers. Rates: See Index.

Directions: Ravensburg is about 35 km. north of Lake Constanz via Rtes. 30 or 33.

HOTEL LANDGASTHOF FISCHERHAUS, Seefelden
(Lake Constanz)

A rooster was crowing. Soon another responded and for awhile it was a contest of wills and lungs. Roosters have been crowing, chickens clucking, and spring has been coming to this farmland for centuries. It is a gentle place on the shore of Lake Constanz in southern Germany, and much of it today is still being farmed or is in vineyards. The father and mother of innkeeper Roland Birkenmayer farmed it for many years and had a small inn nearby. In 1963, according to Roland's sister, Ella, who along with her brother and his wife, is an innkeeper at this quiet, restful resort hotel, the parents closed their smaller place in favor of the new Fischerhaus. It is next door to a farm and there are other farms and villas along the northern shore of the lake.

The hotel has three-and-a-half stories with typical German half-timbers and white plaster both inside and out. The two front dining

rooms have benches around the walls and one has a corner fireplace. They are low-ceilinged rooms with appropriate farm utensils decorating the walls.

Abovestairs, the fifteen lodging rooms have been recently redecorated, with gay curtains providing a marked contrast to the pristine white plaster walls and exposed beams. The rooms were most pleasantly furnished and had a view either of the lake and the flowering trees in the front or the hills in the back of the house.

When I remarked on the beauty of the birch trees, Ella replied, "Yes, our name 'Birkenmayer' actually is a reference to birch trees. Those were all planted about ten years ago."

In addition to lake sports, the principal ones of which are fishing and sailing on the lake, guests at this farmhouse-hotel also enjoy swimming in a heated outdoor pool. There is tennis, walking, and much touring of the area. It is excellent for families with children, and everyone gets acquainted very easily.

Roland is not only the hotelier, but also the only cook. The specialties of the house naturally include fish from the lake, such as perch, pike, trout, and eel. He also makes the desserts, including chocolate mousse, apple cake, and cheesecake.

It was a warm, spring afternoon when I bade farewell to Ella and Roland and their 300-year-old farm, which is now a resort inn. It was a very happy place.

LANDGASTHOF FISCHERHAUS, 7772 Seefelden/Bodensee. Tel.: 07556-8563. A 15-guestroom, 35-bed resort hotel on Lake Constanz. Breakfast, lunch, and dinner served daily except Monday. Swimming pool on grounds. Sailing, fishing, touring, walking nearby. (Not a member of Romantik Hotels. Make direct reservations.) Rates: See Index.

Directions: Seefelden is located on B-31, which runs along the north shore of Lake Constanz. The road east from Meersburg is marked "Uhldingen." From Switzerland, take the Konstanz-Meersburg Ferry and go west 7 km. on B-31.

My trip to Germany was particularly successful through the efforts of Jens Diekmann, the executive director of the Romantik Hotels. His encyclopedic knowledge of Germany, Austria, and Switzerland was most helpful, and I'm certain that readers contacting him in Karlstein will share my enthusiasm.

My very short stay in Munich was made most enjoyable by Hermann and Ellen Sendle, who showed me some of the interesting sights of this fascinating city by night.

A Few Suggestions About the Frankfurt Airport

It is necessary to go through customs twice, one for hand baggage and again for luggage from the airplane. Lufthansa has all its domestic and international flights in Hall A.

If you are going to the city of Frankfurt, a train is the fastest and most reasonably priced method.

When departing, non-residents are eligible for a refund of the V.A.T. (value added tax) if purchases exceed 100 marks. Fill out the form and have it stamped at customs.

Your rental car, particularly AutoEurope, can be picked up at the Frankfurt Airport.

INNS and LOCATION

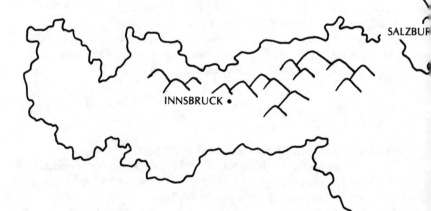

SALZBUR

INNSBRUCK •

AUSTRIA

TRAVEL SUGGESTIONS FOR AUSTRIA

How to Get There

There are several different airlines flying from North America to Vienna. I'd suggest that you talk it over with your travel agent. Eurailpass is also good in Austria.

Country Inns in Austria

Austrian country inns are delightful. Some are simple, less expensive pensions offering the opportunity to know Austrians more readily. The somewhat austere, but pleasant, clean, and comfortable rooms usually have two beds with a private shower and wc. Almost all overnight stays in a pension include a breakfast of rolls, butter, jam, tea or coffee. Many offer an evening meal (full pension), and special rates are available for longer stays.

Reservations

When a reservation is made for an Austrian accommodation, the agreement is very clear. The hotel owner or pension proprietor must hold the rooms, and the guest (unless he cancels) is positively obligated for the cost of the room. This is the law of Austrian innkeeping.

Reservations for accommodations in this book can be made by mail (a deposit helps) or by telephone.

Car Rentals

See section in front of book entitled "Renting a Car for Europe."

Driving Tips

Driving in Austria is the same as driving in Germany, although speed limits are different. Once again the back roads are beautiful and driving in the Austrian Alps is a marvelous experience. Austrian roads are kept in beautiful condition and it's possible to go everywhere in the country by car.

My Itinerary in Austria

I spent about six days in Vienna sightseeing and eating. Then I took the train to Graz, Semmering, and Baden.

Vienna Nights and Days

In every European city there are always "musts." In Copenhagen it is probably Tivoli Gardens; in London, the Changing of the Guard. In Vienna, the list is so long that there is a temptation to try to see everything. There is the Spanish Riding School, the Vienna Boys' Choir, and the opera. There are almost endless art galleries and museums. There are also the Vienna Woods, the many gardens, castles, memorial sites, and libraries.

There is also the Prater, over 1,300 acres on the Danube River. It is easy to find because it has a 210-foot-high Ferris wheel and the ride is something no one ever forgets. Some of the fun rides in the Prater are the most unusual ever devised by the minds of amusement park operators. It is said that Johann Strauss used to play at the various restaurants and his melodies are heard continually.

One of the most fascinating things about Vienna is the fact that the visitor can go almost everywhere by streetcar or public transportation. At 5 p.m., there were people in evening clothes riding the streetcars toward the center of the city to go to the opera, and at 11:30 p.m., the same people were riding back to the suburbs.

It is possible to go almost everywhere in Vienna and nearby on really well-organized sightseeing tours.

Dining in Vienna

Briefly, Viennese restaurants can be divided into several categories: first-class, middle-class (or restaurant "bourgeois"), the gasthaus or inn, the pub, the cellar, restaurants bon marché (for cheap meals), and specialty restaurants. Out-of-towners in Vienna can always be seen with two items in their hands—a Viennese restaurant booklet and a map of Vienna. I have discussed Viennese food more completely in describing my visits to various restaurants.

HOTEL RÖMISCHER KAISER, Vienna

This hotel belongs to the Romantik Hotels, a voluntary association of small historical hotels and restaurants, formed to provide an alternative to the standarized facilities of large hotels and catering groups. The reader will note that there are several Romantik Hotels in Germany in this book.

I liked this hotel immediately and was very happy to meet the young manager and his wife, who showed me proudly through many different rooms.

Some of the bedrooms were most romantic, indeed, with ornately carved beds and rather plush furniture. The building is quite old and therefore has higher ceilings and larger rooms than I found in some of the more recently constructed hotels.

I happened to drop by there again about eleven o'clock in the evening, and I found the night manager babysitting for two of the guests' children. He was a most affable man and explained that this was part of the informal service provided by the hotel.

ROMANTIK HOTEL RÖMISCHER KAISER, Annagasse 16, A-1010 Vienna. Tel.: 527751. A 27-guestroom hotel in the center of Vienna. Rates: See Index.

SAVOY HOTEL, Vienna

This hotel is located one block from the main shopping area. It has a rather small lobby with some very interesting prints. The only meal served is breakfast. It was here that I first saw an eiderdown comforter, the standard type blanket found almost everywhere in Austria. They are usually encased in cotton slip covers.

The general appearance of the Savoy is slightly more austere than the other two I visited.

SAVOY HOTEL, Lingengasse 12, A-1070 Vienna. Tel.: 934646. A 43-guestroom hotel just a short distance from downtown Vienna. Rates: See Index.

St. Stephen's Church

HOTEL KAISERIN ELISABETH, Vienna

Here is another small center-city Vienna hotel that is quite plush and elegant. The lobby is furnished with beautiful antique rugs, wall hangings, and elegant furniture. The hotel has been in existence since the 14th century and has a very impressive history of famous visitors.

The guest rooms are both modern and traditional.

HOTEL KAISERIN ELISABETH, Weihburggasse 3, A-1010 Vienna. Tel.: 0222/522626. A 130-bed hotel in central Vienna. Rates: See Index.

CAFE LANDTMANN, Vienna

It was chilly in the late afternoon and I was happy to succumb to the beckoning blandishments of the Cafe Landtmann, across the street from City Hall Park in the center of Vienna. It has marble-top tables and very spacious booths of different sizes. Everything has a turn-of-the-century look with walls of inlaid wood and ornate hanging brass lamps.

The cafe menu listed at least eight different kinds of coffee and they also served tea, chocolate, and milk. The menu, as in most restaurants, was printed in several languages. I ordered a cup of marvelous hot chocolate served in an old-fashioned cup. There is

A back street in Vienna

also a theater in this building and I looked at the playbill, which indicated that a new play was offered every two or three nights.

Occasionally, the headwaiter would bring around a most delicious selection of cakes and pastries with great mounds of mocha filling and mocha cream icing.

Now the tables were filling up and more people were coming in. It was the end of the day and the beginning of a gay Viennese evening.

CAFE LANDTMANN, Dr. Karl Lueger Ring 4, A-1010 Vienna. Tel.: 639128. A typical Vienna cafe open daily from 9 a.m. to 11 p.m. Immediately across the plaza from Town Hall (Rathaus).

❋   ❋   ❋   ❋

WIENER RATHAUSKELLER, Vienna

I left the Cafe Landtmann and wandered across the park to the Town Hall, known as the *Rathaus*. It was built between 1872 and 1885, and has carved figures all around the fourth story of the building. A huge clock was pointing at six o'clock.

The doors opened promptly and I went downstairs into the Rathauskeller, one of the famous tourist restaurants in Vienna. I was in the cellar where there was a vaulted ceiling, beautifully carved chairs, many murals, and the sound of music in the background. There were various dining rooms off a long hallway, some of them decorated for parties. In the middle of this hallway I saw a large glass tank filled with fish.

One of these rooms is known as the *Grinzinger Keller* where, on each table, there are most unusual wine decanters that look like gigantic medicine droppers. The music I heard was coming from the four musicians at the other end of the dining room. I was told that the atmosphere made this room very popular with the Viennese and visitors.

The menu was typical of many Viennese restaurants, with quite a few schnitzels and other Austrian dishes featured.

WIENER RATHAUSKELLER, Rathausplatz 1, A-1010 Vienna. Tel.: 421219. A popular "middle class" tourist restaurant in the cellar of the Vienna Town Hall. Open for lunch and dinner. Closed Sundays.

The Vienna Opera House

THE THREE HUSSARS, Vienna

I had been told that this was one of the supreme restaurants, not only in Vienna, but in all of Europe. It is located just off the main shopping plaza not far from St. Stephen's Church, which along with the opera house is the center of Viennese downtown activity.

Here was genteel Vienna at its very best. The restaurant was rapidly filling up with well-dressed, confident-looking people, both Viennese and visitors, all of whom seemed very much in place in this rather elegant atmosphere. My table was decorated with a small plant and a lighted candle.

The one thing that everyone always talks about when the Three Hussars enters the conversation is the hors d'oeuvres. There must be at least fifty different varieties and they are all expertly moved by a waiter from table to table on a series of four carts.

I eventually settled for a delicious chicken served Hungarian style, one of the specialties of the house. For dessert I had something that probably could only be born in Vienna. I am not sure it has a name but it consisted of fresh peaches and strawberries intermixed with chocolate whipped cream and nuts.

The Three Hussars is a great adventure in Viennese eating.

THE THREE HUSSARS (Zu den 3 Husaren), Weihburggasse 4, A-1010 Vienna. Tel.: 521192. A "first class" restaurant especially famous for its hors d'oeuvres. Dinner only. Closed Sundays.

GRIECHENBEISL, Vienna

I visited this very old restaurant in the market district of Vienna on a Sunday morning after church. There was a wedding party in progress with gay accordion music, and everyone was having a very good time.

I was shown to a small table in one corner where I had a vantage point from which to watch all of the people arriving for the noontime meal. All around me were coins embedded in the walls and here or there was a hole where apparently someone had acquired a souvenir.

The restaurant is made up of many different rooms, some with very low doors, necessitating tall people to stoop as they enter. The furniture, tables, chairs, and fixtures all give the appearance of being antique.

Long before I visited it, I heard it mentionted as the place Mozart frequented. I discovered that not only Mozart, but Beethoven, Schubert, Wagner, Strauss, Brahms, Mark Twain, and Count von Zeppelin had also been guests.

Naturally, a restaurant like this is well known and quite a few visitors find their way to it during a visit to Vienna. I had an excellent cup of hot chocolate and a piece of Viennese pastry for lunch.

The little booklet in English, distributed to each patron, indicates that apparently there has been an inn on this site since 1447. It was once built into the high wall of the outer defenses of the city against the Turks.

GRIECHENBEISL, Fleischmarkt 11, A-1010 Vienna. Tel.: 631977. A "middle class" restaurant two blocks behind St. Stephen's Church. A well-known tourist attraction. Open every day from 10 a.m. to 1 p.m.

ZUR STADT KREMS, Vienna

This little restaurant of three stars was a dandy experience for me. For one thing it had great numbers of young people enjoying dinner. It was obvious that they were students since it is in the university area. The food was exactly what I had seen on the menus of other Viennese restaurants, but considerably less expensive.

It is quite common in a restaurant of this type to be joined at the table by other people if other tables are filled. In my case I was joined by a very nice Austrian couple who spoke enough English to allow us, with my rather frayed German, to have a good conversation about Vienna, Austria, traveling, the United States, and many other subjects.

The lady explained to me that she and her husband came here frequently, but they also enjoyed other restaurants in the area. She felt that they were a typical retired couple who ate out at a modest restaurant three or four times a week. She said that the food here was very good.

By the time the evening had wound up we had had several conversations with the students at the next table, who were very fascinated by the idea that I was writing a book including my Austrian experience in country inns. Some of the students who lived outside of Vienna made some good suggestions.

At this restaurant I had my first sampling of Hungarian goulash and I am certain that it is served in no other place as it is in Vienna.

ZUR STADT KREMS, Zieglergasse 37, A-1070 Vienna. Tel.: 937200. A pub or bistro restaurant featuring family-style food. Also popular with students. Dinner only. Closed Sunday and holidays.

Graz—The Natural City

Almost from the moment of my arrival I felt that Graz had been a great choice of Austrian cities to visit. It was an almost completely "natural" city, neither self-consciously preening itself for tourists nor dominated by some tremendous scenic attraction, such as high mountains or picturebook lakes. I found that it had dozens of extremely interesting scenic and cultural attractions, but on the whole it was relatively undiscovered as far as tourists are concerned.

Graz is the capital of the province of Styria and the second largest city in Austria with about 239,000 inhabitants. It is situated at the eastern border of the Alps on both sides of the River Mur, about three hours southwest of Vienna by train.

My guide was a young woman who was a student at the university. Incidentally, this guiding service is available at all times through the Graz Tourist Office.

We walked across the river into the Old Town, and immediately I was struck by the many different architectural styles. As she explained, Graz is actually one of the oldest cities in Europe and has one of the best-preserved Renaissance environments.

We walked into the town square, where there were a number of market stalls selling hot chestnuts, soft drinks, fruit, fish, produce, candy—just about everything. Around the square I saw some extremely interesting houses, many of them with handpainted facades. There were all kinds of small cafes and sweet shops around the plaza and on nearby streets.

One of the most impressive sights in Graz is the Landhaus, built in the middle of the 16th century. Its striking three-story inner courtyard is the scene of many pageants.

We walked up the castle hill to the famous clock tower, the Uhrturm, the symbol of Graz, and from the vantage point of the Herberstein Gardens, the panorama of the city stretched out below us. By this time we were both ready to take a few moments rest and enjoy a cup of hot chocolate.

Later that evening, I walked back into the Old Town again, through the town square. The stalls were all shuttered and the stores were all closed. It was a very quiet and peaceful time. The fire engines came through the pedestrian plaza without even sounding their sirens.

I paid a visit to one of the cafes, and once again experienced people joining me at my table when all the other tables were filled. We all started talking to one another almost immediately, the accordian player struck up a few tunes, and quite a few people began to sing. It was a fitting conclusion to an enjoyable day.

HOTEL WIESLER, Graz

It was a warm, sunny early spring day when the train arrived in Graz. I inquired at the Tourist Information Office at the station about the best way to go the Hotel Wiesler.

A few minutes later I had registered and met the innkeeper, Peter Wiesler. He invited me to one of the spacious parlors of the hotel to spend a few minutes before lunch. I liked this very generous and outgoing man immediately. He is the seventh generation of his family to own the hotel and they are one of the oldest innkeeping families in Styria, the name of this province of Austria.

The dining room had a high ceiling with exposed beams and graceful paneling halfway up the wall. A plate rail had many old

The Landhaus, Graz

decorative platters, plates, and pictures. All the waiters were dressed in black suits, starched white shirts, and black ties.

The menu for the midday meal, which is quite substantial, had quite a number of Austrian specialties and a surprising number of international dishes as well.

For lunch I decided on a beef dish served with a delicious horseradish sauce and German fried potatoes. Peter explained that this was one of the favorite dishes of Emperor Franz Josef.

There are eighty-eight rooms in the hotel. Those on the top floor were remodeled and modernized a number of years ago. They have a striking view of the famous Graz Tower and the Old Town (Graz).

Other rooms have high ceilings, parquet flooring, and old-fashioned furniture. About two-thirds of the rooms have private wc's.

That evening I joined the other hotel guests, as well as some of the townspeople, in the hotel coffee shop for a light meal.

That night, after settling down into my comfortable bed and reviewing the events of the day, I was convinced that Graz was one of the most interesting experiences I ever had.

HOTEL WIESLER, Griesgasse 4-8, 8020 Graz. Tel.: 913240. A very comfortable family hotel well within walking distance of most of the sights and attractions of Graz. Rates: See Index.

PARKHOTEL, Graz

This very pleasant hotel is in a quiet section of the old city within easy walking distance of the opera, theater, the university, and the Music and Fine Arts Academy. It has been completely modernized in a comfortable, restrained style. My guide and host was a very knowledgeable young man, named Mr. Florian, and he explained that he and his mother and father, Elizabeth and Herbert Florian, were the owners of the hotel. He had finished his law studies, as well as the hotel school of Vienna.

True to its name, the hotel overlooks a very pleasant park, on the same spot where it has been standing for more than 400 years. It was known for centuries as the Golden Pear.

We sat for some time in the tastefully furnished coffee shop talking about the many cultural opportunities and advantages in Graz. Then we went for a short tour of the hotel.

The first floor has a lobby with contemporary furniture, and one of the living rooms opens out into a garden, where meals were served during warm weather.

Lodging rooms were quite large, and most of them have windows overlooking the park in front or the garden in the rear. Mixed in with contemporary furniture are suits of armor and old tapestry. It makes for an interesting blend.

I liked the spirit of youth and vitality here. Like the Hotel Wiesler it would be an excellent place to stay during a visit to Graz.

PARKHOTEL, Leonhardstrasse 8, A-8010 Graz. Tel.: 0316/33511. A 65-guestroom hotel with modern furnishings. Rates: See Index.

Semmering—My Own Hidden Place

Austria will always have a very special niche in my memory. It was the first country I visited in Europe, and Vienna was the first large city. Graz was the first "natural city," and now Semmering was the first "country" experience.

I arrived on a sunny morning after an overnight snowfall. The train ride from Graz had been through the beautiful Alpine foothills, with those remarkable little Austrian villages built along the sides of rushing streams and upland pastures.

I was the only passenger to alight at Semmering and the railroad station was entirely deserted. I had been told that someone would meet me, so I poked around the station awhile, reading the posters. Finally a taxi arrived but the driver did not speak English. So, off we went on the snowy road, curving upward into the village, and stopping in front of the Pension Belvedere.

PENSION RESTAURANT BELVEDERE, Semmering

I will never forget Magda Engelschall. She and her husband are the innkeepers at the Belvedere. From her I received the most heartwarming introduction to Austrian country hospitality that anyone could desire. The first thing she did was to bring me inside, seat me in a booth and get me a cup of marvelous hot chocolate. She even paid the taxi driver and told me not to worry, we could settle it later. We sat for some time in front of a big picture window overlooking the snow-filled valley with ski-tow areas visible on the other side. I explained to her that I was visiting some out-of-the-way places in Austria to put in a book about inn accommodations, and her face lit up immediately with a beautiful smile. "We have heard about you. I know exactly who to call. Everything will be all right."

In the meantime, I finished my hot chocolate and she conducted me on a short tour of the pension.

The exterior is of a typical Austrian design, with roofs that are made to support considerable amounts of snow, and rooms that have balconies so that guests may enjoy the mountain scenery in any season.

"I'm sorry that it is the wrong season for you to see our garden," she said. "Our guests love to sit out there in the warm weather and also on our terrace in the sunshine. We have many flowers."

The Belvedere is a combination restaurant and hotel, classified as a pension. Magda explained that it is a popular meeting place for all of the people who live in the vicinity and that most of the menu is made up of regional food.

The guest rooms are similar to those that I subsequently found in other pensions—neat and clean, but with no particular style. Most of them have twin beds with those marvelous eiderdown-filled comforters.

Before my Austrian travels were finished I was to meet many other owners of inns and pensions and hotels. I found them generous, understanding, and hospitable. Magda really extended herself

279

to make me feel comfortable. She represents all of the good things about Austrian hospitality. I'm sure that visitors expecting an enjoyable experience in Austria will find their Magdas everywhere.

I have heard from Magda quite regularly since that visit, and it seems that every year some people from America visit because of my story. She tells me that the Belvedere now has an indoor swimming pool and sauna, and all of the guests are enthusiastic about the food.

PENSION BELVEDERE, 2680 Semmering. Tel.: 02664/270. A very cordial restaurant and pension. Breakfast, lunch, and dinner served daily. Rates: See Index.

GARTENHOTEL ALPENHEIM, Semmering

With thirty-eight rooms, this was one of the largest of the hotels and pensions I visited in the Semmering area. It is actually two buildings in one, with more traditional, Austrian-style dining rooms and guest rooms in the old building, and lounges and guest rooms in a more modern style in the newer building.

One of the features of this place is an indoor swimming pool with big, sliding glass windows that create the effect of being outside. There were four or five people swimming, including some children. The garden, which accounts for the "Garten" portion of the name of this inn, was under the snow, but I could see through the windows that it extended some distance into the fields and forests.

280

It was Mr. Steiner who explained to me that Semmering is indeed a year-round resort, with skiing during the winter and a great number of summertime activities taking over in the warmer weather, including tennis, golf, bowling, horseback riding, the ever-present hiking, of which all Europeans seem to be very fond, and many other recreations.

GARTENHOTEL ALPENHEIM, 2680 Semmering. Tel.: 0 26 64/322. A bustling, family-operated inn. Rates: Ssee Index.

Baden

Baden is a small city of 25,000 people, which can be reached from Vienna by a number of ways, including streetcars. I immediately liked its small-town feeling and its many gardens and parks.

From the beginning of the 19th century, Baden was a center of social and intellectual life. From 1803 to 1834, it was the summer residence of the Hapsburg Court.

The Spa Park and the Doblhoff "rosarium" are filled with thousands of roses during the summer. Walking paths lead from the city up into the hills and out to nearby castle ruins. The famous Vienna Woods are not far away.

My afternoon of wandering in Baden took me to the pedestrian zone in the center of the town, where no automobiles are allowed. There is a feeling of space and freedom for the stroller. Around this zone are several attractive buildings, many with historical implications. One is the Beethoven House, where the Ninth Symphony was begun; another is the Civic Theater.

For entertainment in Baden there are regular concerts by a symphony orchestra and operettas in the open air all summer. The Baden theater plays throughout the winter.

In the center of the pedestrian zone there is a three-story statue, erected by the people of the town to commemorate the fact that Baden was not besieged by the infamous plagues during the Middle Ages.

PENSION WEILBURG, Baden

As I understand it, only a technicality of the regulations concerning accommodations places this handsome small hotel in the pension category. It has had a connection with the Bakers' Congress for centuries and the outside of the building has murals showing bakers at work, kneading dough and removing bread from the oven.

Inside, the rooms are much larger than the average pension, and on the top floor there is a group of rooms furnished in Austrian country antiques.

PENSION WEILBURG, Weilburgstrasse 37, A-2500 Baden. Tel.: 02252/43011. Rates: See Index.

I must apologize for doing a grave injustice to the city of Baden, with only a single listing. The fact is that there are all kinds of hotels, pensions, and other types of accommodations. The list of hotels, obtainable from the Tourist Office in Baden, includes at least sixty. Baden is more a place where Austrians themselves come to enjoy a holiday. It is so convenient to Vienna that Americans can make a day trip or two and enjoy the entertainment and attractions of the city, while stopping in Vienna. Whether one stays for the day or for several days, Baden is well worth a visit.

NOTES

SWITZERLAND

INNS and LOCATION

284

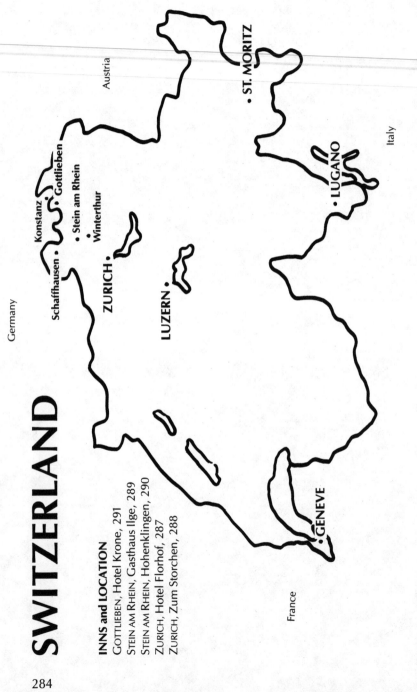

Germany

Austria

Konstanz

Gottlieben

Schaffhausen

Stein am Rhein

Winterthur

ZURICH

LUZERN

GENEVE

France

LUGANO

ST. MORITZ

Italy

TRAVEL SUGGESTIONS FOR SWITZERLAND

How to Get There

PanAm and Swissair have frequent flights to Switzerland. Your Eurailpass is good in Switzerland.

Kloten Airport, Zurich

With admirable Swiss efficiency, visitors arriving at Kloten Airport can deplane and descend to the railroad station and platform with their luggage. There is no charge for carts, and baggage can be transferred to the railway immediately following customs. Porters wear blue uniforms with a Swissair badge.

There are two ways to get to the center of Zurich. One is by train, which takes about ten minutes, with frequent departures, and costs about three dollars. However, the airport station provides connections to many points in Switzerland. The taxi to downtown Zurich is about fourteen dollars.

Country Inns in Switzerland

In Zurich for a short stay, I was so enchanted with my brief glimpse of this picturesque country that I felt I must devote a small section of the book to introducing Switzerland to my readers, with the promise that many more inns will be added in subsequent editions. I know that there are countless small inns tucked away in mountain villages, towns, suburbs, and even in large cities. If you want to strike out on your own, look for signs that include the words gasthaus, gasthof, or wirtschaft—these places will serve food and usually will have rooms. In the French-speaking sections, the word for inn is auberge, and the Italian is albergo.

Invariably, in a small inn, where the rooms are always dependably neat and clean, the chef is the owner, and his or her reputation is dependent on the quality of the food, which I have been told is excellent and impeccably served.

I encourage you to explore this country and discover for yourself the warmth and hospitality of its people

Traveling in Switzerland

Switzerland probably has the most orderly driving in Europe, and certainly has one of the best road systems in the world. Most roads are kept open even in the worst winter weather; however, snow tires or chains are needed in the mountains, and it is best to check ahead on road conditions in the Alpine passes.

While renting a car makes getting around easier, distances are very short in Switzerland, and the entire country can be traversed by express train in about four hours. Trains are clean, fast, and always right on time. They can provide some of the best traveling alternatives and some spectacular touring. Detailed information may be obtained through the Swiss National Tourist Office, which has branches in the United States in New York, Chicago, and San Francisco. The New York address is 608 Fifth Avenue, NYC 10020; telephone: 212-757-5944.

Swiss Menus

Breakfast is not a big meal for the Swiss and will rarely be more than the coffee-with-rolls variety. For cereal eaters, sometimes the national cereal staple, muesli, is available on request.

Tearooms abound, with all kinds of marvelous pastries that can be enjoyed at small tables or taken out to be eaten while sitting on a park bench.

Cheese may very well be what Switzerland is all about, and you will find every area has its own special kind. There are restaurants that specialize in fondues; raclette, a hard cheese, is served hot with a boiled potato and pickles. Geschnetzeltes und Rosti, slivered veal in cream sauce, with a pan-fried potato cake, is probably a national dish.

Menus in out-of-the-way places won't be in English, so sign language usually has to suffice. If you want to see a menu, ask for the Karte. The word menu means the specialty of the day, and that's what you will get if you say it.

Introduction to Switzerland

Switzerland is the heart of Europe, the ideal place to start a trip on the Continent. The two main gateways are Geneva and Zurich, each with its own immense lake and pretty ring of mountains; each beautiful in its own right . . . two quiet, refined cities, very cultural, with a high interest in the arts . . . two strange cities where, unlike other capitals, everything works.

Switzerland is like a gigantic music box, minutely tuned. It is a country as serene and peaceful as its most majestic mountains. Don't think you'll be bored, because even the tiny villages are extremely lively and well worth all the time you'll be able to spend there.

I decided to take this short trip around Zurich, which is, if possible, more Swiss than Geneva, a more puritanical and sober city—"So clean," James Joyce commented, "that if you spilled your soup on the Bahnhofstrasse (the "Champs Elysées" of Zurich), you could eat it up without a spoon." While it is true the "Athens of the Limmat" has a friendly, orderly, and hard-working population, it is also true that there are high-class restaurants, discotheques, shops, three outstanding museums, and that this city is the starting point for myriad enchanting excursions.

In fact, the city inhabitants are so welcoming that they have set up a system called "Meet the Swiss," which offers any tourist wishing to visit a Zurich family the possibility to do so—free of charge, of course. You only need to ask the Tourist Office for a list of local hosts happy to invite visitors from other countries into their homes for dinner. A starting point for discoveries and new friendships!

HOTEL FLORHOF, Zurich

Those who like small hotels will appreciate the Florhof. It possesses all the qualities of a vanishing type of establishment, with a pleasant, just off-center location, quiet surroundings, good service, and good food. An 18th-century patrician building, remodeled ten years ago to provide each of the thirty-three rooms with bathrooms, the hotel still retains some of its ancient atmosphere. Most noteworthy are the ceramic stove with decorative old tiles in the dining room and, on the ceilings of the rooms, the extraordinary plaster moldings in elaborate baroque designs. Both bear witness to the past grandeur of this house.

HOTEL FLORHOF, Florhofgasse 4, 8001 Zurich. Tel.: 01-47-44-70. A 33-guestroom (private baths) unpretentious hotel in a classic building on the bank of the Limmat River. Open year-round. Mr. Schilter, Manager. Rates: See Index.

Directions: Ten min. from railway station.

ZUM STORCHEN, Zurich

Paracelsus, Richard Wagner, and Gottfried Keller knew the Stork, as well as many other famous and unkown visitors, in its six centuries of existence. I walked into the lobby, heavily burdened with large packages filled with all the marvelous objects I'd bought at Heimatwerk, an extraordinary shop specializing in Swiss crafts close to the hotel. I was welcomed into the warm and animated lobby by a helpful porter, who instantly helped me with my load. Amiable and efficient people at the reception desk checked me in and gave me all the information I requested, before taking me up to my room.

Strangely enough, although this hotel had been thoroughly rebuilt in the forties and has been remodeled since, it has more of a

genuine Swiss atmosphere than older, unremodeled places—tradition does carry a spell. The history of the hotel, which starts in the middle of the fourteenth century, would fill a volume.

The restaurant (*rotisserie*) is one of the best in town. Very well decorated with lots of attractive wood and comfortable chairs, it offers a carefully selected choice of local and some international dishes. The big spécialité is venison, in season, of course. My dinner there started with thin slices of smoked young wild boar ham served with fresh figs. I then tried and finished the deer steak with red currants, chives, and green noodles, a very tasty combination. For dessert I chose something also in season, an unusual pasta—a long, fat vermicelli of chestnut paste, all in a tangle on a meringue, and topped with whipped cream. I can only say one thing: try it.

ZUM STORCHEN, Weinplatz 2, 8001 Zurich. Tel.: 211-55-10. Telex: 81-33-54. A 55-guestroom famous, 600-year-old, traditional Swiss hotel (all modern conveniences) overlooking the river. Rates: See Index.

Directions: Within walking distance of the railway station.

Stein am Rhein

From Zurich, I took a train to Stein am Rhein, a tiny medieval city on the Rhine River, a lovely, lively townlet with colorful, painted facades and extraordinarily well-preserved architecture. If I were arriving from the United States, I would drive there straight from the airport and spend a comfortable day or two at Ilge to settle down to the new feeling of old, quiet Continental Europe.

Stein am Rhein is a real fairyland. The frescoes on the buildings, the buildings themselves, the flowers, the ducks and swans on the river, the chocolate in the chocolate shops, the cows and sheep in the fields, the trees in the forest, the people in the street, and even the food on the plates in the restaurants—all are actually real.

I spent a bright and sunny day there at the beginning of fall. The sky was an intense blue, and a strong, whirling wind carried the old leaves away and wrinkled the waters of the river.

GASTHAUS ILGE, Stein am Rhein

This is a warm and very human place, always a bit noisy and smoky, never empty because the clientele is mostly local. A real inn, in our sense of the word, complete with a welcoming hostess,

Rosemarie Benker. She and her husband, Hermann, took over this place six years ago after running the local youth hostel for a long time. Recently, they transformed the second floor of the house into four homey rooms overlooking the neighboring rooftops. A most romantic place, where it is wise to make reservations in advance.

The restaurant, Hermann's domain, provides hearty meals of *kalbsleber* (liver of veal), *rosti* (a special kind of grilled potatoes), and good soups and salads. Don't forget to try the Russian chocolate, *russische schokolade* (hot chocolate with vodka and cream).

GASTHAUS ILGE, CH 8260 Stein am Rhein. Tel.: 54-41-22-72. A 4-guestroom lively but homey inn with a good restaurant. Advance reservations advisable. Rosemarie and Hermann Benker, Innkeepers. Rates: See Index.

Directions: From Zurich, take the highway to Schaffhausen. Turn off to Stein am Rhein.

There is a pretty path through the vines and the woods, climbing up the hill from Stein, towards the fortress of Hohenklingen. In the fall there are lots of hazelnuts and walnuts on the ground that, along with some excellent pears, provided me and a friendly sheep with a healthy midmorning snack.

BURG HOHENKLINGEN RESTAURANT, Stein am Rhein

It takes approximately half an hour to reach this fortress if one stops to rest on a bench conveniently placed halfway up the hill, with a wide view of the town and the river.

Built in 1050, it has been in the possession of the bourgeois of the town of Stein since 1457. It was then used as a watchtower against possible attacks, and the means of the warning was a huge bell, hence the name, "Hohenklingen," which literally means "high ring." In 1860, the perils apparently over, the town council converted it into an inn, and they still run the place as such nowadays. It has some of the very few authentic, turn-of-the-century decorations I've seen in the area—wood-paneled walls covered with trophies, flags, and other paraphernalia of hunting or conquest. It is an interesting place for a simple lunch in the preserved atmosphere of a 19th-century inn.

HOHENKLINGEN, CH 8260 Stein am Rhein. A town-owned fortress-restaurant on top of a hill overlooking the town and the river. Ask the hotel to make reservations.

Directions: Either drive or walk the 3 km. up the hill above Stein am Rhein.

HOTEL KRONE, Gottlieben (Lake Constance)

It was raining on the Rhine. In this rain, the abundant flowers seemed to burst from their buds. The pots of pansies, daffodils, and other flowers on the terrace in front of the Hotel Krone, directly overlooking the river, were persisting gaily in spite of the grey sky. There were ducks and swans swimming in the river.

For dinner, I decided on a small steak cooked in a horseradish sauce with generous amounts of black pepper and homemade noodles. Delicious. For dessert I asked for something with chocolate, and the couple at the next table suggested a large goblet containing three scoops of vanilla ice cream and a pitcher of hot chocolate on the side. I ate every last bite.

I struck up a conversation with my benefactors. He was a businessman who preferred to stay at the Krone when he came to Konstanz because, he said, "It is very tranquil."

All of the guest rooms in this hotel have been converted from the old-fashioned romantic theme to a more contemporary feeling. They are quite a contrast to the traditional furnishings in the public rooms.

I wandered around before dark and found Gottlieben to be a very pleasant, quiet town. There was a fascinating boatyard just a few steps away from the hotel, where large luxury boats are built, apparently for use on the Rhine. Gottlieben is also a stop on the regular Rhine River boat lines.

ROMANTIK HOTEL KRONE, 8274 Gottlieben, Bodensee, Switzerland. Tel.: 072/692323. A 25-guestroom hotel on the banks of the Rhine near Konstanz, Germany. Contemporary guestrooms are clean and comfortable. Breakfast, lunch, and dinner served daily. Familie Schraner-Michaeli, Innkeepers. Rates: See Index.

Directions: From Zurich, drive through Winterthur on the road to Konstanz, Germany. Gottlieben is the last village before the border crossing.

NOTES

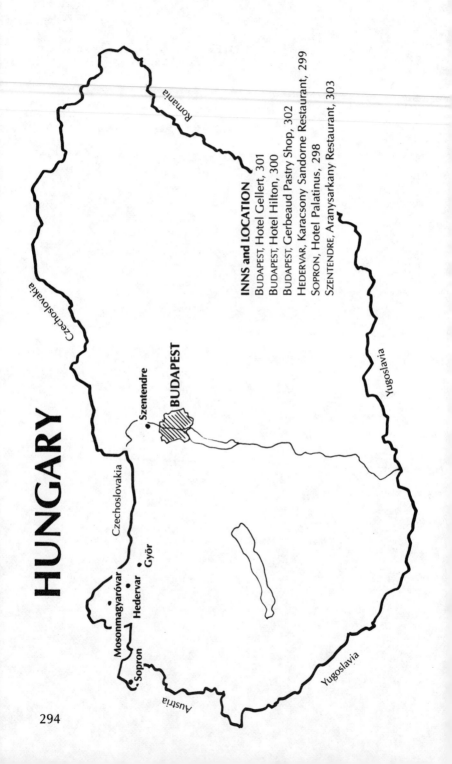

HUNGARY

INNS and LOCATION
BUDAPEST, Hotel Gellert, 301
BUDAPEST, Hotel Hilton, 300
BUDAPEST, Gerbeaud Pastry Shop, 302
HEDERVAR, Karacsony Sandorne Restaurant, 299
SOPRON, Hotel Palatinus, 298
SZENTENDRE, Aranysarkany Restaurant, 303

Czechoslovakia

Romania

Czechoslovakia

Szentendre

BUDAPEST

Yugoslavia

Czechoslovakia

Mosonmagyaróvar

Hedervar

Győr

Sopron

Austria

Yugoslavia

TRAVEL SUGGESTIONS FOR HUNGARY

Hungary represents the first venture by this book into an Eastern European country. At best, it might be called a preliminary toe-wetting. If reader response is favorable, I would expect to go farther into the country in the next edition. All in all, it is an adventure and an education.

Visa Regulations

A visa is required of United States and Canadian citizens. A visa can be obtained at the Hungarian Embassy in Washington D.C., or in Ottawa, and also at the Hungarian Consulate General in New York. Visas are also issued at the Budapest Airport and at border crossing points if traveling by car. However, no visas are issued at border points either to train travelers or those traveling by hydrofoil. Visas are valid for three months from the date of issue for a stay of up to thirty days.

How to Get There

By Air: There are no direct flights from North America to Budapest. However, the regular flights of Malév Hungarian Airlines link up Budapest with forty cities in thirty countries. There are twenty-two other airlines in addition to Malév that have regular flights to Budapest.

By Rail: Budapest is easy to reach by rail from any part of Europe.

By Car: Seven of the eight major highways running through Hungary radiate out from Budapest and all are linked up with the international road network.

By Boat: From May to September there is a daily hydrofoil boat running between Budapest and Vienna. Sailing time is four and a half hours. The international waterway is the famous Danube River.

Currency

The Hungarian unit of currency is the forint. Convertible currency can be brought into Hungary in any amount and exchanged at the tourist rate at banks, IBUSZ (Hungarian Travel Bureau) offices throughout Hungary, and at major hotels.

Credit Cards

Most first-class hotels, restaurants, and shops honor the common American credit cards.

Car Rentals

Have your travel agent rent a car through IBUSZ Hungarian Travel Bureau, 630 Fifth Ave., Rockefeller Center, New York, N.Y. 10111; (800) 367-7878. Also through AutoEurope: (800) 223-5555.

Traffic rules in Hungary are generally the same as in most European countries. An international driver's license is necessary. The consumption of even the slightest quantity of alcoholic beverages before or while driving is absolutely forbidden.

Clothing

In summer, a lightweight jacket or wrap may be necessary during the evening. In winter, a moderate-weight coat is advisable.

Incidentally, Hungary is six hours ahead of U.S. Eastern Time.

For Further Information and Reservations

The IBUSZ Hungarian Travel Bureau, 630 Fifth Avenue, New York, N.Y. 10111; (212) 582-7412, can supply additional information and send very colorful literature. However, they only accept reservations from travel agents and not from individuals. Make your choice and have your travel agent telephone: (800) 367-7878.

Hungarian Cuisine

Hungarian cuisine has a long past and has undergone many foreign influences. During the course of centuries, it has taken in and adapted many features of Turkish, Italian, and French culinary arts. In addition to the large restaurants, there are smaller ones at all points in Budapest and the countryside offering a broad selection. There are also separate restaurants offering Bulgarian, Romanian, Italian, Cuban, Russian, German, and Polish specialties.

The special taste of Hungarian foods is the result of a blend of red paprika, black pepper, onions, sour cream, and oil. Some particular Hungarian dishes include gulyás (fish soup), goulash, chicken paprikás, stuffed cabbage, Transylvanian meat delicacies, and a variety of strudels, pancakes, Somló desserts, raisin noodles, and Dobos cake.

Inns in Hungary

There has always been a tradition of country inns in Hungary, the world-renowned csárdas, where the traveler was always sure to be welcomed with the sound of the violin and offered a plate of hot "goulash." These had more or less disappeared, replaced by state-controlled hotels that lacked both efficiency and taste. Fortunately, because they were eager to increase tourism in their country, the Hungarians have liberated the hotels and the restaurants, and now allow them to be owned and managed by private individuals. This is part of a new scheme in the Hungarian economy, so far very successful, of letting some part of the public sector go private. The result of this is that in the past year a lot of new places have opened.

To find the good private places, just stop someone or ask the local travel bureau. Everyone knows and will eagerly direct you. Some words of German will help, especially in the eastern part of the country, but young people also understand a bit of English.

I have included here the first privately owned and run restaurant and the first privately owned and run inn. They are both very attractive and their standards are indeed much higher than those of their government-run counterparts.

Another agreeable way to visit Hungary is to use the Hungarian bed-and-breakfast network, with rooms and reservation offices in most major cities. Reservations can be made from Budapest or, as you travel, from one day to the next. It is better to avoid the Balaton area altogether in the high season of July and August unless you have planned your trip and made your reservations long in advance.

An Itinerary in Hungary

This trip by auto crosses the border from Austria into Transdanubia, a part of the country east of the Danube, called the Duna. The journey starts in Sopron at a typical government-run hotel. It continues toward Budapest, stopping at the small village of Hedervar for lunch and also at Györ to see the cathedral.

Route 10 continues on to Budapest. This section on Hungary concludes with a short trip north on Route 11 to visit a restaurant in Szentendre, another wonderful, typical Hungarian village.

HOTEL PALATINUS, Sopron

Here is what is typically the best in government- run hotels. The Palatinus is set on the smallest of the old city squares, in one of the old buildings. Quite discreet from the exterior, the renovation is very effective on the inside, achieving both style and comfort. The restaurant, with pink tablecloths, offers good service and good food; the rooms are warm and welcoming. It's a nice place to come home to after a long walk in and around Sopron.

HOTEL PALATINUS, Sopron 9400, UJ utca 23. Tel.: (36-99) 11-395; telex 24-9146 ujhot. A first-class hotel right in the center of an old baroque city. Rates: See Index.

Directions: There are only 2 main streets in the old center; UJ utca is one of the two.

Close by on the same street is a very interesting studio and shop with an equally interesting owner called Andras Orsi. He was originally an engineer and worked as such successfully for many years,

until he decided to be what he really wanted and became a sculptor.
In this new field also he was very successful. One of the first purchas-
ers of private property in Hungary, he was allowed to buy and renew
an old house to transform it into a studio, to which he added a shop.

Budapest is a short and easy drive from Sopron, but I preferred
to linger on the way. There are so many interesting stops. Fertöd
Castle, for example, the grandest masterpiece of baroque architec-
ture, built by Prince Miklos Estherhazy at the end of the 18th century,
where one could spend a whole day...or the area of the Szigetköz,
along the border with Czechoslovakia, the region of islands on the
Danube. Although modernized, it retains some old quaint houses,
the tanias, low and whitewashed, with overhanging thatched roofs. I
had a really good lunch in Hedervar, one of the villages there.

KARACSONY SANDORNE RESTAURANT, Hedervar

If you've seen the Hitchcock film, *The Lady Vanishes*, you'll
understand exactly what I mean. This place is in a tiny village far off
the main road; foreigners never arrive there. No wonder then that
everybody turned their heads and stopped talking when I entered.
Through the smoke I saw an assembly of darkly clad peasants, all
with imposing mustaches, all casting inquisitive glances at me. Suddenly a sympathetic blonde lady materialized from the back of the
room, and asked what I wanted. Upon hearing that I was hungry, she
said that she had little, but would do her best. Her best was marvelous: a thick slice of veal liver cooked to perfection, sweet vegetables
from her garden, salads and fruits. I gave her three rosettes.

KARACSONY SANDORNE RESTAURANT, Kocsmaros, 9178 Heder-
var, Kossuth L. Utca 1. A plain inn offering good food and warmth.

Directions: Midway between Györ and Mosonmagyaróvar. The inn
is in the middle of the village.

On my way to Budapest, I couldn't help stopping in Györ, a
must for any lover of the baroque era, if only for the magnificent
cathedral.

When I arrived at last in Budapest it was dark already, but I knew
where to go, across the river and up to the Var (castle), close to which
is the Hilton Hotel.

HOTEL HILTON, Budapest

In the heart of the 700-year-old castle district of Buda, the Hilton is the best of all the new grand hotels in Budapest. The hotel stands on the site where a Dominican abbey stood in the Middle Ages, and when the construction of the hotel began, archaeologists unearthed the remains of the 13th-century cloister and it was integrated in the new structure, a rare sight in a Hilton. If you dine in the Tower

restaurant, you'll find yourself partly in the authentic tower of the Gothic church of St. Nicholas, newly furnished in the style of the 13th century—a medieval restaurant with air conditioning, serving Hungarian specialties. Everything here is up to standard.

HOTEL HILTON, 1014 Budapest, Hess Andras Ter 1-3. Tel.: 853 500; telex 22-59-84. One of the most surprising Hiltons in the world. Rates: See Index.

Directions: On the Buda hill, near the castle and the cathedral.

Budapest

Budapest is a surprisingly fizzy city, with rich museums, elegant shops, and animated restaurants where wine and music flow. I found that the tramways were the easiest and best way to go around the city. There are also a lot of taxis, public and private. The private ones are driven by people who double their day's work in the taxi business, but even though they don't usually have a meter, they are not more expensive than the normal taxis. One of the best shopping streets is Vaci utca (street), which runs parallel to the river in Pest, behind the Intercontinental Hotel. Pest is the more commercial part of the city, on the eastern side of the Danube. Most of the shops, restaurants, museums, except the one located in the castle, are on the Pest side. A woman friend tells me there is a new thing going on in Hungary these days: the beauty business. Lots of beauty parlors are blossoming, using the usually good new lines of skin and hair creams and lotions that the Hungarian inventors have come up with. They are, of course, much cheaper than American or European similar places and they are fun to try. Another very worthwhile experience in Budapest is the baths. Many different medicinal springs run in Budapest, 123 to be precise. They have many different curative virtues that people have known about for the past 2,000 years. One of the better-known baths flows into the beautiful pool of the Gellert Hotel.

HOTEL GELLERT, Budapest

This is one of the more famous spa hotels in the world. A beautiful building topped with many domes, it was built in 1918 and still retains some Art Nouveau flavor. Surely, it is the most reminiscent of a lost era, and of the specific taste of the Hungary of the beginning of the century. Even if you don't go there to swim, go to see the inside pool—the architecture is startling. The bathers, too, are worth being with, as it is not reserved to the hotel guests, but to anyone who buys a ticket. I enjoyed staying there more than anywhere else in Budapest. Even though it is a luxury hotel, it is really Hungarian, which an international hotel can never be. I learned things about the country there; the atmosphere is more real, the food tastes authentically Hungarian.

HOTEL GELLERT, 1111 Budapest, Gellert ter 1. Tel.: (361) 460-700. An elegant hotel, in the old-fashioned sense. Rates: See Index.

Directions: On the Buda side of the Danube, just below the castle.

For real Hungarian atmosphere, I also like the fruit and vegetable markets with little old peasant women in dark skirts and shawls loudly bargaining over their onions and potatoes. The vegetables were indisputably of the "health" kind, grown naturally and presented for sale with soil and leaves attached. I thought of all the work it would take to prepare them.

For another quite different Hungarian atmosphere, I went to one of the pastry shops that has made the city famous: Gerbeaud.

301

GERBEAUD PASTRY SHOP, Budapest (Vörösmarty)

Henrik Kugler, a confectioner from Sopron, first opened his shop in Jozsef Square, but as he gained popularity he looked for new premises and finally moved into the present large and beautiful building. The splendid interior and the large choice and perfect quality of the cakes made the place renowned throughout Europe from the last century to today. Kugler's successor, Emil Gerbeaud, set up a chocolate factory and exported the world over. The salons are so spacious they can accommodate hundreds of guests. They are gracefully furnished and decorated with fine paintings and pretty objects. The choice between the myriad colorful and delicious-looking pastries is trying. The best-known cake is the Dobos.

Further Facts About Budapest

Budapest is the capital of the Hungarian People's Republic. The Danube River flows through the center of the city for twenty-eight kilometers, with the hilly region of Buda on the right bank and the plains of Pest on the left.

The history of Budapest dates from the Celts and the Romans, and there are examples of both Romanesque and Gothic architecture. Even more numerous are relics of the Turkish eras, including some Turkish baths.

Among the most important of the over twenty museums in the city are the National Museum, where the visitor can get an insight into the 1,000-year history of the Hungarian nation; the Budapest History Museum; the Museum of Fine Arts; and the Museum of Ethnography, which displays objects of folklore from the various regions of Hungary.

There are twenty-five permanent theaters in Budapest, as well as a good number of open-air theaters. Budapest musical life is known throughout the world. Liszt, Bela Bartok, and Zoltan Kodaly made Budapest their home. The Budapest Festival is held every autumn, and the Budapest Spring Festival is conducted at the end of March.

There are many sporting facilities, including stadiums, swimming pools, boathouses, and much diversion for children, including the Budapest City Park and the Zoological Gardens.

ARANYSARKANY RESTAURANT, Szentendre

This is the first private restaurant in Hungary. Attila Mahr, the owner, has shown a lot of courage and good taste, and has also generated some good publicity for his country. He chose Szentendre, a townlet on the "elbow" of the Danube, as the Hungarians call the area where the river bends.

An ancient settlement of Serbs and Dalmatians, the village is very picturesque—almost a museum in itself, with its baroque and rococo houses, many of which are galleries showing contemporary artists, usually one-man shows. One of these houses is our restaurant.

The guests all eat at one large table, which makes conversation and meeting easy. The menu offers a wide choice of Hungarian and other cuisines. When I was there, Attila told me that he was going to publish a book with his recipes, and asked whether I thought it would be worthwhile to translate it. I said, "Yes, by all means!"

ARANYSARKANY RESTAURANT, Szentendre. A touristy but quality restaurant. Prices about 500 to 600 forints. Attila Mahr, Owner.

Directions: Take Rte. 11 to the north. The restaurant is in the middle of the village.

onzano Veneto

ENICE

RAVENNA

Cervia

ortona

Yugoslavia

INNS and LOCATION

TRAVEL SUGGESTIONS FOR ITALY

How to Get There

Pan American Airlines and several others provide excellent service to Italy from North America. Your travel agent will advise. Your Eurailpass is good in Italy.

Country Inns in Italy

In addition to visiting a few of the so-called grand and deluxe hotels in Italy, I found country inn hospitality in villas, country houses, and ancient castles. However, in only a small number did the proprietors actually become involved with the guests.

Reservations

Many of the inns I visited in Italy belong to the Relais de Campagne Chateaux-Hotels. For full reservation information see "Travel Suggestions for France."

Reservations at other than Relais de Campagne Chateaux may be made directly or through toll-free New York booking offices, as indicated in the final fact paragraph for each inn.

306

Italian Menus

Italy has more regional cooking than any other country I visited in Europe. On the coast, fish and seafood dominate the menu; in the Alpine section, it is cornmeal for polenta; farther south, it is rice; and in southern Italy, flour is the base for a great many dishes. Some areas of Italy have extensive grazing lands, so that beef becomes one of the main dishes; however, where there is less pasture, pork and lamb are seen more frequently on the menu.

Italy is a place where individualism plays a great role, and this individuality expresses itself most vividly in the preparation of pasta. With all due respect to several Italian-American restaurants I have visited, I never really tasted pasta until I got to Italy. For one thing, it is not a whole meal, it is one course—part of a carefully orchestrated meal. Pasta is the term applied to many different types of flour-based products such as macaroni, spaghetti, noodles, and ravioli, and comes in all shapes, forms, sizes, and names in various regions of Italy. I am sure that every Italian restaurant worth the name serves homemade pasta in all of its many permutations. The sauces alone would fill a cookbook.

As in every country I visited, in all types of food-serving establishments—the ristorante, the albergo, the trattoria, and, of course, the pizzeria—I was assisted by a collection of good-humored headwaiters, waiters, bartenders, and also other patrons. After all, isn't it true that there is a little Italian in all of us?

Car Rentals

Travelers for whom Italy is part of a continent-wide itinerary should see the section at the front of the book, "Renting a Car for Europe." The best way to see Italy is by car.

Driving Tips

First and most important, many gasoline stations in Italy close at 12 noon and open about 3 p.m. Special coins are needed to use the pay telephones.

For information about driving in Rome, see the directions for reaching the Lord Byron Hotel, Rome. The international road signs are described in the Michelin Green Guide for Italy.

My Itinerary in Italy

This itinerary begins in the Italian Lake District north of Milan and continues on to the Italian Alps and then south to Venice. From there following in order: Florence, Pisa, Portofino, Grossetto, and Rome.

VILLA AZALEA, Pallanza, Lake Maggiore

Enrico Leccardi, his mother, and his sister, Carmen (when she is not working in Milan as a sociologist), are the innkeepers at this exceptionally warm and comfortable inn a short distance from Lake Maggiore in Pallanza.

The building is most unusual. It sits on top of a hill in a little forest overlooking an almost perfect park with orange, lemon, and sequoia trees that were in blossom when I was there, as well as evergreens and palms. There are flowers, shrubs, and bushes in great profusion. It has a wedding-cake feeling and the top story is really an oversized cupola that reminded me of the Mainstay in Cape May, New Jersey.

There is also a stately mansion in the park, a short distance away, that the family has restored and refurbished to provide additional rooms. This is a much more formal building and some of the

interior designs, fireplaces, paneled walls, and decorated ceilings are most impressive.

Breakfast is the only meal offered here; however, Enrico's mother is queen of all she surveys in the kitchen.

This is one of Italy's most sought-after vacation areas and the Villa Azalea offers an interesting alternative to staying in the more palatial hotels. In May, June, September, and October a room can usually be obtained without a reservation.

PENSIONE VILLA AZALEA, 28048 Verbania, Pallanza. Tel.: (0323) 43-575. An 11-guestroom modest inn in the middle of a beautiful park about five min. from downtown Pallanza. Italian Lake District recreation available within a few moments' drive. Breakfast only. Closed end of Oct. to Easter. Rates: See Index. Famiglia Leccardi, Innkeepers.

Directions: Look for signs for Pensione Villa Azalea in downtown Pallanza.

Pallanza

For hundreds of years, indeed, thousands, the lakes of northern Italy have meant a mild climate, natural beauty, and peaceful surroundings. They have a romantic, poetic aura. Poets, musicians, and painters like Dante, Stendhal, Manzoni, Ruskin, Toscanini, and Hemingway, among many others, found respite and inspiration there.

The Italian lakes have become synonymous not only with mild climate, beauty, and quiet, but with a rich variety of attractions, such as swimming, boating, sports, excursions, cultural and social life, folklore, and outstanding cuisine. The traditional boats, with their white awnings, are in themselves symbolic of some of the unchanging customs. The picturesque watercolor effects of the fishermen's villages are much the same as they were in the last century, and the lakes themselves, bordered by mountains, parks, and vineyards, are always beckoning the visitor to return.

Let us stop for a moment here and say the word "Maggiore" several times. It is pronounced with a soft "g" and the "a" is pronounced "ah." Just the sound of the word is soothing and relaxing, and Lake Maggiore is all of that and much, much more. Say it again: Maggiore . . . Maggiore.

GRAND HOTEL MAJESTIC, Pallanza, Lake Maggiore

I'm not sure what makes a Grand Hotel "grand," but the Majestic is grand in every possible definition of the word. The building reminds me of the old John Wanamaker store because it is built around a hollow square. There are inner galleries around all four sides at each level and it is possible to look right down into the reception area below. Everything is massive and the stairways have broad stone steps with somewhat faded carpeting.

The terrace, which leads off the main drawing room, has a magnificent view of the lake, and people sit for hours watching the little steamers ply back and forth between Pallanza and the many islands. The gardens also are right next to the lake, adjacent to the tennis courts and indoor swimming pool. Bedrooms are in the size and style that were popular over 100 years ago when the hotel was built; mine was large enough to accommodate a basketball practice session. Many of them have a very commanding view of Lake Maggiore.

The Majestic is always filled during the high season, sometimes with guests who stay many weeks. The Majestic celebrated its 100th year in 1970, and has been host to dozens of great figures of note in the world of nobility and the arts.

Even the most pretentious hotels in North America do not approximate the particular European style and air of elegance. True, the Majestic is fading a little here and there, but like a few others I would see, they remain as symbols of super hospitality that is slowly disappearing.

GRAND HOTEL MAJESTIC, 28048 Verbania Pallanza. Tel.: (0323) 42453. A 100-year-old sumptuously luxurious hotel overlooking Lake Maggiore. Breakfast, lunch, and dinner. Large park directly on lakeside with private beach, dock for boats, covered heated swimming pool. Tennis and golf nearby. Closed from early Oct. thru April. Rates: See Index.

Directions: The Italian Lake District, including Lakes Maggiore, Como, and others too numerous to mention, is north of Milano. The Hotel Majestic is on the main street of Pallanza on Rte. 33.

✳ ✳ ✳ ✳

CASTELLO DI POMERIO, Erba (Lake Como)

My tower bedroom at the Castello di Pomerio was in the oldest part of the castle, dating back to the 13th century. One of the windows was very narrow, just large enough to provide a view of the countryside, but presenting a very small target for arrows or musket balls by any besiegers. However, a large window overlooked a neighboring villa, and lakes and mountains in the distance. The rough stone walls were partially covered with tapestries and there was a heavy table and chair next to the fireplace to complete the medieval atmosphere. The plumbing, however, was not medieval.

This castle-inn is built around a central courtyard, paved in small stones, in which there are two beautiful mulberry trees. There are wooden balconies around three sides of the square and the stone walls and red-tiled roofs create a quiet, tranquil place, quite unlike anything I had found thus far in Italy. There are flowers everywhere, both indoors and out.

The dining room had very high wood ceilings supported by heavy beams that contrasted remarkably with the stone walls. There was a large table with a great collection of salads and cheeses and desserts. I saw fresh strawberries, blueberries, grapes, and all kinds of confections.

Restoring and refurbishing this castle has been the work of its owner, Madame Lita Donati. As she explained to me, "We have greatly emphasized the necessity for reproducing the naturalness of the past six or seven centuries. Where new windows and walls had to be created, we've tried to maintain the graceful arches of old. We uncovered some absolutely magnificent frescoes in the main dining room hall that had been hidden for many years. This is one of five ancient castles in this vicinity, all connected by tunnels."

Our conversation turned to the subject of accommodating today's sophisticated travelers. "I think people enjoy staying here very much," she said, "because this is one of the oldest castles in northern Italy and because we have added some of the recreational facilities that travelers have come to expect. There are two swimming pools, two sponge-surface tennis courts, an outdoor grill area, and a sauna.

"Many of our guests stay here for quite a few days and travel by car to all of the points of interest and beauty in the Lake District. We are just a few moments, literally, from the shores of Lake Como."

In the main lounge there was some electronic equipment, indicating that although this may be an old castle, there was very modern

entertainment. That night, a young man played classical selections on the piano with great fervor and sincerity.

CASTELLO DI POMERIO, 22036 Erba, Como. Tel.: (031) 611516. Telex: Pomeri 380463. A 58-guestroom restored ancient castle with modern conveniences in the middle of the Lake Como district. Breakfast, lunch, and dinner. Indoor and outdoor swimming pools, tennis courts, sauna on grounds. Golf, horseback riding, touring lake country all nearby. Open all year. Rates: See Index.

Directions: Erba is located on the road that runs from Como to Lecco. Look for sign for Castello di Pomerio on the north side of this road. It is well marked. Do not go into the town of Erba.

GRAND HOTEL VILLA SERBELLONI, Bellagio (Lake Como)

"You must go to Bellagio, even in the rain, it is beautiful." Lita Donati at the Castello di Pomerio was insistent. "It is a beautiful, unspoiled village and you definitely should see Villa Serbelloni!"

Signora Donati was right. Bellagio *is* beautiful in the rain and the Villa Serbelloni belongs to another world in another century. It is situated in one of the most romantic settings imaginable, almost at the point where the two arms of Lake Como join. There is a sandy beach, swimming pool, and beautiful gardens, all adjacent to the lake. The drawing rooms, dining rooms, and lounges have marvelously painted frescoes and ceilings and an airy openness that is unexpected in a buildng constructed over a hundred years ago.

I was told that Americans don't find their way to Bellagio very frequently, and that for many years it has been a favorite of the English. I am sure that Shelley and Byron walked these shores, and drew inspiration from the mountains, lake, and sky.

The Villa Serbelloni has been owned by Rudi Bucher and his family for many years. Although it was a busy day for him, he took a few moments to point out some of the more attractive aspects of both the hotel and the town. "There are many wonderful day-tours here in the Lake District," he said, "we suggest that our guests take the demi-pension, which leaves them free to make the noontime meal optional. Most of the time they return in the middle of the afternoon to enjoy the tranquil view of the lake and the mountains and to walk in our gardens."

On beautiful Lake Como, the Grand Hotel Villa Serbelloni is a leisurely look backwards into the 19th century.

GRAND HOTEL VILLA SERBELLONI, 22021 Bellagio, Lake Como. Tel.: (031) 950-216. An 85-guestroom luxury hotel, literally at the heart of Lake Como. Breakfast, lunch, and dinner. Heated swimming pool, private lake beach, tennis court, boating, water skiing on grounds. Golf nearby. Open April 10 to Oct. 10. (As with all hotels of this nature in Europe there is a wide variety of rooms and eating plans. There are special reductions for children, rooms for servants and chauffeurs, rooms with a park view and a lake view. All of this sounds like the Serbelloni is unusually expensive, but actually there are some rooms without views of the lake that are quite reasonable.) Rates: See Index.

Directions: Lake Como is shaped like an inverted "Y." Bellagio is at the confluence of the two arms of the lake. It is also accessible from Varenna and Cabenabbia by ferry. About 1 hr. from Milan.

GRAND HOTEL VILLA D'ESTE, Cernobbio (Lake Como)

Villa d'Este is one of the world's most famous hotels. With 180 rooms, I would not call it a country inn, but anyone who visits the Lake Como area should at least stop for lunch or dinner. This is

313

exactly what I was doing when I met another American couple from Cleveland, who were making their first return visit after spending their honeymoon at Villa d'Este thirty years ago. We were seated on the terrace overlooking the lake, and naturally I asked them if it had changed very much.

"We were worried about that," they both responded. "We thought perhaps it might have been 'modernized' as so many other things are, but it is almost exactly as we remembered it. We found our favorite spot in the garden and we were actually able to have our old room again—the food is still exceptional. We are planning to come back for our fifieth!"

Villa d'Este has a most intriguing and unusual history. It was built in 1568 by one of the wealthy families of Italy. In the 18th century it was renovated by a former La Scala ballerina who married an Italian nobleman. During this period, the gardens were perfected with an avenue of cypress trees bordering a cascade of fountains. This same lady made a second marriage to a young, handsome, Napoleonic general, and since she feared he might suffer from military nostalgia, she had a series of simulated fortresses and towers built on the slopes overlooking the gardens, where he and his friends could play war games. They are still here.

Unquestionably, the most interesting chapter in the history of the Villa centers around Caroline of Brunswick-Wolfenbuttel, Princess of Wales and the future Queen of England. This unhappy lady discovered Lake Como in 1814 and devoted the next five years of her life to adorning and decorating Villa d'Este. All of this put a great strain on her resources and she returned to London in 1820, hopefully to take her place on the throne beside her husband, King George IV, but a scandalous divorce action filed against her by the King was thought to have caused her to die broken-hearted in 1821.

In 1873, the estate became a luxury hotel, providing hospitality for European nobility and wealthy guests from all over the world.

Today, Villa d'Este is indeed a swinging place. The parade of Rolls Royces has been augmented by rented Fiats and Renaults. Things are still done in the grand manner, but it is not stiff or formal. Every imaginable resort facility is available, and there is both a discotheque and a night club. It is very popular with Americans.

Caroline of Brunswick-Wolfenbuttel, wherever you are, your beloved Villa d'Este is in good hands.

GRAND HOTEL VILLA D'ESTE (Relais et Chateaux), 22010 Cernobbio, Lake Como. Tel.: (031) 511-471. A 180-guestroom exceptionally comfortable resort-hotel with first-class service, on the western shore of Lake Como. This is a complete resort facility, including indoor and outdoor swimming pools, private beach, motor boating, sailing, water skiing, surfing, tennis, golf, discotheque, and night club. Rates: See Index.

Directions: Cernobbio is just a few km. north of the town of Como near the southern tip of the western arm of Lake Como.

This part of Italy is as much Austrian as it is Italian. When asking directions in the city of Merano, I was given answers almost entirely in German. I stopped in two places to determine the location of Castel Freiberg; in one, a waitress took me outside and pointed in the general direction, and in the other, the proprietor took me to one of his guests who spoke English and who, in turn, made a marvelous map with extremely good directions. To double-check myself before heading up the mountain, I stopped once more and asked directions from a lady who was selling cold drinks in the street. Before I knew it we had drawn a crowd of people with helpful suggestions. Everyone was extremely friendly and cooperative.

HOTEL CASTEL FREIBERG, Merano (Fragsburg)

I was strolling around the walls and grounds of what was, for the moment, my own castle thrust high into the blue skies of northern Italy. Circling me on all sides was a ring of mountains, white-clad sentinels announcing the first snowfall of the season. The view from this side was of rolling green upland meadows, where a herd of cattle placidly grazed. I could hear the tinkling of the bells even at this distance. At the far end, farmers were making the last hay crop of the season.

I left the crenelated battlements that might have protected the men-at-arms in earlier days, and passed a young gardener who had paused for his morning snack of round brown bread, some meat, and a bottle of wine. He was responsible for the gorgeous array of flowers that were sending forth a divine message.

Now, I came to a grassy terrace with an outdoor swimming pool, tennis courts, and a few swings and slides for children. The view from here was of the city of Merano, and on this clear, fall day everything in the valley seemed to be miniaturized, and I felt almost as if I could step into space.

The interior of Castel Freiberg is rather formal, with a series of drawing rooms, including a card room with color television, heavy castle-type furniture, and floors of mellowed terra cotta. The beige walls have been amply decorated with pieces of armor and other

warlike reminders of earlier days. Everything is beautifully kept with great style and grace.

The castle dates back to the 14th century and has an extensive history that includes several noble Italian families. As is the case with many European castles, it fell into disrepute and disrepair; rescued by the present proprietor in the 1960s, it was opened as a hotel in 1973.

Since my last visit, several American readers have visited here and their accounts of the Castle have pleased me very much. Getting there from Merano is half the fun (see directions).

HOTEL CASTEL FREIBERG (Relais et Chateaux), 39012 Merano. Tel.: (0473) 44196. A 40-guestroom very comfortable castle inn located at 2,400 ft. in the Italian Alps. Breakfast, lunch, and dinner. Swimming pool, tennis courts on grounds. Fishing, horseback riding, water skiing, mountain climbing nearby. Closed Nov. thru March. Rates: See Index.

Directions: Merano is located high in the Italian Alps, a relatively short distance from both Switzerland and Austria. First, get directions to the Scena (Schenna) section of the city. The inn is located in a small community called Fragsburg. Passing the Hotel Angelica, look for sign at bridge on the right that says Laberz. This will also have the hotel and Fragsburg signs. Turn right over the bridge, head up the side of the mountain. There are street lamps and the road is very twisty. To the right will be the sensational view of Merano. If necessary, reassure yourself by stopping at a small restaurant on the right-hand side of the road. Persist, have faith, believe the signs. Once you have arrived at the top of the mountain, ignore the parking lot and drive to the left on a brick roadway that eventually will lead to the entrance. Park car, leave bags, check with concierge who is amazingly informed and I will leave everyone in his hands.

A Day in the Italian Alps

I was headed out of Merano in a northeasterly direction toward Passo di Giovo. The clouds gathered at the tops of the mountains, but the valley was quite sunny as the sun filtered through. There were many apple orchards in full fruit and apple sellers along the road.

The floor of the valley with its meadows and farms is as appealing as the upland meadows and pastures with small houses set high above. There are numerous single cable lifts, which valley farmers use to bring bales of hay down from the upper pastures. The architecture is Italian Tyrol, which means the top floors of the old houses are often wooden, with white-painted stone and plaster ground floors. Hundreds of flowerpots suspended from the overhanging roofs splash their bright colors against the beautiful, weathered wood and white walls. The overhanging roofs provide shelter against rain and snow. Some of the older houses have stones on the roofs.

Here, the cow is queen of all she surveys, as the road signs imply, and twice a day the traveler is apt to find cattle being driven across the main road. There is something about looking into the eyes of a Tyrolean brown cow that apprises one of the true order of things.

Now the road begins to hug the mountains with a series of linking S-turns, and there are many waterfalls coursing down from the very tops of the mountains, like silver ribbons tracing their way among the various shades of green trees. Jagged mountains cut into the skyline with their saw teeth, while occasional old barns and houses cling to their sides. It is a countryside that is verdant and challenging, with massive vastness of gentle meads, rushing rivers, and thousands of shades of green with an occasional accent of red or beige.

It is a place where small kittens sit sunning themselves on stone walls and cattle placidly munch their way through the meadows—a place where waterfalls seem to emerge from the sides of the mountains; where barnyards have fat roosters and goats; where the wash is hung out in the sunshine and the wind; and where birds lift the hearts and spirits of all who hear their full-throated, joyous songs.

RELAIS EL TOULA, Ponzano Veneto (Treviso)

It was dinnertime at El Toula. My repast began with some very thinly sliced ham and an excellent house paté, which was followed by a beef marrow placed on a bed of fresh, sautéed tomatoes.

The third course was a delicious pasta in the form of a thin spaghetti cooked to a perfect degree of firmness and over which the waiter sprinkled freshly grated cheese. I found that in Italy there was nothing to compare with homemade pasta in any form.

Next, came a small piece of beefsteak served with an unusual herb sauce and local endive. Dinner ended, or at least I thought it did, with a delectable crème brulée—the second ending came in the form of a piece of local cake, which was like a very large Scotch shortbread cookie.

Almost on cue, the owner of El Toula entered. "You have enjoyed dinner, yes?" I responded in the same rhythm. "I have enjoyed dinner, yes!" He and I talked at length about the joys of Italian innkeeping.

My room at this beautiful villa had two full-length windows with balconies overlooking the terrace and the fields in the rear. There was a small swimming pool, which I am sure would be most welcome in the Venetian summer. The theme of the original villa was carried out with antique furniture and painted ceiling beams.

In the morning, looking out of the windows towards the small forest, I saw many different colors of autumn leaves. The stunning red of the New England maples was missing, but otherwise it could have been from my bedroom at home in the Berkshires.

The entrance to El Toula is impressive. Turning off the main road, I drove for at least a kilometer between vineyards, where the vines had been trained on an archlike trellis over the road, so that I was driving literally through a tunnel of grapes. They were being harvested at the time of my arrival. These grapes supply the house wine.

Once inside a big gate, I found myself in a very large courtyard paved with small black and white stones. The main house is a Venetian villa, and in previous years has been flanked by new additions stretching out on each side like large wings. There were flowers and plants everywhere, many in huge earthenware pots that were being watered by a very colorful-looking lady wearing a straw hat.

El Toula is less than an hour's ride from Venice. Many guests commute daily, preferring the quiet of the countryside evenings to the somewhat hectic tourist-oriented pace of the city.

RELAIS EL TOULA (Relais et Chateaux), Via Postumia 63, 31050 Ponzano Veneto, Treviso. Tel.: 0422-96023. A 10-guestroom exceptionally comfortable villa hotel with first-class service, located about 1 hr. north of Venice. Breakfast, lunch, dinner. Swimming pool on grounds. Open every day of the year. Rates: See Index.

HOTEL LA FENICE ET DES ARTISTES, Venice

I am indebted to Lynn and Charlie Henry, whom I met on the Rialto bridge, for recommending this hotel to me—I think it was a great find. In fact, I might well term it the "Algonquin of Venice." For

one thing, it is just around the corner from the Teatro la Fenice and the artists appearing there are quite likely to be booked at the hotel. I browsed through several guest registers with fascinating signed photographs and compliments from singers, actors, and conductors. Like the Algonquin, it has that artistic ambience.

La Fenice consists of two buildings—the old section, which does not have a lift (there are bellmen to help with luggage), and a newer section with a lift. Both buildings are air-conditioned, and every room is furnished with great individuality in the "romantic style," and all have baths.

Because these are very old buildings, there are some interestingly shaped hallways and rooms, with views out of corners into hidden courtyards overlooking the canals. Seven rooms have their own terraces, and provide an ideal place to rest in the late sun after a lovely day in Venice.

I found it very easy to get information and assistance at the main desk here. The concierge is at home in several languages and has a good sense of humor in many of them.

Breakfast, the only meal served, is taken during clement weather in a secluded L-shaped garden, and at other times in a small dining room located between the two buildings. There are two restaurants just a few steps away, both of which are highly recommended.

HOTEL LA FENICE ET DES ARTISTES, 1936 San Marco, Venice. Tel.: (26) 403-32-333. A 75-guestroom hotel of the second class, centrally located a short distance from the Plaza San Marco. Open all year. Rates: See Index.

Directions: From Grand Canal Station at parking garage, take either water taxi or ferry to Pier 15 (be certain to have a complete understanding in advance with the water taxi driver as to cost). Porters will be available at Pier 15 to carry luggage to hotel.

Twilight in the Plaza San Marco

Idling away the hours in the San Marco Plaza is a continuing preoccupation in Venice—the tables and chairs of the various cafés are filled from 10 a.m. until midnight. At noon, the orchestras appear in the cafés, and there ensues a battle of the bands, with at least three different groups playing at the same time; however, the result isn't cacophony, since they are some distance from each other. The orchestra for my café strikes up a medley, not of Vivaldi or Puccini, but of "Oklahoma," for which they receive a smattering of applause. Shadows are getting long now, and the sun has dropped behind the palaces. Sweaters and coats are being put on and the sunny afternoon is changing into a fall twilight. The huge metal figures on top of one of the buildings have drawn back their hammers to let the world know that it is, indeed, five-thirty. A toddler from a nearby table climbs up on the chair next to mine and dips a finger into my hot chocolate—what a look of instant pleasure comes across his little face as he tastes this heavenly concoction.

The pigeons, which enliven the Plaza by day, have all but disappeared; maybe it's because the people selling corn have folded their little carts and traveled home for a Venetian dinner.

The first of the many artists have returned to the center of the Plaza to set up their easels and show their work once again, and the crowds at the cafe become more numerous as twilight deepens into evening. Now, a man selling yo-yos with lights in them comes

strolling by, followed by the usual group of young people. At the far end of the Plaza, they are playing with Frisbees—but mostly the San Marco Plaza is people; people walking arm-in-arm, solitary strollers, people visiting for the first time, and others who know exactly where they are going.

Ah, Plaza San Marco! One day I shall return to the pigeons, to hear your beautiful music and watch your wonderful people.

RISTORANTE AL TEATRO, Venice

I had several recommendations for this restaurant, just a short distance from the Hotel la Fenice. Lynn and Charlie Henry mentioned it first and their recommendation was backed up by the concierge and director of the hotel. The word was that this restaurant, in addition to being a regular family-style Italian restaurant, also had some of the best pizza in Venice.

There were different types of dining rooms. I ate in one where there were fish nets and other fishing gear hanging from the ceiling. Mounted securely on one wall was a Venetian gondola.

The headwaiter was very helpful. We settled on pizza with anchovies and a small salad. However, the rest of the extensive menu was most exciting. The dessert cart, wheeled around in most Italian restaurants for everybody to "ooh" and "aah" over, was particularly tempting.

There was also a more elegant dining room, La Mansard, on the top floor of the building, that started out as a club, but is now open to anyone. It is richly appointed with beautiful furnishings and paneled walls; in one corner a pianist was playing Gershwin.

Here was an opportunity for me to see Italians in a totally unselfconscious atmosphere. There were several families with children and it was a very gay, happy, inviting place. I enjoyed not only an unusually good pizza with fresh mozzarella cheese, but also the fun of watching people at other tables having a good time.

RISTORANTE AL TEATRO, Campo S. Fantin 1917, Venice (located a few steps from La Fenice Hotel). Tel.: (041) 37-214-21-052. A good restaurant in the middle price range located a short distance from the Plaza San Marco. No rooms available. Open every day.

Ravenna

On the way from Venice to Florence, on the coastal road (S-309), Ravenna is undeniably a must. It is a lovely, elegant, quiet, and conveniently flat city, a rare comfort in Italy. I spent a very enjoyable day there visiting the churches, tombs, and museums, and shopping in between.

It is a miracle that so much remains of the Imperial City and the primitive Christian art decorating the churches. Some of the mosaics are often reproduced and well known—the graceful doves in Galla Placidia's tomb, drinking from the cup of life; the portrait of Theodora strikingly present in the soft light flowing through alabaster windowpanes of the church of San Vitale.

But there is much more to be discovered, and there are even surprises: did you know that it is here, in 1321, that the poet Dante, exiled from Florence, died and is buried?

CLASSENSIS TOURIST HOTEL, Ravenna

I chose to stay outside of the city, six kilometers south, in the ancient port of Classis. The hotel is in Classe, next door to the Basilica Sant'Apollinare, which I find to be the most wonderful and perfect of all the churches in Ravenna. The hotel is very simple, so don't expect any fancy furniture or dishes. It is more like an Italian version of a side-of-the-road motel, with typically 1950s furniture and an unobtrusive ugliness. When the main road was rerouted elsewhere, the hotel remained on the old road, now quieter, nicer.

There is a garden and a shady parking spot, a vegetable garden with an old gardener, and the meals are served by a dark, silent maiden. In its own way, it is a true Italian place.

CLASSENSIS TOURIST HOTEL, Sant'Apollinare in Classe, 48100 Ravenna. Tel.: 0544-47-30-15. A 10-guestroom (most with bathrooms) very simple hotel. Open all year except Mon. from Sept. to May. Rates: See Index.

Directions: South of Ravenna, 6 km.

I had lunched at the hotel and wished to dine elsewhere. I was leisurely seated in a comfortable sidewalk café trying to decide which of the many restaurants in the city to choose. I noticed two Italian men at the next table engaged in a demonstrative conversation. They seemed men of taste, slightly upper bourgeois, dressed in an understated style. I was sure they would know the best restaurants. I decided to ask them in my faltering Italian. They were most obliging. The man next to me turned out to be an expert historian and told me all about the city and more. The other one gave me the name of THE place to go for dinner in Ravenna, and then they left. Thank you, Mister Unknown.

CASA DELLE AIE RESTAURANT, Cervia

I hesitated, but the trip was well worth it. The restaurant this good man indicated is thirteen kilometers south of Ravenna, just before Cervia, on the road to Rimini (S-16). It is an old, good-looking farmhouse, converted into a restaurant. I caught a glimpse of a large, hot kitchen where aproned women were busy kneading dough for the pasta and the bread, and others were standing watch over the wide fireplaces, ready to take the food out.

Casa delle Aie is both unsophisticated and excellent. Although jammed with Italian and a few foreign diners, both inside and on an outside porch, I found a table and was promptly noticed by the young, affable waiter. Everything they serve is homemade, cooked on an open fire, and strictly *romagnolo*, that is, typical of the gastronomy of Romagna. I had the flat, unleavened bread called *piedine, zuppa di fagioli e pasta, carne alla brace.* One thing though, they don't serve Coca Cola or any other "bibite" there, only their own good wine! Dinner is about 30,000 lire for two.

CASA DELLE AIE RESTAURANT, Via delle Aie, 48015 Cervia. Tel.: 0544-92-76-31. A restaurant serving hearty and simple but excellent Italian fare. Open all year, for dinner only, except Sat. and Sun. when lunch is served. It is advisable to make reservations. Mario Brandolini and Paolo Abbondanza, Managers.

Directions: On the left-hand side of the road, after Savio, just before Cervia. Watch for the alley of cypresses leading to it.

Florence

Florence, like Rome and Venice, is one of the main cultural tourist attractions in Italy. Between visits to several small hotels and inns, I did manage to see the Duomo—the great cathedral in the city, as well as the famous doors on the Baptistry created by Ghiberti. I walked across the Ponte Vecchio, the bridge over the Arno, traditionally the center of the gold and silversmith shops, and also visited the truly inspirational Uffizi Museum.

For full details on everything in Florence, I recommend the Michelin Green Guide to Italy, *which has devoted ten pages to Florence.*

HOTEL VILLA LA MASSA, Candeli Firenze (Florence)

It was a beautiful October Sunday morning at Villa La Massa, on the Arno River, just a few kilometers from Florence. Bells in the nearby village were joyfully peeling out the good news that church doors were open and everyone was invited to attend.

I was in the garden overlooking the river, watching a solitary fisherman who had three poles working at the same time. The Arno takes a bend at this point, so it was possible to look in both directions for some distance. The mist was rising from the water as the sun rose on a cloudless blue Florentine sky.

"Florentine" is indeed the mood, because the city is such a short distance away and all the artistic delights are readily available to Villa La Massa guests. The hotel has a minibus that goes in and out several times a day. On this particular morning there were a number of U.S. and European fashion buyers staying at the Villa to attend the yearly display of new Italian fashions in the city. Apparently this was a return visit for many of them and there were several reunions.

Everyone was saying, "Why are we going to be spending the day inside when we could be staying here."

The main building of the Villa is built around an open three-story square, and the entry to the guest rooms is from inside galleries that circle each floor. All of the rooms are furnished in a comfortable villa style.

Saturday night we all had a good time in the main dining room, with a pianist who enticed dancers onto the floor with his repertoire of all the old and new songs. The menu was relatively simple, with a reasonable number of choices in each category and the service was friendly and helpful.

I am sure that every guest staying at Villa la Massa is not only impressed with the beauty of the gardens and the tranquil atmosphere, but also with the extremely accommodating air of the staff.

Love is part of the theme here. The very atmosphere inspires warmth and affection, and to illustrate the point, two people who were sitting in the garden enjoying the sunshine suddenly looked at each other, smiled, and embraced. Ah, *amore*!

HOTEL VILLA LA MASSA, 50010 Candeli, Florence. Tel.: (055) 63-00-51. A 44-guestroom very comfortable inn located in a 16th-century villa on the banks of the Arno River, about 20 min. from downtown Firenze (Florence). Breakfast, lunch, and dinner. Swimming pool on grounds, tennis, fishing, golfing, and horseback riding nearby. Open year round. Rates: See Index.

Directions: From Autostrada (A-1) use Firenze Sud Exit and proceed through the village of Bagno a Ripoli. Follow signs for Candeli. At the river, still following signs, turn right on Via Villa Magna, the principal way from Candeli to Florence, a distance of about 10 km. Keep a careful eye out on the left-hand side of the road for Villa La Massa.

RESTAURANT TRATTORIA CAMMILLO, Florence

Frederick and Christine Boes from Dusseldorf were the two people I saw embracing in the gardens of Villa La Massa. We became acquainted and they suggested that I join them for dinner at the Trattoria Cammillo. "This is not a so-called exclusive restaurant," said Frederick. "It is a place where Florentians enjoy a family meal."

We took a taxi to the center of the city, walked over the famous Ponte Vecchio Bridge, and within a few moments were at the door.

The Trattoria Cammillo is not elegant in any sense of the word. Fortunate guests (those *with* reservations), stand inside the front door and wait for a table to become available. The waiters deftly carry the trays over their heads and good-naturedly work around the anxiously waiting, hungry, expectant, would-be diners. "Don't let all this bother you," said Frederick, "believe me, it is well worth it."

Finally, the owner informed us that our table was ready; we were unceremoniously seated and the fun of choosing from the menu began. From my chair I could look right into the kitchen, where there were many shiny pots and pans and busy chefs exchanging badinage.

Briefly, the evening at the Restaurant Cammillo was a great success. We all sampled each other's choices and pronounced them delicious. My opening course was spinach with cheese and tomato sauce. For the main dish I had veal scaloppine—thinly- sliced veal in a most marvelous sauce. Frederick had chicken breasts baked just right, topped with some cheese and basil.

Dinner moved on in what was now a leisurely pace as there were no more diners waiting. At the cheese course, I had Bel Paese for the first time in Italy. It was a very delicate cheese, and I was to order it several times in the future. Another very good, inexpensive, local cheese is called Pecorino.

Dessert was baked pear, a house specialty. Other specialties on the menu were Scaloppine Capriccio, scampi with curry and wild rice, and Florentine tripe.

Frederick, Christine, and I resolved we would write a book on the small, little-heralded restaurants in Italy. It would take 1,000 years and begin with Trattoria Cammillo.

RESTAURANT TRATTORIA CAMMILLO, Borgo S. Jacopo 57, Florence. Tel.: 21-24-27. This is an excellent, moderately-priced family restaurant. Not certain whether it is closed on any nights during the week. Telephone ahead for reservations and then be prepared to wait.

Directions: Trattoria Cammillo is located about two blocks from the Ponte Vecchio on the south side of the Arno River. It is a few squares from the Pitti Palace.

HOTEL REGENCY, Florence

Florence is a busy, bustling city . . . one of the great tourist objectives in Italy. Naturally, with this kind of reputation and with so much to see and enjoy, finding peaceful and quiet accommodations (with a convenient place to park) can sometimes present a problem. The Regency answered all of these conditions.

The director is Arturo Secchi, a most accommodating and well-informed man, with lovely Florentine manners that put me immediately at ease. I have had an extensive correspondence with him ever since my first visit, and his latest letter says that the Regency has been officially classified as a "deluxe hotel." They still have thirty-one rooms, but are probably going to have forty since they have purchased a building immediately adjacent. All of the rooms have a bath or shower, a radio, air conditioning, and color television. Everyone enjoys the lovely private gardens.

There is a park in front of the Regency with dozens of beautiful sycamore trees and a place for children to play. It is in a very quiet section of Florence and provides quite a change from the busy downtown area.

My first impression, once inside the front door, was of hundreds of fresh flowers. They were placed everywhere—in the sitting rooms, lobby, and in the dining rooms.

Arturo took me on a brief tour, including guest rooms, most of which had high ceilings, harmonizing curtains and wallpaper; many overlooked the garden or the park.

Over lunch, he talked about the food on the Regency menu,

which is "homemade and natural." One of the interesting house specialties is a T-bone steak that comes from the fat cattle in the Tuscan countryside.

The Regency is that quiet corner in Florence that many people will find delightful.

HOTEL REGENCY (formerly the Umbria) (Relais et Chateaux), Piazza M. d'Azeglio 3, 50121 Florence. Tel.: 587-655-602. A deluxe, quiet, 31-guestroom conservative hotel, convenient to all the Florentine museums and beautiful churches. Parking facilities. Breakfast, lunch, and dinner served. Open year-round. (New York reservation telephone: 800- 223-5581.) Rates: See Index.

Directions: Arriving by car in Florence, inquire for the Piazza D'Azeglio, a small park. The Regency is about six squares from the Duomo.

Counterpoint on the Ponte Vecchio

In the middle of the bridge called Ponte Vecchio, which spans the Arno between the Pitti Palace and the Uffizi Gallery, there is a bronze bust of Benvenuto Cellini, the master craftsman of Florence.

Today, a few centuries after Cellini, the Ponte Vecchio is more than a bridge, it is actually the street of the gold sellers where, in addition to the shops, there are young people who spread out on blankets their designs and crafts in leather, silver, jewelry, ceramics, and paintings.

In the very middle of the bridge on a Sunday afternoon, a group of young people can be found singing to guitars and bongo drums. From time to time, their friends drop by and "sit in," singing the choruses softly after the main singer and guitar player have done a few verses.

The passersby also create a good show . . . sightseers of all ages in all types of garb, conversing in many languages and accents . . . some of them, perhaps themselves Florentines, strolling in their Sunday best after the noontime meal . . . young ladies in knee-high white boots and black dresses . . . there are Germans and Scandinavians with long hair and blue jeans—sometimes it is impossible to tell the nationality.

I am not sure what Signor Cellini is thinking about all this. His bust faces the young people in the street, but his eyes seem to be raised to heaven. I think that's just perhaps an accident of design; I would think that Benvenuto appreciated this kind of a good time.

PENSION HERMITAGE, Florence

"The Hermitage is just like a private club." These are the words in which Jim Mellow of St. Louis described this unusual accommodation in the center of Florence. "You don't even realize you are in a small hotel."

His recommendation was backed up also by Malcolm Frager, my concert-pianist neighbor, who was also most glowing in his praise. Thank you, gentlemen.

The Hermitage is located literally a few steps from the Ponte Vecchio and is just around the corner from the Uffizi and Pitti Museums and the Duomo.

An elevator carries guests to one reception room on the fifth floor, which also has the dining room with a rooftop view, and a living room with a very cozy fireplace. Just one flight above is a roof garden with many flowers, and even more inviting views of the town. Accommodations are in small but tidy rooms.

Breakfast, the only meal offered here, is served on the terrace in the summer, and there are many good restaurants nearby.

High season at the Hermitage is from March to October and fortunate, indeed, are the guests who are able to obtain accommodations here during this time. English, French, and German are spoken by two members of the staff.

PENSION HERMITAGE, 1, Vicolo Marzio (Ponte Vecchio) 50122 Florence. Tel.: 28-72-16. A 16-guestroom intimate inn in the heart of old Florence within walking distance of all of the main attractions. Breakfast is the only meal served. Probably closed during Nov. High season is from March to Oct., but anyone writing in advance will receive a room confirmation. Rates: See Index.

Directions: The Hermitage is about 20 steps to the famous Ponte Vecchio Bridge. Park as close to the Ponte Vecchio as possible; proceed on foot until you find Vicolo Marzio. There is a brass plate on the side of the building. Take the elevator to the fifth floor, where the reception desk is located.

PLAZA HOTEL LUCCHESI, Florence

The Plaza Hotel Lucchesi is located directly on the bank of the Arno River, within a pleasant walking distance of the center of the city. The management and the staff seem to be particularly adept in handling tour groups. I must also commend them for efficiently and courteously tracking down two sweaters that I left inadvertently in the wardrobe of my river-view guest room. The Plaza Lucchesi is an excellent example of a large hotel that manages to maintain pleasant contact with its guests.

PLAZA HOTEL LUCCHESI, Lungarno della Zecca Vecchia 38, Florence 50010. Tel.: 298-856. A 105-guestroom modern hotel overlooking the Arno River, a 12-min. walk from center of city. Breakfast, lunch, and dinner. Garage on premises. Open year-round. (Reservations made be made through Jane Condon, New York, N.Y. 800-223-5608.) Rates: See Index.

IL CEDRO RESTAURANT, Moggiona (Arezzo)

On my way between two interesting monasteries, hidden away in the wild Apennines east of Florence, I made a refreshing detour into a thick forest of trees that covered hill after hill. I finally arrived at Moggiona, a little mountain village overlooking a valley, with a river flowing into the Arno. There was nothing in sight but green turning into blue in the distance. I stopped to have a bite, and sat down to a feast. From beginning to end the cucina casalinga (homemade) was a delight, as was the coniglie in porchetta, roasted rabbit. Dinner is about 20,000 lire, wine included.

As in so many other small Italian restaurants, the cook is none other than the owner's wife. Bravo Franca Tassini.

IL CEDRO RESTAURANT, Moggiona (52010 Arezzo). Tel.: 0575-556-08. A tiny but good restaurant in the mountains east of Florence. Closed Mon. except in summer. Italo Tassini, Owner.

Directions: From Poppi, go 5 km. into the mountains to Moggiona.

PENSIONE CASENTINO, Poppi (Arezzo)

If you don't feel like driving all the way back into the touristic main street, head towards picturesque Poppi, another marvel handed down from the Middle Ages, a miniature city set on top of a hill with an imposing and graceful fortress. I liked the Pensione Casentino because it is an example of what a good and unpretentious hotel can be in Italy—everything is up to standard: rooms agreeable and quiet with comfortable furnishings, a garden, and a good location in the town. You'll find a cool and comfortable room at the Pensione Casentino facing the castle in a pretty garden.

Poppi itself is a little jewel of a city, one of the myriad well-polished, subtly gleaming gems adorning the hills of Tuscany and Umbria.

PENSIONE CASENTINO, 52014 Poppi (Arezzo). Tel.: 0575 52-90-90. A quiet, small hotel. Open from June to Oct. Lucca Gatteschi, Owner. Rates: See Index.

Directions: Poppi is 38 km. north of Arezzo.

VILLA LA PRINCIPESSA, Massa Pisana (near Pisa)

Dinner at Villa La Principessa was over; I returned to the living room, where there was a crackling fire sending out a welcome warmth against the mild chill of a Tuscany October evening.

A very attractive Italian couple invited me to share their delicious roasted chestnuts, and while we were getting acquainted, the last piece of wood was put on the fire, and we asked the porter to replenish the supply. He replied, "The wood is burning too fast," This started a series of jokes about fireplaces and wood and darkness that had us all laughing in both English and Italian. Another bundle of wood arrived and the laughter and good conversation continued well into the late hours of the evening. All of this played against the rather impressive background of the villa; the main living room has an extremely high ceiling and the walls are adorned with a large collection of oils from a variety of Italian periods, mostly portraits of noblemen. They all seemed to be gazing approvingly at an elaborate coat-of-arms over the fireplace.

Villa La Principessa is set in the midst of a very lovely park with a terrace on two sides. The view from the swimming pool offers a panorama of the Tuscany hills.

Guest rooms are quite luxurious; the furnishings more modern than traditional.

We all met for breakfast the next morning as the sun streamed in the windows of the dining room. The gardener was already preparing for the oncoming, relatively mild winter. This is a quiet part of Italy, although the city of Pisa, with its famous leaning tower, is just a short distance away.

VILLA LA PRINCIPESSA (Relais et Chateaux), 55050 Massa Pisana, Lucca. Tel.: (0583) 379-136. A 44-guestroom very comfortable inn in a beautiful villa approx. 25 min. north of the city of Pisa. Breakfast, lunch, and dinner. Swimming pool on grounds; tennis, golf, horseback riding, and Leaning Tower of Pisa nearby. Open all year. Rates: See Index.

Directions: Use Lucca exit from Autostrada (A11). Follow signs to Pisa. Villa la Principessa is on the right about 5 km. from Autostrada exit. Massa Pisana is not on many Italian maps. It is a wide place in the road on Rte. 12 between Lucca and Pisa.

Portofino

One look at the brochure on Portofino and I was enchanted beyond measure. Portofino is an old fishing village at the end of a small peninsula that thrusts its way into the Mediterranean, and is reached from Santa Margherita by a magnificent winding coastal road, considered to be one of the most beautiful drives in the world. On a brilliant fall afternoon the sea was blue and the flowers and trees were in their final burst of glory. Best of all, because it was not the height of the season, the traffic on this road had been reduced to a minimum.

The village of Portofino is clustered around a natural harbor, and although it is a prime objective of tourists, the main business is fishing, an occupation that has persisted for several hundred years. The crescent-shaped harbor is surrounded by small cafés, restaurants, and curio shops that attract many sightseers. The brochure on Portofino can be obtained by writing the Tourist Office, 16034 Portofino.

ALBERGO SPLENDIDO, Portofino

I was savoring a lunch of fresh Gorgonzola cheese, Italian bread, grapes, and some small, very tart Italian oranges and luscious pears. The view from the terrace at Albergo Splendido, overlooking a portion of the harbor at Portofino and the Mediterranean Sea beyond, was so enchanting that it brought a lump to my throat.

Before me in the wonderful Riviera afternoon, boats were bobbing on a blue harbor, beyond which was an ice-cream-cone-shaped, green, forested hill, at the top of which was a most appealing villa. Here was a scene that had been enjoyed by Phoenicians, Roman nobles, and tourists from all parts of the world for many centuries.

The mid-October sun was so strong that I spent most of the afternon at the pool, getting a light tan and alternating between reading a novel and looking at the hilltop skyline, replete with the wonderful silhouettes of the green trees against the blue horizon.

Later, I walked from the hotel down the hill into the narrow streets of the village and out into the harbor area. I arrived at five o'clock to the accompaniment of two different sets of church bells. On a bench by the water, I idled away an hour watching the fishing boats returning with the day's catch, and then I wandered back into town to enjoy a hot chocolate at one of the outdoor cafés.

My dinner at the hotel was enlivened by the company of two English people—we sat outside on the terrace and chatted until well past midnight. A piano played lightly in the background, and in the semidarkness, the soft voices and occasional laughter of other guests created a warm feeling of belonging.

Down in the harbor, the riding and cabin lights of the boats were bright punctuation points in the blue velvet of the night, and the street lights of the town seemed like an enchanted pearl necklace disappearing around the small hill.

In the bright sunshine the next morning, again there was breakfast on the terrace, a conversation with some tennis players, and a reluctant goodbye to my friends of the previous evening. They were

on their way north and would stay near Nice that evening. "Oh, we stop here every year," they said, "sometimes for two or three days. It is on the road to Rome."

The Albergo Splendido was what I was looking for on the Italian Riviera. The rates are in the luxury class, but considering its comparatively small size and romantic setting, I think it is worth it.

ALBERGO SPLENDIDO, Salita Baratta 13, 16034 Portofino. Tel.: 69551; Telex 331057 Splend I. A 67-guestroom exceptionally comfortable inn with first-class service overlooking the exquisite harbor of Portofino. About 1 hr. south of Genova. Breakfast, lunch, and dinner. Swimming pool and tennis on grounds. Fishing, water skiing, golf, horseback riding, and exceptional Italian Riviera scenery. Closed Nov. 1 to Mar. 29. All rooms face the sea. Half and full pensions available. Rates: See Index.

Directions: Portofino is just off Autostrada (A12). Using the exit for Rapallo, follow signs through Santa Margherita. Before reaching Portofino village watch carefully for signs to Albergo Splendido leading up a precipice road on the right.

PARK HOTEL, Siena

I believe that the man from New Jersey on the American Express tour summed up the Park Hotel very well: "We never expected to be staying in a place like this . . . a real castle. We have been on this tour for about a week now, starting in Paris and going to Rome and Naples. We're on our way back through Switzerland to Amsterdam. This has been the most impressive place we have visited.

The Park Hotel is an old, 15th-century Tuscan castle that has been thoroughly modernized. Built in the form of an **E**, with about sixty guest rooms, it is on a piece of high ground on the outskirts of

Siena and is very quiet. The hotel is surrounded by olive groves and vineyards, both of which enhance the menu—vegetables and fruits for the table are grown also in the fields below.

Besides this feeling of being set apart, perhaps the most impressive feature of the hotel is the gardens. One is a formal garden of carefully trimmed hedges and trees, as pictured in the paintings of the Italian masters. The other is a carefully tended flower garden that even in mid-October was a riot of color. A gardener was busy cutting, trimming, and tying back.

Adding to the naturalness of the scene, the vines growing in profusion over the beige walls were turning into the many hues of autumn. A small park immediately adjacent to the castle has paths used for centuries to meander among the old trees.

The exterior of this castle has remained unchanged in recent centuries. The architecture is typically Tuscan. For the most part, all of the bedrooms and the interior public rooms have contemporary furniture with an occasional sprinkling of traditional paintings and tapestry. Castles differ in various parts of Europe, and perhaps this one would be better described as a palace.

PARK HOTEL, Via Marciano 16, 53100 Siena. Tel.: (0577) 44-803. A 52-guestroom very comfortable 15th-century castle-inn with a panoramic view of the city of Siena. Breakfast, lunch, and dinner. Swimming pool and tennis on grounds; horseback riding, fishing, golf nearby. Open all year. Rates: See Index.

Directions: Siena is in the heart of the Tuscany area of Italy. The Park Hotel is on the east side of the city.

LOCANDA DELL'AMOROSA, Sinalunga (Siena)

Here is a place that is hard to describe. Genuine and stylish, it belongs in the pages of *Vogue*, as well as in any art book about Italy. This old Tuscan farmhouse includes a self-enclosed village square, complete with arcades and a chapel, a brick well on a triangular lawn, white canvas chairs under a parasol. Elegance, leisure, and quality are three words to finally sum it all up.

It is strange how each place in the center of Italy—each city, each restaurant—opens up a new variation of the same pleasure. Here the surprise is total; one enters a whole separate world, and a very refined one, too. Giuseppe Vaccarini, the young manager, sees to it.

The menu is crowded with numerous delicacies: *filetto di cinghiale* (ham from a wild boar), fish raviolis, *crespelle di ricotta e spinaci*, a rolled, hand-drawn pasta enclosing ricotta, a soft white cheese mixed with spinach...

The decor features international chic in a typical Italian way. There are also a few rooms along the same line.

LOCANDA DELL'AMOROSA, 53048 Sinalunga (Siena). Tel.: 0577-67-94-97. A luxurious inn and restaurant in an old Tuscan farmhouse, 45 km. from Siena. Rooms have baths, TV and all necessary luxuries. Closed Jan., Feb., Mon., and Tues. mornings. Giuseppe Vaccarini, Manager. Rates: See Index.

Directions: Take S-326 out of Sinalunga for 2 km. Watch for the usual landmark—the long alley of beautiful old cypress trees on the right-hand side.

From Toscana into Umbria

Traveling from Florence towards Rome, it is very refreshing to stop and linger in Umbria, often called "the green heart of Italy." This region has very much to offer: beautiful lakes, soft rolling hills rising up to 900 meters, innumerable townlets complete with castles and old churches with frescoes and museums filled with real treasures. Before entering Umbria one should stop in Arezzo to see the magnificent frescoes of Piero della Francesca.

Right on the piazza, coming out of the church, is a good restaurant, the Buca di San Francesco, where they serve a particularly savory Bollito misto, different sorts of meats boiled together and served with a tasty green sauce.

The city of Cortona is about fifty kilometers from Arezzo. Located on a hilltop at an altitude of 650 meters, Cortona is the belvedere of Toscana and Umbria. From the piazza it is possible to see Lake Trasimeno and, farther down, the pretty Umbrian hills rolling southward. Cortona is loaded with touristic pleasures. This city is a miniature epitome of what one expects from an Italian town. There are seven beautifully decorated churches, two museums of great interest, old palaces, antique shops, winding streets, and a superb ice cream parlor, bar, and pastry shop: the Bar Barichelli on the Via Nazionale. Also, two very good restaurants and one very quiet and intimate hotel, Villa Guglielmesca.

❋　❋　❋　❋

VILLA GUGLIELMESCA, Cortona

Leaving Cortona, bearing north, one drives into the hills and through the woods. The road seems long and the hotel very remote —which it is. One has ample time to fantasize about what the place will look like before getting there. Pink bricks and green shutters finally appear at the end of the road. The hotel is an old, unpretentious villa with an atmosphere of faded grandeur that carries a certain appeal. Most of all, it is set in an atmosphere of perfect peace and tranquility.

We met Mario Boari, the innkeeper, in the bar on the veranda, where there are lots of plants—a nice place to have breakfast. The restaurant offers good, simple food. One of the best dishes there is *bistecca alla fiorentina*, a roasted rib of beef, Italian style.

VILLA GUGLIELMESCA, Cortona. Tel.: (075) 60-33-65. A 26-guest-room comfortable inn in the midst of trees and silence, 8 km. from Cortona. Breakfast, lunch, and dinner. It is a very good place for an overnight stay. Open April 1 to Oct. 10. Rates: See Index.

Directions: Leave Cortona going north on the road to the Eremo di San Egidio, towards Citta di Castello. At about 8 km. from Cortona there are signs to the hotel.

RESTAURANT LA LOGETTA, Cortona

Maria Vitaliano always liked to cook. Maybe this accounts for her marrying Marilli Vitaliano, who always wanted to open a restaurant. Maybe this explains the smoothness of things at La Logetta—Marilli welcomes the guests with grandeur and politesse, while Maria produces a continuous flow of delicious dishes.

Built into the cool whitewashed walls of the wine cellars of Palazzo Pochetti, La Logetta is a good place to have lunch on a hot summer day. The palazzo dates back to the 16th century and is still in the hands of the same family, the Pochettis, who dwell above the restaurant.

Four years ago, some of the more enterprising members of the family had the idea of turning the "cantine" wine cellars into a chic restaurant. They were lucky to find Marilli and Maria. She cooks following her own invention and also makes conventional dishes, but with her own flair added. Marilli likes to tell the story of an American lady, owner of a restaurant in New York, who lunched and dined at La Logetta for a whole week in the hope of softening Maria's heart, because she wanted the recipe of the *budino alla cioccolata*, a good Italian dessert that is a kind of chocolate custard. She was given a lot of *budino,* but not the secret.

For news on overnight accommodations, see the following paragraph.

LA LOGETTA, Piazza Pescheria, 3, Cortona. Tel.: (0575) 603-077. Rates: about 16,000 to 25,000 lire per person with a good wine.

RESIDENCE S. SABRINA, Cortona

Marilli opened this small pensione just a few steps from La Logetta. There are six double rooms, each with its own private bathroom. The rooms are also supplied with a TV, a telephone, and independent central heating. This provides a very quiet and clean place to stay in Cortona.

RESIDENCE S. SABRINA, Via Roma 37, Cortona. Tel.: (0575) 604-188. A 6-guestroom pensione in the center of Cortona. Breakfast and room service available. Rates: See Index.

Closer to Lake Trasimeno, 25 miles south of Cortona, is the tiny village of Castel Rigone. Perched on one of the lovely hills above the lake at an altitude of 65 meters, Castel Rigone is a picturesque fortified village with a tiny, very pretty piazza and a very beautiful church. Off the piazza is the hotel-restaurant, La Fattoria (the farm), offering good food, comfortable rooms, and a wide open view on the lake.

LA FATTORIA, Castel Rigone (above Lake Trasimeno)

When Aldo Pammelati first came to the Fattoria in 1960, he came to run it as a real farm with 600 hectares of land. As agriculture in the hills was slowly dying, the farm was closed and sold in 1965. Aldo Pammelati bought the main buildings and immediately opened a few rooms to travelers. He then stubbornly set to his task of turning the farm into a pleasant and comfortable hotel.

Now, fifteen years later, it is an undeniable success. The buildings have all been restored to their original simplicity. The rooms are plain but comfortable, most of them with a beautiful view of the lake over the hills; all of them with the pure and cool breezes of the mountains. Even in the midst of summer it's never too warm here. Its perfect location makes this hotel a good overnight place when visiting the center of Italy. Easy access to the lake makes it a nice place to stay for a few days.

Lidia (Mrs. Pammelati) runs the restaurant with the help of her stepmother, who was the cook at the Castle of the Knights of Malta in nearby Magione. Lidia's cooking has kept the simple hearty touch she used when she had to feed all the workers of the farm. But now she caters to a cosmopolitan crowd that fills the impressive dining room on weekends. It is wise to make reservations.

LA FATTORIA, Castel Rigone 06060 (Perugia). Tel.: 845-212. A 30-guestroom rustic place. The restaurant is closed on Wed., and the hotel and restaurant are closed in Nov. Tennis and horseback riding ten minutes away. Rates: See Index.

Directions: On the road from Arezzo to Perugia, 58 km. from Arezzo, a sign on the left of the road points to Castel Rigone. The road leaves the lake and winds up to the village. The inn is on the piazza, the highest point in the village.

HOTEL LORD BYRON, Rome

I was up to my neck in bubbles in one of the world's deepest bathtubs. The water was soothing to my tired muscles and exhausted emotions. What a day it had been! At eight-thirty in the morning, I had taken the tour that leaves the front of the hotel and had "done" just a small section of the sights and attractions of Rome in the morning. Returning for lunch, I had followed it with another tour in the afternoon. I had seen St. Peter's, the Capitoline Hill, the Coliseum, the bridges of Rome, the fountains, and many of the ruins. In the normal course of events it would take another four days to see everything. Now, I was luxuriating in this beautiful bathroom with its mirrored walls, scented soaps, and great, fluffy towels.

A hotel like the Lord Byron is what every traveler needs in Italy. Rome is one of the most energetic, frenetic cities in the world—a fantastic mix of the old and the new in every possible sense. It is certainly one of the most popular tourist attractions because of the presence of the Vatican and all of the incredible ruins of the Old City. After a day on the buses, on foot, bicycle, taxicabs, or what-have-you, it was a pleasure to return to the quiet, efficient service at this conservative hotel.

The Lord Byron is located on a residential dead-end street, which means practically no traffic—and traffic is the one thing that impresses everyone visiting Rome.

I cannot praise the front desk, the concierge, and the management enough for all of the services they provide for their guests, because one thing that everyone needs when they come to Rome is information, advice, and directions.

There are many large hotels in Rome catering to the innumerable crowds of tourists that seem to be there in all seasons of the year, but in many conversations I have had since my return, and sharing experiences with people who have been to Rome, I now know that it was a very fortunate day for me when I discovered the Lord Byron.

LORD BYRON HOTEL (Relais et Chateaux), 5 Via de Notaris, 00197 Rome. Tel.: (06) 360-9541. (New York reservations: 800-223-5581.) A 55-guestroom deluxe modern hotel with first-class service in a quiet section of Rome on the outskirts of the Villa Borghese and near the Via Veneto. Breakfast, lunch, and dinner served all year. Rates: See Index.

Directions: Arriving by air: either take a taxi directly from the airport to the hotel or take the air terminal bus going to the middle of Rome, and then take taxi to hotel. In either case, before paying taxi fare go inside the hotel and check with Lord Byron concierge to make sure it is a fair amount.

Note: Don't rent a car at the airport if you are going to be at the Lord Byron. The car company will bring a car to the hotel. The traffic in Rome for the first-time visitor is unbelievable.

Arriving by car from north: Exit Autostrada (A1) and follow signs that say Salaria, one of the main avenues in Rome. Stay on Salaria (if you have a map of Rome you will notice a large green area to the north of the city—this is Villa Borghese). The most sensible thing to do when you arrive in this area is to hire a taxi and follow it to the Lord Byron.

If You Are Arriving in Rome . . .

Rome is served by the Leonardo da Vinci Airport, about eighteen miles, or one hour, from the bus terminal. Built more than twenty-five year ago, this airport was never expected to handle the tremendous volume of people that it now accommodates. One needs patience, forbearance, and good humor to negotiate its environs.

I've always heard that there is very little searching of suitcases at this airport, and clearing customs is a fast operation. Get a porter, identified by orange uniforms, who will charge about sixty cents per suitcase. Tipping is not customary.

The buses to Rome have "A.C.O.T.R.A.L." painted on the sides and leave every fifteen minutes for the central train station, Termini, about an hour away. The fare is about three dollars.

Use only the authorized yellow cabs and the fare should run about twenty-five dollars. About an eight percent tip is sufficient. It's a half-hour drive.

Rome has automobile traffic exceeded only by that of Lisbon, so allow plenty of time to get back to the airport, regardless of the method used.

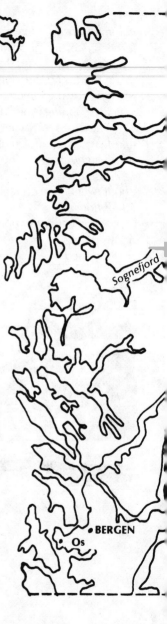

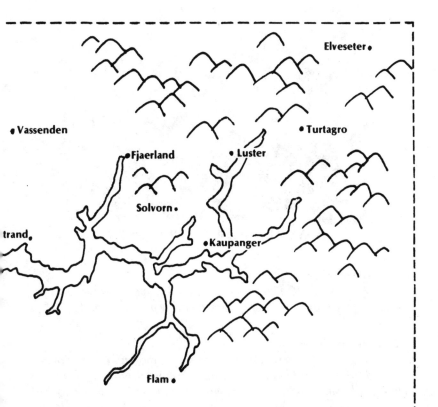

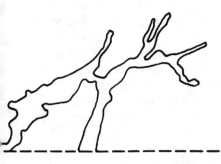

NORWAY

TRAVEL SUGGESTIONS FOR NORWAY

How to Get There

SAS has direct flights to Oslo. Norway can also be reached directly by car from Sweden and by car/ferry from Denmark.

Country Inns in Norway

My visit to Norway was confined for the most part to the Sognefjord district where I found hotels and pensions. In Norway, a hotel is legally classified as having enough bedrooms and reception rooms to adequately house at least twenty guests, and is required also to have a certain number of available wc's. Some Norwegian hotels have many resort facilities on the grounds or nearby.

The pensions share a number of common virtues: most of their rooms have twin beds with down comforters encased in a washable sheeting. Almost all have running water in each room, and sometimes there is only one wc and one bathroom for seven or eight rooms. All serve three meals a day, and often offer between-meal snacks of delicious homemade cakes with coffee or tea.

All have living rooms where guests can relax before and after meals. Both pensions and hotels have plans that include three meals a day and special rates for three days or more.

Reservations can be made by mail or telephone.

Norwegian Menus

Every hotel and pension has a single-price meal as well as an à la carte menu. The evening meal consists of three courses: soup, usually homemade, a main dish—a large platter with meat or fish

346

and a vegetable, as well as lettuce and tomato or other salad vegetables—and dessert, usually fresh or frozen fruit served with whipped cream.

Breakfast, Norwegian-style, is a real eating adventure. This is where I found the many varieties of cold fish, cheese (including delicious goat cheese), breads, crackers, and jams.

Driving Tips

Public transportation in Norway is excellent, and in a great many cases it would be advisable to leave the car in Oslo or Bergen and travel by train, bus, or ferry to a central point, such as Balestrand, and then make a series of daily or overnight excursions into the fjord country, using the carefully coordinated schedules of both ferries and buses. That's what I did. I had to grow accustomed to the long daylight hours and the occasional rain and mist that are part of the fjord country ambience. I was glad that I brought a raincoat. There was, however, plenty of sunshine. Incidentally, gasoline stations and supermarkets close early, usually at five o'clock.

My Itinerary in Norway

I took the train from Oslo to Bergen and spent one night nearby before taking the car/ferry to Balestrand. It is also possible to get to Bergen from Oslo by air, ferry, or car and then follow this itinerary. I went to the end of the Sognefjord, up and over the mountains, and down the other side into Sweden.

THE SOLSTRAND FJORD HOTEL, Os, Bergen

My table in the dining room had a perfect view of the Bjornafjord. I could look across the green lawn, past the tennis courts, and out into this water wonderland. The Norwegian flag stirred lightly as breezes from across the water picked up its elegant long tail, making it look like a kite in the sky. The Hardanger mountains across the fjord had patches of snow, and in the distance, the peaks of higher mountains were almost completely covered with snow.

After an afternoon of learning more about the fascinating city of Bergen, I had set out on Route 14, the road to Os, and now was enjoying my first evening meal in Norway.

It began with a delicious vegetable soup served in a big bowl.

347

The table was laid with old-fashioned silverware. The main course was fresh trout served with a tartar sauce and white potatoes. The dessert was tasty fresh fruit, including oranges, grapes, and peaches, topped with freshly whipped cream. A young man played the piano throughout the entire meal, alternating his selections between such old favorites as Errol Garner's "Misty" and Chopin's "Minute Waltz."

All of the guests in the dining room seemed to be Norwegian. As far as I could tell I was the only non-Scandinavian present. However, the entire staff of this resort-inn spoke English and I was made to feel at home at once.

One of the outstanding features of this waterside hotel is a large heated indoor swimming pool, a sauna, and some extensive exercise equipment.

Guest rooms at this hotel are typical of what I found everywhere in Scandinavia. There are older rooms with traditional furniture and decor, typical of many American and British country inns. Then there is a newer wing of modernized rooms with furniture reflecting mod-

ern Scandinavian design with greater simplicity and austerity of line. The tables, chairs, lamps, and beds are not as decorative as they are functional. I found this functional style almost everywhere I went, for more and more pensions and small hotels have been redecorated and refurnished.

THE SOLSTRAND FJORD HOTEL, N-5200 Os. Tel.: Bergen 30-00-99. Located in a scenic fjord area, 17 mi. from Bergen Airport, 18 mi. from Bergen. Accessible by bus from Bergen. Indoor heated swimming pool, sauna, private beach, rowboats, speedboats, waterskiing, fishing, walking, tennis, mini-golf. Rates: See Index.

Balestrand

On the map showing the Sognefjord area I have indicated the location of the town of Balestrand. Balestrand is the principal stop on the ferries that leave from Bergen each day. There is a car ferry that leaves at 9:30 in the morning and arrives at 6:30 at night, and another ferry leaves at 8:30 a.m., arriving at noon, but does not permit automobiles. Balestrand is approximately a 5-hour drive from Bergen and can also be reached conveniently by bus.

I found that I could use Balestrand as a base for traveling anywhere in this particular fjord system and the nearby mountains. There are ferry, bus, and automobile connections in all directions. The local tourist office which, by the way, is typical of similar offices everywhere in Norway, is most accommodating. It is open from 9:30 until 6:30 every day with two hours off for lunch. It is possible to arrive in Balestrand and get assistance at the tourist office in planning either a one-day or a two-week stay in the area. This includes making reservations at various hotels and pensions. Travelers are also invited to contact the Balestrand tourist office in the off-season for information, which can be studied in advance of arrival. The mailing address is: Balestrand Tourist Office, N-5850, Balestrand, Norway.

PENSJONAT DRAGSVIK, Balestrand, Sognefjord

This was my first stay in a Norwegian pension. It is located in a very pretty village just across the Esefjord from the village of Balestrand. It is within walking distance of the Dragsvik ferry stop, which means that guests here have the entire Sognefjord area accessible by water. My room, furnished in a modern Scandinavian fashion, overlooked Balestrand and the main fjord.

I'll take a few moments to describe the dinner served here because it was typical of pension fare that I enjoyed during my trip. The first course was a piquant homemade asparagus soup. The main course for two was served on a large platter. This consisted of sliced roast beef, cauliflower, pickles and prunes, and generous amounts of lettuce, arranged most artistically. There was a separate dish of boiled white potatoes, which I found was a staple in the Norwegian diet, and a bowl of tasty gravy prepared from the juices of the meat. Dessert was freshly whipped cream and peaches.

The view from the dining room was lovely, overlooking the fjord and the mountains. In the foreground there were fruit trees in blos-

som. Overhead, the sky cleared for a short time and a bar or two of sunshine dramatically lighted the fjord.

PENSJONAT DRAGSVIK, N-5850 Balestrand. Tel.: 056-94-293. Dragsvik is a hamlet across the Esefjord from Balestrand. All of the fjord outdoor recreation and excursion advantages are available. Rates: See Index.

MIDTNES PENJSONAT, Balestrand, Sognefjord

I stayed one night in this pension in a modest single room that overlooked the flowery hillside. There was running water in the room, and since my visit, nearly all of the rooms have a shower and a wc.

This family-owned pension has a beautiful dining room overlooking the fjord and an outdoor terrace that is very popular on clement evenings. A few steps away it has its own dock and facilities for hiring sailboats, rowboats, and water skis. The owners were most accommodating and I noticed that they spent a great deal of time sitting in the salons, talking with their guests.

I particularly remember the dozens of yellow tulips that were in bloom on the terrace and in the yard of the inn during my stay. It is immediately adjacent to St. Olav's English church.

MIDTNES PENSJONAT, N-5850 Balestrand. Tel.: 056-91-133. Rates: See Index.

KRINGSJA HOTEL, Balestrand

This is a good example of the difference between a pension and a small hotel in Norway. In this case there were much larger living rooms and salons. The furnishings were more modern and the decor was tastefully harmonized. The bedrooms were a bit larger and more imaginatively furnished.

In one of the lounges there were modern reproductions of Norwegian runic writings on the walls. There is usually entertainment during the weekend—dancing or perhaps folk singing. Although this is a bit more formal than a pension, it still has a very homey feeling. It has a view of the fjord and sits in a small orchard of fruit trees and lilac bushes, which were in bloom during my visit.

KRINGSJA HOTEL, N-5850 Balestrand 8. Tel.: Balestrand 8. Rates: See Index.

The Fjaerland Fjord

A trip by ferry on the Fjaerland Fjord is an exciting way to spend a day, or even a longer visit with an overnight stay at the Hotel Mundal or the Fjaerland Pensjonat. I made the trip for the day and was entranced with this strange and marvelous corner of Norway. The Fjaerland Fjord is one of the most famous and unusual in Norway, with its ever-changing shoreline, from serene pastoral meadows to steep cliffs and snow-topped mountains rising to 3,000 feet on both sides. And at the end of the line, there is a bus trip up to the Jostedal Glacier and its spectacular waterfalls.

HOTEL MUNDAL, Fjaerland

I had a feeling that I had been at this beautiful inn before. Perhaps because of its similarity to so many country inns I have visited in both Britain and North America. As a matter of fact, its atmosphere was distinctly British. When I mentioned this to Marit Mauritzen, she said that quite possibly it was because of their many guests from the British Isles, even as far back as the late 19th century.

"The British are great walkers," she said. "And I think that our proximity to the Jostedal Glacier, the largest ice field on the European continent, makes the prospect of mountain walks and climbing even more attractive. With this in mind, we have always offered courses in glaciology and geology. We're very popular here with botanists and ornithologists as well."

351

I could feel the innkeeping tradition radiating from this old building and its owners. It was obvious that this hotel had been well cared for by its owners and loved by guests for many years. In the main living room, a fireplace with intricate hand-painted designs of Norwegian flowers was surrounded by deep leather chairs that invited both reverie and conversation. While I was walking through the hotel I could hear someone playing the piano in the background, and there was one particularly interesting room with a circular seat in a beautiful bay window. I also found a billiard room with a wood-paneled ceiling.

In the dining room, there were some large painted panels depicting the fairy tale of the three princes who were turned into bears and

could only be turned back into princes if they could find princesses who would be willing to take them into their bedchambers. There is one panel showing the three princesses with their hair literally standing on end upon being confronted by the bears. The happy ending is that somehow or other the bears did turn into princes the next morning!

The guest rooms on the two upper floors were most comfortable, with some rooms overlooking the fjord and the garden below.

Perhaps most interesting of all is the fact that the Hotel Mundal and the Fjaerland Pensjonat are reached only by ferry from either Hela or Balestrand. However, I understand that a road has been approved and will be under construction shortly.

HOTEL MUNDAL, N-5855 Fjaerland. Tel.: 056-93-101. A country hotel in a beautiful Norwegian village with capacity for 80 guests. Many bedrooms modernized. Boating, badminton, fishing, walking, hiking, and glacier excursions. Rates: See Index.

FJAERLAND PENSJONAT, Fjaerland

Mr. Ansgar Mundal was my guide through this pension with a friendly atmosphere on the fjord side in Fjaerland. He told me that his family has owned this property for many years and that he, in fact, grew up here. There were photographs of his father and mother and grandparents in the reception rooms. Both the main salon and the dining room overlooked this enchanting fjord and there is a wonderful view of several waterfalls cascading from the mountains.

There were a number of people seated in the salon on this particular day, because there was a slight drizzle. Ordinarily, they might have been walking in the mountains or venturing on to the great glacier, but today they were inside drinking coffee and carrying on enthusiastic conversations. Ansgar explained that the pension was very popular with Dutch, English and Norwegians, many of whom return year after year.

I looked at several of the guest rooms on the second floor and found them clean and comfortable. Some of them have their own baths and wc's. The dining room had paintings of fjord scenes, a sparkling floor, white tablecloths, and flowers on each of the tables.

It certainly looked like a delightful place to me.

FJAERLAND PENSJONAT, N-5855 Fjaerland, Sognefjord. Tel.: 056-93-161. A 25-guestroom pension at the end of the Fjaerland Fjord within 7 mi. of the glaciers. Bathing, rowing, badminton, fishing, walking, hiking and glacier excursions. Rates: See Index.

A Day Trip from Balestrand

My drive into the mountains north of Balestrand on Route 5 turned out to be a very scenic one, with prosperous farmlands, mountains with rushing brooks and streams and waterfalls coursing down their sides, carrying melting snow to ponds and lakes below. The frequent bus signs reminded me this beautiful trip can be made by bus in a day, or with an overnight stay at the pension in Vassenden. A bus schedule can be obtained at the Balestrand Tourist Office.

VASSENDEN TURISTPENSJONAT, Vassenden, Jolster

This interesting pensjonat might well be considered a hotel. The road led through some spectacular mountain and lake country and quite a bit of it was well above the snow line. One could really appreciate why it was closed during the winter.

The community of Vassenden proved to have many surprises. The inn was one of the biggest. I wasn't expecting anything quite as complete. It is located at the southern end of Lake Jolster, with mountain and lake recreation readily available.

A girl behind the desk offered to take me on a tour of the dining rooms, salons, and some of the guest rooms. The first thing we looked at was the main salon, which had a very cozy fireplace, numerous chairs and tables for conversation and games, and a view of the lake.

When we went upstairs, I realized that the inn was actually in two sections—the original main building and a new wing recently built. In this new section, each room has its own bath and is furnished with rather simple furniture and bright wallpaper.

The old section has an entirely different atmosphere. Some of the rooms have walls made out of painted boards. There is old furniture, including some carved headboards, tables, and chairs and a very warm, homelike feeling. Some of these rooms have also recently been remodeled, and while there is a bathroom and a wc in the corridor, all that I looked at had running water in the rooms.

She explained that the area is very popular with vacationers because there are many excursions in the mountains, for which Vassenden can be the starting point. She explained that it was possible to take a plane ride over the famous Jostel Glacier, nearby. This glacier, by the way, covers quite a bit of the mountains in this section and extends south into the Sognefjord area.

While we were talking, I happened to notice a book that included full-color reproductions of paintings by a Norwegian artist. She explained that these were the works of Nicolai Astrup, who lived nearby until his death in 1928. As I leafed through the book I remembered seeing copies of Astrup's work in other inns in Norway.

They are characterized by bold strokes in somewhat somber tones and depict Norway's mountains and fjords.

Before I left Vassenden I drove to the top of a nearby high hill, so that I could get a good look at the town, the inn, the lakes, the mountains, and even the glacier. It was easy to see why this section of Norway provided inspiration for artists and writers.

VASSENDEN TURISTPENSJONAT, N-6840, Vassenden i Jolster. Tel.: (057) 27192 Vassenden. A very comfortable hotel with many modern features combined with a homey atmosphere. Folk singing weekly. Rowboats, trout fishing, swimming, many excursions can be arranged by bus or ferry and also excellent walking and hiking nearby. Rates: See Index.

HUSUM GJESTEHEIM, Kaupanger, Sognefjord

This place was another pleasant surprise for me. I was en route from Balestrand to Flam, catching the 9 p.m. ferry through the fjord system from Kaupanger. Near the ferry landing there was a small sign indicating that the Husum Gjesteheim was just a few kilometers away. I would have time to visit it before catching the ferry.

Although it was about 8 p.m., the sun was still well above the horizon since it was just a few days before the longest day of the year.

The waters of the fjord were the deepest blue. It couldn't have been more than three minutes before the road, leading around a secluded harbor, went up an orchard-covered hillside, and I could see this inn peeking out from the apple trees.

It was immediately obvious that there were two sections to the inn. The main building had the dining room, reception rooms and salons, and a number of guest rooms. The other section had been added in recent years and looked more modern.

I liked the older immediately. The furniture was homey, similar to American Victorian, and the bedrooms were of a generous size, with windows overlooking the bay. Some of them had the old-fashioned Norwegian stoves in them.

Mr. Husum explained that Kaupanger was an important ferry terminal with bus connections to many points in the Sognefjord district. He said that many guests make their first stop just overnight, but come back again in later years to spend a longer time.

"I hope you will have a chance to visit our folk museum, which you passed coming up here. It has the most notable collection of rural arts and crafts and tools and implements here in the Sogne district."

The traditional Norwegian breakfast is the only meal served here.

HUSUM GJESTEHEIM, 5880 Kaupanger, Sognefjord. Tel.: Sogndal 3101. Open from May 20 to Sept. 10. Rates: See Index.

HEIMLY LODGE AND MARINA, Flam, Sogn

The twilight ferry trip through the Aurland fjord was such a beautiful and tranquil experience I would have been disappointed if there hadn't been an inn that breathed the same kind of atmosphere in this little town at the far end of the fjord. Fortunately, there was—the Heimly Lodge.

It seemed that my head had just touched the pillow when the alarm went off. I wanted to get an early start on the day as there was really so much to see and do in Flam. I took a quick shower in the bathroom down the hall and joined the other guests for breakfast in a sunny and delightful dining room.

The breakfast was indeed unbelievable. There was a large table in the center of the dining room laden with a wide assortment of fish, and many different varieties of cheese, including some delicious cheese made from goats' milk. There were six varieties of Norwegian bread, sliced ham, liverwurst, and other meats. There were all kinds of fresh fruit jams and several varieties of hot and cold cereals. I filled my plate with as many of the breakfast offerings as possible, and took a seat by the window. I was immediately drawn into conversation with people who were pointing out the fact that the morning ferry boat, which was down the fjord, seemed to be floating in space because of the illusion created by the brilliant sunshine, the steep sides of the fjord, and the absence of wind.

As we watched, far down the fjord a huge cruise ship came into view and it was explained that occasionally these luxury liners, which can go almost anywhere on the fjord system because of the deep water, frequently make calls at Flam, and the passengers ride the Flam railway up the mountain to Myrdal or even on to Oslo.

It was an absolutely gorgeous morning, and the sunshine on the garden of the inn found ready reception, from the fruit trees in blossom to the geraniums decorating the terrace and bordering the walk down to the road. I started counting the waterfalls that could be seen from the dining room and finally gave up at eighteen.

Heimly Lodge has the same type of atmosphere that I found at the Hotel Mundal in Fjaerland and the Hotel Walaker in Solvorn. There were many original touches in the salon and quite a few photographs of Norwegian craftsmen and crafts.

After breakfast a group of us went out on the terrace to enjoy the really magnificent presence of the high mountains in this valley and

to try to store up some of the incredible serenity. Then, one by one, we all separated to do whatever pleased us for the day. Some were taking off to go hiking, others bicycling, and some would be boating on the fjord. A great many were going to disappear in the mountains with a good book. I was going to take the Flam Railway to Myrdal. We would all gather at dinner for what I knew would be an outstanding experience.

HEIMLY LODGE AND MARINA, N-5743 Flam, Sogn. Tel.: 056-32241. A 40-guestroom inn at the end of the Aurland Fjord in the beautiful Flam valley. All types of outdoor recreation available. Open May 1-Oct. 30. Rates: See Index.

WALAKER HOTEL, Solvorn, Sogn

Pointing to the right, the sign off the main road read, "Walaker Hotel." A road took me past some upland meadows where cows were grazing and I headed for the fjord at the bottom of the mountains. The road looked well traveled and I later found out it was the main road into this village. I passed through some orchards and soon the church spire of the village came into view. It was also lilac time in Solvorn. Norway is captivating in June with all the fruit trees in blossom.

The Walaker Hotel deserves this setting. One thing I learned is that the house is over 325 years old and the old portion of it is called

the *Tingstova*, the Norwegian word for courtroom, and is so called because at one time this is where a judge held trials.

The Walaker Hotel has been owned by the same family since 1690. The present owners, Hermod and Oddlaug Walaker, were married here in peasant costume on Midsummer Eve in 1968, and their photographs were taken on the front porch of the hotel. I was delighted when Oddlaug presented me with a photograph of the event.

I was pleased to see these two energetic people, along with their four children, keeping this country inn in an enchanting village amidst awe-inspiring scenery.

The hotel has a real country inn atmosphere with some beautiful Norwegian antiques, some of them from the "old church" in the town, which dates back to the 17th century. Open fireplaces, beamed ceilings, a collection of family photographs, and winding staircases add to the comfortable, homelike feeling.

There is also a section that contains new rooms, furnished in the modern mode with kitchenettes.

Across the fjord from the village is Urnes Stave Church, one of the old stave churches of Norway, and now on the UNESCO Heritage List. There is frequent ferry service to the opposite shore. Incidentally, Solvorn is also on the express boat schedule from Bergen, and has direct bus connections with principal Sognefjord points.

The Walaker Hotel is one of the beautiful country inns in Norway.

WALAKER HOTEL, N-5815 Solvorn, Sogn. Tel. from abroad: 4756 84207; in Norway: 056 84 207. A delightful hotel in a secluded fjordside village. Hiking, walking, glacier trips, fjord fishing, rowboats, swimming. Boat, bus, and ferry connections to all points. Rates: See Index.

SOLSTRAND PENSJONAT, Luster, Sognefjord

My stop here was unexpected. I saw a little sign on the side of the road indicating that there were accommodations, and I went in to ask information about the road ahead. What I found was a rather substantial pension.

I arrived right at the height of breakfast and was invited to join some Americans at their table. We introduced ourselves and exchanged some travel notes.

The breakfast was typically Norwegian, with just about as many dishes crowded on one table as was possible. The guests were talking about the cable railway immediately next to the pension that ascends the mountain, and they spoke of the fantastic view of the Sognefjord and its neighboring mountain ranges.

"The rooms here are very clean and comfortable," said one lady. "We have decided to stay an extra night, for this is an excellent location for trips up into the mountains to see the Jostedalsbreen, the largest glacier in northern Europe."

The pension, on the banks of Lusterfjord, is entirely surrounded by fruit trees, which were in full bloom. The aroma was most enticing.

I might have missed this place except for the fact that all of the accommodations in Norway have a roadside sign with a symbol of a bed. The eating places have a knife and fork.

SOLSTRAND PENSJONAT, Post Boks 9, N-5830 Luster, Sognefjord. Tel.: 056-85100-50. Rates: See Index.

Through the Mountains Towards Sweden

My time in Norway was drawing to a close. I was driving east on the main highway leading from the fjord country high into the great mountains and snow fields to Lom, on the other side of the mountains. This road, closed for the winter, had been open only four days when I ventured upon it. In some places the snowplows had carved through drifts twice the height of the car, and only continual sanding and filling prevented the cars from being mired down in the spring thaw.

Between Luster on the Sognefjord and Lom, I passed a few small hotels and pensions, most of which were closed. Here are my impressions of one that was open.

ELVESETER HOTEL, Elveseter, Norge

This hotel, 2,100 feet up in the great Norwegian mountains, was originally a manor farm that was converted into what are for the most part modern accommodations. A considerable number of new buildings have been added in recent years. A great deal of effort has been made to create the atmosphere reminiscent of an old Norse "Home of the Gods" and every room has a name derived from Norse mythology.

The buildings are grouped together around a square and are linked by heated corridors and an elevator. Each room has a private bath. There is an indoor swimming pool, a gymnasium, and several facilities for meetings.

I was quite surprised to find an accommodation so large and so luxurious in this part of Norway. I wouldn't describe it as a country inn, but it is certainly most impressive.

ELVESETER HOTEL, 2689 Elveseter, Norge. Tel.: Lom 9811. Rates: See Index.

It was all downhill from here to Lom. As I descended from the Alpine heights, the wild terrain was replaced by farming country, and quite a few fields had sprinkling systems that were now in use because the rain in Norway stays on the west side of the great mountains.

The Norwegian portion of my trip was, for all practical purposes, completed. There remained only the drive to Lillehammer to cross the border into Sweden.

Stave church

361

SWEDEN

GOTHENBUR

Tallberg •

DALARNA

Stollet •

Sunne •

VARMLAND

Karlstad •

Vanern

Siljan

STOCKHOLM •

Mariefred •

Aby •

Vattern

Norrkoping •

• Granna

• Sunds

• Hok

SKANE

• HJARNARP

• Helsingborg

• Raa

•MALMO

363

TRAVEL SUGGESTIONS FOR SWEDEN

How to Get There

SAS (Scandinavian Airlines) maintains flights from the United States to all Scandinavian countries. There are flights to Stockholm and Gothenburg in Sweden. Numerous ferries provide service to Sweden from other parts of Europe. The Eurailpass is good in Scandinavia.

Country Inns in Sweden

Country inn hospitality in Sweden falls roughly into two categories: there are lovely old manor houses and small castles, and there are the more traditional country inns in southern Sweden, in the province of Skane, that are similar to their Danish cousins. The latter I have described more extensively in the section on Denmark.

Those inns to be found in manor houses and castles often have historical or literary connections, with an ambience in which their gardens play a special role. Decorated in harmonizing Scandinavian fabrics and furnished with both traditional and modern furniture, most have lodging rooms with private baths. The food is excellent; usually prepared and usually served by members of the owner's family, who make up the modest staffs.

I like to think of the section on these three Scandinavian countries as being a smörgasbord—literally a sampling of the three countries. It is designed to encourage travelers from all parts of the world to visit Norway, Sweden, and Denmark. I have attempted to elaborate on the type of hospitality in each country and indicate the wide variety of food, services, and accommodations.

Swedish Menus

Everything I've ever heard about Swedish smörgasbord is true: it is fabulous. Served as a noon meal, and all day on Sundays and holidays, smörgasbord has many varieties of fish, as well as the famous Swedish meatballs served with lingonberry sauce. Also included are salads, cheese, marinated meats, breads, and relishes. I found that each chef was proud of his smörgasbord, which involves many hours of preparation.

I had my first taste of small, fresh raw herring for breakfast in Sweden and found them delicious. Evening meals in many Swedish manor houses and restaurants are served in the Continental style with a great deal of emphasis on French dishes.

Car Rentals in Scandinavia

SAS has many different "Fly-Drive" plans that include automobiles. Travelers for whom Scandinavia is part of a continent-wide itinerary, or those who are not on a "Fly-Drive" plan, will find more information in the section "Renting a Car for Europe," in the front of the book.

My Itinerary in Sweden

Because I entered Sweden from Norway, the account in this edition starts in the western part of Sweden called Varmland, and proceeds eastward through the Dalarna region, and thence to Stockholm and south, past Lake Vattern to Skane, the resort area of southern Sweden.

Varmland, My Introduction To Sweden

I crossed the border into Sweden at Eda, and was now in the rich Varmland country in western Sweden, north of Karlstadt. This was an area blessed with most of the good things that Sweden has to offer— great forests, lakes numbering in the thousands, hiking trails, canals, folklore festivals, crafts of all descriptions, and rivers that not only are famous for their natural beauty, but are also avenues of commerce, with many floating logs.

This is a region replete with opportunities for active outdoor sports, including tennis and golf, swimming, canoeing and boating. In winter there is downhill and cross-country skiing.

The town of Sunne, where I remained overnight, is deep in Selma Lagerlof country. It is on the straits connecting the upper and middle Fryken Lakes. In August there are nine days of Fryksdal festivities based on Selma Lagerlof stories.

The fairs and festivals in this area, I am told, are most enjoyable. For further information about Varmland, write the Varmland Tourist Association, Kungsgatan 4, B S 65224 Karlstad, Sweden.

LANSMANSGARDEN, Sunne

I was completely entranced with this lovely manor house. It is located on the banks of Lake Fryken in Sunne, the center of Sweden's famous Varmland area. It reacquainted me with the Swedish Nobel Prize-winning author, Selma Lagerlof. She had used this inn as a locale for one of her books, and her home, Marbacka, is just a few kilometers to the south.

I arrived about nine o'clock, driving from Norway. My first experience was heartening, indeed. I had arrived long past the dinner hour, but the girl at the desk said that the cook could prepare something for me if I were willing to wait a few minutes. I was. Then an accommodating waiter with a good sense of humor showed me to a table in a most attractive dining room. After a very tasty bowl of soup, he brought me a warm plate with five delicious seafood-filled crêpes accompanied by an excellent tossed salad and some home-made Swedish bread.

The dining room, like the remainder of this inn, is a tribute to Swedish furnishing and decorating. It was a tasteful blend of painted furniture and natural wood. There were flowers on each table, and the cutlery and dishes were Swedish Modern.

After dinner, I went out on the terrace and met a Swedish couple and their English friends who had been coming to Lansmansgarden for many years. We talked about traveling and promised to meet the next morning for breakfast.

My room in this manor house could be a model for country inns anywhere. It had a lacy bedspread, Swedish designs on the

wallpaper, a blue carpet, and painted furniture. Erik Biorklund, the innkeeper, later explained to me that these were the "romantic" rooms that, whenever possible, were reserved for honeymoon couples. The rooms in this building were named after characters in Selma Lagerlof's novels.

The next morning, breakfast with my four new friends was great fun because they took delight in introducing me to several typically Swedish dishes, of which there were several. For one thing, I had my first taste of fresh, raw herring. I'll never be satisfied with pickled herring again. I was also introduced to a breakfast porridge made from rye grain, to which I was instructed to add applesauce and a small amount of sugar and milk. Delicious. There were many other dishes, including meats and cheeses.

LANSMANSGARDEN, S-686 00, Sunne. Tel.: 0565-10301. A 29-guestroom (private baths) manor house in a garden setting in the Varmland section of Sweden. Summer sports include swimming, rowing, badminton, tennis, golf, fishing, walking, hiking. Winter sports include several different ski lifts within a short distance. Rates: See Index.

Marbacka and Rottneros

The fact that novelist Selma Lagerlof was born in this part of the Varmland in 1858, and subsequently made her home here from 1907 until 1940, has asserted a tremendous influence on the area. Her home, Marbacka, is open to the public, and has been preserved exactly as she left it at the time of her passing. It is visited by thousands of people every year.

Rottneros is identified as the "Ekeby" in Selma Lagerlof's novels. It was probably the residence of an important country squire as early as the 13th century. It is the former garden of an important iron foundry. It covers almost a hundred acres that are in turn surrounded by both natural and formal parkland. In the gardens are more than a hundred sculptures, representing a large part of what Swedish sculptors have created during the past century. These marvelous pieces of sculpture are carefully placed within the natural atmosphere of gardens and trees, and are one of Sweden's foremost tourist attractions.

Marbacka and Rottneros are open from May 15 to September 15. There is a coffee room at Marbacka and a restaurant and cafeteria at Rottneros.

Dalarna

Dalarna covers a considerable area to the northwest of Stockholm. Dalarna means "the valleys between the east and west Dal Rivers."

From my talks with Signe Keyes at Siljansgarden, I learned that the entire area is rich in folklore, history, handcrafts, and the preserva-

tion of old Swedish ways. It is also the home of the famous Dala paintings, decorative paintings by self-taught artists who lived between 1780 and 1870. The famous Dala horses, occasionally found in imported crafts shops in the United States, come from a small village near Leksand.

The Leksand area itself is comprised of ninety villages and the resort towns of Tallberg, Siljansnas, and Insjon. They are all located on the shores of beautiful lake Siljan, a most attractive natural area.

For further information about Dalarna, write the Dalarna Tourist Association, Bergslagsgrand 1, S-791 00 Falun, Sweden.

SILJANSGAARDEN GASTHEM, Tallberg

I just happened to be walking down a lane toward the shore of Lake Siljan, when I saw a group of several old, sod-roofed houses. The sign said, "Siljansgaarden Gasthem." This was the beginning of a most wonderful adventure that included meeting Signe and Kenneth Keys, the proprietors, and several of the guests at this unusual country inn.

This inn, which is really the inspiration of Signe's mother and, later, her father, not only preserves the Sweden of the past, but actually makes it useful and viable today. Many of the living rooms and bedrooms are furnished with antiques. However, there are some lodgings with modern furniture. Perhaps the best description of the inn is found in Signe's words:

"The first question we tend to get here is 'How old is this place?' When you arrive here it seems so settled in its environment and so peaceful that people think it must be an old farmstead. But it isn't. I used to answer that 'the house is much older than the place as you see it.' The oldest house in the group is from the 16th century and that house also has guest rooms in it. We don't know the age of some of the houses. Many of them have dates engraved on them or you can tell from the way they are built.

"When my mother arrived in 1916, there was nothing here—just meadows, forests, and stone heaps. She was born and grew up north of here. She had been married in Stockholm, and for a woman of that time she was very unusual. She was well trained in many subjects and wanted to work among people, as well as have a family.

"In those days it was uncommon to buy a house. You usually tried to find an old one—old houses were of timber. It was common to move houses. The first house she bought had been a mill at the foot

369

of the mountain across the lake here. The millstone we have on the front lawn was one of the millstones inside the house—and it's now used as a coffee table. The house became much bigger than she had intended. She couldn't build the cellar deep enough so the house became higher. That was in 1917. She was well known for her taste in furnishings and art, and the big room is today as it was then. In the old days, people slept, worked, and ate in the one room, therefore it was named the 'Big Room' *(Stor Stuga)*. In one corner you had the fireplace; in the other corner you had the beds, similar to what are now known as bunk beds. The bottom was a double bed for the older people and the top for the younger folk. The big drawers were pushed in during the day, and at night were used for the very young children.

"In 1925, my father came here. They found that they had similar interests, and in 1927, they opened this as a guest home where you could come for rest and recreation, and to meet people. They began to offer summer courses in music, singing, dancing, and literature. When this was started it was very unusual—a pioneer movement."

I receive lovely letters from Signe every year, and she reports that between ten and twenty-five guests visit her every year as a result of reading *Country Inns and Back Roads*.

SILJANSGAARDEN GASTHEM, S 793 03 Tallberg (Dalarna). Tel.: Leksand 0247/50040. A wide range of rooms, some with private bath. In addition to the preserved Swedish environment, guests can enjoy sauna, tennis, rowboating, table tennis, croquet, badminton, and many walks and hikes throughout the remarkable scenic Dalarna area. Closed from the end of Sept. to Christmas. Open for Christmas. Rates: See Index.

THE LIDINGOBRO WARDSHUS RESTAURANT, Stockholm

My host and hostess for the evening in Stockholm were Ake and Margaret Gille. Ake, a very gentle man, had been connected with the Swedish Tourist Information Center for some time, and for eight years was located in New York City.

Our first visit was to a lovely restaurant on the water, the Lidingobro Wardshus, just a few miles from downtown Stockholm (Centrum).

Apparently, it was located in a former manor house, as are many Swedish inns. My first impressions were most favorable. As soon as we stepped inside the old gates, now permanently opened, I saw three old-fashioned Swedish sleighs loaded with flowers. There were flowers everywhere—in formal gardens, in large tubs placed all around the terrace, and in hanging baskets. The rather formal buildings are wooden, painted in a muted yellow with white trim, and with red tile roofs.

On one of the terraces a cook was barbecuing some meat on a charcoal brazier, and the aroma did amazing things to my already substantial appetite. There were many chairs and tables placed around the terrace, which was not being used on that evening, but was very popular during lunchtime and in the afternoon because of the beautiful view of the pleasure boats and the shore beyond.

Inside this old restaurant there was a series of small connected dining rooms, each with a view of the terrace and the water. Apparently the buildings were in existence before the 1700s and the decorations have been done in the old-fashioned Swedish way.

We walked through the kitchen and had a conversation with a few of the chefs who were getting ready for the considerable number of people already seated in the dining rooms. I was allowed to sample four or five dishes, including some delicious fish. Because we were going on to dinner, I was not able to eat an entire meal; it took all of my will power to keep from devouring each portion.

LIDINGOBRO WARDSHUS, Kaknas, Djurgarden 62, Stockholm. Tel.: 08-62 06 94. A country restaurant overlooking the water, just a few miles from central Stockholm. Luncheon and dinner served daily. No lodgings available.

ULRIKSDALS WARDSHUS RESTAURANT, Stockholm

Margaret and Ake Gille and I arrived at the gardens at the Ulriksdals Wardshus just as the Swedish flag was being lowered at approximately 9 p.m. It was a lovely moment because the guests in the restaurant had assembled on the terrace to join in singing the Swedish national anthem. I understand that, weather permitting, this is the custom almost every evening.

Ulriksdals Wardshus has really fine extra touches, many of which are supplied by the hostess and owner, Kerstin Bergendahl. She is an extremely handsome lady of great energy, ability, and graciousness. I was delighted when she and her husband and a friend from Canada decided to join our table. A little earlier she had introduced herself and said that she was going to sing for a wedding party being held on the porch upstairs. She invited us to come along.

Walking as softly as possible we went up the stairs of this unusual manor house, built in 1868. Apparently, it has changed very little since then, and the romanticism associated with the reign of

King Karl XV still persists. The wedding party, with all of the ladies in their beautiful gowns and handsome gentlemen in their white ties and tails, indeed seemed to belong to another day and time.

We stood quietly, while Kerstin sang a lovely little peasant song in Swedish. Then all the guests rose and shouted "good luck" to the happy couple and drank a toast.

The dinner was a complement to the ambience. My main course was red trout served in a special sauce with brown potatoes, and dessert was grapes and figs with small balls of ice cream all topped with delicious freshly whipped cream. Cream is one thing that the Scandinavians have in great quantities, and it is usually served with dessert.

ULRIKSDALS WARDSHUS, S-171 71 Solna/Stockholm. Tel.: 08-85 08 15. A striking restaurant just a few miles from downtown Stockholm. Luncheon and dinner served daily (on my last visit). No lodgings available.

HOTELL REISEN, Stockholm

When I find myself in large cities, I definitely prefer the conservative type of hotel: the Algonquin in New York, the Lenox in Boston, and the Goring in London, for example. In Stockholm, where large hotels are a way of life, the Reisen fits right into my personal preference. Although it is somewhat sophisticated and definitely European in style, this rather small hotel has a very personal air about it, and I found it quite easy to feel at home almost immediately. This was partially because of the friendliness and informality of the staff members who, by the way, are fluent in many languages, including English.

The hotel is housed in three beautiful 17th-century residences in the Old Town section, where there are narrow cobblestone streets and several attractive shops.

Other amenities at the Reisen include music in one dining room that has been designed to resemble the elegant saloon of a 19th-century ship. There is also a very welcome sauna and an indoor swimming pool.

HOTELL REISEN, Skeppsbron 12-14, S-111 Stockholm. Tel.: 08-22 32 60. Rates: See Index.

GRIPSHOLMS VARDSHUS, Mariefred

My reason for visiting Mariefred was to see Sweden's oldest inn and possibly to look in on the famous Gripsholms Castle. After just one inquiry, I found myself walking through the garden of the inn, which faces the quay and the Castle.

I easily located the enthusiastic innkeepers, Bengt and Inger Erikson, who said that I could tag along with them while they took care of the last-minute preparations for the Sunday smörgasbord that would be served in just a few minutes.

Inger assured me that the Gripsholms Vardshus was indeed the oldest inn in Sweden, dating back to 1623. "But," she added, "the castle over there is much older, by at least 300 years."

I followed her into the kitchen, where a dozen people were busily preparing special dishes for the smörgasbord. In one corner, fish was being sliced and boned, and in another, cheeses were being prepared. There was a table where all of the many salads were being put together, an elaborate bread tray was being filled with at least eight kinds of bread, and at least three people were working on some delectable homemade cakes and tarts.

The dining room was furnished with beautiful native antiques, and many oil paintings and prints adorned the walls. In the corner of one of the blue and white dining rooms, there is a very handsome, old-fashioned white stove that served as the principal means of heating the rooms during past centuries. It is now decorated with blue figures and gay flowers. Each of the dining rooms has a different color scheme and theme.

In the center of the main dining room were the tables set with the delectable choices for the smörgasbord. Bengt Erikson was on hand with a few of the last-minute touches, and in a matter of moments the doors would be open. It was like waiting for the curtain to go up on the first act of a play.

Subsequently, I did have time to visit the old castle and to walk around the town, where I found a little Sunday flea market in progress with many handcrafted items displayed on little tables placed around the square.

There are ten rooms in the inn, most of them modernized, and many of them with a view of the castle.

The inn, the castle, and the town make visiting Mariefred a very happy experience.

A few years ago, I had the pleasure of hosting Mr. and Mrs. Erikson in New York. They told me that Mariefred has become a

distinguished resort area, and to meet the heavier demands, they have increased the number of their rooms and their kitchen and service staffs. The building has been renovated, but with great respect, and every effort has been made to retain the fine old environment. The menu is now offered in four languages, including English.

GRIPSHOLMS VARDSHUS, Mariefred. Tel.: 0159-100 40. Rates: See Index.

I was breezing along on Highway E-4 from Stockholm to southern Sweden, admiring a lake on the left side of the road, when I spied a stately white house and some formal gardens on my right. I was almost positive that I had seen the word "Vardshus" as well. Impatiently, I sought out an exit on my right so that I could turn back for a second look. (E-4 is a divided highway at this point, so there were no left turns.) I drove on for about six kilometers, although in my impatience it seemed like twenty-six. Finally, I turned off and learned from a friendly gas station man that what I had seen was indeed a "Vardshus" or inn. Following careful directions I returned and the result was one of my most memorable adventures in Sweden.

VARDSHUSET STENKULLEN, Aby

The grounds of this inn were a tribute to the art of gardening. Everywhere I looked there were plants and flowers, well-trimmed hedges, and carefully pruned trees. In mid-June the colors were

kaleidoscopic. There were gardens on all four sides, and on the second-floor balconies there were great hanging begonias and containers and tubs of other cascading flowers. There were three or four fountains, some with water lilies in bloom.

While I stood there for a few minutes contemplating camera angles, I discovered I had a companion. A gigantic St. Bernard nuzzled me, nearly knocking me into a rose bush. For a moment I thought he was going to stand on his hind legs and put his paws on my shoulders, which surely would have been a disaster for me. Just at this crucial point, I heard a voice call something in Swedish and the dog disappeared. A young woman then came out on the rear veranda of the inn and said, "Good afternoon, may I help you."

The young lady, as it developed, was Maria Svensson and her family owns the inn. After I had explained that I was writing a book about country inns in Sweden and that this inn looked like something quite special, she gave me permission to wander around and promised to give me a few minutes later on.

"We are serving a special party right now," she said, "but please make yourself at home."

As soon as I walked into the reception area, I realized that I was supposed to remove my shoes and choose a pair of sandals from a neat collection just inside the door. After I saw the handsome Oriental rugs on the floors of every room I knew why.

My next impression was that almost every square inch of wall in the hallways and living rooms was covered with some type of wall

376

hanging, portrait, reproduction, or print. There were also notices of exhibitions of paintings and concerts, past, present, and future. Every room also had many pieces of sculpture placed on the wide windowsills, tables, and among the books on bookshelves that ran from ceiling to floor.

It was obvious that the owners and guests of this lovely inn took delight in music, art, history, and literature.

I could hear the guests in the dining room singing Swedish songs. Between courses, Maria managed to come out and explain a few things to me. My principal regret was that I simply could not take the time to remain there overnight.

The Vardshuset Stenkullen is a family operation with Maria and her mother and father doing most of the work themselves. Maria explained that nearby Lake Brovikien provided water sports and recreation and that there were lovely walks and drives in the countryside. "Many of our guests," she said, "some of whom have been returning for quite a few years, prefer to just walk in the gardens and sit on the terraces and perhaps read. And, of course, we have music available at any time. Everyone seems to be content."

I certainly had no trouble believing that.

Maria Svensson's letters indicate that things have not changed at this lovely place, and they always take me back to my visit there on a sunny day.

VARDSHUSET STENKULLEN, Aby. Tel.: 011/690 19. Closed Christmas, New Year's until Jan. 15. Rates: See Index.

LOFSTAD SLOTT RESTAURANT, Norrkoping

I imagine that everyone has reveries about owning a castle or a palace. It does, however, present a few difficulties. The upkeep is terrific. Just keeping the grounds presentable and the walls in repair is a full-time job. Imagine repairing a leaky roof on a castle! In many places in Europe, palaces and castles are maintained by government grants and by the proceeds from conducted tours. Quite a few of them offer accommodations and some have restaurants within their walls.

The latter is the case at the Lofstad Castle, or *slott,* as it is known in Sweden. This particular castle was recommended by Ake Gille, who said that if I felt like having a meal or a cup of coffee in a castle, then I should by all means stop at this place on Route E-4, just south

of Norrkoping. The sign for it is on the right-hand side of the road. The castle sits on a wooded hill overlooking a field and brook.

I walked into a courtyard and joined a handful of people strolling around the area. I peeked in on one of the many dining rooms on the first floor, where there were busy preparations for a wedding. Tables were also set on the outer porches that have an excellent view of the orchard and countryside.

I wandered through some of the dining rooms, where there were painted ceilings and painted furniture, and in the corner of one I saw electronic equipment that could only mean a rock band plays here. I could also see that one of the other uses for old palaces and castles is to present musical and theatrical programs. Here at Lofstad Slott this is true almost every weekend. Bach, Beethoven, and Gershwin were on the program for the coming Sunday afternoon. There were also notices of several small chamber groups as well.

I walked down to the stable area, where a very pleasant outdoor dining area had been created. There were quite a few people enjoying themselves in a Forge Room, which had been converted into the restaurant.

As nearly as I am able to understand the brochure from this castle, it apparently dates back to the 1600s. It looks as if it has had a long, peaceful, and productive life and now continues on as a reminder of some of Sweden's opulent past.

LOFSTAD SLOTT, Norrkoping. Tel.: 011 351 65. A castle restaurant serving from 11 a.m. to 8 p.m. No lodgings.

HOTELL RIBBAGARDEN, Granna

"And this is the room occupied many times by Greta Garbo." I was being conducted through the Ribbagarden in the very orderly village of Granna, on the shore of Lake Vattern.

The Ribbagarden, two squares from the main street, is on one of the town roads leading down to the lake. The innkeeper took me through the entire inn, explaining that its history dates back to 1569. The building has been increased in size many times over the years so that the interior has many different levels on the same floor. On the top floor of the main building, he showed me to a large room with windows on three sides. One of them offers a view of Lake Vattern. It was a much larger room than the others that I saw. "This was the room that Greta Garbo occupied many times," he said. The other rooms were more or less conventional in size and for the most part had been modernized.

The living rooms had arrangements of old-fashioned Swedish furniture with many landscapes and prints on the walls. The furnishings are more in keeping with the exterior of the inn, which has many little balconies and windows overlooking a large parklike area with fruit and pine trees and quite a few tables and chairs for outdoor relaxation. Just outside the main entrance, the path into this secluded woodland passes through an old grape arbor.

Because the Ribbagarden is a very popular place to dine, attracting many people from the nearby cities of Jonkoping and Norrkoping, the two dining rooms are most spacious. I happened to be there on a Sunday, one of the favorite dining-out days for Swedish smörgasbord. I understand that there are many specialties connected with the area, which has excellent vegetables and fruits, as well as fish from the lake. Almost every town in Sweden has a different specialty for the smörgasbord.

Just for the record, I don't think that Greta Garbo has visited the Ribbagarden in many years.

HOTELL RIBBAGARDEN, 56030 Granna. Tel.: 0390/10820. This is an old hotel still keeping some of the traditional Swedish ways. Rates: See Index.

HOTELL VASTANA SLOTT, Granna

I always thought of castles as having moats, drawbridges, and crenelated battlements, where men-at-arms in chain mail poured down a rain of arrows from their crossbows at besieging armies.

Here, however, was a gentle castle filled with luxurious antiques, paintings, and sculptures and just a low decorative wall on the front, erected no doubt to complete the setting.

I entered, crossing a stone threshold over 300 years old, and found myself in a large reception area with a huge fireplace at one end. Originally, the "working rooms" of the castle were found on either side—the scullery, pantry, storehouses, and servants' rooms. The owners and their guests occupied the spacious second floor. This is reached by a set of stone steps that have been well worn by many generations. Imagine 300 years of castle visitors all using these steps to present petitions, or perhaps pay respect to the nobility.

Halfway up the twisting passage, a formidable figure in medieval armor with a battle-axe in its fist confronts and scrutinizes

all visitors. When I saw that no one was watching I lifted the visor to see if there was a man inside. There wasn't.

The living rooms, dining rooms, library, and lodging rooms are all lavishly furnished and decorated in the florid castle style that represents 300 years of adding more furniture and seldom removing any. Carved chairs, benches, tables, beds, armoires, and the rooms themselves, are all on a larger-than-life scale. Naturally, with so much wall space many of the paintings, all in the classical style, are tremendous in size and scope.

Today, in these more modest times, the castle is open only in

June, July, and August, and the only meal offered is breakfast, although large dinner parties may be arranged.

Most of the bedrooms are very large and many have casement windows that open out to a generous view of the lake. I did see a few smaller bedrooms. No doubt they were reserved in the old days for guests of lesser rank.

HOTELL VASTANA SLOTT, 560 30, Granna. Tel.: 0390/107 00. Rates: See Index.

HOOKS HERRGARD, Hok

I teed-up my ball, took a long look down the first fairway, and stopped to speak to my hostess at Hooks. "This looks like an excellent cross-country skiing area," I said. "Do your winter guests enjoy outdoor sports here?"

"Oh, yes," she replied, "winters are really fun here. We Scandinavians enjoy being outdoors then, just as much as we do in the summer. Besides skiing, we have skating on the lake, tobogganing, and curling. Everybody enjoys walking in the snow and our woods are particularly beautiful after a fresh snowfall!"

We then decided that one of the best ways for me to get acquainted with this old manor house/modern resort inn, was to play a few holes of golf and enjoy the countryside. It was a most entertaining few hours. In addition to the golf course, the resort offers tennis, badminton, swimming (in the pool and in the lake), bocci, sailing, boating, and fishing. There is also a rather elegant billiard room.

In fact, elegant is a good word to describe much of the Hooks Herrgard. In addition to the main building, built in the 1700s, several other buildings have been added, providing rather luxurious accommodations for approximately 120 guests.

When I commented that there seemed to be quite a few guests in the "young married" category, she replied, "Yes, and many of them bring their children. I think that we have guests who enjoy both the old-fashioned and the modern things that they find in Hooks. The setting is romantic, but the facilities are very much up to date."

ROMANTIK HOTEL HOOKS HERRGARD (Also Relais et Chateaux), 56013 Hok. Tel.: 46/393/21080. A 100-guestroom resort-inn and conference center in an old Swedish manor house, 370 km. from Stockholm, 230 km. from Helsingborg, and 180 km. from Gothenburg. All summer and winter sports. Rates: See Index.

SUNDS HERRGARD, Sunds

There are a few interesting little notes about this inn. For one thing it is an unusual family arrangement. Two Swedish sisters inherited this property, each married a German fellow a few years ago, and now they all live in harmony, keeping this lakeside inn.

It has prospered and grown in many respects, starting with the main house that has conference rooms, kitchen, and dining rooms. After a few years, additional lodgings were created in some small adjacent buildings that helped to form a kind of open square. More recently, a number of lakeside cottages with all conveniences have been added. It is now an active resort with its own lake recreation and the advantages of being just a short drive from Lake Vattern and Granna.

The surrounding woods and fields that have been left in their natural state, with many trails for pleasant walks, are another reason that this place is popular with families. Children especially like it because there is a large fenced-in area, where deer and wild boar are kept (some of these eventually appear on the menu). This is where I had my first glimpse of a live wild boar. Although they weren't very big, I must say they did resemble all of the old prints I had ever seen with those formidable curved tusks. This inn has a very informal air and most of the guests had been there for a one- or two-week holiday. It is located on beautiful rolling farming country, and from the sports car badges displayed at the front entrance, it is quite popular with the motoring crowd.

SUNDS HERRGARD, 560 28 Lekeryd. Tel.: 036/82006. Accommodations are in the main house and many bungalows. Horseback riding, fishing, boating, and Finnish steam baths available. Brochure available in English. Rates: See Index.

Skane

Skane, like Varmland, Dalarna, and Granna is one of Sweden's enticing playgrounds.

Skane is assuredly unique. It has great cultivated fields, beautiful wooded areas, and miles and miles of beaches. Here in Skane it is possible to take eight different auto tours and never repeat a single place. For example, there is the Gold Coast Tour that includes the 700-year-old city of Malmo and is in the area immediately adjoining Denmark. There is also a tour of the great golden farmlands, a tour of the white sand coast, an apple blossom tour through the extensive orchard section, a green forest tour through the wooded areas, and perhaps one of the most enticing of all, the red castle tour that directs the traveler to at least eighteen different castles in Skane, most of which are more than 300 years old.

For additional direct information about Skane, write to the Skanes Turisttriafikforbund, Box 4277, 203 14 Malmo 4, Sweden.

MARGRETETORPS GASTGIFVAREGARD, Hjarnarp, Skane

History, intrigue, beauty—the Margretetorps Gastgifvaregard has them all. It also has the most difficult name for an American to twist his tongue around. When asking directions to reach it I finally gave up on the second word and took the easier first word. Even that took some adjustment.

The first thing that impressed me was a brightly painted old farm cart outside the entrance, piled high with flowers. All Scandinavians love flowers and this section of Sweden is blessed with warm sun and fertile soil, so every farm has a generous flower garden.

The word "farm" is appropriate here because this inn, certainly one of the oldest in Sweden, dating back to the 1200s, was also a farm for many centuries. The buildings form a hollow-square shape, a pattern I saw repeatedly among the Swedish farms.

I arrived well past the dinner hour and found my way to the reception desk, located in the kitchen. I found this arrangement also in several Danish inns.

There's a very practical reason for the reception desk being located in the kitchen: this is the center of most of the activity, especially for inns on a more modest scale.

Modest is also a good word for describing this inn, because there are only ten rooms, and as I learned, just one bath. It is necessary to ask for the key to the bathroom. (The wc's are always open.)

Even though the kitchen had been closed for some time, I was given a large jug of milk and great quantities of ham, cheese, and bread—so I had a satisfying late-night snack.

In the morning, I was roaming around the inn when I made the acquaintance of a man who works there. He explained that he was from Holland. I was surprised to learn that he had done the very impressive mural on the walls in one of the dining rooms. He

supplied me with a great deal of extremely valuable and interesting information.

The inn has been the host to much of Swedish royalty during the 700 years of its existence, and also to many Swedish writers, artists, and musicians. There are several large dining rooms, and the smörgasbord, served daily, is one of the most famous in all of southern Sweden.

As I left this lovely little inn later that morning, a small drama unfolded in the fields immediately adjacent. A sturdy Swedish farmer was having trouble getting a young bull under control, and he went into his farmhouse and returned with his equally sturdy wife and the two of them finally herded him into the next field.

MARGRETETORPS GASTGIFVAREGARD, 262 07 Hjarnarp, Skane. Tel.: 0431/540 08. A 10-guestroom (no private baths) modest inn, 10 km. from Angelholm. Rates: See Index.

RAA WARDHAUS, Raa

This little inn, typical of others in Skane, has an interesting nautical theme explained by the fact, I am sure, that Raa is a seaside village. There are many ship models on display throughout the dining rooms, as well as dozens of photographs and prints of old steam and sailing ships. Brass nameplates, old bells, telescopes, pulleys, anchors, and many other nautical items are tastefully placed throughout all of the public rooms.

There are just twelve guest rooms in this rather modest hostelry, mostly furnished in modern Scandinavian style. Some look out over a park. Raa is a very picturesque little town and it is possible to rent sailboats and enjoy excursions from its waterfront. I had a definite feeling that both the town and the inn had not been discovered by tourists as yet.

RAA WARDHAUS, Raa, Helsingborg. Tel.: 042-260000. Rates: See Index.

DENMARK

INNS and LOCATION

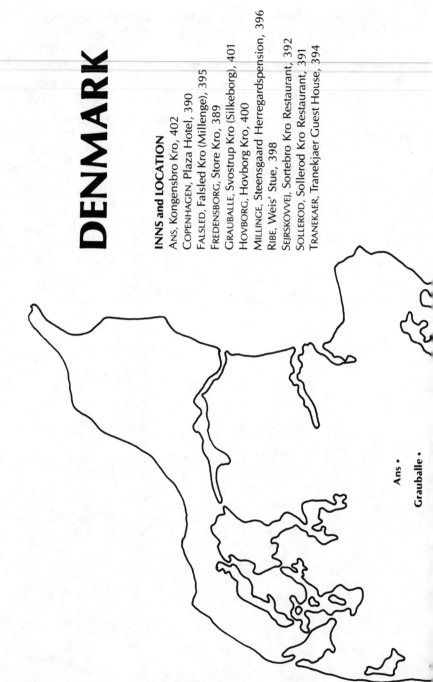

Ans •

Grauballe •

386

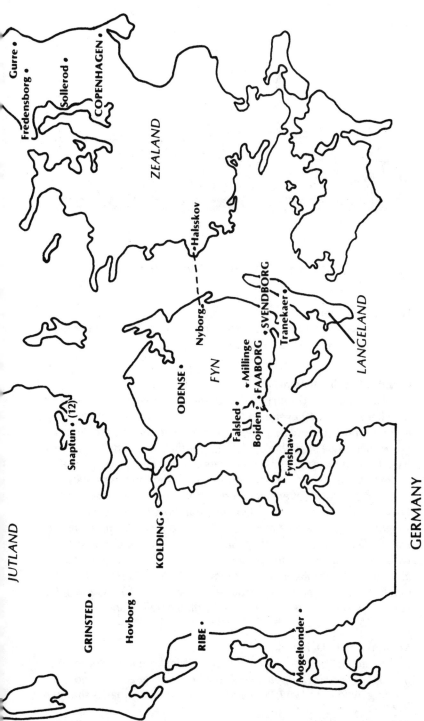

JUTLAND

GRINSTED •

Howborg •

RIBE •

Mogeltonder •

GERMANY

Snaptun • (12)

KOLDING •

ODENSE •

FYN

Falsled •
Millinge •
Bojden • FAABORG

Fynshav •

Nyborg •

SVENDBORG

Tranekaer •

LANGELAND

Halsskov •

ZEALAND

Gurre •

Fredensborg •

Sollerod •

COPENHAGEN •

TRAVEL SUGGESTIONS FOR DENMARK

How to Get There
The SAS flights go directly to Copenhagen. There is a car-ferry from Norway, and a direct road from Germany.

Country Inns in Denmark
Denmark is a country with a tradition of inns, some of which date back 300 to 400 years. A few were designated as royal inns by reigning monarchs, which meant that a bedroom and a change of horses had to be available at all times for the royal party. Some inns have been in the same innkeeping family for generations.

I found these Danish inns in small villages and towns, with the name of the town often included in their own name. Kro is the Danish word for "inn." Although these traditional inns are frequently sought out by foreign travelers, they are principally used by the Danes themselves. All of them serve hearty and wholesome food, with the menus frequently printed only in Danish. The guest rooms are always, as throughout Scandinavia, clean and practical. In the older sections of the inns, the baths and wc's are usually down the corridor. Reservations can be made by mail or telephone.

My Itinerary in Denmark
I entered Denmark by ferry from Helsingborg in southern Sweden. From north of Copenhagen I continued through Zealand, proceeding by ferry to Fyn Island and then south to Denmark's summer

resort area, called Langeland. Again a ferry took me to Jutland, that portion of Denmark on the European mainland adjacent to Germany. From here the road leads north and I could have continued on to Norway by ferry from northern Jutland.

STORE KRO, Fredensborg

"Oh, yes, the King and Queen are dining here tonight." I stopped short and turned to learn whether I had heard correctly. The innkeeper at Store Kro went on, "Well, the castle is nearby," he said, "and there are strong links between the castle and the inn.

"In 1723, King Frederik IV constructed Fredensborg Castle and at the same time he had an inn built nearby, which was named Store Kro and consisted of two separate buildings. For a number of years the King himself was the keeper of this inn. One of the original buildings is still in use and its exterior has not changed during the many years. It serves as an annex and the interior is equipped with beautiful, modern guest rooms."

The proximity to Fredensborg Castle accounts for the fact that the inn has been the scene of royal receptions and royal weddings. There is one dining room, known as the King's Room, with either photographs or paintings of every Danish king.

Catering to these unusual functions has carried the inn's reputation for good food to places considerably far from Denmark. The innkeeper told me that the chef has traveled widely, preparing meals in other countries and taking certain Danish specialties with him, such as bread, butter, salmon, and fresh herring.

As we moved into another room with many photographs and paintings of what appeared to be the same man on the wall, he explained the decor to me.

"We Danes are very fond of the theater," he said, "and Olaf Poulsen was probably the most outstanding actor of the Danish age. He played every major role up to the time of his death in 1923. Some years ago I began to collect photographs, prints, and paintings of him playing various theatrical characters. Now we have put them in this room where they are well preserved and displayed for everyone to enjoy. I think it's better than a museum because they are in an atmosphere that he, himself, would appreciate."

Store Kro is located on one of the quiet streets in Fredensborg. There are spacious grounds and a garden in the rear of the inn.

Although this inn is larger than many of the inns I visited in

Denmark and a bit more formal because of the many functions that take place here, it is nonetheless most hospitable. Each of the rooms has highly individual decorations.

Just imagine the King and Queen would be dining here tonight!

STORE KRO, 3480 Fredensborg. Tel.: (02) 280047. A royal inn immediately adjacent to a royal palace still in use. All of the North Zealand recreational facilities and historic castles are nearby. Rates: See Index.

PLAZA HOTEL, Copenhagen

I believe that anyone visiting Denmark would want to spend some time in the beautiful city of Copenhagen. My time in Copenhagen on my first visit was somewhat limited. However, I did look at a small hotel in the central part of town, not too far from Town Hall Square—the Plaza Hotel. I found it to be an elegant, conservative hotel in a town that specializes in big hostelries. My first impression of the lobby was one of restraint and calm. For the most part, the luncheon guests seemed to be Copenhagen businessmen rather than tourists.

My lunch was excellent and I was very much impressed with the comfort of the dining room as well as the relaxed service.

After lunch I was invited to have my coffee in the Library Room, an impressive two-and-a-half-story room with a glass dome. It is lined with books from floor to ceiling. There are several arrangements of luxurious leather chairs placed around handsome round tables. It reminds me of the lobby of the Hotel Algonquin in New York.

While I was there I saw several guest rooms and suites, all tastefully designed. This hotel has an old section and a new section and appears to be very well run.

PLAZA HOTEL (Sheraton), 4 Bernstorffsgade, DK-1577 Copenhagen V. Tel.: (01) 149262. (USA reservations: 800-325-3535.) A luxurious hotel in central Copenhagen. Rates: See Index.

SOLLEROD KRO RESTAURANT, Sollerod

I was wandering about the churchyard immediately adjacent to Sollerod Kro. The rain, which had been spouting all afternoon, had stopped, and scudding clouds frequently opened long enough to light the scene with tints of silver.

All of this was a most appropriate postlude to a delightful evening at the inn across the village road. Actually, it had begun for me just before lunch, when I left Store Kro in Fredensborg to drive to Copenhagen. I located the village of Sollerod with just one inquiry, and after driving through a Danish "Forest of Arden," suddenly came upon a serene and peaceful crossroads with a triangular-shaped flowerbed literally overwhelmed with blossoms. The words "Sollerod Kro" were in large letters stretched across the front of the inn.

The principal entrance was through a cobblestone courtyard or hollow square formed by the buildings of this ancient inn. In the center there was a tinkling fountain and around the edges and in sheltered nooks and crannies were tubs of daisies, pansies, and cornflowers. Much to my surprise there was a large birdcage with colorful exotic birds.

It was too early for lunch, but the innkeeper was happy to explain the history of the inn and invited me to walk through the spacious dining rooms.

It was during this tour that I learned that the church where I was strolling once owned the inn, which dates back to 1677. It has remained unchanged ever since except for certain strengthening of walls and re-thatching of roofs. The building is exquisite, one of the best examples of traditional romantic Danish architecture that I encountered during my trip.

All the rooms are decorated with Danish antiques, and the reception rooms are hung with Professor Aksel Jorgensen's historical paintings and a selection of original manuscripts of the best-known works of Danish writers.

From May to September meals are served in the courtyard, and include dishes from the open grill.

That brings us to where I started—strolling in the churchyard and listening to the organ. To my knowledge, the church does not own the inn any longer. But the tradition remains, and many of the inn guests attend the church and enjoy the church gardens. There are no rooms at this inn, but luncheon and dinner are served continuously from 11:30 a.m. to 10 p.m.

SOLLEROD KRO (Relais et Chateaux), Sollerod Vej 35, 2840. Tel.: (02) 802505. A country restaurant just a few kilometers north of Copenhagen. Open year round. No lodgings.

SORTEBRO KRO RESTAURANT, Sejrskovvej

"Welcome to Sortebro Kro." That was Herr Nielsen, the innkeeper and owner of this unique museum-inn. My visit with Innkeeper Nielsen was memorable for several reasons. First, there were prodigious amounts of lunch that I kept insisting I didn't want as I kept eating. Then there was the fact that the inn is a restaurant as well as a museum-inn, adjacent to a very extensive restored farm village that is preserving some of the old ways of Fyn Island. Finally, there was Mr. Nielsen, himself, with his bright red suspenders and leather apron.

Mr. Nielsen is very proud of his inn and of the model farm village, and promised me that we would have a short tour as soon as we had completed lunch. When I asked him about the specialty of the house he had a surprising reply. "We take pride in the fact that we can prepare almost any dish for which a guest may ask. We do have specialties but we are always pleased when one of our guests asks for a Danish dish that is not on the menu so that we can cook to order."

My luncheon began with a large portion of delicious pickled Danish herring and four small white potatoes. I insisted that that would be enough.

Meanwhile, the waiter brought some sausage and red cabbage with bread and butter. I watched Mr. Nielsen as he cut a piece of sausage and combined it with a sliver of bread on his fork, eating with his left hand in the Continental style, something that I simply haven't mastered as yet.

"There are hundreds of thousands of people passing through the Fünen model village every year," he said, "and of course this means that the inn is very popular. We open at 10 o'clock in the morning to serve a light breakfast, and then continue to serve our regular menu from about 11 a.m. to 9 p.m. We do not have any rooms."

The main dining room at the Sortebro Kro, which has been constructed in the same architectural style as the farm village, has low ceilings with varnished beams and a large collection of antique Danish tools and memorabilia. The floors are rough, scrubbed boards and the dining room furniture is heavy and sturdy in the Danish country style. There were fresh flowers on every table and many old wooden trays on which cold Danish plates are carried. These, as Mr. Nielsen explained, are known as *trougs*, a wooden platter used only for cold dishes.

True to his word, after lunch we toured the Fünen Village, starting in the gift shop where there were all kinds of Danish ceramics and wooden crafts, including spoons, forks, and miniature trougs, all hand carved. We ventured out into the village, and the first thing I saw was a pond with baby ducks just across a country road from a beautiful meadow, where some baby chicks were being herded by their mother.

This restored village is an important link with the agricultural past of Denmark and old farm implements, tools, and carts have been collected from every point in Fyn to form what is still today a working farm.

One interesting feature was a natural arena where dramatizations of Hans Christian Andersen's stories are given during the summer months. I was particularly intrigued with the large collection of old Danish sleighs. I found the kitchen with its great iron stove, where stones were heated to put into the beds, quite fascinating. Incidentally, the inn also has two or three rooms set aside with small artifacts and old utensils.

SORTEBRO KRO, 5260 Hjallese, Sejrskovvei. Tel.: (09) 132826. Open from 10 a.m. to 9 p.m. No lodgings available. This inn, 4 km. from Odense, is a part of the well-known "Fünen Village," a restored agricultural environment.

TRANEKJAER GJAESTGIVERGAARD, Tranekaer

Herr Carl Gammelholm, the innkeeper, supplied me with some excellent information about Langeland Island, just off the southern tip of Fyn Island.

"We are one of the great vacation places in Denmark," he said. "We have a delightful holiday atmosphere along with good beaches, swimming, sailing, fishing, hunting, tennis, horseback riding, and many other sports. I mention hunting, because there are many people who come to the inn to enjoy the game and deer that we have on the menu. They are in abundance in the forests nearby."

A great deal of our conversation took place in the dining room of the inn, which had a red brick fireplace at one end. There were beamed ceilings, flowered wallpaper, leather chairs, and a plate rack with dishes of old Danish design. The atmosphere was old-fashioned and quite comfortable.

There were two styles of bedrooms. Some were rooms that had been there for a great many years and had beds with wicker head-boards and old paintings on the walls. There were also motel-type rooms, each with its own terrace and flower boxes. There was quite a bit of land around the inn and many, many flowering bushes.

Herr Gammelholm told me that in addition to the deer and game, other menu specialties were fish and eel. "You're seldom far from water here in Denmark," he said. "We Danes love the products of our seas."

Before I left the Tranekjaer Gjaestgivergaard, I asked the inn-keeper about the sign I had seen on my journey from Odense to Langeland. One of the roads was called "Elvira Madigan's Way." "Oh, many people ask us about that. The locale was the southern part of Fyn and some of the film was shot in this region," he said.

"By the way, it is possible to come directly to Langeland Island from North Zealand Island by taking the ferry to Lohals and bypassing Fyn Island entirely."

TRANEKJAER GJAESTGIVERGAARD, DK 5953 Tranekaer, Lange-land. Tel.: (09) 59 12 04. Rates: See Index.

FALSLED KRO, Falsled

The Falsled Kro is not a conventional Danish country inn. I think it would be outstanding in any country. Like the Solerod Kro, just north of Copenhagen, it is included in the Relais et Chateaux, a directory of rather elegant and exclusive European hotels and restau-rants.

The owners of this inn are Sven and Lene Grønlykke. Unfortu-nately, Sven was not at the inn during my visit, but Lene and I had an opportunity to get acquainted. It was from her that I learned that although the inn was a farm during the 16th century, it had become a "privileged inn," meaning there would always be room for the king and his horses.

I am certain that it is Lene's experience in the fields of film and fashion that accounts for the exquisite decor of this inn. My room had Danish tables and leather-covered stools, complemented by the white-washed walls on which there were several original paintings. I had the opportunity to look at several other rooms during my stay and one of them in particular was most attractive, with the bedroom on the second floor, reached by old stone stairs.

Outside my door was a broad lawn, and just a few steps away was a very pleasant harbor. There were birds, flowers, flowering bushes, and beautiful trees everywhere.

The main sitting room had a wonderful center fireplace with comfortable low leather seats that invited everyone to stretch out and enjoy coffee after dinner. There are groupings of wicker furniture in various corners and many arrangements of freshly cut flowers. It is the kind of atmosphere that draws people together in conversation.

The cuisine at Falsled Kro is basically French, prepared by a team of chefs. My mixed salad followed by salmon soufflé would have been at home in Paris. The dessert table had at least eight different types of pastries, including a delicious chocolate mousse.

I had been hearing about Falsled Kro since my arrival in Scandinavia and I was told that it would be a beautiful and idyllic place, and indeed it was. I could only add one further word—sophisticated.

FALSLED KRO (Relais et Chateaux), DK-5642 Falsled, Millinge. Tel.: 009-45-9-68 1111. South of Odense, on the Faborg-Assens Hwy. Rates: See Index.

STEENSGAARD HERREGARDSPENSION, Millinge

The clock over the stable sounded twelve times, just as it has been doing for hundreds of years. I paused in my walking tour of this elegant manor house, located just a few minutes from the sunny beaches of South Fyn Island, to watch two colts hardly more than two months old chase each other across the meadow.

The hostess at Steensgaard enthusiastically explained that the manor probably belonged to Hartvig Steen, a man most likely of noble means, and that it was apparently mortgaged by him to another family in 1310. This makes it date back considerably before Columbus discovered America.

After a brief account of owners and mortgagees, I was amazed at how well the manor house-cum-castle appeared today.

"Oh, yes," she agreed. "The original sections were built to last and the other buildings, which were added to form three sides of the square, are quite in harmony. Don't you agree?"

Indeed, I did. All of the buildings are made of rough stone and half timbers.

Steensgaard is in one of Denmark's most beautiful sections. It offers a magnificent view of fields and forests extending onward to high hills.

"We call it 'smiling countryside,'" said the hostess. "Our guests love to walk in the manor park, which extends through the woods down to the beach. There are fourteen other forests nearby if they really like longer excursions.

"There are also tennis and croquet. By the way, you have never played croquet until you have played with enthusiastic Danes."

The interior of this manor house is quite exciting. I passed from one room to another with original oil paintings, beautiful furniture, and rich rugs. The library has a chessboard in one corner and comfortable chairs drawn close together to invite conversation.

Guest rooms are unusually large, since they were built for private occupancy hundreds of years ago. Many of them have canopy beds.

In a country where there are dozens and dozens of beautiful old country inns, I found Steensgaard Herregardspension a most interesting contrast. It offers the opportunity to spend a few days in a luxurious manor house.

STEENSGAARD, HERREGARDSPENSION, 5642 Millinge, Fyn. Tel.: (09) 61 94 90. An elegant 15-guestroom (10 with private bath) manor house serving three meals a day. All types of outdoor recreation available. Rates: See Index.

Ribe

I could have spent a month in Ribe (Ree-ba). To me it is the penultimate medieval town. It has fascinating 16th-century houses, which are actually lived in today, intriguing alleyways, unexpected courtyards, and cobbled streets everywhere.

Dominating the center of town, just across a small square from Weis' Stue, an ancient village inn, is the cathedral. It is partly constructed of stone carried to Ribe from the Rhineland in Germany. One tower has loopholes, evidence of the war with Germany. The bells of the cathedral play every day—a hymn at 8 a.m. and 6 p.m., and folk songs at noon and 3 p.m.

Ribe's port area, the Skibbroen, is the oldest harbor in Denmark. The storm flood column marks the height the waters have reached during some of the worst floods down through the ages. Here is a lovely town richly endowed with areas of outstanding beauty, and many charming bridges across, and paths along the river. There are gardens, museums, castles, fenlands, churches, and a fascinating little island off the coast, called Mando.

WEIS' STUE, Ribe

"Yes, the village watchman starts out from here every night during the summer. He drops in around 9 p.m. and sits here in this room, in fact, in your chair, and enjoys conversing with his friends. At 10 p.m. he picks up that long pole there in the corner and walks out to the street singing."

I, too, was enjoying myself immensely at Weis' Stue. The building and the atmosphere picked me up almost bodily and carried me

back to medieval times. The very personable innkeeper, Knud Nielsen, was telling me what great fun it is to be the keeper of an ancient inn.

"The watchman is an example of the good times we have here," he said. "He is a great storyteller and also has an extensive knowledge of the town. People follow him all around the town, just as if he were the Pied Piper of Hamlin. He tells them about the old buildings and stories about the town. Everyone eventually ends up here again. The night watchman is a well-established Ribe tradition."

Knud invited me to join him on a tour of this modest inn. To go up to the second floor, I had to duck under a very low doorway and climb steep stairs with the aid of a rope bannister. At the top of the stairs were just four double rooms and one single. The running water for all rooms was available in a wash bowl in the hallway. That's where guests would brush their teeth and do their shaving. There were no private bathrooms and all shared a wc "in the corridor."

When I asked him about his guests' reaction to this old-fashioned mode of innkeeping, he replied, "They love it. Many come back quite often. Actually, we're quite luxurious compared to two or three hundred years ago."

As we returned to the first floor, I became aware of a great number of students who were lounging in one small dining room, playing chess, arguing, and even studying. "This has always been a student's favorite," he said. "For centuries they have been meeting here just as you see them today."

The food being prepared for the evening meal looked sumptuous. There were many Danish dishes as well as a few German and French. We passed through an open courtyard and into the Danish Marine Room, which was very imaginatively decorated with old ship's models, marine sabres, guns, pictures of ships, ship's wheels, old brass, maps. He explained that it is given over to the Marine Club about six times a year to members who wish to come and have dinner.

The town of Ribe and the Weis' Stue proved to be a most pleasant Jutland experience. It is hard to imagine one without the other.

WEIS' STUE, Torvet 2, 6760 Ribe. Tel.: (05) 42 67 00. Rates: See Index.

HOVBORG KRO, Hovborg

The thing I remember about this inn is that the innkeeper and staff were hosting dinner for a number of people in wheelchairs. One entire dining room had been set aside that evening, and vans and small buses carrying guests were arriving every few minutes. They were all having a marvelous time and I understand that the inn provides this entertainment for this group at least once a year.

I mention this because Hovborg Kro is typical of the spirit of Danish innkeeping. For example, this inn has been in the same innkeeping family since 1836 and the members have played an important role in community affairs throughout these years.

I found it very easy to identify with many of these traditional country inns in Denmark, because they are quite similar to many American inns that I have visited. This inn was built in 1790 and for centuries was used by drovers on their way to and from the market.

I made the acquaintance of some Danish guests at dinner and amidst some really great laughs at my attempts to understand them, they explained that they had stayed for four days of fishing and

400

boating on the river and horseback riding in the woods. English is spoken by the key staff people of this inn and occasionally the headwaiter gave me a hand in understanding my dinner companions.

The oldest part of the inn has lodgings of a more traditional nature and a recent addition has rooms that are furnished in modern Danish fabrics and furniture. All of these have their own baths.

I felt very much at home at the Hovborg Kro.

Incidentally, there are ferries to Norway in the northern part of Jutland and this and other inns in central and northern Jutland could be a place for a convenient overnight stay for anyone en route.

HOVBORG KRO, Holmeavejz, P.O. 6682, Hovborg, Jutland. Tel.: (05) 39 60 33. A 29-guestroom inn in central Jutland. Lunch and dinner served daily. Angling, riding, backroading, walking, and boating. Rates: See Index.

SVOSTRUP KRO, Grauballe

By now I had traveled some distance into Jutland, and I found that the farther I went from Copenhagen, the towns where English was spoken became fewer and fewer. Such was the case at the Svostrup Kro. This was more of a fun challenge than a problem. I always find it a thrill to be some place where English is a rarity rather than commonplace.

Finding this inn took some persistence, and I am sorry that I cannot be more detailed. I advise the traveler to ask the Tourist Office in Silkeborg for exact directions.

At first I felt that it was hopeless. After thirty minutes of circling, I stopped the car at a stone bridge to look at the water and realized that I was looking squarely at the inn!

The entrance was through a low arch formed by some old stone barns. I was in a lovely country courtyard with four or five large trees at one end in front of the inn. There were many flowers everywhere.

The lady at the reception desk and I tried to communicate, but she gave up and brought in the owner. He and I did somewhat better. He showed me all around the inn and answered my many questions as well as he was able. He even arranged for me to make a long distance telephone call!

This inn, so close to the river, was once used by bargees, the men who use the river as a highway for transporting goods by barges. One of the dates on the buildings was 1286. Herr Lauesen, the innkeeper, showed me a collection of Stone Age artifacts found in the vicinity. There were many arrowheads and primitive spearheads as well as knives.

All of the rooms overlook the orchard and the river. As in many cases, there were a few rooms furnished in older, more traditional furniture, and some in a more modern style. Only a few had private baths.

I was not able to be at Svostrup Kro for any meals, but from the look of the kitchen, where eels fresh from the river were being prepared for the evening meal, I was certain that it would be wholesome and hearty!

SVOSTRUP KRO, P.O. 8642 Grauballe, Silkeborg, Jutland. Tel.: (06) 87 70 04. A 10-guestroom inn, 10 km. from Silkeborg. Rates: See Index.

KONGENSBRO KRO, Ans

Mr. Hans Andersen, innkeeper at Kongensbro Kro, made it quite clear during the first few minutes of our meeting that his middle name was not "Christian." He was one of the more sophisticated innkeepers that I met in Jutland and the inn reflected the fact that he and his wife had tastes and preferences that would be appropriate in many other settings as well.

We got acquainted in the residents' lounge of the inn, where a small fire was burning at one end, and windows overlooked the river. We soon found that innkeeping joys and tribulations are much the same in Denmark as they are in the United States.

"It is a 24-hour-a-day job," he said, "especially when one wishes to hold a good reputation."

A good reputation is something that Herr Andersen possesses in abundance. I had tried six weeks in advance to reserve a room for just one night, but it was impossible. "We take bookings this year for next year," he said. I asked him if there was an explanation for this popularity.

"This is a good place to stay for anyone who wants to take his ease in a time of hurry, and feel in close contact with the peaceful rhythm of nature.

"It is a good place for nature lovers and bird enthusiasts and it is a paradise for anglers," he declared. "Many a lovely hour can be spent fishing and watching the animal life and nature at large.

"The staff at the inn can supply good tips about short or long trips and several of these trips will bring to mind days gone by. One of them is on the old tow path at the bank of the river, which is now able to be used for a distance of twenty-five miles. Incidentally, we also rent canoes for use on the river."

Later on, I had a chance to talk to Mrs. Andersen, whom I met in the garden. She invited me to walk over to a little building next door on the banks of the river, where a special party was being held and a man who lived in Argentina was cooking barbecued spare ribs.

All across Denmark, I kept hearing from other travelers about how much I would enjoy Kongensbro Kro. "You'll especially enjoy Mrs. Andersen," I was told. "Besides, she has written a cookbook."

During my stay I had a long talk with Mrs. Andersen, and she presented me with a copy of her book, entitled *Inn Food*.

Mr. Andersen's middle name may not be Christian, but the Kongensbro is a real Danish fairy tale come true.

A recent note from Hans informed me that he and his wife, after thirty-five years of innkeeping, have turned the inn over to his son and his wife. However, he and Mrs. Andersen will be nearby and will drop in frequently to say hello to the guests.

KONGENSBRO KRO, Ans By, Jutland. Tel.: (06) 87 01 77. A 27-guest-room inn in Danish farm country, 25 km. from Viborg, 18 km. from Silkeborg. Golf, fishing, walking nearby. Rates: See Index.

❖   ❖   ❖   ❖

Random Reflections on Scandinavia

Although there are many language similarities, the three countries, Norway, Sweden, and Denmark, are highly individual. Each year they are becoming increasingly popular with visitors from North America.

Scandinavia is the home of some of the world's famous artisans and craftsmen. Glassware, ceramics, rugs, tableware, handicrafts, and jewelry are to be found everywhere. The performing arts are a great tradition in all three countries, and there is a wide choice among lawn concerts, dramatic presentations, opera, symphony, and folk dancing.

NOTES

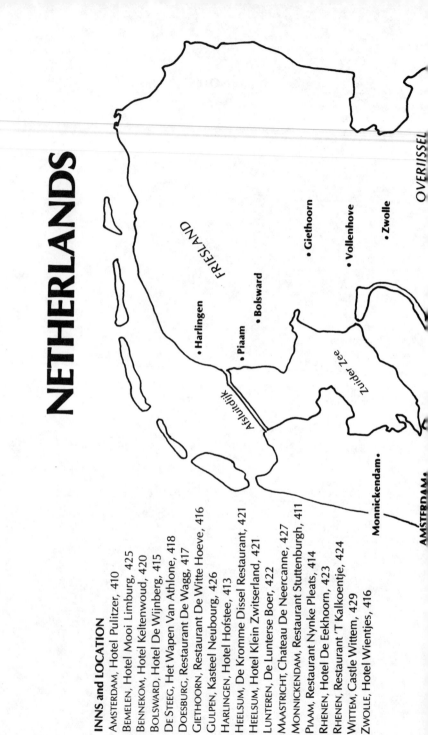

NETHERLANDS

OVERIJSSEL

FRIESLAND

Afsluitdijk

Zuider Zee

• Harlingen

• Piaam

• Bolsward

• Giethoorn

• Vollenhove

• Zwolle

Monnickendam •

AMSTERDAM •

INNS and LOCATION

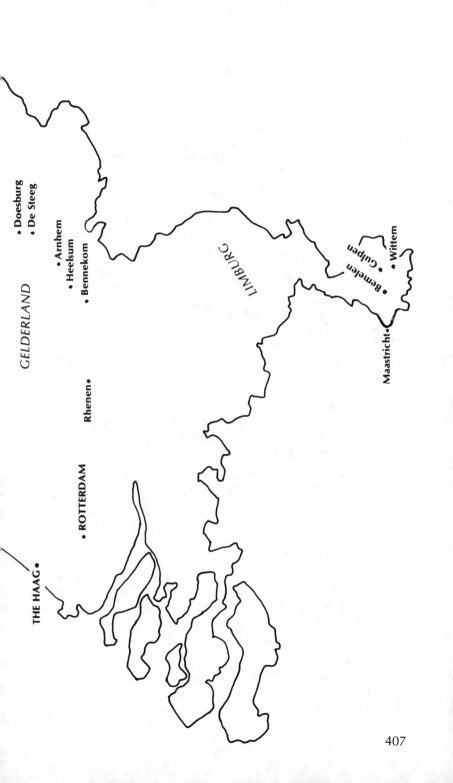

THE HAAG

GELDERLAND

ROTTERDAM

Rhenen

Doesburg
De Steg

Arnhem
Heelsum
Bennekom

LIMBURG

Maastricht

Bemelen
Gulpen
Wittem

TRAVEL SUGGESTIONS FOR THE NETHERLANDS

How to Get There

Your travel agent is in the best position to advise you about the many airlines that travel from North America to the Netherlands.

Country Inns in The Netherlands

I saw very few accommodations that precisely resemble American country inns. Many places I visited were small and middle-sized hotels offering bed and breakfast as well as other meals. Many had rooms with private baths and wc's, but there were also other rooms with conveniences "in the corridor."

These hotels had parlors and lounges where guests could get acquainted. Many were owned and managed by families who frequently did the cooking, serving, and housekeeping. I also stayed at three- or four-star hotels, including castle hotels.

Reservations

Hotel reservations in the Netherlands can be made through the National Reservation Center (NRC), P.O. Box 3387, 1001 AD Amsterdam. Telephone: (020) 211-211; Telex: 15754.

Tourist offices called VVV are located in every community to provide help in finding local accommodations.

The VVV has set up a nationwide hotel reservation system, known as the VVV Logies Service, to assist those travelers who have arrived in the Netherlands without hotel reservations for the same day or the next few days. Go to a VVV office to make these reservations; no telephone or written reservations. There is a nominal charge. Reservations for accommodations mentioned in this book can be made directly by letter or telephone, as well as through the NRC and the VVV.

Dutch Menus

Among the intriguing Dutch dishes are many different species of eels. Other Dutch foods are broodjes, small rolls stuffed with cheese, shrimp, pork, and ham. These are served in small snack bars called broodjeswinkeles. There are also croquetten, spiced meat fried in bread crumbs and served with french fried potatoes. Erwtensoep is a Dutch pea soup with slices of sausage. Other dishes are sauerkraut with bacon and sausage, minced beef with fried apples and red cabbage, and hutspot, a stew of onions, potatoes, carrots, and ribs of beef.

In the larger cities of the Netherlands I found quite a few Indonesian restaurants. Pancake restaurants are popular. The Netherlands also has restaurants with Continental menus and service. These meals are often served in sumptuous surroundings and in great style.

Driving Tips

Backroading in the Netherlands is one of the great sports. I will certainly remember to bring a compass on my next trip, because even with the very best road map I still needed help. I was forever getting turned around and on days when the sun was behind the clouds the best Boy Scout would have had a hard time.

My Itinerary in The Netherlands

I started in Amsterdam and drove in a clockwise direction around the Zuider Zee into Friesland and then down the other side through Overijssel through Arnhem into Maastricht.

Amsterdam Reflections

I was not prepared for the great number of canals in Amsterdam, even though I'd been told of their importance to the city. They are everywhere, intertwined, crossing and recrossing.

Driving from the airport, Amsterdam looked like one giant traffic jam of cars, while the swarms of bicycles and the triple streetcars rolled by silently amid the squeals of brakes and the roar of traffic. Parking, as might be expected, is a problem; however, I easily found space in front of my hotel, the Pulitzer.

Many of the Centrum shops are closed on Saturday afternoon. Those catering to tourists are always open. Earlier, driving from the airport, I saw many open-air markets, obviously not aimed at tourist trade. Walking is a fine pastime in Amsterdam, seeing all the interesting and intricate architectural styles with the mansard and traditional Dutch "step" roofs, and buildings with little penthouse studios and windows with flowers in them.

Amsterdam is one of the several principal gateways to Europe. I stayed just long enough to be intrigued by all its many possibilities for sightseeing, amusement, and culture.

HOTEL PULITZER, Amsterdam

The brochure for this hotel says that it provides comfortable, contemporary accommodations in Old World surroundings, and I think that is a fair evaluation. Amsterdam has 218 hotels of which 18 are towers of Continental-style hospitality. The other 200 are most modest in both size and intent. The Pulitzer, which certainly is not one of the grand palaces, did very nicely for my one-night stay. My room overlooked the Prinsengracht Canal and some most fascinating centuries-old town houses on the other side. One of them had the date of 1733 in ornate scroll.

The Pulitzer was rather busy since it was the height of the tourist season and there was at least one tour booked into it. It is within walking distance of all of the downtown Amsterdam attractions (Centrum). It was reasonably quiet, and the carillon bells of the Westekerk Towere were happy and welcome sounds.

The hotel is made up of a series of old Amsterdam town houses that have been modernized and interconnected. It stretches for a block between two canals and there are many hidden gardens and courtyards within the complex.

One of its most appealing features is the very pleasant breakfast room overlooking the canal.

HOTEL PULITZER, Prinsengracht 315, Amsterdam. Tel.: 202-228333. A 176-guestroom canal-side hotel where all the rooms have baths, wc's, radios, telephones, TV, and mini-bars. Well within walking distance of all Amsterdam attractions. Rates: See Index.

North of Amsterdam along the Zuider Zee (Now known as the Ijsselmeer.)

Poring over the road maps of Holland brought back some of its history; just the names evoked memories: Edam, the home of the great red cheeses; Kampen, the town famous for its foolish wisemen; Nijmegen and Charlemagne's Castle, and Leyden, where a sneeze might have changed the course of history for awhile.

The Zuider Zee, once a great inland sea, had important harbors from which Dutchmen sailed the seas of the world, until 1932, when a dam turned it into a large lake. This changed the plant and marine life, and among other phenomena, caused the proliferation of the famous Zuider Zee eels. Many new towns were created on the reclaimed lands (polders).

RESTAURANT STUTTENBURGH, Monnickendam

Honestly, this place is incredible. It is a very pleasant old building sitting back from the busy harbor street in the center of a sizable lawn with quite a few tall trees and many flowers. I had a clue to its

uniqueness when I noticed a few exotic birds in cages on the terrace, but it was when I stepped inside the front door that the real nature of the place impressed me.

It was the music boxes. I gave up counting at 45, but later learned that there were at least 150 with that many more at various stages of repair at a workshop. Everyone of the music boxes in the restaurant was in working condition. The natural question is, "What happens if they all play at once?" I was reassured that they only play one at a time. However, most of the time I could hear one tinkling away in the backround.

There are small music boxes, large ones, and miniatures. There are music boxes mounted inside of birds, elaborate cabinets, and dancing dolls. There is even an antique machine that plays two discs at the same time with a stereophonic effect!

Even without the music boxes this restaurant is worth a visit. For one thing, almost every table has an unobstructed view of the canal and marina traffic gliding by continuously.

I had my first taste of eels here. These were pickled eels served cold with a peach salad. At first I thought the portion would be too big but I enthusiastically consumed every last one. There are many different ways of preparing eels.

The table d'hote menu has traditional Dutch farm food. The à la carte menu has many French dishes.

My visit here was made more enjoyable because of meeting Peter Koster of Rockport, Massachusetts. He had been a native of this province and had returned with his family to pay a visit. We discovered mutual friends in Rockport—Fred and Lydia Wemyss, who are innkeepers at the Yankee Clipper.

RESTAURANT STUTTENBURGH, Monnickendam. Tel.: 02995-1398. A restaurant overlooking water, serving typical Dutch food and specializing in eels. No lodgings.

To Friesland Via the Afsluitdijk

The Afsluitdijk is the road over the Zuider Zee Dike (twenty-nine kilometers to Friesland), and I took it at Ben Oever, after driving back roads through the towns of Edam, Enkhuizen, and Twisk. I was heading for Harlingen in Friesland, on the Waddenzee, a channel of the North Sea between the mainland and the offshore islands of Terschelling and Vlieland. A romantic place with many canals, a picturesque town square and many medieval buildings. Harlingen is one of the towns to see in Friesland.

HOTEL HOFSTEE, Harlingen, Friesland

I had to get directions at least twice to find this hotel, located a few blocks from the main harbor, but directly on one of the major canals. One of the problems is finding bridges over canals.

Mr. Hofstee himself answered the bell at the front door and proved to be a very communicative man who has owned this hotel for quite a number of years.

I followed him up a set of winding stairs with a brass railing and looked at several rooms. Those on the front were sunny and overlooked the canal. He also has collected quite a few interesting original paintings for the rooms.

Mr. Hofstee explained that while they had served meals for many years, the hotel now was strictly bed and breakfast, and that he was prepared to recommend several different restaurants to his guests, some of whom come to Harlingen every year and spend one or two weeks at the hotel.

A couple of rooms have been modernized, but for the most part they were furnished in traditional furniture. I don't think Mr. Hofstee is a man who gives up the habits of many years without a struggle.

HOTEL HOFSTEE, Frankereind 23, Harlingen, Friesland. Tel.: 05178-5846. A 25-guestroom canal-side, modest hotel. Located away from the harbor noises and traffic. Rates: See Index.

413

NYNKE PLEATS RESTAURANT, Piaam, Friesland

Piaam is considerably off the main track, and I found myself out in the country early in the evening trying to find someone from whom to obtain directions after I got lost. But what matters all this if I am in Friesland, where the horizon line is always dotted with rows of picturebook trees and where the golden sun was dropping into the Zuider Zee and the breeze was bending the fields of golden grain?

Frankly, after my adventures in reaching Piaam I wish I could be of help to my readers. But I am afraid that everyone must take his own chances. What I was prepared to find was the Nynke Pleats Restaurant, which I thought was one of the best-kept secrets in the country.

Nothing could have been further from the truth! Even with just thirty minutes before the kitchen would close, the parking lot was filled and people were still arriving.

The building was modeled after a traditional Friesland barn. It has a high-pitched thatched roof with walls of light tan brick. The interior emphasized the farm-style construction, with sturdy exposed beams, post, and rafters. Old watering troughs were used as planters. Huge windows at one end provided light and allowed an unobstructed view of the Friesland meadows. The floor was board tiling. The walls were lined with paintings by local artists and also an excellent collection of hand-painted tiles. Long wooden tables accommodate the large Dutch families who apparently enjoy eating here because of the good food. The menu matches the farm-style design. Food is served on individual large platters. I had pork chops with a sauce of apples, sliced fried potatoes, small peas, and a salad. Salads in Holland are quite likely to be elaborate. This one had slices of mushrooms, eggs and fish, all placed attractively on a bed of

lettuce and served with a salad dressing. Dessert was a very tasty apple pie with ice cream—a dish that was invented in a small upstate New York hotel during the 19th century.

NYNKE PLEATS RESTAURANT, Piaam, Friesland. Tel.: 05158-1707. This is a farm-style restaurant near the shores of the Zuider Zee about 12 to 15 km. from Bolsward. Closed Mon. Allow extra time for making wrong turns. No lodgings.

HOTEL DE WIJNBERG, Bolsward, Friesland

Bolsward is a small town not far from the shores of the Zuider Zee, and would be a good place to stay for two or three days while touring the remainder of Friesland. It is noted for having a very famous town hall and one of the oldest churches in Friesland, dating back to 1446, with ceiling paintings and hand-carved choir stalls.

The Hotel De Wijnberg, my first overnight stop outside of Amsterdam, is clean and comfortable and apparently has been modernized. My room on the third floor overlooked some of the roofs of the town.

When I returned from having dinner at the Nynke Pleats Restaurant in Piaam, I found that everyone was gathered in the main salon watching the soccer match between Czechoslovakia and Germany. There was a big table in the middle of this room with all kinds of magazines and newspapers for the guests. The match turned out to be one of the most important, and there was a great deal of interest among all of us. The enthusiasm got so hot that two or three of the guests started shouting advice to the players. In one respect some of the hotels that I visited in Holland were quite similar to American country inns. The guests gathered in the main salon or living room to enjoy after-dinner coffee, read the papers, and talk among themselves.

Breakfast at this hotel was three different kinds of bread served with butter and jam, sliced cheese, and ham.

HOTEL DE WIJNBERG, Bolsward, Friesland. Tel.: (05157) 2220-3120. A pleasant conventional hotel offering all services. Most of the rooms have their own baths and wc's. Rates: See Index.

RESTAURANT DE WITTE HOEVE, Giethoorn, Overijssel

This is a restaurant that specializes in pancakes. Pancakes with ham, pancakes made with cheese, with apples, with ginger, with mixed fruit, with peaches, with strawberries—pancakes with just about everything. It is located in a thatched-roof, barn-type building made into a restaurant, immediately next to a small canal. The decorations include mounted birds of all kinds.

This is a place that Hank Fisher in New York at the Netherlands National Tourist Office had told me about. He said that it was quite an experience. Well, it was.

My pancake was as big as a small pizza, rather thin and covered with sliced of candied ginger. I ate about half of it, and then savored the ginger from the uneaten half. A glass of cold milk was welcome. This was really a most enjoyable meal.

After lunch I walked outside and found that a number of small excursion boats were used to take passengers along the tree-arched canals. These are the streets of Giethoorn, where punts are used instead of cars, a sort of village Venice. The whole area is, in fact, one big nature reserve, the Wieden—10,000 acres, with an unbelievable wealth of flora and fauna.

RESTAURANT DE WITTE HOEVE, Zuiderpad 32, Giethoorn, Overijssel. Tel.: 05216-1428. This is a pancake specialty restaurant, open from April 1 until Sept. 15. No lodgings.

GOLDEN TULIP HOTEL WIENTJES, Zwolle, Overijssel

In Zwolle, I stayed overnight at the Hotel Wientjes, which had several very attractive rooms. Most of them had their own bath and wc. My room had been modernized, and it overlooked the tree-lined Stationsweg. The front desk staff was most accommodating and I found the general atmosphere very friendly. I particularly enjoyed sitting on the broad front terrace and, like everyone else, watching the traffic pass by. The dining room was extremely attractive with high ceilings and great french windows. I had an excellent evening meal with John Smulders, and he acquainted me with the charms of Overijssel and made suggestions about places to visit. The hotel also has a restaurant that is typical of the country. The service is more informal.

GOLDEN TULIP HOTEL WIENTJES, Zwolle, Overijssel. Tel.: 05200-11200. A 45-guestroom conventional in-town hotel in a thriving central Holland community. Well within walking distance of the town's attractive center. Breakfast, lunch, and dinner served daily. Rates: See Index.

RESTAURANT DE WAAG, Doesburg, Gelderland

My way now led south through Deventer and Zutphen on well-traveled main roads, for I had no time for meandering.

I was now in the Arnhem district, most of which is in Gelderland Province. This is an area rich in recreational opportunities with many hotels, pensions, restaurants, sports, and cultural activities. The VVV office at Arnhem is extremely busy at all times. They loaded me with literally pounds of information about all holiday and vacation attractions.

Anticipating my route from Zwolle, the director of the Arnhem VVV, directed me by telephone to two inns on the outer perimeter of Arnhem that he thought I would find intriguing. He was correct.

The first inn was in Doesburg, a comely town with quite a few 16th-century Gothic buildings. Here I visited Restaurant De Waag as they were serving afternoon tea and preparing for the evening meal.

To begin, I was awed by the facade of the building, which is about five and a half stories high, as can be seen from the accompanying drawing. The ground floor dining room is about two stories high with graceful arches supporting the upper stories. (I later discovered that, as in Amsterdam, the two top stories were false. The is typical of Dutch classicism.)

The first thing I saw inside was a huge farmer's scale hanging from the high ceiling. It was made in 1640. I was most impressed with this antiquity, until I learned from the hesitantly bilingual head-waiter that this restaurant has operated since 1449! In some ways the town and restaurant reminded me of Ribe in Denmark.

The interior is rather formal with heavy wooden chairs and tables that looked quite ancient though sturdy. There were many plants and flowers on various tables.

There was a huge fireplace at one end with a gigantic oil painting hanging over it. Around this fireplace was a grouping of big, comfortable leather chairs that looked perfect for dissertative conversations.

On the front sidewalk there were many chairs and tables that were filling up with townfolk seeking refreshment in the late afternoon.

The menu, as I suspected, was dominated by French cuisine. I could not arrange to eat here, but if the food was just half as good as the decor, it would be a delight.

RESTAURANT DE WAAG, Doesburg, Gelderland. Tel.: 08355-1388. Luncheon and dinner served daily except Sun. and Mon. No lodgings.

HET WAPEN VAN ATHLONE, De Steeg

Now this one was a dandy. A real American-style country inn in Holland. It is on one of the main roads, a few miles from Arnhem, so it has all of the advantages of the activities in the vicinity.

Even before I met the distaff side of the innkeeping team, I could see that lots of tender loving care was being lavished on this old inn. This was verified in a conversation I had with Ale Van Dyk as we sat on the terrace in the late afternoon sunshine.

"We're over 160 years old," she said. "Part of the building is from 1700, but most of it is from 1824. We had our 150th celebration in 1974.

"At Christmas we always have lots of people who come and stay for about ten days. We have a wonderful party and dinner at Christmas with presents for any children who are here.

"Many people enjoy the long walks in the woods right next to us. We have fifteen beds and serve breakfast only for our guests. Would you like to see some of the lodging rooms?"

I followed her to see five or six of the rooms, which looked very comfortable.

We stopped to look at a most unusual Dutch fireplace with two seats conveniently placed for warming chilly toes. There was a deer head mounted on the chimney.

In the dining room I saw that there were candles on the table, and that the Lions and the Rotary meet here, all of which contribute to a very homelike feeling.

The menu seemed to be a mixture of both French and Dutch dishes.

"We try to make everyone feel at home here," Ale went on. "Both Kees and I enjoy innkeeping very much and part of the fun is in meeting new people from many lands."

HET WAPEN VAN ATHLONE, Hoofdstraat 19, De Steeg, Gelderland. Tel.: 08309-1343. A village inn with 15 beds, serving breakfast (houseguests only), luncheon, and dinner daily except Wed. from Sept. 1 to May 1. Rates: See Index.

Arnhem

For me, Arnhem was one of Holland's unexpected experiences. I knew that it had been a battleground in World War II and that a motion picture entitled A Bridge Too Far *had been filmed in the vicinity, but I had no idea of the tremendous extent of its natural and cultural appeal. The staff of the VVV office in Arnhem was most generous and helpful (as they are with everyone) in apprising me of all the possibilities offered to visitors; first and foremost of which is the great Zuid-Veluwe Nature Reserve—240 square miles of undisturbed natural beauty—merging with the city's beautiful parks and near the scenic Rhine and Ijssel Rivers.*

The greatest Van Gogh collection in the world—272 of his

works—is housed in the Rijksmuseum Kroller-Muller, and there are many other fine galleries along with castles and museums to be visited in Arnhem.

The Netherlands Open Air Museum is a valley at the northern edge of Arnhem featuring a fascinating collection of authentic architecture from all corners of the country.

I visited several small towns in the Arnhem area and found country inn accommodations in a few of them, which I am happy to share.

HOTEL KELTENWOUD, Bennekom

Bennekom is one of the many resort areas just outside of Arnhem. It is surrounded by miles of country roads and forests, and has quite a few beautiful homes.

Following some strategically placed signposts, I sighted Het Keltenwoud through the trees, where many guests were enjoying breakfast on the outside terrace. It looked like a very comfortable place.

I introduced myself to the son of the owners, and he showed me through many bedrooms, the dining room, and the parlors, all of which were pleasantly furnished.

In this type of hotel, there are frequently quite a few photographs of the various members of the innkeeper's family on display, including grandchildren. This, of course, contributes to a feeling of being in a home.

This inn had a unique bit of history that my host explained to me this way:

"During the war, there were some Jewish families in this area. There was a secret room in the stable where some of those families were kept. It was common for the Dutch people in this area to hide their friends this way."

In America I have found quite a few inns that were stops in the Underground Railroad, the system that passed escaped Negro slaves from house to house until they were safe and free. Here in the forests outside of Arnhem was another example of man's humanity to man.

HOTEL KELTENWOUD, Dikkenbergweg 28, Bennekom. Tel.: 08389-4219-5406. A forest-side family inn a few miles outside of Arnhem. Many sports nearby. Rates: See Index.

DE KROMME DISSEL RESTAURANT (Hotel Klein Zwitserland), Heelsum

I was having dinner in a restaurant in the Hotel Klein Zwitserland in the Arnhem suburb of Heelsum.

It was a most enjoyable evening. The service and the food were excellent and there was the added touch of soft piano music with selections ranging from Strauss to Burt Bacharach. The interior has been quite elegantly designed to represent a traditional Dutch farmhouse. There were old farm tools hung along the brick walls and the beamed ceilings and stone floors completed the rustic-chic atmosphere. A rather small fire, more for atmosphere than warmth, burned in a handsome fireplace.

Heavy wooden tables set with snow-white napery and gleaming silverware were further enhanced by silver candlesticks.

The atmosphere may have been bucolic Dutch, but the menu and service were sophisticated French and featured much preparation at the table. My dinner was crab cocktail, steak au poivre, and fresh strawberries.

The atmosphere, food, service, and music in this restaurant all combined to encourage good conversation. The Hotel Klein Zwitserland was a large four-star hotel. I had very comfortable lodgings there for one night.

DE KROMME DISSEL RESTAURANT (Hotel Klein Zwitserland), Heelsum. Tel.: 08373-19104. A lavish country restaurant about 30 min. from downtown Arnhem. Open daily except Mon. Lodgings in Hotel Klein Zwitzerland. Rates: See Index.

DE LUNTERSE BOER, Lunteren

I found this inn to be most interesting for a number of reasons. First, it is adjacent to a beautiful public swimming pool that looked very enticing to me during the warm midday hours of my visit. There are also quite a few tennis courts nearby. Like the Hotel Keltenwoud, De Lunterse Boer is on the edge of the Zuid-Veluwe, the great Arnhem Nature Preserve, so there are many outdoor activities available.

The second thing of interest is the fact that the inn has been operated by two women for many years and they are both highly involved, articulate individuals.

After I had introduced myself and explained that I was writing a book about European inns, they asked to see my American book and asked me about its distribution, readership, and so forth. They wanted to make sure *Country Inns and Back Roads, Continental Europe* was the right kind of a book to represent them. I appreciated their attitude.

I also appreciated De Lunterse Boer. The main dining room and parlors are in a building similar to the Restaurant Nynke Pleats in Piaam. It has a thatched roof and country furniture. There is a view of the forest in all directions. The housekeeping is meticulous.

Guest rooms are in another building a short distance away. They are extremely comfortable and homelike. All have a shower and wc, and a balcony overlooking the woods.

The average European traveler is a little different from the average American. When I asked my hostess what single factor found the most favor with their guests, she unhesitatingly replied, "They all love walking in the silent woods."

DE LUNTERSE BOER, Lunteren. Tel.: 08388-3657. A country inn in beautiful natural surroundings near Arnhem. Rates: See Index.

HOTEL DE EEKHOORN, Rhenen

I left Lunteren and drove south for my first glimpse of the Rhine River. In many ways this was the essence of Europe—a majestic waterway that rises in the Alps and flows to the sea. It is a source of

legend and history that is unique. Here, in this part of the world, it is in the final stage of its journey. In this small Dutch village on the banks of the Rhine I found the Hotel de Eekhoorn, a restaurant specializing in pancakes, with a few modest rooms.

The terrace, riverside bedrooms, and dining room all enjoy a pleasant view of some meadows overlooking the Rhine, about 300 yards away.

The atmosphere is pleasant and informal, and I was introduced to everyone from the cook to the owner. The lodging rooms were casual but clean. The specialty of the house was pancakes, and the restaurant catered mainly to the many people driving along the highway next to the Rhine.

The longer I remained, the more this place grew on me.

HOTEL DE EEKHOORN, Utrechsestraatweg 3,. Rhenen. Tel.: 08376-2276. A modest restaurant and pension overlooking the Rhine River. Rates: See Index.

RESTAURANT 'T KALKOENTJE, Rhenen

If this place had rooms it would be a total country inn. As it is, this is a tiny and beautiful restaurant just a few feet from the shores of the Rhine, with its own grove of fruit trees and a resident tethered goat.

The building is a thatched-roof white farmhouse that looks as if it has been unchanged for at least a hundred years. The interior has the unmistakable patina of graceful old age. The furniture has mellowed to a wonderful deep brown that comes from years of dusting and waxing. The parlors and inside dining room have beautiful antiques.

There are shelves of books on every available square foot of wall space. These are interspersed with dozens of delicately handpainted Dutch tiles.

Although I was five hours behind schedule and not the least bit hungry, I stayed an extra hour sitting on the sunny terrace with all of the rambler roses and flowers. I ordered and ate every bit of a delicious mushroom omelet. Even the goat looked on approvingly.

Meanwhile, the Rhine traffic was just a few yards away and occasionally the crew of a barge or boat would wave merrily at me.

There is one word to describe this tiny restaurant on the Rhine—exquisite.

RESTAURANT 'T KALKOENTJE, Utrechtse Straatweg 143, Rhenen. Tel.: 08376-2344. Specialty restaurant. Open depending on season. No lodgings.

Maastricht and the Province of Limburg

Holland was a land of surprises. One of the principal delights that unfolded like a tulip in bloom was Maastricht and Limburg.

The road south from Arnhem, instead of offering the usual vistas of endless grazing lands intersected with canals and dikes, was bordered by fertile fields on sloping hills with swift-running brooks and many open woods. Along the banks of the Maas River, with its famous bridges, were many castles, churches, and ruins with a rich history. Surprisingly, the province of Llimburg has many other high hills, some with pleasant views.

Upon my arrival in Maastricht, the provincial capital of Limburg, I went to the VVV office, where I met Mr. Nicholas de Korte, who was to accompany me on a "Merry-Go-Round" tour of the area. This would include a small country inn, a famous castle-hotel, a stop for dinner at a chateau, and on to another castle for an overnight stay.

HOTEL MOOI LIMBURG, Bemelen, South Limberg

This was the Dutch country inn that Nicholas said was first on the list. It is on a hill with a view that includes rolling hills and sloping meadows. The owner was very proud of the swimming pool, which

425

would certainly be most appreciated by guests during the warm weather. This is really a very small inn where guests become almost one of the family.

I saw all of the guest rooms, including those on the top floor underneath the thatched roof. The thatching keeps out the heat of the sun, I was told. There was one corner room with a balcony that I liked very much.

We sat for awhile on the terrace and I learned that it was just a short distance to the American cemetery in Limburg. The Dutch people in this section feel very close to the Americans, because it was an American division that liberated this part of Holland in World War II.

This little country inn seemed like a very nice place in which to stay for a number of days while exploring not only Maastricht but the entire province of Limburg.

HOTEL MOOI LIMBURG, Bemelen, South Limburg. Tel.: 04407-1212. A family hotel 5 km. from Maastricht. Swimming pool. Rates: See Index.

KASTEEL NEUBOURG, Gulpen, South Limburg

We turned off the main road and drove down a long tree-lined dirt road over a moat and through a gate to reach the main entrance of this castle hotel. An impressive placard indicated that it has been designated as an "official monument," which means that no alterations can be made in its basic structure without going through channels.

We walked into the main reception room, with its white walls and several magnificent crystal chandeliers. I was in awe already. It was really a fantastic castle, even more impressive than a film set.

The main lounge was decorated in various tones of green, with chairs upholstered in a rich green fabric. There was a large beautiful fireplace at one end and several marvelous examples of framed Dutch needlework to be seen.

I strolled through one parlor after another. Each one seemed more ornate and impressive than the previous one. The ceilings, walls, and floors all had decorations that reminded me of the Schonbrunn Palace in Vienna.

The dining room was already lavishly set for the evening meal

and there were beautiful fresh daisies everywhere, quite a contrast to the formal atmosphere.

The director of the castle escorted me on a tour, including a few of the guest rooms. Most of them can best be described as mammoth. After all, what did I expect in a castle? They all have impressive views of the Limburg countryside, including the moat. From the third floor I could see the pattern formed by the 2,000 rose bushes that were recently planted in the formal rose garden.

One of the rooms had a double bed with a marvelous inlaid wood headboard. The bathroom and wc were six steps up at another level.

Returning to the first floor, the director showed me the menu, which for the most part had French cuisine and French-style service.

HOTEL-RESTAURANT KASTEEL NEUBOURG, Gulpen, Limburg. Tel.: 1222-04450. A castle-hotel in the south Limburg hills. Rates: See Index.

CHATEAU DE NEERCANNE, Maastricht

Nicholas and I were seated on the terrace of this beautiful chateau, reviewing our excursion and mentally preparing for what I felt would be an exceptional dinner.

We had followed the "Merry-Go-Round" route through a series

of back roads and over the most beautiful parts of this entire area. He explained that it is very popular because it reminds Hollanders of Switzerland.

At one point we were headed down a beautiful valley, the trees and the sun making long shadows over the road, when I noticed a building sitting near the top of some cliffs. "That's the Chateau de Neercanne," he remarked. "That's where we are going for dinner."

We passed through the gate and walked through the main entrance into a reception area that had lavish displays of fruits and

cheeses on a large table. We were escorted to the garden and the terrace, and were now contemplating a rural scene that seemed almost like a Renaissance painting.

Other guests were arriving, and soon the wrought-iron chairs and tables were filled with attractively dressed people, chatting amiably and placing their orders for dinner, which would be served in the main dining room.

This is the only restored terraced castle in Holland and dates back to 1611. Everything about it adds up to the word "elegance."

One of the most interesting features is the fact that there are caves carved out of the side of the cliffs, where the wine for the chateau is kept, and these may be visited by guests. There is an impressive herb garden and almost twenty-five acres of woods with many paths. I was told that 50,000 trees have been planted on the property.

The headwaiter informed us that our table was ready and we joined others in the candlelit dining room.

Here at Chateau de Neercanne with all of the beautiful surroundings—the flowers, the attention and service, and the ambience—there were a few moments when I felt like I was visiting royalty 400 years ago.

CHATEAU DE NEERCANNE, Cannerweg 800, Maastricht. Tel.: 043-51359. A most elegant restaurant a few miles from the center of Maastricht. Serving lunch and dinner every day except Sun. and Mon. No lodgings.

CASTLE WITTEM, Wittem, South Limburg

The bells were tolling 8 a.m. at Wittem Castle. I had been awakened earlier by the sound of many birds in the tall trees surrounding the castle and I leaned out of the windows to watch some of them dive and catch an elusive fish or two from the moat for breakfast. Swans were just making their appearance, their white feathers glistening in the morning sunlight.

The previous night I had the privilege of meeting the owner of this castle, Mr. Ritzen. Although I have visited other castle-inns, this was the first time that I had talked to a man who actually owned a castle! This man, with a delightful sense of humor, explained that the earliest parts of the castle dated back to an 11th-century tower and that over the years it has been built to its present size. "We have done everything we can to modernize, but we believe we have still kept the real feeling of the castle," he said. "We have furnished it with antiques and at the same time have made improvements that mean our guests can be comfortable—even in a castle."

Comfort, in my particular case, involved a handsome tower room with very attractive furniture and an adjoining bath and wc that were the last words in contemporary fixtures.

Even as I was gazing out of my high window, the modern-day housekeepers in attendance at the castle began to appear, armed with scrubbing brushes, dust cloths, and vacuum cleaners. The gardener was already at work. The cooks were bustling around in the kitchen and the waiters were beginning to arrive. Perhaps this scene was not so far removed from the activity in this castle 200 or more years ago.

Breakfast consisted of a basket of assorted breads, a plate of cheese, ham, and liverwurst, jam and a 3-minute egg. I'm certain that the food is much better than it was in 1611.

Besides all of the scenic attractions in South Limburg, there is a golf course, swimming pool, and tennis in the immediate vicinity.

CASTLE WITTEM HOTEL RESTAURANT (Relais et Chateaux), South Limburg. Tel.: 04450-1208. A luxurious castle with modern accommodations a few miles from the center of Maastricht. Breakfast, lunch, and dinner served every day. Rates: See Index.

Netherlands in Retrospect

My entire experience in the Netherlands was delightful and unique. I loved the canals, flowers, wonderful farms, lakes, the continual parade of boats, smoked eels, great salads, and the narrow little roads that seemed to go nowhere but everywhere. I found a complete change of pace in the hilly southern part of the country, which seems quite like the northeastern United States.

I think I expected the Netherlands to be composed entirely of canals, bridges, and people wearing wooden shoes. However, it is much, much more, including one of the most impressive collections of ancient and historical buildings in Europe. There are historical and art museums in almost every town and it is a country with a rich cultural heritage.

I enjoyed the jolly smiles and attitudes of the Dutch people.

If You Are Arriving in Amsterdam. . .

The *Schiphol Airport* in Amsterdam can be a very pleasant experience. The lines move along rapidly, and baggage is automatically transferred without going through customs. Making connections with another flight can take about forty to fifty minutes.

There are porters at this airport, although there is no set charge for their services. About a dollar for the first bag and forty cents for each additional bag ought to keep everybody happy.

Three public buses are available hourly to the center of the city, costing about a dollar and a half. It takes around half an hour to go on the KLM buses to the central station, for about three dollars. You can also catch buses to the Hague and Utrecht.

Cab fare is about twelve dollars; tip ten percent.

The train to Amsterdam, and then a tram to the city center, takes forty-five minutes and costs a little over a dollar. There are also trains to the Hague, Rotterdam, and Utrecht.

Schiphol is famous for its duty-free shops that sell countless items to delight the tourist. You can even buy an automobile there with two weeks' notice.

An Austrian Interlude (One of My Favorite Stories)

Kurmittelhaus

The itinerary seemed simple enough. I was to change trains at Wiener Neusta (a five-minute leeway I was sure would be sufficient) and then take the train into the mountains. "You won't have to worry," explained a very efficient woman at the tourist office in Vienna, "because it is the last stop on the line."

She handed me a piece of blue paper on which had been written one word: "Kurmittelhaus." "Someone will meet you at the station and take you there. There is absolutely nothing to worry about."

So now I found myself on the train from Semmering to Wiener Neusta and I checked my watch several times. We were not going to be making it with five minutes to spare; we would be lucky to make it with one minutes to spare. I expressed my concern to several of the passengers in my compartment, and they assured me that everything would be all right. All of this was done with a modicum of English.

We came into the outskirts of the town and I kept peering ahead trying to see the station and if, indeed, there was a train. Finally we ground to a stop in the Bohnhof and I scurried out of the train with echoes of "good luck" in my ears, showed my ticket to a guard who pointed to the adjacent track and made motions that I was to go down the stairs and under and back up the stairs. Meanwhile, I caught a glimpse of the train, which looked to me as if it were just about ready to leap forward. I rushed down the stairs, through the tunnel, up the stairs completely out of breath, and threw myself into the coach of the train, which, in fact, was already moving ahead about an inch at a time.

Apparently, there was nothing particularly unusual about my behavior because the other passengers, few as they were in the coach car, paid little or no attention to me. The conductor took my ticket and when I tried to tell him about my destination and when I was to get off, he simply said, "Ja, Ja."

I was somewhat reassured, but not completely. All kinds of doubts began to invade my mind, including such thoughts as "Suppose this isn't the last stop and I go too far—what will I do? I don't speak enough German to order a decent meal, much less find a mysterious place called Kurmittelhaus."

Meanwhile, the train, if indeed it can be called such, started uphill. I discovered there was an engine and one car and I was in the coach portion of that car and the other portion was the mail car—a sort of Austrian version of the Toonerville Trolley. I settled back to look at the mountain scenery; however, dusk was falling fast in April and the mountains soon became nothing more than darkened silhouettes and finally disappeared altogether. The train stopped every few kilometers and the passengers began to thin out. At each stop a man dressed in a green uniform with a standup collar and sporting a very smart-looking cap with a forepiece would come out of a little house, look up and down the tracks, blow his whistle, and turn a small hand sign so that the color green was showing. The train would then answer with its whistle and we continued chugging uphill, never attaining a speed that was above a mild jog. I don't remember any downhill grades.

Now there were just two passengers remaining—two ladies who were chatting enthusiastically in German. They had obviously been shopping in Vienna as their seats and overhead racks were filled with packages. I attempted some type of conversation, but they just smiled and looked mildly interested, but did not really offer me any relief for my concern. Then I took my piece of blue paper with the word "Kurmittelhaus" written on it and got the same reaction from them as I did from others—they both laughed and looked at me in a very strange way and laughed some more. They said something which seemed somewhat reassuring in German and continued their conversation.

I slumped down into my seat and pulled the collar of my jacket up over my ears because it was already beginning to get quite chilly; in fact, cold. There was no heat on the train, although it was clean and the seats were comfortable. Finally the two fraus nodded to me and departed, and I was on the train all by myself.

The stops now had gone up into the double figures and it was very black outside.

I decided to take matters into my own hands and opened the door between the passenger compartment and the mail compart-

ment and found three or four men sitting around a table playing cards, all of them obviously railroad or postal service employees. I started to take my blue piece of paper out again but felt I could not withstand any further guffawing. I showed my ticket stub to the man who was the conductor. He smiled broadly and once again said, "Ja, Ja!"

About two and a half hours had now gone by and finally the conductor poked his head in the door and indicated that indeed the next stop was mine. Eagerly, I stood up at the window, looking ahead, and saw a sizable railroad station rather than the usual little platform. There were lights and some signs of life. This was it. I gathered my duffel together and stood waiting to disembark. Finally, with many wheezes and screeches, the train came to a stop.

As I started walking toward the station, almost as if by pre-arranged signal, every light went out, including those in a small newsstand and magazine store. Before I got inside the station everybody had disappeared and when I went out the front door all I could see were the receding red taillights of automobiles. I was positively alone. The train had disappeared up the track, and there wasn't a soul around.

The baleful yellow lights from the street lamps were hardly enough even to read by. The cold was now setting in in earnest. I stamped my feet, slapped my hands, sang songs, exhorted the gods of travel (if indeed there are such deities) to look kindly upon my plight, and after a thirty-minute wait there was still no one there.

I wasn't sure I was in the right town and I certainly didn't know where I was supposed to go. Chiding myself for not asking intelligent questions of the fraulein in the Vienna tourist office, instead of looking into her deep blue eyes, I walked up the street where the stores were all tightly shuttered and all was black. I could not see anyone. I had walked about two blocks from the station when out of the gloom emerged a man wearing knickers and a Tyrolean hat. I raised my hand in the traditional Indian sign for peace, and once again with some misgiving brought out my piece of blue paper. He struck a match and looked at it and much to my surprise did not laugh. He gave me some directions in German, accompanied by hand signals indicating I was to go one more block, turn right, go one more block and turn right again. Timorously, I thanked him and he disappeared into the Stygian blackness.

I reached the next corner, did a smart right turn, and saw two country people coming toward me. I just couldn't bring myself to go through the same routine again, so I pressed on to the next corner and turned right. I peered into the blackness and nary a flicker did I see. Putting one foot in front of the other, I started down the road (there was no sidewalk), and after about 150 yards realized that there was, indeed, a light at the end of my tunnel. (Now, where have I heard that before?)

I quickened my step and the light became larger and brighter, and soon I could see the outlines of a low house and realized that the light was coming from behind large glass doors. I reached the gate, stepped through the garden onto the veranda, and realized the light was somewhat diffused by the fact that there was a great deal of steam on the inside and I could not see through the doors. I pushed a bell and waited anxiously, holding the piece of blue paper in my hand. The door was soon thrown open and in front of me stood a six-foot Austrian Valkyrie with other dimensions to match, wearing a white uniform and a most imperious look in her eye.

From somewhere in my theater training of the past, I gulped once, took a deep breath, and said, "My name is Norman Simpson..." She cut me off with "Oh, Norman Simpson!" She reached for my bag with one hand and literally gathered me unto her ample bosom with the other. "We've been waiting for you."

She drew me into the most magical room I have ever seen. It was filled with men and women who either were clad in a towel or in nothing at all. I thought that I had died and gone to heaven and that this was my reward for a life of at least a few good works.

The lady in white indicated that I was to sit in a chair and then she disappeared. Meanwhile, another lady, completely nude, dropped into the chair next to me and I heard the most wonderful sounds I had heard in the past four hours: English.

"They have been waiting for you. They forgot to go to the train and she is apologizing. You are to wait here until someone comes to take you somewhere else. I lived in Chicago for five years."

The remainder of the conversation, which lasted about twenty minutes or so, was conducted with my eyes on the ceiling. Put it down to my first experience in visiting a Kurmittelhaus, which, she explained to me, was a place where people come for rest, warm baths, massages, and to "take the waters."

Just as I was beginning to get into the spirit of the occasion and wondering whether or not I could make arrangements to stay there for the night and have a rest, massage, and take the waters, a man arrived at the front door to take me even farther into the mountains to a more conventional ski resort.

So, as they used to say in the Fitzpatrick Travelogs, I "bade farewell to my friends at the Kurmittelhaus and reluctantly departed, hoping someday to return."

I don't think I could find it again.

ACKNOWLEDGEMENTS

This book is really a team effort. Behind the scenes were literally dozens of individuals and organizations who gave generously of their time and advice in order to bring these experiences to their publishing fruition.

The National Tourist Office of each country that I visited did invaluable advance research for me. Fortified with this material, I called upon well over 100 individual tourist agencies throughout my trip. In every instance I received the gracious and patient service which is available to every visitor. These people are wonderfully knowledgeable. They converse in many languages and have thousands of valuable facts and schedules at their fingertips. I found these offices in almost every large village or small town.

I am also indebted to Iberia, Pan America, Lufthansa, and Alitalia Airlines and Air France for consideration in arranging flights to Europe.

INDEX / RATES

Approximate rates for two people for one night are given in the currency of the country and are subject to changes in the exchange rate. Breakfast is not necessarily included. Rates are estimated through 1987.

Amounts shown in shillings for two people for one night. These are not firm quotations, but for general estimating.

Amounts shown in krone for two people for one night. These are not firm quotations, but for general estimating.

Amounts shown in francs for two people for one night. These are not firm quotations, but for general estimating.

Amounts shown in marks for two people for one night. These are not firm quotations, but for general estimating.

HUNGARY

Amounts shown in forints for two people for one night. These are not firm quotations, but for general estimating.

ITALY

Amounts shown in lire for two people for one night. These are not firm quotations, but for general estimating.

Amounts shown in Dutch currency for two people for one night. These are not firm quotations, but for general estimating.

Approximate rates for two people for one night are given in the currency of the country and are subject to changes in the exchange rate. Breakfast is not necessarily included. Rates are estimated through 1987.

NORWAY

NORWAY	RATES	PAGE
BALESTRAND, Kringsja Hotel	NKr 150-270	351
BALESTRAND, Midtnes Pensjonat	NKr 250	350
BALESTRAND, Pensjonat Dragsvik	NKr 120-220	349
ELVESETER, Elveseter Hotel	NKr 250	360
FJAERLAND, Hotel Mundal	NKr 500	351
FJAERLAND, Fjaerland Pensjonat	NKr 250-450 with meals	353
FLAM, Heimly Lodge	NKr 300	356
KAUPANGER, Husum Gjesteheim	NKr on request Apt. by wk.	355
LUSTER, Solstrand Pensjonat	NKr 150-250	359
OS, Solstrand Fjord Hotel	NKr 700	347
SOLVORN, Walaker Hotel	NKr 320-500	358
VASSENDEN, Vassenden Turistpensjonat	NKr 200-350	354

Amounts shown in krone for two people for one night. These are not firm quotations, but for general estimating.

PORTUGAL

PORTUGAL	RATES	PAGE
ARMACAO DE PERA, Hotel do Levante	6,952 Esc	208
ELVAS, Pousada de Santa Luzia	5,214 Esc	216
ESTREMOZ, Pousada da Rainha Santa Isabel	6,952 Esc	215
EVORA, Pousada dos Loios	7,521 Esc	213
GUINCHO, Estalagem Muchaxo	6,952 Esc	196
LISBON, York House/Residencia Inglesa	6,257 Esc	199
PALMELA, Pousada do Castelo Palmela	7,821 Esc	201
QUELUZ, Cozinha Velha	Restaurant	196
SAGRES, Pousada do Infante	6,083 Esc	205
SANTA BARBARA DE NEXE, Hotel La Reserve	13,904 Esc	209
SANTIAGO DO CACÉM, Pousada de Santiago	5,214 Esc	204
SÃO BRÁS DE ALPORTEL, Pousada De São Brás	5,214 Esc	210
SERPA, Pousada de São Gens	4,345 Esc	211
SETUBAL, Pousada de São Filipe	6,952 Esc	202
SINTRA, Palacio dos Seteais	13,904 Esc	193
SINTRA, Quinta de São Thiago	7,821 Esc	194

Amounts shown in escudos for two people for one night. These are not firm quotations, but for general estimating.

Approximate rates for two people for one night are given in the currency of the country and are subject to changes in the exchange rate. Breakfast is not necessarily included. Rates are estimated through 1987.

Amounts shown in pesetas for two people for one night. These are not firm quotations, but for general estimating.

Approximate rates for two people for one night are given in the currency of the country and are subject to changes in the exchange rate. Breakfast is not necessarily included. Rates are estimated through 1987.

Amounts shown in krone for two people for one night. These are not firm quotations, but for general estimating.

Amounts shown in Swiss francs for two people for one night. These are not firm quotations, but for general estimating.